"This book seriously explores the marginali.
modern world and in contemporary Christian life by tracing the
history of humility from the Greco-Roman philosophical traditions
and Judeo-Christian origins to major monastic sources of teaching
on humility from the desert monks, the Rule of Benedict, Bernard of
Clairvaux, and Christian de Chergé and the monks of Tibhirine. The
breadth and depth of each chapter guides the reader to the significance
and reevaluation that humility offers for Christian living, whether one
is a monk or married person, by the transforming grace of Christ's
own *kenosis*. I hope that every monastic house and theological library
offers this fine study of humility, in its many facets, for its readership
to read, ponder, and reflect with others."

> —Mary Forman, OSB
> Associate Professor of Monastic Studies
> Saint John's School of Theology and Seminary

"This wonderfully clear and insightful introduction to so central
a topic will be of immense help to students and scholars. At a
moment when the spiritual formation of Christian theology is
emerging once more as central to our understanding of Christianity,
Reclaiming Humility provides a deeply thoughtful and well-researched
consideration of this difficult, indispensable, sometimes dangerously
misused, life-generating virtue."

> —Mark A. McIntosh
> Professor of Christian Spirituality, Loyola University
> Author of *Divine Teaching: An Introduction to Christian Theology*

"Jane Foulcher's important book returns our attention to the neglected
topic of humility. A long spiritual tradition regards this virtue as
fundamental to the imitation of Christ, but moderns often disparage it
as detrimental to our sense of human dignity and self-worth. Turning
to such sources as the desert fathers, John Cassian, Benedict of Nursia,
and Bernard of Clairvaux, Foulcher recovers the crucial links that unite
Christian humility with human dignity and charity. In a stunning final
chapter, Foulcher turns to the practice of humility among the monks
of Tibhirine, martyred in Algeria in 1996. Foulcher concludes that a
reclaimed humility is vital to the Christian way in the twenty-first
century. Highly recommended."

> —Ann Astell
> Professor of Theology, The University of Notre Dame

CISTERCIAN STUDIES SERIES: NUMBER TWO HUNDRED FIFTY-FIVE

Reclaiming Humility

Four Studies in the Monastic Tradition

By

Jane Foulcher

α

Cistercian Publications
www.cistercianpublications.org

LITURGICAL PRESS
Collegeville, Minnesota
www.litpress.org

A Cistercian Publications title published by Liturgical Press

Cistercian Publications
Editorial Offices
161 Grosvenor Street
Athens, Ohio 54701
www.cistercianpublications.org

1	2	3	4	5	6	7	8	9

Library of Congress Cataloging-in-Publication Data

Foulcher, Jane.
    Reclaiming humility : four studies in the monastic tradition / Jane Foulcher.
        pages   cm. — (Cistercian studies series ; number two hundred fifty-five)
    Includes bibliographical references.
    ISBN 978-0-87907-255-1 — ISBN 978-0-87907-728-0 (ebook)
    1. Humility—Religious aspects—Christianity.   2. Monastic and religious life.   I. Title.

BV4647.H8F68   2015
241'.4—dc23   2014036385

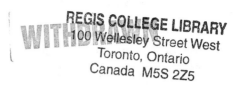
This book is dedicated to John, Dylan, and Alice:
you have been the faithful bearers of God's grace and
love in my life.

Siquidem humiliatio via est ad humilitatem.
Humiliation is the way to humility.

—Bernard of Clairvaux, *Letter 87.11*

Contents

Acknowledgments

Until recently most studies of monastic theology have come from inside the monastery. In the preface of his influential and pioneering study of Benedictine monasticism, Cuthbert Butler offered his credentials:

> As there is a certain presumptuousness in venturing to treat an evidently complex and difficult subject, that has hitherto, perhaps, deterred explorers, it may be well for me to set forth the credentials I bring to the undertaking of the work. In the first place, then, I have been for more than forty years a Benedictine monk, living the life according to the Rule, and trying to shape my spiritual life and my intellectual and other activities by its inspiration and teaching; and during the last twelve of these years I have had the experience of ruling as Abbot over a large monastery.[1]

By comparison, my credentials for the task I have set myself seem impossibly thin. Since I have not lived as a monk, my perspective is that of an outsider. I am heartened, though, by Michael Casey's assessment of two twentieth-century giants of the monastic world, Thomas Merton, the celebrated writer, and Jean Leclercq, the prolific and peripatetic scholar. "Both men," Casey says, "were somewhat marginal to the daily life of ordinary monks, and it was this semiexclusion that gave them the

---

1. Cuthbert Butler, *Benedictine Monachism: Studies in Benedictine Life and Rule* (London: Longmans, Green, and Co., 1919).

freedom to see things from a different perspective."[2] It was from this marginal place that both were able to offer their prophetic voices to the church.

My life, lived in the context of family, one given, one chosen, is completely remote from "the daily life of ordinary monks," but I have, in this study, ventured over the monastery wall in the hope of discovering how it is that we have lost touch with our faith's most basic orientation: humility.

The opportunity to spend three years happily reading and writing was the gift of being awarded a scholarship through the Public and Contextual Theology (PACT) Strategic Research Centre of Charles Sturt University (CSU). I am thankful to have been blessed with Dr. Heather Thomson and the Rev. Dr. Sarah Bachelard as supervisors for the doctoral project that gave birth to this book. Their warm encouragement gave me courage to complete the journey. Fr. Michael Casey, Sr. Mary Foreman, and Professor Anne Hunt gave invaluable advice on the doctoral manuscript. I am grateful to the staff of St. Mark's National Theological Centre and the Australian Centre for Christianity and Culture for their hospitality, to the library staff at St. Mark's and CSU for their tireless support, and for the good company of fellow researchers. I am appreciative of the careful reading and responses to draft work offered by the St. Mark's scholarly community. Associate Professor David Neville gave invaluable advice regarding chapter 1. I am grateful for his encouragement and interest in my project, alongside that of the Rev. Associate Professor Scott Cowdell, Professor Wayne Hudson, and the Rev. Professor John Painter in George Browning House. The Rev. Dr. Matthew Anstey, the Rev. Dr. Erica Mathieson, the Rev. Nikolai Blaskow, and the Rev. Tim Watson assisted where I met my linguistic limits.

It has been a pleasure to deal with Fr. Mark Scott, ocso, and Professor Marsha Dutton at Cistercian Publications. Professor Dutton's careful reading of the manuscript and editorial sugges-

---

2. Patrick Hart, ed., "Afterword," in *Survival or Prophecy? The Correspondence of Jean Leclercq and Thomas Merton*, MW 17 (Collegeville, MN: Cistercian Publications, 2008), 142.

tions have improved the clarity of the text. I am also grateful to Chris Brennan for his initial editorial work on the book manuscript. Part of chapter 5 appeared as "Humility: Christian de Chergé and the 'other'" in Phillip Tolliday and Heather Thomson, eds., *Speaking Differently: Essays in Theological Anthropology* (Canberra: Barton Books, 2013). The support of PACT enabled me to present part of chapter 3 at the Annual Monos Conference, at Douai Abbey, Reading, United Kingdom, in 2010. I am thankful to Fr. Massimo Maria, a brother of the Fraternités de Jerusalem in Florence, for graciously giving me access to the Cloister of the Oranges to view and photograph the fresco cycle of the Life of Saint Benedict. Fr. Terry McNaughton and the team at Saint Mary's Towers, Douglas Park, provided a place for spiritual refreshment and encouragement.

One small essay by André Louf (1929–2010) has continued to nourish this research journey: *The Way of Humility*.[3] This small publication, originally conferences given to the new monastic community of Bose in northern Italy, was first published in Italian as *L'umiltà* (2000) and then in French as *L'Humilité* (2002). Louf confirmed my early suspicion that *humility* and *virtue* had become unhelpfully tangled, and he confirmed my intuitions regarding humility's centrality to the Christian vocation. Whenever I deemed myself lost I would head to the cafeteria with Louf's slim volume in hand and reread his essay. In the end my book feels like a giant footnote to Louf's masterful contribution. I am deeply grateful for both his theological and spiritual clarity and sad that his death in 2010 has prevented me from extending him my thanks.

3. André Louf, *The Way of Humility*, trans. Lawrence S. Cunningham, MW 11 (Kalamazoo, MI: Cistercian Publications, 2007).

Abbreviations

ABR	*The American Benedictine Review*
CF	Cistercian Fathers series
Col	*Collectanea Cisterciensia*
Conf	Cassian, *Conferences*
CS	Cistercian Studies series
Csi	Bernard of Clairvaux, *De consideratione /* *On Consideration*
CSQ	*Cistercian Studies Quarterly*
Desert Fathers	*The Desert Fathers: Sayings of the Early Christian* *Monks*. Translated by Benedicta Ward. London: Penguin, 2003.
Hum	Bernard of Clairvaux, *Liber de gradibus humilitatis et* *superbiæ / On the Steps of Humility and Pride*
LR	Longer Rules or Longer Responses
Miss	Bernard of Clairvaux, *Hom super missus est in* *laudibus virginis matris / Homilies in Praise of the* *Virgin Mary*
Mor	Bernard of Clairvaux, *Ep de moribus et officiis* *episcoporum / On the Conduct and Office of Bishops*
MW	Monastic Wisdom series
PG	Patrologia Graeca, ed. J.-P. Migne
PL	Patrologia Latina, ed. J.-P. Migne

RB	The Rule of Saint Benedict
RM	The Rule of the Master
Sayings	*The Sayings of the Desert Fathers: The Alphabetical Collection.* Translated by Benedicta Ward. Rev. ed. CS 59. Kalamazoo, MI: Cistercian Publications, 1984.
SBOp	Sancti Bernardi opera. Edited by Jean Leclercq, C. H. Talbot, and Henri M. Rochais. Rome: Editiones Cistercienses, 1957–63.
SC	Bernard of Clairvaux, *Sermo super cantica canticorum / Sermons on the Song of Songs*
SCh	Sources chrétiennes series
SP	*Studia Patristica*
SR	Shorter Rules or Shorter Responses
V Mal	Bernard of Clairvaux, *Vita sancti Malachiæ / Life of Malachy*

Introduction

Why Humility?

Joan Chittister makes a bold claim in her reflective guide to the Rule of Saint Benedict: "If the preservation of the globe in the twenty-first century requires anything of the past at all, it may well be the commitment of the Rule of Benedict to humility."[1] Benedict's world, she says, was much like ours: a disintegrating empire, where the benefits of Roman civilization were steadily being lost to growing inequality, poverty, and social chaos. Into this, she says, "Benedict of Nursia flung a rule for privileged Roman citizens calling for humility, a proper sense of self in a universe of wonders. When we make ourselves God, no one in the world is safe in our presence. Humility, in other words, is the basis for right relationships in life."[2]

Chittister's intuition, voiced at the end of the twentieth century, seems even more urgent in the early decades of the twenty-first century. The reality of global warming, with its almost certain human cause, is a case in point; the overreach of human beings in relation to the use of the earth's resources is endangering our very survival. Hubris, human pride, prevents us from acknowledging our limits. In the West in particular, our elevation of the individual at the expense of the relational, our adulation of the market, and

1. Joan D. Chittister, *The Rule of Benedict: Insights for the Ages* (New York: Crossroad, 1992 [repr. 1997]), 61–62.

2. Chittister, *Rule*, 62.

our belief in unlimited economic growth have eroded our commitment to building communal life. Our sense of self and our
relationships are too often characterized by rivalry and the fulfillment of superficial desires. The confident rejection of God by the
new atheists and the overconfidence of religious fundamentalists
similarly speak of hubris: arrogant certainty regarding the nonex-
istence of God or of knowing the mind of God. Both endanger our
common life, closing our minds to possibilities beyond our grasp
and, in too many situations, justifying violence toward *the other*.

In this context, the possibility that a retrieval of humility, carefully understood, might contribute to the reordering of our relationships—with the earth, with ourselves, with each other, and
with God—in a fruitful and life-giving way is worthy of serious
consideration. Is humility foundational to human well-being?

This book seeks to open out Chittister's claim regarding the
centrality of humility to human life and well-being, exploring
questions regarding the nature and place of humility in human
life. How might we understand humility as foundational for
human well-being and for right relationships? On what grounds
can we retrieve a productive Christian reading of humility, one
that promotes human well-being, both individual and communal?

Such a project of retrieval, however, is by no means straightforward. While humility had a central place in early Christian
theology and practice, it has generally been marginalized by the
modern Western world and in contemporary Christian life. David
Hume dismissed humility along with "the whole train of monkish
virtues."[3] Nietzsche saw it as a mark of the slave nature of Christian
morality. While the rehabilitation of virtue ethics has helped to put
humility back on the agenda, contemporary philosophers continue
to read Christian sources on humility negatively as encouraging
self-hatred and a negative view of the self. On the other hand, the
critiques generated by post-Enlightenment philosophy and by
psychology and feminism during the twentieth century have made
Christians shy about proclaiming humility as a virtue. By contrast,

---

3. David Hume, *Enquiries Concerning Human Understanding and Concerning
the Principles of Morals*, 3rd ed. (Oxford: Clarendon Press, 1975), 270.

ascetical traditions in Christianity, especially monasticism, have retained and developed humility as central to the human journey. While initially considering the marginalization of humility, and specifically its problematic relationship to virtue, this book focuses on four historical expressions of the Western monastic tradition[4] and their engagement with the question of the nature and place of humility in human life. I have chosen to take this focus not only because the monastic tradition has continued to recognize humility as foundational to the Christian journey but also because it offers a rich ground for considering the interrelationships between theology, practices, and the lived life. Here I draw on André Louf's suggestion that "concrete experience" of monastic life "which is both connected to particular situations and properly scriptural" offers the most helpful route for exploring equally the "what" and "how" of humility.[5] This inquiry, then, has both conceptual and practical elements: it seeks to clarify the theological understanding of humility and to examine how humility might be cultivated in human life. And while the focus is on monastic life, the hope, and assumption, is that what I have discovered might be applicable beyond the monastery wall.

Chapter 1 outlines the problematic heritage of the concept of humility and suggests that the roots of contemporary suspicion can be found in the meeting of emerging notions of humility in the Judeo-Christian tradition with classical philosophy and its virtue tradition. The subsequent appropriation of concepts of virtue by Christian theology and practice has contributed to a persistent lack of clarity regarding humility, a situation that the monastic tradition has had to address repeatedly and that poses a danger to those contemporary retrievals of humility that rely on the renewed interest in virtue ethics. Chapter 1 also raises the subjects that recur in the monastic expressions explored in subsequent chapters: the relationship between humility and virtue, humility

---

4. In using *monastic tradition* to denote the stream of theology and practice of Christian monasticism, I recognize that there are multiple strands or expressions of monasticism.

5. André Louf, *The Way of Humility*, trans. Lawrence S. Cunningham, MW 11 (Kalamazoo, MI: Cistercian Publications, 2007), 10.

and humiliation, the humility of God revealed in Christ, humility as an interior disposition versus its material expression, and the question of humility as a social ethic. Underlying these themes is the question of the place of humility in human life.

The four central chapters of the book examine the theology and practice of humility at critical junctures in the development of Western monasticism. Chapter 2 examines the emerging expressions of monasticism in fourth-century Egypt. The literature from this context significantly shapes the evolution of Western monastic theology and practice. Chapter 3 investigates the highly influential sixth-century Rule of Saint Benedict, and chapter 4 considers the person and writings of Bernard of Clairvaux, a central figure in the Cistercian monastic reform of the twelfth century. Chapter 5 brings the study into a contemporary frame, examining the writings of Christian de Chergé and the story of the Cistercian community of Notre-Dame-de-l'Atlas at Tibhirine, Algeria, and focusing on those monks' interpretation of monastic theology and practice in a Muslim context. It will be apparent that in focusing on these four historical moments, the study does not offer a comprehensive exegesis of humility in the Western monastic tradition. That would be a different, larger undertaking.

At the same time, each of these investigations has been conducted with a particular theme in view. The examination of the literature of fourth-century Egypt focuses on humility and the self, the way in which individual identity is reshaped by the theology and experience of the desert. Consideration of the Rule of Saint Benedict allows an examination of the relationship between humility and community, and the way in which the presence of others offers a context for the cultivation of humility. The very public nature of Bernard of Clairvaux's own life and of his reflections on the tensions between contemplation and action facilitates reflection on the place of humility in public life. Finally, the particular vocation of the Tibhirine community to living alongside their Muslim neighbors affords an opportunity to look at humility and *the other*. These themes are partly suggested by the material itself, but this approach is also designed to offer a range of perspectives and, in particular, to move discussion about humility beyond a narrow focus on the individual.

Given the breadth of this project, it is important to acknowledge that I have relied on the closer textual and historical work of a broad range of scholars. Many of them have already noticed or hinted at connections and ideas that I will bring into the foreground. It has often been necessary to leave to one side the numerous scholarly issues that attend each of the subjects under investigation. I generally flag these issues, however, in the contextual introductions that accompany each chapter. Readers familiar with the literature may choose to pass over this material. I begin each of the four central chapters with a visual text: an engraving of *The Temptation of Saint Antony*, a fresco of a scene from the *Life of Saint Benedict*, a Renaissance painting of Bernard of Clairvaux, and a photograph of Christian de Chergé and the Tibhirine community. The intention is to offer an alternate perspective alongside the narratives that unfold through the examination of written texts. These visual texts raise questions and open imaginative worlds with an immediacy that has been helpful in my own journey and that, I hope, will also illuminate the path for my readers.

Any one of the book's four central chapters could have provided more than enough material for the whole. Indeed, many of the scholarly works that I draw on have more modest parameters, offering retrievals of humility in particular settings. In this book I endeavor to analyze and synthesize this material into a broader picture. Placing material from four monastic contexts side by side adds a texture—a fullness and complexity—to understanding humility that would be missing if each had been considered alone. It is my hope that, in sweeping across the canvas of Western monastic thought, it might be possible to see more clearly both the contours of a theology of humility and the way such contours are embedded in the lived life, so that these might in turn be reclaimed in contemporary Christian thought and practice. Nonetheless, the picture is far from complete: the four studies provide four windows or soundings on the subject, not a history of humility. It is my hope that these explorations may offer a small contribution to the rehabilitation of the theology and practice of humility for the twenty-first century.

Chapter 1

Virtue or Vice?

Humility among the Virtues

humility, *n.*
1. a. The quality of being humble or having a lowly opinion of oneself; meekness, lowliness, humbleness: the opposite of *pride* or *haughtiness*.
b. with *pl.* An act of humility or self-abasement.
2. Humble or low condition, rank, or estate; unpretentiousness, humbleness.
3. A local name of several N. American birds of the family Scolopacidæ.

—*Oxford English Dictionary*

The English word *humility* is derived from the Latin *humilis*, meaning "low" and, as has often been observed, is related to *humus*, from the soil. The sense of lowliness is a constant in the story of humility. An eighteenth-century history of Connecticut, cited in the *Oxford English Dictionary*, speaks of a bird called *humility*, so named because it "seldom mounts high in the air."[1] But this lexical tradition has not prevented the emergence of radically different understandings and evaluations of humility over the

1. *Oxford English Dictionary Online*, s.v. "humility," http://www.oed.com:80 /Entry/89375.

course of Western cultural and religious history. While a history of
humility is well beyond the scope of this book, this chapter outlines
some of the critical issues that accompany the task of retrieval.

The modern suspicion of humility and recent attempts to rehabilitate humility as a virtue both rest on an uneven history. When
notions of humility emerge into the post-Constantinian Christian
world, the seeds of complexity and ambiguity are already present. I
will consider these difficulties along two related lines of inquiry: the
contrast between Greco-Roman and Judeo-Christian understandings of humility, and the place of humility in relation to the classical
tradition of the virtues.[2] These investigations bring to the surface
the problems, which persist in the Christian tradition, associated
with understanding humility as a virtue. While many of the issues
identified in this chapter necessarily remain unresolved, its primary
purpose is to reveal the roots of the difficulties that cling tenaciously
to the idea of humility and that, more important, threaten its radical
reading in the Christian tradition. This exploration in turn will inform the reading of the theology and practice of humility in the
monastic expressions that are the primary focus of this book.

1.1 The Lost Virtue? Humility in the Modern World

Humility has had an ambiguous and often marginal place in
the modern Western world.[3] While it is common to recognize

2. In this broad-brush review, I use the term *Greco-Roman* to designate
the cultural world, centered on the Mediterranean, that emerged in the late
fourth century BCE and lasted until the late fourth century CE. See Luther
H. Martin, "Graeco-Roman Philosophy and Religion," in *The Early Christian
World*, ed. Philip F. Esler (London: Routledge, 2000), 53–79, here 55. The term
Judeo-Christian, while somewhat problematic, is used to signify the traditions
emerging from the Hebrew Bible and Judaism, together with their continued
trajectory in early Christianity. I recognize that both Jewish and Christian
traditions came under the influence of the Greco-Roman, or Hellenistic, world
in which they were situated. The term *classical* refers more specifically to the
philosophical tradition that can be traced to the ancient Greeks, beginning
with Socrates and Plato.

3. See, for example, Mark Button, "'A Monkish Kind of Virtue'? For and
Against Humility," *Political Theory* 33, no. 6 (2005): 840–68; Elizabeth A.

a certain sense of personal modesty in the people we most admire, we tend to be suspicious of anything that diminishes self-actualization. Ironically, in Western culture the word *humility* is used most comfortably as a way of portraying an individual's gracious bearing of success.[4]

We are particularly alert to false humility, that is, claims that underplay one's capacities in the face of obviously masterful performance. The obsequious Uriah Heep in Charles Dickens's novel *David Copperfield* exemplifies, albeit in an extreme form, the manipulation of humility as a means of gaining power. Heep is schooled in the art of humility:

> They taught us all a deal of umbleness—not much else that I know of, from morning to night. We was to be umble to this person, and umble to that; and to pull off our caps here, and to make bows there; and always to know our place, and abase ourselves before our betters. And we had such betters! Father got the monitor-medal by being umble. So did I. . . . "Be umble, Uriah," says father to me, "and you'll get on." . . .
>
> When I was quite a young boy . . . I got to know what umbleness did, and I took to it. I ate umble pie with an appetite. . . . "People like to be above you," says father. "Keep yourself down." I am very umble to the present moment, Master Copperfield, but I've got a little power![5]

Humility here has become a form of pride and a mechanism for manipulation. But underneath this, Dickens is exposing a social reality—the place of submission in a hierarchical social order—and the deeper experience of humiliation. There is no interior

---

Dreyer, "Humility," in *The New Westminster Dictionary of Christian Spirituality*, ed. Philip Sheldrake (Louisville, KY: Westminster John Knox Press, 2005); Tom Frame, "Humility: The Despised Virtue?" *Quadrant* 51, no. 4 (2007): 36–42.

4. So, for example, the newspaper headline, "'I'll be peeling potatoes': PM's humble Christmas traditions," referring to the Australian Prime Minister's Christmas Day preparations, would be unlikely to be used in relation to an ordinary citizen (*Sydney Morning Herald*, December 25, 2010).

5. Charles Dickens, *David Copperfield*, ed. Nina Burgis (Oxford: Clarendon Press, 1981), 490–91.

freedom here, and the notion of humility ("umbleness") is deeply despised and mistrusted.

In other contexts, humility has become synonymous with hypocrisy, as Lord Longford's famous remark illustrates: "In 1969 I published a book on humility. It was pioneering work which has not, to my knowledge, been superseded."[6]

Unease with humility, particularly as a social ethic, has a long history. In Renaissance Italy Machiavelli argued that humility was inimical to political advancement since it exhorted acceptance of one's place in the existing power structures.[7] The Enlightenment accelerated a process of sweeping out what was deemed, by Immanuel Kant and others, to be the infantile intellectual heritage of medieval Christendom.[8] Humility was an obvious casualty. With newfound confidence the individual, with a capacity for self-determination and fulfillment, is put at center stage. Here pride seems virtuous and humility unnecessary, even potentially damaging.

So, for example, the eighteenth-century philosopher David Hume dismissed humility as neither "useful" nor "agreeable." For Hume, to deem a quality a virtue required that it entail the use of reason unencumbered by "the delusive glosses of superstition and false religion."[9] The criteria of utility and enjoyment had both individual and communal dimensions. Humility, for Hume, failed on all counts:

> Celibacy, fasting, penance, mortification, self-denial, humility, silence, solitude, and the whole train of monkish virtues; for what reason are they everywhere rejected by men of sense, but because they serve to no manner of purpose; neither advance a man's fortune in the world, nor render him a more valuable member of society; neither qualify him for entertainment of company, nor increase his power of self-enjoyment?

6. Quoted in Frame, "Humility: The Despised Virtue?" 37.
7. See Button, "A Monkish Kind of Virtue?" 842, 862n3.
8. Ted Honderich, ed., *The Oxford Companion to Philosophy* (Oxford: Oxford University Press, 1995), s.v. "Enlightenment."
9. David Hume, *Enquiries Concerning Human Understanding and Concerning the Principles of Morals*, 3rd ed. (Oxford: Clarendon Press, 1975), 270.

We observe, on the contrary, that they cross all these desirable ends; stupefy the understanding and harden the heart, obscure the fancy and sour the temper. We justly, therefore, transfer them to the opposite column, and place them in the catalogue of vices.[10]

Hume's dismissal of humility with "the whole train of monkish virtues" is the dismissal of both a worldview and a whole way of life. Monastic culture, which had been a critical component of medieval Christendom, is viewed as antithetical to living "in the world," in "society," so that values honed in that context have no bearing on ordinary human life or civilization. While Hume's resolutely irreligious stance colors his judgment here, his critique raises a significant question: can humility be practiced as a social, and therefore public, ethic, or is it properly a virtue relevant only to private space?

The nineteenth-century philosopher Friedrich Nietzsche was even more damning, saying that humility is a mark of the slave nature of Christian morality generally and that humility is actually motivated by a desire to use weakness to gain power. Further, there is a perverseness, he argues, in the exaltation of lowliness and weakness and the denigration of success and power. This is an inversion of the natural order of virtues and damaging to human vitality. Humility is utterly despised: "When it is trodden on a worm will curl up. That is prudent. It thereby reduces the chance of being trodden on again. In the language of morals: Humility."[11]

Nietzsche's critique is echoed by feminist concerns. If humility is construed as a virtue in order to facilitate the control imposed by the strong on the weak, it is not surprising, in patriarchal societies, to find it featured as a feminine ideal. In the Christian,

---

10. Hume, *Enquiries*, 270.
11. Friedrich Nietzsche, "Maxims and Arrows," in *Twilight of the Idols* and *The Anti-Christ* (Harmondsworth, UK: Penguin, 1968), 26. See also Button, "'A Monkish Kind of Virtue'?" 847–49; Philippa Foot, *Virtues and Vices, and Other Essays in Moral Philosophy* (Berkeley: University of California Press, 1978), 81–95; Robert C. Roberts, *Spiritual Emotions: A Psychology of Christian Virtues* (Grand Rapids, MI: Eerdmans, 2007), 79–81.

particularly Catholic, tradition this view has been reinforced by the idealization of Mary, submissive and humble. Feminist analysis has rightly cast suspicion on notions of self-sacrifice. Indeed, for women, the sort of self-abnegation that is often equated with humility could be viewed as a vice rather than a virtue. In her classic 1960 essay Valerie Saiving argued that because of the different socialization of women, the "underdevelopment or negation of the self" is more likely to characterize feminine forms of sin than pride.[12]

This sketch of post-Enlightenment suspicion of humility raises a series of questions. What precisely is being rejected? Have understandings of the notion of humility changed? Are there misunderstandings to be clarified? Are there understandings to be retrieved?

In fact, humility has a complex and ambiguous heritage. So, for example, comparing the pre-Christian Greco-Roman world with premodern Christendom reveals an astonishing difference in the understanding and estimation of humility. In the Greco-Roman world, humility was, generally, viewed negatively, even as a vice. In the Christian world humility became a virtue. In order to understand this shift, it is necessary to review briefly the differing conceptions of humility in the Greco-Roman and Judeo-Christian traditions. It is here, and especially in the meeting of these two traditions, that the roots of much of the complexity and ambiguity surrounding the notion of humility are found. Here, too, are found the seeds of its problematic relationship to virtue.

1.2 Humility and Virtue in the Greco-Roman World

It is important to recover a sense of how starkly different the estimation of humility is in Greco-Roman and Judeo-Christian traditions. Humility, it is widely argued, had no place in classical conceptions of virtue.

---

12. Valerie Saiving, "The Human Situation: A Feminine View," in *Womanspirit Rising: A Feminist Reader in Religion*, ed. Carol P. Christ and Judith Plaskow (San Francisco: Harper and Row, 1979), 25–42, here 37.

It will be helpful at this point to give the term *virtue* a little more content. Contemporary moral philosophy generally speaks of virtue in terms of positive traits that motivate action. For example, Jean Porter defines virtue as "a trait of character or intellect which is in some way praiseworthy, admirable or desirable."[13] These traits, she emphasizes, are "dispositions," that is, consistent orientations that underpin behavior, rather than "inclinations," which are a much less stable basis for action. As Porter observes, all societies tend to develop some scheme for naming such desirable traits together with their corresponding vices. The study of the virtues, however, emerged as a central and persistent component of Western moral philosophy.[14]

Philosophical concern for the virtues grew in Greece during the fifth century BCE as the more settled life of the emerging city-states (the *polis*) made the heroic virtues of the Homeric era less relevant.[15] In a context where the warrior was no longer the primary model of a virtuous life, new questions arose regarding what constituted human flourishing. A crucial development, according to Alasdair MacIntyre, was the extension of the notion of virtue beyond the simple fulfillment of a social role to a consideration of what might constitute the good life.[16]

In his analysis, in *After Virtue*, of the varying accounts of virtue in the ancient Greek city-states, MacIntyre observes that, despite the existence of rival lists and definitions, humility "could appear in no Greek list of the virtues."[17] John Casey agrees. In *Pagan Virtue*, his contribution to the contemporary rehabilitation of virtue ethics, Casey claims that "pagan" virtues have a worldly orientation that is utterly opposed to Christian renunciation of

13. Jean Porter, "Virtue Ethics," in *The Cambridge Companion to Christian Ethics*, ed. Robin Gill (Cambridge, UK: Cambridge University Press, 2001), 96.

14. Porter, "Virtue Ethics," in Gill, 96. Also John Casey, *Pagan Virtue: An Essay in Ethics* (Oxford: Clarendon Press, 1990), v.

15. Porter, "Virtue Ethics," in Gill, 97.

16. Alasdair MacIntyre, *After Virtue: A Study in Moral Theory*, 3rd ed. (London: Duckworth, 2007), 132–33.

17. MacIntyre, *After Virtue*, 136.

"worldliness" and its emphasis on "self-abnegation."[18] This is seen most classically, he suggests, in the contrast between Aristotle's *megalopsychos* ("great-souled or magnanimous man"[19]) and Christian notions of humility.[20]

1.2.1 *Aristotle,* Eudaimonia, *and* Megalopsychos

It is worth pausing here to consider this claim, which must be examined in the context of Aristotle's vision of the good life. Indeed, an appreciation of this context contributes significantly to understanding early Christian responses to the classical virtue tradition. Aristotelian metaphysics and ethics influenced the development of Christian thinking well in advance of Thomas Aquinas's ambitious thirteenth-century synthesis, even though it was Aquinas's rethinking of philosophical and theological virtues that decisively reduced humility to a form of modesty.

Aristotle (384–322 BCE) rejects simple identification of the good with wealth, pleasure, or honor (although they are not entirely unconnected), naming instead the good life as *eudaimonia*, a term that has been variously translated as "blessedness," "happiness," "prosperity,"[21] "well-being,"[22] or "flourishing." It is, in

---

18. Casey, *Pagan Virtue*, v–vi. The term *pagan* is problematic. Michele R. Salzman notes that contemporary scholarship recognizes this term as an essentially Christian construction. It became the common term to describe non-Christians in only the fourth century. In addition, this term tends to mask the diversity of non-Christian, non-Jewish "religious" expressions in the late Roman world. See Michele R. Salzman, "Pagans and Christians," in *The Oxford Book of Christian Studies*, ed. Susan Ashbrook Harvey and David G. Hunter (Oxford: Oxford University Press, 2008), 186–202, here 187–89. Casey recognizes that *pagan* is a Christian label, but he uses the term to refer to the ethical tradition arising from Greek philosophical treatment of the virtues.
19. By definition women were excluded from being "great-souled."
20. Casey, *Pagan Virtue*, 199–200.
21. MacIntyre, *After Virtue*, 148.
22. Linda Hogan, "Virtue," in *The New Westminster Dictionary of Christian Spirituality*, ed. Philip Sheldrake (Louisville, KY: Westminster John Knox Press, 2005), 636–37, here 636. See also Honderich, ed., *Companion to Philosophy*, s.v. "Eudaimonia." Hogan suggests that *eudaimonia* is "the state of having an objectively desirable life" and should be carefully distinguished from

MacIntyre's words, "the state of being well and doing well in being well, of a man's being well-favoured himself and in relation to the divine."[23] For Aristotle *eudaimonia* and the virtues are integrally connected. Indeed, as MacIntyre says, the virtues are "precisely those qualities the possession of which will enable an individual to achieve *eudaimonia* and the lack of which will frustrate his movement toward that *telos* [goal]."[24] The virtues are not simply a means to an end but constitutive of the good life. As MacIntyre says, "What constitutes the good for man is a complete human life lived at its best, and the exercise of the virtues is a necessary and central part of such a life, not a mere preparatory exercise to secure such a life."[25]

Essential to Aristotle's ethical system is his doctrine of the mean "according to which the virtues are stable dispositions leading to reactions and behaviours in accordance with a mean as that is determined by practical wisdom."[26] Virtue is to be found at the midpoint between two corresponding vices, an excess or a deficiency.[27] So, for example, the virtue of courage is the mean between the vices of rashness and cowardice. Rashness is an

---

"subjective" modern concepts of happiness. I am not sure that *objective* and *subjective* are the most helpful terms here. The point is more clearly made by Christopher Cordner, who argues for the communitarian context of Aristotelian ethics, and by Casey, who calls this setting "worldliness." See Christopher Cordner, "Aristotelian Virtue and Its Limitations," *Philosophy* 69, no. 269 (1994): 291–316, here 303–10; and Casey, *Pagan Virtue*, viii.

23. MacIntyre, *After Virtue*, 148.
24. MacIntyre, *After Virtue*, 148.
25. MacIntyre, *After Virtue*, 149.
26. Porter, "Virtue Ethics," in Gill, 98.
27. Aristotle, *The Ethics of Aristotle: The Nicomachean Ethics*, trans. J. A. K. Thomson, rev. ed. (Harmondsworth, UK: Penguin, 1976), 2.6, 1106b–1107a: "So virtue is a purposive disposition, lying in a mean that is relative to us and determined by a rational principle, and by that which a prudent man would use to determine it. It is a mean between two kinds of vice, one of excess and the other of deficiency; and also for this reason, that whereas these vices fall short of or exceed the right measure in both feelings and actions, virtue discovers the mean and chooses it." For the Greek text, see Aristotle, *The Nicomachean Ethics*, trans. H. Rackham, Loeb Classical Library (London: William Heinemann, 1926).

excess of courage, while cowardice is its deficiency (*Ethics* 2.7–8; 1107b–1108b).

The first challenge in examining Aristotle's description of the virtue of *megalopsychos* (*Ethics* 4.3; 1123a–1124a) is to adequately translate this term and the corresponding vices, *chaunos* and *mikropsychos*, from the Greek. *Megalopsychos* (literally "great-souledness") is sometimes translated as the "proud man," and *mikropsychos* (literally "small-souledness") as the "humble man."[28] This pairing, of course, is very tempting, since it would provide a neat reversal of later Christian estimations of humility and pride. But the situation is more complex. It is probably safer to use the terms *magnanimous* and *pusillanimous*, or to use the original Greek.[29] *Chaunos* is more straightforward; it can be rendered as *vain* or *conceited*.

The twin watchwords of magnanimity are greatness and honor. Aristotle says "a person is considered to be magnanimous if he thinks that he is worthy of great things, provided that he *is* worthy of them" (*Ethics* 4.3; 1123b). The estimation of greatness is an accurate one: the magnanimous man thinks he is great because he is great. By contrast, the pusillanimous man underestimates his worth, regardless of his actual worth: "whether his worth is great or moderate or little" (*Ethics* 4.3; 1123b). Aristotle suggests that "magnanimity seems to be a sort of crown of the virtues" (*Ethics* 4.3; 1124a). It is never found without excellence in all the other virtues and also seems to enhance them. For this reason, Aristotle says, it is difficult to be truly magnanimous. The central concern of the magnanimous man is what Aristotle recognizes as

28. For example, Daniel H. Frank, "Humility as a Virtue: A Maimonidean Critique of Aristotle's Ethics," in *Moses Maimonides and His Time*, ed. Eric L. Ormsby (Washington, DC: Catholic University of America Press, 1989), 89–99, here 90. Frank confidently identifies *megalopsychia* as pride and *mikropsychia* as humility and proceeds to demonstrate their reversal as virtue and vice in the work of the twelfth-century Jewish philosopher Maimonides.

29. As Casey notes, this approach has "the advantage of literalness" and is "a little more distant from common usage than 'proud' and 'pride.'" See Casey, *Pagan Virtue*, 199n3. That is not to say that *megalopsychos* and pride are unrelated.

the greatest external good: honor. We render this to the gods, he says, and such honor is rightly due to the magnanimous man.[30] The magnanimous man has, Aristotle claims, the particular capacity to deal with expressions of honor and dishonor:

> At great honours bestowed by responsible persons he will feel pleasure, but only a moderate one, because he will feel that he is getting no more than his due, or rather less, since no honour can be enough for perfect excellence. Nevertheless he will accept such honours, on the ground that there is nothing greater that they can give him. But honour conferred by ordinary people for trivial reasons he will utterly despise, because that sort of thing is beneath his dignity. And similarly with dishonour, because it cannot rightfully attach to him. (*Ethics* 4.3; 1124a)

The magnanimous man will have, Aristotle suggests, a similar detachment or moderation with regard to other external goods—"wealth, power, and every kind of fortune" (*Ethics* 4.3; 1124a). Such detachment will sometimes result, though, in being thought "supercilious" (*Ethics* 4.3; 1124a).

Aristotle is somewhat equivocal, however, about the relationship between magnanimity and fortune.[31] Magnanimity is unquestionably a Greek aristocratic virtue. The height of moral goodness, the greatness of virtue, achieved by the *megalopsychos* is facilitated by "good fortune" (*fortuna*), by wealth, and by access to power. It is possible, though, to have these advantages without virtue; as Aristotle says, "It is not easy to bear the gifts of fortune inoffensively" (*Ethics* 4.3; 1124a). Fortune seems to be a necessary but not sufficient condition of magnanimity. On the other hand, it is inconceivable to Aristotle that those of the lower

---

30. "If, then, the magnanimous man makes, and deservedly makes, great claims, and especially the greatest claims, he must have one special object in view. Now when one speaks of worth, it is in relation to external goods; and we should assume the greatest of these to be that which we render to the gods, and which is most desired by the eminent, and is the prize for the finest achievements; and that which answers this description is honour, because it is clearly the greatest external good" (Aristotle, *Ethics* 4.3; 1123b).

31. Casey, *Pagan Virtue*, 201–2.

classes could exhibit magnanimity. He assumes wealth and status to be prerequisites.[32]

Aristotle's portrait of the *megalopsychos* illustrates this position clearly. The magnanimous man sits at the top of the patronage system: he must never be a debtor.

> He is disposed to confer benefits, but is ashamed to accept them, because the one is the act of a superior and the other that of an inferior. When he repays a service he does so with interest, because in this way the original benefactor will become his debtor and beneficiary. People of this kind are thought to remember the benefits that they have conferred, but not those that they have received (because the beneficiary is inferior to the benefactor, and the magnanimous man wants to be superior). (*Ethics* 4.3; 1124b)

Similarly, maintaining this superior position requires a nuanced set of behaviors toward people of different social ranks. The closer a benefactor is to a beneficiary in rank, the more the benefactor has to work to demonstrate superiority:

> He is haughty toward those who are influential and successful, but moderate towards those who have an intermediate position in society, because in the former case to be superior is difficult and impressive, but in the latter it is easy; and to create an impression at the expense of the former is not ill-bred, but to do so among the humble [Gk *tapeinos*] is vulgar—like using one's strength against the weak. (*Ethics* 4.3; 1124b)

Above all, the magnanimous man must differentiate himself from any form of servitude—"and he cannot bear to live in dependence upon somebody else, except a friend, because such conduct is servile; which is why all flatterers are of the lowest class, and humble people are flatterers" (*Ethics* 4.3; 1125a). Here Aristotle is a world away from the Christian commonplace of servant leadership.

---

32. MacIntyre, *After Virtue*, 159.

There are two things to note at this point. The first is contemporary discomfort with the contingency of moral goodness in Aristotle's scheme. As Casey says, "The notion that what is obligatory on all—moral goodness—might be possible only for people favoured by fortune, or much easier for them, will strike many of us as a sort of scandal."[33] This view is, Casey suggests, in stark contrast to Christian teaching, where goodness is seen to be independent of circumstance. Pagan virtues have, from a Christian perspective, a disturbing "worldliness."[34] (By "worldliness" Casey means that they "include an element of self-regard" and "rely upon material conditions for their fulfillment."[35])

The second, and not unrelated, thing to note is the social dimension of Aristotle's scheme. Indeed the social setting of Greek moral thought has sometimes been overlooked in contemporary philosophical retrievals of humility. For example, against MacIntyre and others, Brian Scarlett wants to find a place for humility in the Greek world.[36] He looks initially to Aristotle's virtue of *megalopsychos* but rejects as "nonsense" Aristotle's "vignette of great-souledness," including its outworkings with regard to patronage, speech, and demeanor. For Scarlett, Aristotle's magnanimous man is not the mean but the excess of self-regard.[37]

What Scarlett has failed to note is the social embeddedness of Aristotle's portrait. Aristotle is fundamentally concerned with the arena of *honor* in his discussion of magnanimity. In Aristotle's world, this self-appraisal cannot be separated from the *polis*. And, again, it cannot be separated from *fortuna* and from one's place in the scheme of life. No one is self-made; the accidents of birth, health, wealth, luck, and the favor of the gods all contribute to

33. Casey, *Pagan Virtue*, 202. A key reason for discomfort with this approach is that, as Casey notes in his preface (vi), the Western moral outlook has been substantially shaped by the Christian tradition. See also Cordner, "Aristotelian Virtue," 293.

34. Casey, *Pagan Virtue*, 208.

35. Casey, *Pagan Virtue*, viii.

36. Brian Scarlett, "Humility: A Monkish Virtue," Preprint Series (Department of Philosophy, University of Melbourne), no. 14/94 (1994), 1–20.

37. Scarlett, "Humility: A Monkish Virtue," 11–12.

one's capacity to achieve moral excellence. Scarlett, however, argues that such an awareness of the operation of *fortuna* should "rein in haughtiness" and bring "gratitude" and "humility."[38] Perhaps, but there seems little evidence that such awareness manifested itself widely in the Greco-Roman world or was held up as an ideal. Certainly, as Scarlett himself acknowledges, if such a corrective to excessive self-regard was operative, it was not named "humility." Scarlett is bringing a very modern sensibility to bear here and has failed to take account of the central place of honor and shame in the ancient Mediterranean world, particularly in relation to understanding the self.

MacIntyre is helpful here. In *After Virtue*, MacIntyre draws attention to the multiple traditions that operate in a society at any one time. The Greek city-states of the fifth century BCE inherited, and reshaped to their own purposes, the conception of virtue reflected in Homer's poetic telling of heroic, warrior society. In the Homeric world identity was determined by one's place in the social order, by role and status. One's actions were the test of one's worth—there was no separation between character and behavior. To fail is to fail to fulfill one's duty, one's given role. To succeed was to meet one's social expectations. Success brought honor. Failure was the cause of shame. The self was, as MacIntyre notes, "a social creation, not an individual one."[39] There is no outside view. Indeed, to step outside this order was to become a nonperson.[40]

This Homeric tradition was not lost to Aristotle. Honor and shame were still key players in his world. Christopher Cordner observes that, for Aristotle, "virtue can be realized only in an essentially public realm in which men *appear* before one another—in which honor, shame, praise, blame, admiration, contempt are manifest in practice and ceremony."[41] For Aristotle, ethics has a social and public orientation. So, for example, in the case of courage, which is understood primarily as physical courage and

38. Scarlett, "Humility: A Monkish Virtue," 16–17.
39. MacIntyre, *After Virtue*, 129.
40. MacIntyre, *After Virtue*, 122–27.
41. Cordner, "Aristotelian Virtue," 303.

shown most completely on the battlefield, Aristotle's concern is with the presentation of the self to the world, "the carving out of an impressive *presence* before others."[42] For Aristotle there is no *separate* inner state of courage as in modern understandings. There is little interiority here. As Cordner says: "The moral selfhood of Aristotle's virtuous person is actually constituted in the domain of his communal interactions."[43] Indeed, Aristotle's portrait of the *megalopsychos* demonstrates this very concern with social relations. Virtue has an essentially public face.

1.2.2 Humility as a Condition of the Socially Inferior

This brief examination of Aristotelian ethics has highlighted the significant relationship between virtue and honor in the classical philosophical heritage that underpins the Greco-Roman world, and the essentially social nature of moral life. In this world, human well-being or flourishing (*eudaimonia*) and the possession of virtue are fundamentally related to the accumulation of honor. Understanding this context makes it clear why humility can never be considered a virtue in that world.

Klaus Wengst's study of the occurrence of words denoting "humble" and "humility" (Gk *tapeinos* and Lat *humilis*) in Greco-Roman texts further signals the need to be attentive to social meanings and resonances.[44] According to Wengst, these terms are most commonly found in social or political contexts. Significantly, he notes, these terms are used by people of high social status with regard to those of low status. The terms convey a sense of talking down from above. Humility generally denotes a lowly social position, sometimes even a sense of being downtrodden. Wengst

---

42. Cordner, "Aristotelian Virtue," 300.
43. Cordner, "Aristotelian Virtue," 305.
44. Klaus Wengst, *Humility: Solidarity of the Humiliated: The Transformation of an Attitude and Its Social Relevance in Graeco-Roman, Old Testament-Jewish and Early Christian Tradition*, trans. John Bowden (London: SCM Press, 1988), 4–15. See also Erich Auerbach, *Literary Language and Its Public in Late Latin Antiquity and the Middle Ages*, trans. Ralph Manheim (Princeton, NJ: Princeton University Press, 1965), 39–40.

offers a series of examples to make his case. In Aelius Aristides's *Eulogy of Rome*, Oibaras instructs the Persian king on the necessity of touring his kingdom to inspect those who have been subjugated by his rule: "Let him see what happens to a hosepipe: the parts on which he treads are pressed down [Gk *tapeina egigneto*] and touch the earth, whereas the parts from which his foot is removed rise up again and are pressed down again [*etapeinounto*] only when he treads on them once more."[45]

Significantly, this lowliness of position also results in a lowly disposition.[46] Indeed, as was noted above, a "slave mentality" is evident in Aristotle's description of low-class flatterers (*Ethics* 4.3; 1125a). Similarly, Wengst observes that in the Greco-Roman world, high status and *fortuna* give one access to the social advantages of freedom, wealth, power, influence, leisure, and learning, all prerequisites for the pursuit of the virtues. By contrast, those whose lives are dominated by manual labor or, in a phrase used by Pliny, by "lowly and dirty tasks [Lat. *humiles et sordidas curas*]," are precluded from living a life of virtue.[47]

Lucian's *The Dream*, an account of the vision that inspired Lucian to abandon sculpture in order to pursue a career as a rhetorician, is particularly illustrative. The late date of this text (second century CE) is helpful, showing the persistence of the connection between manual labor, low status, and notions of humility. Lucian (ca. 125–180) relates how, on the day after he had been sent to his uncle to train as a stonemason, he had a dream in which he had to choose between two women, one beautiful (representing Education) and the other ugly (representing Sculpture). It is worth quoting Education's condemnation of Sculpture at length:

> What shall it profit you to become a sculptor . . . you will be nothing but a labourer, toiling with your body and putting in it your entire hope of a livelihood, personally inconspicuous [Gk *tapeinos tēn gnomēn*], getting meagre and illiberal returns, humble-witted, an insignificant figure in public, neither sought

<hr/>

45. Quoted in Wengst, *Humility*, 4.
46. Wengst, *Humility*, 4.
47. Wengst, *Humility*, 6.

by your friends nor envied by your fellow-citizens—nothing but just a labourer, one of the swarming rabble, ever cringing to the man above you and courting the man who can use his tongue, leading a hare's life, and counting as a godsend to anyone stronger. . . . You will put on a filthy tunic, assume a servile appearance, and hold bars and gravers and sledges and chisels in your hands, with your back bent over your work; you will be a groundling, with groundling ambitions, altogether humble [*tapeinos*]; you will never lift your head, or conceive a single manly or liberal thought.[48]

All the key elements are here: humility is connected with sordid manual labor and with social inferiority; the humble are condemned to flattery and trod upon like slaves, utterly without public honor and incapable of higher thought.[49]

Humility in the Greco-Roman world, then, was primarily a condition of the socially inferior, whose servile status and dependence on physical labor precluded them from all that was considered valuable in public life: freedom, learning, power, riches, influence. Humility is not a virtue.

1.3 Humility in the Judeo-Christian World

The Judeo-Christian world reveals a very different climate. Care for the lowly or humiliated emerged as a core value in the Hebrew Scriptures and in the practice of Judaism, with God taking the side of the oppressed and downtrodden. How is this solidarity with the lowly related to evolving notions of humility?

48. Lucian of Samosata, "The Dream or Lucian's Career," in *Lucian*, 8 vols., trans. A. M. Harmon, Loeb Classical Library (London: William Heinemann, 1921 [repr. 1960]), 3:223, 227; Wengst, *Humility*, 8.

49. Lucian's story, as Wengst notes, also signals the possibility of social mobility. Education enables "the beggarly son of a nobody" to rise to a position of wealth and honor (Wengst, *Humility*, 8–10). Wengst also notes a small number of positive uses of *humility* in ancient literature, generally to describe the relationship between humans and the gods, and occasionally as a form of modesty in relation to one's lifestyle (Wengst, *Humility*, 14–15).

Biblical scholars have engaged in considerable debate regarding the origin and meaning of humility in the Hebrew Scriptures, much of it of a technical, linguistic nature. Moving across languages (from Latin and Greek to Hebrew) poses significant challenges. What should one look for? Which word or words in the texts? And what preconceptions regarding humility shape the search for its antecedents? There is more than one place to start, and where one starts seems to influence what one finds. Wengst, for example, begins with the Septuagint and traces back into the Hebrew Bible the terms that have been rendered by the Greek root *tapeino-*. In the Hebrew Bible, Wengst finds the roots of humility in the experience of material poverty and argues that it develops ethically as the "solidarity of the oppressed."[50]

Stephen B. Dawes, on the other hand, begins with the Hebrew noun *'anawa(h)*, the word used in rabbinic literature for the "virtue of humility" (which he understands as the lowering of oneself before another). He confirms this usage in Sirach and the Community Rule of the Dead Sea Scrolls and then traces this term back into the Hebrew Bible, finding the same ethical meaning in each of its occurrences.[51] He then tentatively suggests that what he calls the "humility ethic" has its origins in royal ideology, in questions about the use and abuse of power.[52] These different starting points take Wengst and Dawes in different directions.[53] John P. Dickson and Brian S. Rosner, again starting with the Hebrew *'anawa(h)* but

50. Wengst, *Humility*, 16–35.

51. Stephen B. Dawes, "Anāwa in Translation and Tradition," *Vetus Testamentum* 41, no. 1 (1991): 38–48.

52. Stephen B. Dawes, "Humility: Whence This Strange Notion?" *Expository Times* 103, no. 3 (1991): 72–75, here 74.

53. In both instances, there is a very real possibility that later usages may have influenced the reading of earlier texts. Dickson and Rosner, for example, note correctly that in beginning his argument with the use of *'anawa(h)* in Sirach and the Community Rule, Dawes is merely demonstrating "what the term came to mean in Jewish tradition." Further, "the frequent references in the body of the essay to these and other ancient Jewish traditions concerning [*'anawa(h)*] leave the impression that the later usage of the term (to mean ethical humility toward God or man) is somehow significant for understanding the work in its biblical occurrences centuries earlier" (John P.

looking at a broader linguistic range than Dawes, argue that biblical humility is a theological rather than social ethic, one focused on submission to God, not on social relations.[54]

The resolution of this debate is beyond the scope of this chapter, but its nature indicates the sorts of issues and ambiguities that present themselves when one endeavors to understand emerging notions of humility. It touches, for example, on the challenging relationship between humility and humiliation, the relationship between humility and poverty, and the question of the relationship between humility and social ethics. Even if Wengst sometimes pushes the evidence too hard, there is clearly a relationship between the experience of humiliation, poverty, and oppression, and an evolving notion of humility; they are, if contentiously, linguistically related. And while, as Wengst admits, there seems to be a trend toward the spiritualization of humility over time,[55] its material and social resonances persist. In the shift from humility as the material deprivation of the poor to humility as submission before God, from material to spiritual abasement, as Pierre Adnès observes, "we are taken imperceptibly from one meaning to the other."[56]

Early Christianity took up these complex foundations and stretched them further. Not only did it affirm God's solidarity with the humiliated, but also, looking at the life and death of Jesus as paradigmatic, it named humility a central value. It is important to keep in mind here the broader cultural milieu in which the earliest Christian communities were located and, in particular, the largely negative estimation of humility among the Roman ruling classes. In this context, the positive valuation of humility was radically

Dickson and Brian S. Rosner, "Humility as a Social Virtue in the Hebrew Bible?" *Vetus Testamentum* 54, no. 4 [2004]: 459–79, here 463).

54. Dickson and Rosner, "Humility as a Social Virtue," 459–79.

55. Over time, Wengst argues, humility in the Old Testament-Jewish tradition begins to gather positive ethical connotations, such as commending modesty against inflated pride (Wengst, *Humility*, 16–35).

56. Pierre Adnès, "Humilité," *Dictionnaire de spiritualité*, 1969 ed. My translation.

countercultural.[57] This was a significant, if not definitive, moment in the development of conceptions of humility. Both Wengst and Gerd Theissen offer an analysis of these developments that helpfully maps the cluster of ideas that accompanied an emerging Christian conception of humility.[58]

The earliest Christian communities, Theissen observes, found themselves "between Judaism and paganism."[59] As these communities developed an "ethic," a way of living out their emerging identity, they brought to this project three fundamental ingredients: the heritage of the Hebrew Scriptures and the traditions of Judaism, the religious and cultural environment of Hellenism (in which the majority were formed),[60] and the stories and emerging traditions regarding the life, death, and resurrection of Jesus of Nazareth. The emerging Christian ethic built on and sometimes extended its Jewish heritage and often played against the Greco-Roman environment. Out of this context, Theissen argues, love of neighbor and the renunciation of status emerged as the two basic values of the primitive Christian ethic.

57. The strength of an honor-shame culture in Roman society has been demonstrated by J. E. Lendon in his interpretation of Roman government. While he does not directly deal with the changing estimation of humility, Lendon does note the radical challenge of Christian perspectives (where glory belongs to God and is not to be sought in this life) to Roman aristocratic views of honor: "Activities prompted by the lust for honour in this life were ruled out; ideally the whole proud, competitive, jostling ethos of the ancient city was abandoned." He notes, however, that in practice Christians redefined honor in a way that allowed for a "rapprochement" (J. E. Lendon, *Empire of Honour: The Art of Government in the Roman World* [Oxford: Oxford University Press, 1995; repr. 2005], 92–93).

58. Wengst, *Humility*, 36–53; Gerd Theissen, *A Theory of Primitive Christian Religion*, trans. John Bowden (London: SCM Press, 1999), 63–80.

59. Theissen, *Primitive Christian Religion*, 63.

60. Martin uses the term *Hellenistic* to refer to "the general diffusion of Greek culture among those peoples conquered by Alexander as a consequence of his Hellenizing policies, a cultural program actively pursued by his successors." Hellenism remained the dominant culture in the Greco-Roman period and the context in which "the early Christianities emerged and were given their shape" (Martin, "Graeco-Roman Philosophy," 55).

Renunciation of status is actually necessitated by the love of neighbor. While love of neighbor, and even its extension to include outsider groups, is found in the Hebrew Scriptures and Judaism, in primitive Christianity it comes to center stage. Its centrality raises the very real issue of how one loves across boundaries—when the neighbor is of a different rank or status. Love of neighbor pushes one to consider how to overcome these differences. Theissen suggests that this value is mapped by three interrelated terms: humility, renunciation of status, and change of position. *Change of position* is Theissen's term for the paradoxical elevation of the lowly or humiliated that is found in the Hebrew biblical tradition and reinforced and strengthened in primitive Christianity (he places "the Christ event" within this framework).[61]

Renunciation of status is the downward movement of giving up or renouncing one's superior rank or status. This renunciation can be expressed in a variety of ways: by renouncing the display of one's status (modesty), by renouncing the imposition of one's will, or by giving up "the possession of a status" itself. Theissen understands renunciation of status as a particular manifestation of the broader ethic of humility: "[*Humilitas*] denotes both the one who has a lowly status and inwardly accepts it and the one who has high status but does not exploit it."[62] Humility here has both an inner disposition and a social outworking.

Both Theissen and Wengst detect in the earliest Christian traditions the novel appearance of a type of "mutual humility" that functions as a "social virtue."[63] Wengst styles this "mutual humility" as "the condition for a new community."[64] Paul's exhortation to the Philippians is a clear example: "Do nothing from selfish conceit, but in humility regard others as better than yourselves. Let each of you look not to your own interests, but to the interests of others" (Phil 2:3-4).[65] This instruction, as both Theissen and

---

61. Theissen, *Primitive Christian Religion*, 72.
62. Theissen, *Primitive Christian Religion*, 71.
63. Theissen, *Primitive Christian Religion*, 72.
64. Wengst, *Humility*, 45.
65. All quotations from the Bible use the New Revised Standard Version unless otherwise stated.

Wengst note, is in sharp contrast to the expectations of the prevailing Greco-Roman culture, where the increase, not the decrease, of honor and status is the prime motivator of action.[66] Within the framework of the pursuit of honor, humility can only be viewed as "a servile, contemptible disposition."[67]

By contrast, in the "new Jewish and Christian ethic of humility," Theissen says, "a moral defect becomes a virtue."[68] Wengst observes that the stress here is not on individual renunciation but on establishing "the basic condition for [the creation of] a new society which really is all-inclusive."[69] That is, it creates a community that can practice the radical love of neighbor. The Philippians passage, which has the feel of a manifesto, arises from Paul's concrete experiences of both accepting weakness and humiliation (e.g., 2 Cor 12:7-10) and choosing material and social lowliness (2 Cor 11:7; Phil 4:10-14). He has embarked on the same downward path (which Wengst calls "the complete opposite to a career") as the Christ he follows.[70] This is the Christ celebrated in the hymn in Philippians chapter 2. Here Christ's radical humility, his self-emptying (*kenōsis*), leads to and finds its ultimate expression in the extreme humiliation of death on the cross:

> though he [Christ] was in the form of God,
> [he] did not regard equality with God
> as something to be exploited,
> but emptied himself [*heauton ekenōsen*],
> taking the form of a slave,
> being born in human likeness.
> And being found in human form,
> he humbled himself [*etapeinōsen heauton*]
> and became obedient to the point of death—
> even death on a cross. (Phil 2:6-8)[71]

66. Theissen, *Primitive Christian Religion*, 72; Wengst, *Humility*, 48–50.
67. Theissen, *Primitive Christian Religion*, 72.
68. Theissen, *Primitive Christian Religion*, 72.
69. Wengst, *Humility*, 49.
70. Wengst, *Humility*, 50.
71. The Greek text is from *The Greek New Testament*, ed. Barbara Aland, et al., fourth rev. ed. (Stuttgart: Deutsche Bibelgesellschaft, 1993). Greek

This self-emptying, Wengst says, is "an act of the deepest solidarity" with the lowly and humiliated.[72] It is also the locus of the formation of Christian community. Theissen articulates the consequences of acting from this perspective (that is, the ethical outworking of Paul's Christology here): "Within the Christian community, humility is not a servile attitude towards rulers and the powerful but behaviour towards all fellow men and women, regardless of their social status. It is the imitation of the one who forsook his high status in pre-existence in order to bring about the salvation of human beings on earth by humbling himself."[73] The Christian community is to enact this same pattern: mutual humility, a giving way of the self to the other, replaces rivalrous competition for honor.

A final but important note in this brief review of developments in the early Christian conception of humility: Theissen rightly points out that the radical requirement of love and humility "asks too much of human capabilities" (asceticism and martyrdom are particularly extreme "demands") but that, against this demand, is placed an equally radical development of the concept of God's grace.[74] So forgiveness, both by God and of each other, and acceptance, of self and others, become key elements of the primitive

---

transliterations follow the conventions specified by *The SBL Handbook of Style* (Peabody, MA: Hendrickson Publishers, 1999).

72. Wengst, *Humility*, 51.

73. Theissen, *Primitive Christian Religion*, 76. Theissen's interpretation of *kenōsis* as the renunciation of "high status in pre-existence" is contentious. This position, however, does not detract from his main argument here. For a brief overview of historical interpretations of Philippians 2 and their theological significance, see Sarah Coakley, *Powers and Submissions: Spirituality, Philosophy and Gender* (Oxford: Blackwell, 2002), 3–39. A classic New Testament study of this passage, originally published in 1967 under the title *Carmen Christi*, is Ralph P. Martin, *A Hymn of Christ: Philippians 2:5-11 in Recent Interpretation and in the Setting of Early Christian Worship* (Downers Grove, IL: InterVarsity Press, 1997). For an introduction to the key areas of debate, including the relationship between Christology and ethics, see Ralph P. Martin and Brian J. Dodd, eds., *Where Christology Began: Essays on Philippians 2* (Louisville, KY: Westminster John Knox Press, 1998).

74. Theissen, *Primitive Christian Religion*, 79.

Christian ethical environment.[75] Above all, the ethical demands of
love and humility are sustained by a deepening encounter with
the foundational Christian story: "God himself realizes love . . .
by loving his enemies, the sinners; and God realizes humility by
coming close to human beings in their finitude by renouncing
his status."[76] It is, as Wengst might say, God's solidarity with the
humiliated that enables solidarity among the humiliated.

Already, then, the cluster of ideas that accompany the Christian notion of humility through time have emerged: renunciation, humiliation-exaltation, mutuality, community, grace, and
love. These companions appear repeatedly, sometimes clarifying,
sometimes clouding the understanding of humility as it is woven
into Christian monastic traditions.

In addition to these, but more problematically, obedience
and submission are already found in conjunction with humility
in the earliest layers of the Christian tradition. As Christianity
emerges from its foundational period, through persecution to
post-Constantinian embrace, the radical countercultural social
ethic implied by New Testament readings of humility proves,
not surprisingly, to be difficult to enact. And there emerge, very
early in the Christian tradition, readings of humility that begin
to serve the interests of those in authority. At the end of the first
century, in the first letter of Clement, for example, humility is
equated with the submissive obedience of the individual to the
appointed authorities. This view, as Wengst observes, is not far
from the Greco-Roman inheritance.[77]

1.4 Humility among the Virtues

With the contrast between Greco-Roman and Judeo-Christian
visions of humility in view, it is now possible to consider the

---

75. MacIntyre argues that the inclusion of charity and forgiveness as core
virtues "alters the good for man in a radical way; for the community in which
the good is achieved has to be one of reconciliation." This is consonant with
Theissen's reading of early Christianity (MacIntyre, *After Virtue*, 174).

76. Theissen, *Primitive Christian Religion*, 80.

77. Wengst, *Humility*, 54–57.

meeting of the classical-virtue tradition with the emerging vision of Christian humility. One result of this encounter is that humility began to be identified as a virtue, a move that has significant and arguably dangerous consequences for its Christian understanding.[78] While the language of virtue (Lat *virtus*, Gk *aretē*) is almost completely absent from the Hebrew and Christian Scriptures,[79] both Jewish and Christian theologians necessarily began to engage with Greco-Roman philosophical and ethical systems. The classical notions of virtue and vice, with their associated alternate pathways for the conduct of human life, were readily incorporated into a Judeo-Christian framework. The Jewish theologian Philo of Alexandria (ca. 20 BCE–50 CE) reframed Moses as a moral hero, progressing through various stages of virtue until he was accorded a vision of God. Gregory of Nyssa (ca. 331–395) took up and extended this reworking in his influential *Life of Moses*. But even before the Constantinian shift, Origen of Alexandria (ca. 186–255) made a formative contribution to the synthesis of classical and biblical thought, identifying Christ not simply as an exemplar of virtue but also as its embodiment and thus both the source and the goal of the virtuous life.[80]

---

78. The manuscript for this book was completed before the publication of Stephen T. Pardue's study, *The Mind of Christ: Humility and the Intellect in Early Christian Theology* (London: Bloomsbury, 2013). Pardue does not contend with the identification of humility as a virtue. His primary focus is on humility in the life of the intellect. Working particularly with Gregory of Nyssa and Augustine of Hippo, Pardue argues that a Christian understanding of intellectual humility allows one to avoid "post-Kantian apophaticism" (182). Rather, as a response to human limits, humility paradoxically empowers the individual, through the operation of divine grace, to transcend these limits. I arrive at a not dissimilar conclusion via a very different route.

79. While the word *aretē* appears occasionally in the New Testament, its use is different from that of the classical philosophical tradition. See André Louf, *The Way of Humility*, trans. Lawrence S. Cunningham, MW 11 (Kalamazoo, MI: Cistercian Publications, 2007), 5. For a broad consideration of the place of virtue ethics in the Bible, see John Barton, "Virtue in the Bible," *Studies in Christian Ethics* 12, no. 1 (1999), 12–22.

80. John Anthony McGuckin, *The Westminister Handbook to Patristic Theology* (Louisville, KY: Westminster John Knox Press, 2004), s.v. "Virtue."

Augustine of Hippo's (354–430) engagement with the virtues—
both his critique of classical thought and his rethinking of the
hierarchy of virtues—had a definitive influence on the development of Western Christian thought. Augustine was critical of
Roman conceptions of virtue that were predicated on the pursuit of human praise.[81] Virtue in itself, he argued, is not the end
or goal of life.[82] Appropriating the Greek philosophical notion
of *eudaimonia*, Augustine recasts human flourishing or *beatitudo*
(blessedness) as founded on the knowledge of God, with the goal
and end of human life "the enjoyment of God." Moral choices are
determined by this end (*telos*).[83] God is the source of true virtue.
So, in the *City of God*, Augustine suggests that since pagan virtues are founded in human glory rather than in the knowledge
of God, they should be deemed vices rather than virtues.[84] For
Augustine, Christian virtue, based on revelation and faith, is superior to "natural" virtue derived from experience and reason.
Augustine did not, however, completely reject "natural" virtue,
and he incorporated it into a twofold scheme: he added three
"infused" or theological virtues (faith, hope, and charity) to the
four classically derived cardinal virtues (prudence, temperance,
fortitude, and justice). The resulting scheme of seven virtues has
influenced moral theology to the present.[85]

Humility finds no place in this scheme. This is not to say that
Augustine did not recognize its significance for Christian theology
and ethics. Indeed, for Augustine, humility is the very quality

81. Jean Porter, "Virtue," in *The Oxford Handbook of Theological Ethics*, ed.
Gilbert Meilaender and William Werpehowski (Oxford: Oxford University
Press, 2005), 210.

82. George J. Lavere, "Virtue," in *Augustine through the Ages: An Encyclopedia*,
ed. Allan D. Fitzgerald (Grand Rapids, MI: Eerdmans, 1999), 871–74, here 872.

83. Gerard J. P. O'Daly, *Augustine's Philosophy of Mind* (Berkeley: University
of California Press, 1987), 5.

84. Augustine, *The City of God*, trans. Henry Bettenson (London: Penguin,
1984), 19.25, 891. This assessment needs to be read with some caution. Porter
argues that Augustine's critique of virtue in his society is actually highly
nuanced and partly directed at the degeneration of ancient ideals. See Porter,
"Virtue," in Meilaender and Werpehowski, 209–13.

85. Lavere, "Virtue," in Fitzgerald, 872.

that distinguishes Christianity from paganism: many "excellent precepts of morality and self-improvement" can be found in the "books of the pagans, whether Epicurean, Stoic, Manichean or Platonist," but "nowhere humility like this."[86] Augustine is clear about the source of such humility. In his second exposition of Psalm 31, he says, "The way of humility comes from no other source; it comes only from Christ. It is the way originated by him who, though most high, came in humility. What else did he teach us by humbling himself and becoming obedient even to death, even to the death on the cross?"[87] For Augustine humility is the fundamental underpinning of Christian life.[88]

Further, for Augustine, the embrace of the humble way of Christ continues to have social consequences. In the *Confessions* he relates the story of the conversion of Victorinus, a noted professor of rhetoric and defender of Roman cultic practices. In his old age Victorinus becomes privately convinced of the truth of the Gospel, but his friend Simplicianus will not count him as Christian until he has joined the Christian community, the church, and challenges him to make his profession of faith public. When Victorinus does so, he risks his privileged place in Roman society. Indeed both Simplicianus and Augustine consider his baptism and profession of faith as acts of humility: "He was not ashamed to be the child of Christ and to become an infant at your font,

86. Augustine, *Expositions of the Psalms (1–32)*, trans. Maria Boulding, The Works of Saint Augustine: A Translation for the 21st Century, pt. 3, vol. 15 (Hyde Park, NY: New City Press, 2000), Exposition 2, Psalm 31:6b, sec. 18, pp. 380–81.

87. Augustine, *Expositions of the Psalms*, Exposition 2, Psalm 31:6b, sec. 18. This reference is cited by Louf, *Way of Humility*, 7. Louf also cites Sermon 351.4: "*Humilitas pene una disciplina Christiana est.* Humility is practically the only Christian discipline there is" (6). Hill argues, however, that this is unlikely to be an authentic sermon by Augustine (Augustine, *Sermons [341–400] on Various Subjects*, trans. Edmund Hill, ed. John E. Rotelle, The Works of Saint Augustine, A Translation for the 21st Century, pt. 3, vol. 10 [Hyde Park, NY: New City Press, 1995], 134n1).

88. Augustine's approach to humility and virtue is carefully explored in Deborah Wallace Ruddy, "A Christological Approach to Virtue: Augustine and Humility" (PhD diss., Boston College, 2001).

submitting his neck to the yoke of humility and bowing his head before the ignominy of the Cross."[89]

Humility is often named as a virtue in patristic writings, sometimes as the "mother" of virtue or as the "summit" of all virtues. In the preface to the *City of God*, Augustine speaks of humility as a virtue "which makes it soar above all the summits of this world," overturning human arrogance by divine grace.[90] Crucially here, Augustine carefully links humility and grace. He views humility, using later terminology, as a theological virtue. Both Basil of Caesarea (ca. 330–379) and John Chrysostom (ca. 345–407) speak of humility as the foundational virtue.[91] For Basil, humility is an all-encompassing virtue (*panaretos*);[92] for John Chrysostom, it is the "mother, root, nurse, foundation and center of all the other virtues."[93]

As the use of virtue language becomes common in the Christian tradition, however, a number of problems arise. First, there is a danger that the notion of grace will be compromised. This issue, in fact, becomes the key reason for the rejection of the notion of virtue in the Protestant Reformation, but it is already a matter of intense concern in the fourth century. Athanasius's *Life of Antony*, for example, deliberately frames monastic life as a way of virtue to rival that of "the Greeks."[94] But how are human efforts (especially the monastic ascetical regime) and divine grace related? This question is of critical importance to the early monastic movement. The monastic theologian John Cassian (ca. 360–ca. 435) addresses this question in Conference 13, arguing that the cultivation of virtue requires human cooperation with divine

89. Augustine, *Confessions*, trans. R. S. Pine-Coffin (Harmondsworth, UK: Penguin, 1961), 8.2, 159. Ruddy calls this "the ecclesial dimension of humility" ("Christological Approach to Virtue," 130).

90. Augustine, *City of God*, bk. 1, preface 5.

91. Adnès, "Humilité," 1157.

92. Louf, *Way of Humility*, 10.

93. Quoted in Tomáš Špidlík, *The Spirituality of the Christian East: A Systematic Handbook*, trans. Anthony P. Gythiel, CS 79 (Kalamazoo, MI: Cistercian Publications, 1986), 89.

94. Athanasius, *The Life of Antony and the Letter to Marcellinus*, trans. Robert C. Gregg (London: SPCK, 1980), chap. 20, p. 46.

grace.[95] The background here is Augustine's protracted debate with Pelagius (ca. 350–425) regarding the respective roles of grace and human will in salvation. Augustine argued that human beings are so marred by original sin that they are incapable of even desiring God. Pelagius held a more optimistic view of human nature and the power of human will.[96] The relationship between humility, divine grace, and human freedom subsequently becomes a persistent and necessary theme in the monastic tradition and the source of continued tension.

Second, virtue language becomes particularly problematic when theologians attempt some sort of rapprochement with the classical tradition, especially in relation to the classification of the virtues. Humility, as it had evolved in early Christianity, is endangered by these moves. This problem is seen most clearly, and much later, in Thomas Aquinas's harmonization of Christian and Aristotelian ethics. While humility does not appear in Aristotle's list of virtues, nor in Augustine's scheme of theological and cardinal virtues, Aquinas, by contrast, makes a place for humility by interpreting it as a form of moderation. Here, as André Louf suggests, humility becomes "a by-product . . . of the virtue of temperance."[97]

Aquinas was not, however, the first to go down this path. His relegation of humility to a form of modesty has its antecedent in Origen, who identified the humility of the Virgin Mary in the *Magnificat* as the classical virtue of *metriotes* (measure), which in turn became the Latin *mediocritas* (moderation). As Louf observes, "[Origen] started a perilous path, sown with traps, but onto which Saint Thomas (with practically all the spiritual writers after him)

---

95. John Cassian, *The Conferences*, trans. Boniface Ramsey (New York: Paulist Press, 1997), Conf. 13, pp. 467–91.

96. William Harmless, *Desert Christians: An Introduction to the Literature of Early Monasticism* (Oxford: Oxford University Press, 2004), 398–400; McGuckin, *Handbook to Patristic Theology*, s.v. "Pelagius-Pelagianism"; Columba Stewart, *Cassian the Monk* (Oxford: Oxford University Press, 1998), 76–81.

97. Louf, *Way of Humility*, 7.

ventured gladly."[98] Much is lost in this move: the theological character of humility, that is, its fundamental relationship to the life of God, witnessed in Jesus Christ; and its social resonances, including the radical implications of "mutual humility."

This picture is further complicated by the development of schemes of virtues and vices within the Christian ascetic and monastic traditions. Notably, Evagrius's eight thoughts (Gk *logismoi*), which were taken up by Cassian as the eight principal vices (Lat *vitii*), become the direct ancestors of the ubiquitous "seven deadly sins."[99] While these schemes were intended primarily as pastoral aids for combating sin, an unintended consequence was often the relegation of humility from being foundational to the Christian life to being one virtue in a list of many. Consequently, the virtue of humility is commonly named as an antidote to the vice of pride.

The virtue's trajectory, then, significantly complicates the development of Christian understandings of humility. By the twentieth century, the recovery of humility, against its rejection in the Enlightenment, becomes a project of recovering the virtue of humility. This approach may not be the most productive means of retrieving a Christian understanding of humility.

1.5 The Return of the Virtues

Interest in virtue as a basis for moral and ethical discourse in philosophy saw a significant revival in the latter part of the twentieth century.[100] Alasdair MacIntyre's *After Virtue*, first published in 1981, made a seminal contribution to this conversation in both philosophy and theology.

---

98. Louf, *Way of Humility*, 7. Louf also briefly discusses the consequent difficulties Aquinas has to face in his account of the relationship between humility and magnanimity (*Way of Humility*, 8).

99. Harmless, *Desert Christians*, 218, 312; McGuckin, *Handbook to Patristic Theology*, s.v. "Virtue."

100. The pioneers of this movement were Elizabeth Anscombe, Philippa Foot, and Iris Murdoch (Porter, "Virtue Ethics," in Gill, 107).

In the light of this renewed interest in the virtues, some contemporary philosophers have turned their attention to humility.[101] Norvin Richards, for example, endeavors to rehabilitate humility outside a Christian framework. He argues for an understanding of humility as "an accurate understanding of oneself" against what he styles as Christian conceptions that see humility as self-contempt or having a low opinion of oneself. He then explores the implications for living of such a reading of humility.[102] More recently Mark Button has argued for what he calls "democratic humility" as a sort of modest openness to otherness. He too pits this against theistic readings of humility.[103] Both Richards and Button, however, tend to read the Christian tradition thinly. Interestingly, both engage with a key monastic writer, Bernard of Clairvaux.

Richards begins his 1988 article by quoting Bernard: "If you examine yourself inwardly by the light of truth and without dissimulation, and judge yourself without flattery; no doubt you will be humbled by your own eyes, becoming contemptible in your own sight as a result of this true knowledge of yourself."[104] Richards goes on to dismiss Bernard's words as "depressing" and "not obviously correct."[105] Only the likes of a Luther, Richards suggests, would hold such a thoroughly negative view of human capacity for redemption. Richards's quotation, however, is selective, extracted from an introductory essay to Bernard's *The Steps of Humility and Pride* by George Bosworth Burch, which endeavors carefully to understand humility in the context of the growth of contemplative life. Burch is in the midst of discussing Bernard's distinction between "cold" and "warm" humility (Burch: cognitive

101. Button notes, however, that humility has not enjoyed the same "renaissance" as other virtues. See Button, "'A Monkish Kind of Virtue'?" 840.

102. Norvin Richards, "Is Humility a Virtue?" *American Philosophical Quarterly* 25, no. 3 (1988): 253–59, here 254; see also Norvin Richards, *Humility* (Philadelphia: Temple University Press, 1992).

103. Button, "'A Monkish Kind of Virtue'?" 840.

104. Richards, "Is Humility a Virtue?" 253. The quotation is from SC 42.

105. Richards, "Is Humility a Virtue?" 253.

and conative humility).[106] Richards makes no effort to understand
or engage with this distinction, or with the sermon itself. Bernard's
understanding of humility is much subtler than Richards's brief
quotation suggests and is worthy of fuller attention.[107]

By contrast, after a standard initial dismissal of Christian readings of humility, Button finds Bernard of Clairvaux's thinking
fruitful for its consideration of the relational aspects of humility
and concern with "practical questions." Button seems somewhat
surprised that monastic interest in humility stretches beyond an
interest in divine-human relations or interior dispositions.[108] He
need not be: monastic communities, like all human communities, have long engaged with such questions. In the context of
philosophical accounts of humility, however, Button's positive
account of Bernard is refreshing and indicates the potential for
further dialogue between contemporary philosophy and the monastic tradition.

1.6 A New Monastic Turn?

A further turn in contemporary thought is relevant: the renewed interest in practice in contemporary philosophy and
theology. In *After Virtue*, MacIntyre is concerned to show how
modernity struggles with a now largely incoherent set of remnant
traditions and narratives in which the context for constructing
moral life has been lost. MacIntyre suggests that virtues emerge
from, and are sustained by, traditions, practices, and narratives. A
number of theologians, eager to reestablish grounds for construct-

---

106. George Bosworth Burch, "Introduction: An Analysis of Bernard's
Epistemology," in *The Steps of Humility*, by Bernard of Clairvaux (Notre Dame,
IN: University of Notre Dame Press, 1963), 1–117, here 51–52.

107. See below, chap. 4, section 4.2.4, pp. 196–98.

108. Button, "A Monkish Kind of Virtue?" 850: "One intriguing possibility
[for constructing humility as a civic virtue] comes from the writings of St.
Bernard of Clairvaux. By briefly turning to the contributions of this Cistercian
monk, we can draw some useful guidance for a more socially and ethically
robust understanding of humility, and one that ironically belies the Humean/
Kantian charge that humility is strictly a 'monkish kind of virtue.'"

ing Christian ethics, have embraced this contention.[109] It has also been a key inspiration for a renewed interest in practice among theologians.[110] Understandings of humility are always embedded in contexts (traditions) and surrounded by practices—a fact Hume clearly understood. So while it is necessary, for the reasons outlined in this chapter, to exercise caution about naming humility as a virtue, it is possible that attending to the nexus between traditions and practices may result in a fuller understanding of humility.

Indeed, the monastic tradition offers a particularly fruitful ground for considering the interrelationship among theology, practices, and the lived life. And as Louf suggests, "concrete experience" offers the most helpful route for exploring both the "what" and the "how" of humility. His program is akin to that of the present study: "I would like to present humility from the perspective of the traits embodied in concrete experience which is both connected to particular situations and properly scriptural—an experience that the early monks actually lived out and described as an essential stage of Christian living. We will ask ourselves about that which concretely takes place in that experience while attempting to describe how one conducts oneself in such an experience."[111]

1.7 Conclusion

The notion of humility has a complex and ambiguous heritage. It cannot be named straightforwardly as a virtue, nor indeed as

---

109. For example, see Nancey Murphy, Brad J. Kallenberg, and Mark Thiessen Nation, eds., *Virtues and Practices in the Christian Tradition: Christian Ethics after MacIntyre* (Harrisburg, PA: Trinity Press International, 1997); Jonathan R. Wilson, *Living Faithfully in a Fragmented World: Lessons for the Church from MacIntyre's* After Virtue (Harrisburg, PA: Trinity Press International, 1997).

110. See, for example, Miroslav Volf and Dorothy C. Bass, eds., *Practicing Theology: Beliefs and Practices in Christian Life* (Grand Rapids, MI: Eerdmans, 2002).

111. Louf, *Way of Humility*, 10.

a vice. As I have already noted, a cluster of ideas accompany the Christian notion of humility through time. At each historical turn, the same issues resurface in some form: the relationship between humility and virtue, humility and humiliation, the humility of God revealed in Christ, humility as an interior disposition versus its material expression, and the question of humility as a social ethic. Underlying these subjects is the question of the place of humility in human life.

In the meeting of Greco-Roman and Judeo-Christian worlds the word *humility* signals a very real contest regarding the *telos* or end of human life and the conduct of social relations. Is the goal of human life the accumulation of honor or "the enjoyment of God"? Are social relations primarily determined by honor and status or by love of neighbor? For Aristotle, the goal of human life is *eudaimonia*, achieved by the accumulation of honor and virtue. The Gospel of Jesus Christ offers a radically different narrative and *telos*. In Christ, the early Christian communities experienced God as one who identifies with the lowly and bends before the other, even to the point of death. Here they encounter the paradox that God relinquishes honor to stand with the weak and dishonored. Participation in the kingdom of God (the *telos*), tasted in the context of Christian community and realized in heaven, entails the same commitment to this costly way of self-giving love witnessed in Jesus. It is this way that Augustine and the later monastic tradition style the way of humility. Human flourishing, *eudaimonia*, is being reconfigured.

Figure 1. Martin Schongauer, *The Temptation of Saint Anthony*, ca. 1470–1475,
© 2009 Museum of Fine Arts, Boston.

Chapter 2

Humility and the Self

Desert Monasticism

I saw the snares that the enemy spreads out over the world and I said groaning, "what can get through from such snares?" Then I heard a voice saying to me, "Humility."

—Abba Anthony

Martin Schongauer's famous engraving of *The Temptation of Saint Anthony* offers a vivid image of a human being caught in "the snares of the enemy." Is it also a portrayal of humility? How did the desert monks understand the human project and the place of humility in human life? Who is the "I" who is ensnared, the "I" who longs to "get through"? And if "humility" is the way through, what might it look like?

Schongauer was a painter and engraver who worked in the Rhine Valley in the second half of the fifteenth century. He is recognized as a master of late Gothic style and a key contributor to the development of engraving as a vehicle for artistic expression. It was this medium that ensured that his work, including his image of Antony, was disseminated widely throughout Europe.[1] His

1. Trustees of the British Museum, "Martin Schongauer, *The Temptation of St Anthony*, a copperplate engraving," British Museum, http://www.british museum.org/explore/highlights/highlight_objects/pd/m/martin

interpretation of *The Temptation of Saint Anthony*, executed sometime in the 1470s, while not the first depiction of this subject in
Western art, is possibly one of the most influential. At least seven
copies of the plate have survived. The Italian Renaissance painter
and architect Vasari knew Schongauer's engravings and in his
Lives of the Artists relates how the young Michelangelo had copied
the engraving of Anthony in both pen and ink and in color.[2] Al-
brecht Dürer drew on the club-wielding demon above Anthony's
head for his depiction of the devil in his masterly 1513 engraving,
Knight, Death and the Devil.[3] Dürer had paid a visit to Schongauer's
workshop in Colmar in 1492, shortly after the engraver's prema-
ture death.[4] In 1512, in the nearby town of Isenheim, Matthias
Grünewald was commissioned to paint an altarpiece for the hospital attached to the Monastery of Saint Anthony.[5] Grünewald, in
what was to be his most famous work, incorporated and developed
the iconography for a panel dedicated to Anthony's temptations.

From Hieronymus Bosch to Salvadore Dali to the present day,
the temptation of Saint Anthony has captured the imagination
of Western artists. (One can observe, though, a rapid narrowing
of focus regarding the nature of Anthony's temptations to those
primarily of a sexual nature.) The great nineteenth-century French
writer Gustave Flaubert wrote a novel styled as a drama, *La Tenta-*

_schongauer,_the_temptat.aspx; "Martin Schongauer," Grove Art Online,
Oxford University Press, http://www.oxfordartonline.com.ezproxy.csu.edu
.au/subscriber/article/grove/art/T076738pg1#T076739.

2. Giorgio Vasari, *The Lives of the Artists: A Selection*, trans. George Bull,
rev. ed. (Harmondsworth, UK: Penguin, 1971), 329. A work believed to be the
colored version referred to by Vasari was purchased in 2009 by the Kimbell
Art Museum, Forth Worth, Texas (Ed Pilkington, "Texas Museum Gets
Michelangelo's First," *Guardian Weekly*, May 22, 2009).

3. See British Museum entry, n. 1 above.

4. See Grove Art Online, n. 1 above.

5. Schongauer himself had painted an altarpiece for the same monastery
sometime between 1465 and 1470. It included a panel with a simple portrait
of Anthony. The monastery with its hospital was one of a significant number
of Antonine foundations originally dedicated to working with the mainly
poor sufferers of ergotism or Saint Anthony's Fire. See British Museum entry,
n. 1 above.

tion de Saint Antoine, inspired by a painting he had seen in Genoa. He worked on the script sporadically over a period of twenty-five years and considered it his best work.[6] A contemporary musical drama based on Flaubert's script premiered in Germany in 2003.[7] Fascination with the story is not yet spent.

This appeal was evident from shortly after Anthony's death in 356. When Athanasius wrote his *Life of Antony* sometime between 356 and 358, complete with its vivid descriptions of Anthony's spiritual battles with demons, it became an instant best seller.[8] It was almost immediately translated into Latin from its original Greek and subsequently became the prototype for the innumerable *Lives* of saints written in the Latin West. Moreover, as William Harmless points out, it changed lives. Anthony's story was a critical motivator in the conversion of Augustine.[9] And while Anthony was by

6. At the time, the painting was attributed to Pieter Brueghel the Younger. See the translator's introduction to Gustave Flaubert, *The Temptation of Saint Anthony,* trans. Kitty Mrosovsky (Harmondsworth, UK: Penguin, 1983), 3.

7. Produced by Robert Wilson with music created by Bernice Johnson Reagon; the staging company described the work as "a production that asks fundamental questions about sin, goodness and the temptations of the flesh, starting from the figure of Saint Anthony in Gustave Flaubert's novel of 1874. Saint Anthony struggles for perfect asceticism and reclusion but can also be seen as a symbol of the artist living in visions and images and getting lost in the imaginary world of his inspiration" (http://www.changeperformingarts .com/Wilson/st.anthony.html).

8. William Harmless, *Desert Christians: An Introduction to the Literature of Early Monasticism* (Oxford: Oxford University Press, 2004), 59. In English, *Anthony* is also rendered *Antony.* I use *Anthony* except when quoting from texts that use this variant. Unless otherwise stated, quotations use Gregg's translation, which is based on the Greek text in PG 26:835–976. A new critical edition with French translation supersedes that of the PG: G. J. M. Bartelink, ed., *Athanase d'Alexandrie: Vie d'Antoine,* SCh 400 (Paris: Éditions du Cerf, 1994). Harmless provides a summary of the recent challenges to the attribution of authorship of the *Life* to Athanasius by René Draguet, Timothy Barnes, and Martin Tetz. Athanasius's authorship of the Greek text is, however, widely attested by his contemporaries, internal evidence, and its stylistic unity (111–13). The task of orienting myself in the literature of desert monasticism has been significantly eased by Harmless's survey.

9. Harmless, *Desert Christians,* 98–100. As a tearful Augustine hears "a divine command" to open the Scriptures and read, he recalls, "I had heard the

no means the founder of Christian monasticism, the *Life* had an inestimable impact on its growth and development.[10]

What Athanasius offers in his *Life of Antony* is a guide to the recovery of the virtuous self, the self that was originally "made beautiful and perfectly straight" but often "turns from its course." Anthony walked "the way of virtue," a way that Athanasius styles a "contest" (Gk *agōn*) with demonic forces, and emerged a fully restored, integrated human being.[11] Anthony, as Harmless argues, offers a portrait of deified humanity: "what a human being renewed in the image and likeness of God should look like."[12] Anthony is a new model of human flourishing.

In Schongauer's engraving, Anthony is placed centrally, airborne and surrounded by a swarm of fantastic demons pulling violently at his monastically clothed body. Anthony, remarkably, appears calm, passive even, certainly detached—he shows no sign of resistance, anxiety, or anguish. He seems to be suspended midair, somewhere above the rocky earth yet below the heavens.

Close to the end of the fifteenth century, in view of the closing chapters of medieval Christendom, Schongauer's engraving stood at the turning of the tide for the monastic culture that had dominated European life for a millennium. The seismic upheavals of the Reformation were not far off.[13] It is curious that the temptation of Saint Anthony became a frequent subject of late medieval and

---

story of Anthony, and I remembered how he had happened to go into a church while the Gospel was being read and had taken it as a counsel addressed to himself. . . . By this divine pronouncement he had at once been converted to you" (Augustine, *Confessions*, trans. R. S. Pine-Coffin [Harmondsworth, UK: Penguin, 1961], 8.12, 177–78).

10. See, for example, Marilyn Dunn, *The Emergence of Monasticism: From the Desert Fathers to the Early Middle Ages* (Malden, MA: Blackwell Publishing, 2000), 12–13; Derwas J. Chitty, *The Desert a City: An Introduction to the Study of Egyptian and Palestinian Monasticism Under the Christian Empire* (Oxford: Basil Blackwell, 1966), 2. Chitty calls the *Life* "the first great manifesto of the monastic ideal—a classic of the spiritual life which was exerting its influence over the Christian world within a very few years of its writing."

11.Athanasius, *Life of Antony*, chaps. 20–21, pp. 46–47; PG 26:875.

12. Harmless, *Desert Christians*, 90.

13. Luther wrote and circulated his Ninety-Five Theses in 1517.

early Renaissance art: there is a certain irony in seeing the figure that symbolized the birth of Christian monasticism standing at another historical crossroad. Certainly, as Christendom receded in the wake of modernity, Nietzsche and Hume would have found the notion of holding up Anthony as a model of human wholeness entirely ludicrous. Closer to Schongauer's day, Machiavelli bemoaned Christianity's glorification of "humble and contemplative men" at the expense of "men of action."[14]

Through an examination of the lives and sayings of Anthony and other desert monks, this chapter explores the vision of the virtuous self that emerges in early desert monasticism; it particularly seeks to understand how humility is constitutive of this ideal. In the desert, the antithesis of the city (Gk *polis*), humility is cultivated through the radical renunciation of status and the eschatological orientation of the self.

2.1 The Literature of Early Desert Monasticism

The sources for fourth- and fifth-century monasticism are rich, and the literature of desert monasticism is extensive and complex. In this chapter, I focus primarily on early (fourth- and fifth-century) monasticism in Egypt. Even here the sources are rich: Athanasius's *Life of Antony*, the multiple collections of *Apophthegmata Patrum* or *Sayings of the Fathers*, Palladius's *Lausiac History*, the anonymous *History of the Monks in Egypt*, the various *Lives* of Pachomius, Syncletica, and others, letters and fragments by Ammonas, Anthony, Ammon, and Pachomius, the rich corpus of writings by Evagrius Ponticus, and the *Institutes* and *Conferences* of Cassian, which reflect his experience of Egyptian monasticism.

It is tempting to focus on the work of Evagrius (ca. 345–399) and Cassian (ca. 360–ca. 435), since they are generally recognized as the first monastic theologians. Both are of immense importance in articulating and systematizing theologically what the desert monks

---

14. Niccolò Machiavelli, *Discourses*, trans. Leslie J. Walker, 2 vols. (London: Routledge, 1991), 2.2.6–7. The relationship between humility, contemplation, and action is examined in chap. 4 below.

had learned by experience. Via Cassian, the thinking of these two theologians came to underpin the emerging theology and practice of Western monasticism.[15] Indeed, their influence can be detected broadly in Western spirituality. Evagrius's eight thoughts (Gk *logismoi*), taken up by Cassian as the eight principal vices (Lat *vitiis*), are the direct ancestors of the seven deadly sins. The schema of virtues and vices that becomes standard in medieval Christendom has its origins here.[16] Evagrius and Cassian are significant players in the story of how the notion of humility develops.

   The *Sayings of the Fathers*, however, the short, often pithy, sayings and short stories arising from the tradition of the desert fathers (Gk *abbas*) and mothers (*ammas*), offer a raw directness in accessing the experience of the desert that is more muted in the work of the theologians.[17] This chapter consequently focuses

---

15. Samuel Rubenson, "Evagrius Ponticus," in *Encyclopedia of Monasticism*, ed. William M. Johnson (Chicago: Fitzroy Dearborn Publishers, 2000); Boniface Ramsey, "Cassian, John," in *Encyclopedia of Monasticism*. The rediscovery of Evagrius during the twentieth century, following his posthumous condemnation for Origenism at the Council of Constantinople II in 553, has restored him to his rightful place in the development of monastic theology. See John Eudes Bamberger's introduction to Evagrius Ponticus, *The Praktikos and Chapters on Prayer*, trans. John Eudes Bamberger, CS 4 (Kalamazoo, MI: Cistercian Publications, 1981), xxiii–lxxi.

16. Harmless, *Desert Christians*, 312.

17. For an introduction to the issues around the transmission of the *Sayings*, see Douglas Burton-Christie, *The Word in the Desert: Scripture and the Quest for Holiness in Early Christian Monasticism* (New York: Oxford University Press, 1993), 76–103. The term *Desert Father* is traditionally used to refer to the monks of fourth- and fifth-century Egypt who lived as anchorites or semi-anchorites. Use of the title *father* designated eldership or seniority in wisdom and experience; it was not a sign of priestly ordination. Such elders are often designated *old men* (Gk *geron*) in the literature of the desert. The Coptic equivalent to the Greek *abba* is *apa*. See Columba Stewart, "Desert Fathers," in *Encyclopedia of Monasticism*. Recent scholarship has significantly expanded our understanding of the place of women in Late Antiquity and in Christian communities experimenting with ascetic practices. The extent to which women practiced an anchoritic form of monasticism is, however, a matter of debate. Only three *ammas* (Theodora, Sarah, and Syncletica) are listed in the *Alphabetical Sayings* but 120 *abbas*. None can be located with certainty as living as desert anchorites. It is not possible at present to

primarily on Athanasius's *Life of Antony* as a foundational text, together with a selection of the *Apophthegmata Patrum* or *Sayings of the Fathers*. Both offer hermeneutical challenges.

Athanasius (ca. 296–373) wrote his *Life of Antony* while he was living as a fugitive among the Egyptian desert communities. Although Athanasius is a key figure in early Christianity, his life was punctuated by political controversy and a series of exiles: as a key advocate of Nicene orthodoxy, he was involved in bitter disagreement with heterodox factions, including Melitians and Arians.[18] His *Life of Antony* reflects his theological agenda—the defense of orthodoxy against heresy—and cannot be read as a simple narrative.[19] Like Cassian's imaginative retelling of the

---

determine whether there were more women in desert settings than the extant texts allow for, or whether women generally lived out their asceticism in different (urban and communal) contexts. See Harmless, *Desert Christians*, 440–45. In this chapter I use the term *monk* to refer to the desert anchorites, whether men or women.

18. Harmless, *Desert Christians*, 33–36.

19. As Harmless says, "it is a theological tract in the form of a narrative" (Harmless, *Desert Christians*, 85). The "search for the historical Anthony" presents challenges similar to those of the "search for the historical Jesus." See Columba Stewart, "Anthony of the Desert," in *The Early Christian World*, ed. Philip F. Esler (New York: Routledge, 2000), 1089–91. Rubenson suggests, "It is . . . as an ideal not as a historical figure that Antony has been handed down to posterity" (Samuel Rubenson, *The Letters of St. Antony: Monasticism and the Making of a Saint*, Studies in Antiquity and Christianity [Minneapolis, MN: Fortress Press, 1995], 9). Rubenson has endeavored to recover the historical figure through his study of Anthony's surviving letters. By comparing these with other sources, including the *Life* and *Sayings*, he concludes that Athanasius's picture of Anthony as "an unlettered monk" is false (185). Rather, Rubenson argues, the letters reveal Anthony to be both a literate and a theologically educated monk, whose thought lacks the anti-Arian agenda of Athanasius (187). The letters, however, have survived only in fragments, and Rubenson's privileging of them has been criticized. Gould, for example, argues that Rubenson has exaggerated the theological and intellectual sophistication of the letters and says that they are not theologically incompatible with the *Life*. Graham Gould, "Recent Work on Monastic Origins: A Consideration of the Questions Raised by Samuel Rubenson's *The Letters of St. Antony*," *Studia Patristica* 5 (1993): 405–16, here 412–14. My interest, however, is in the tradition of practice and theology that emerges from the desert rather than

lives and wisdom of the desert fathers in the *Conferences*, Athanasius narrates Anthony's life in order to commend a particular
version of monasticism and, in his case, a particular (orthodox)
view of the Christian vocation—indeed a particular view of the
human vocation.

The *Sayings of the Fathers* arises primarily, though not exclusively, from the monastic settlements in Lower Egypt. Most of the
named monks are connected with Scetis, established by Macarius
the Egyptian in about 330. Scetis, like other settlements in Lower
Egypt, was essentially a "colony of hermits."[20] Monks lived in
individual cells (small mudbrick huts or dwellings formed from
caves or rock faces), gathering on Saturday and Sunday for common worship and meals. Often, like Anthony, monks moved out
from the settlement in search of more complete solitude, either
permanently or for a period of time. The experiments in such
withdrawal (Gk *anachōresis*) offer rich resources for considering
humility and the self. Communal settings, which offer different
challenges and insights, are the focus of chapter 3. Consequently,
the more communal (cenobitic) experiments of Upper Egypt pio-
neered by Pachomius (ca. 292–346) are not considered here.

The *Sayings of the Fathers* has been transmitted in two major
types of collections, the *Alphabetical* and the *Systematic*, and in a
variety of languages, including Greek, Latin, Coptic, Syriac, and
Ethiopic. The sayings and stories had their origins in Coptic oral
traditions that grew around particular *abbas* or *ammas* and their
disciples, but they were probably first written down in Greek, the
literary language of the time. The *Alphabetical Collection*, about a
thousand sayings arranged according to their attribution to 130
named monks, survives in Greek, with an additional group, the
Anonymous Collection, appended.[21] The *Systematic Collection* is

---

the historical Anthony; in this context, Athanasius's *Life* remains a critical
influence on the emerging monastic tradition.

20. Harmless, *Desert Christians*, 175.

21. Harmless, *Desert Christians*, 169–71; *The Sayings of the Desert Fathers:
The Alphabetical Collection*, trans. Benedicta Ward, rev. ed., CS 59 (Kalamazoo,
MI: Cistercian Publications, 1984). Quotations from the *Alphabetical Collection*
use Ward's translation unless otherwise indicated and are referenced by the

arranged according to themes and in the Greek version has almost 1,200 sayings, many of which overlap with the *Alphabetical Collection*.²² A sixth-century Latin collection, the *Verba Seniorum*, translated from Greek by two Roman clerics, Pelagius and John, brought together elements of both the *Alphabetical* and *Systematic Collections*. In terms of the transmission of the sayings tradition, this collection is particularly important as it predates the extant Greek collections. It was hugely influential in Western monasticism and was known to Benedict of Nursia.²³

Of the eighteen thematic groupings in the *Verba Seniorum*, the fifteenth is devoted to humility. The broad scope of this section gives a sense of the complexity of notions of humility in the desert setting. Many sayings and stories in this grouping, however, do not specifically mention humility (Lat *humilitas*). Further, many of the themes and ideas gathered in this section are found elsewhere in the collection, as are other sayings that use the term *humility*. These features reflect the eclectic nature of the material and the

---

abba or amma's name and number followed by the page number in Ward's translation, abbreviated as *Sayings*. The Greek text of the *Alphabetical Collection* (prepared by Jean-Baptiste Cotelier, 1647) can be found in PG 65:71–440. For a discussion of textual issues and limitations, see Ward, *Sayings*, xxvii–xxix. The *Anonymous Collection* had a core of around 240 sayings with a further four hundred added later. For English translations of the *Anonymous Collection*, nos. 1–132, see *The World of the Desert Fathers: Stories and Sayings from the Anonymous Series of the* Apophthegmata Patrum, trans. Columba Stewart (Kalamazoo, MI: Cistercian Publications, 1986). For nos. 133–396, see *The Wisdom of the Desert Fathers:* Apophthegmata Patrum *from the Anonymous Series*, trans. Benedicta Ward (Oxford: SLG Press, 1975).

22. *The Book of the Elders: Sayings of the Desert Fathers: The Systematic Collection*, trans. John Wortley, CS 240 (Collegeville, MN: Cistercian Publications, 2012). The Greek text with French translation is available in *Les Apophtegmes des Pères: collection systématique*, ed. and trans. Jean-Claude Guy, SCh 387 (Paris: Les Éditions du Cerf, 1993, 2003, 2005), nos. 387, 474, 498.

23. The Latin text of the *Verba Seniorum* (prepared by Heribert Rosweyde, 1615) can be found in PL 73:855–1022. Again, I rely primarily on *The Desert Fathers: Sayings of the Early Christian Monks*, trans. Benedicta Ward (London: Penguin, 2003). Sayings from this source are cited as *Desert Fathers* followed by chapter and saying numbers together with page numbers. On the significance of the text, see Ward, trans., *Desert Fathers*, xxxi; Harmless, *Desert Christians*, 170.

difficulties that the compilers of these collections faced in trying to organize them in ways that would be useful to their audiences. So while the humility section of the *Verba Seniorum* offers some insight into how the compilers mapped the notion of humility, it would be unwise to focus solely on their perspective.

Finally, in dealing with this diverse and unsystematic collection, it is important to resist imposing too much theological order: the experience and reflection on experience that the *Sayings of the Fathers* transmit are as diverse as the monks themselves. As Harmless rightly points out, it "is a polyphony of solo voices that sometimes combine, sometimes diverge, sometimes even clash around a core of favored motifs."[24]

2.2 From the City to the Desert: Locating the Self in the World

What is the significance of the choice of the desert as the location for the project of remaking the self? The desert was already resonant with rich biblical and theological traditions: forty years of Israelite wandering, Elijah's flight to the Sinai desert, John the Baptist's living in the desert margins, and Jesus' own temptation in the wilderness. It offered an exterior, physical setting that mirrored the interior, spiritual enterprise: in the desert, the self is starkly revealed to itself. And it offered a new social location, where renunciation of material wealth and social status could be practiced. Both in relation to God and to others, the desert was a place where humility could be cultivated.

2.2.1 The Desert: A Place of Humility

Historically, the desert adjacent to the Nile and its delta was a primary setting of the monastic experiments of the fourth century and of Anthony's encounter with the "snares of the enemy."[25] (In

24. Harmless, *Desert Christians*, 227.
25. It is not the only location for monastic experiments. See Andrew Louth, "The Literature of the Monastic Movement," in *The Cambridge History of Early*

Schongauer's engraving this desert is represented by the barren, craggy rock in the bottom right-hand corner.)

Anthony's story begins with the radical renunciation of all his possessions. Athanasius writes that one day, shortly after Anthony's parents' death, while walking to his local church, Anthony is pondering the way of life of the early disciples. As he enters the church, he hears the gospel being read: "If you would be perfect, go, sell what you possess and give to the poor, and come, follow me and you will have treasure in heaven" (Matt 19:21).[26] Anthony takes this word to be expressly directed to him. He sells his inherited estate, gives the proceeds and his possessions to the poor, places his sister with some "trusted virgins," and begins a life of asceticism (Gk *askēsis*), initially on the outskirts of his village.[27] This was not a new way of life: Anthony imitated and looked for guidance from others who already lived as solitaries.[28]

Anthony was eighteen or twenty when he embarked on this ascetic path, but when he was about thirty-five, he withdrew further into the desert, living for the next twenty years in an abandoned fort. This complete withdrawal (*anachōresis*) is definitive in Anthony's story and is the particular focus of Athanasius's *Life*. When Anthony finally emerges from his desert fortress, it is as a renewed human being. What brings about this transformation? This withdrawal into solitude exposes the self to itself in a way

---

Christian Literature, ed. Frances M. Young, Lewis Ayres, and Andrew Louth (Cambridge: Cambridge University Press, 2004), 373–81.

26. Athanasius, *Life of Antony*, chap. 2. Trans. based on the Greek text, PG 26:841. Gregg lacks "come, follow me."

27. Athanasius, *Life of Antony*, chaps. 2–3.

28. For an overview of the origins of Christian monasticism, see Dunn, *Emergence of Monasticism*, 1–24; *RB 1980: The Rule of St. Benedict in Latin and English with Notes*, ed. Timothy Fry (Collegeville, MN: Liturgical Press, 1981), 3–41; Harmless, *Desert Christians*, 417–69. The word *monk* has its origins in the Coptic word *monachos*, with connotations of oneness or unity of being, as well as the implication of being single or solitary. See Dunn, *Emergence of Monasticism*, 8. The use of this word as a religious title, in a papyrus legal document dated June 324 CE, is the subject of the seminal study by Edwin A. Judge, "The Earliest Use of *Monachos* for 'Monk' and the Origins of Monasticism," *Jahrbuch für Antike und Christentum* 20 (1977): 72–89.

that Athanasius describes as a contest (*agōn*) with the demonic. This experience equips Anthony to become a teacher or father (*abba*) of other monks. In his last years he alternates between engagement with the growing desert monastic communities (in the *Life*, "the Outer Mountain") and withdrawal into solitude ("the Inner Mountain").

In the monastic movement that grew in fourth-century Egypt, particularly Lower Egypt, the choice to renounce the life of a householder for the life of *askēsis* took on a dramatic flavor. In contrast to other early Christian ascetic experiments, this life was lived in the context of the desert. It is important to reimagine the strangeness of this movement. We need to look in two directions: there is a choice to remove oneself from the city and there is a choice to live in the desert. In the ancient world both choices seemed incomprehensible.[29]

In the Greco-Roman imagination the city, the *polis*, was considered the locus of civilization.[30] The city was the setting where men (and they were primarily men) were educated in classical literature and philosophy, trained to be citizens. Even pagan ascetic options, as Peter Brown notes, were bound to the civilized world.[31] By the early fourth century, Christian bishops looked as though they had embraced this cultural frame—they were, as Brown says, "austere, highly literate, exclusively urban."[32] And here, perhaps, is a difficulty. For Christians the city was also a place of ambiguity: the city had been the location of martyrdom (and still was, even in Anthony's day), and paganism was still

29. See Peter Brown, *The Body and Society: Men, Women and Sexual Renunciation in Early Christianity* (New York: Columbia University Press, 1988), 213–40; Peter Brown, *The World of Late Antiquity* (London: Thames and Hudson, 1971), 9–112.

30. The complex historical situation of fourth-century Egypt needs to be acknowledged. It was a period of rapid urbanization (with the political strengthening of towns, *metropoleis*) and the corresponding emptying of villages. Egypt in this period was no longer a political and cultural backwater. See Rubenson, *Letters of St. Antony*, 89–99.

31. Brown, *Late Antiquity*, 96.

32. Brown, *Late Antiquity*, 96. On the wealth and power of Egyptian bishops, see Rubenson, *Letters of St. Antony*, 107.

alive if not quite well; but then, increasingly, there was a growing muddiness in the relations between the church and secular power. The desert, beyond the reach of the civilized world, offered a new perspective: it offered clarity.

This gift of clarity is illustrated vividly in a story from the *Verba Seniorum* of three friends who had become monks (Lat *monachi*). One, taking his cue from the beatitude "Blessed are the peacemakers" (Matt 5:9), had tried to settle disputes, another had visited the sick, and the third had withdrawn into solitude.[33] The first two, finding themselves worn out and "failing in spirit," went to visit the third:

> He was silent for a while, and then poured water into a vessel and said, "Look at the water," and it was murky. After a while he said again, "See now, how clear the water has become." As they looked into the water they saw their own faces, as in a mirror. Then he said to them, "So it is with anyone who lives in a crowd; because of the turbulence, he does not see his sins: but when he has been quiet, above all in solitude, then he recognizes his own faults."[34]

The desert offered a view of the self, an interior vision that was almost impossible to achieve in the city.

In Egypt, as Brown observes, this contrast between city and desert was starkly visible.[35] The fertile Nile valley and the barren desert regions lay side by side: one could see the desert from the city and the city from the desert. In this juxtaposition of *ecologies*,[36] the social realities of urban life were revealed: Egypt (the granary of the Roman Empire) was utterly dependent on the whims of the Nile, towns were crowded, the obligations of civic service burdensome,[37] and while there were those who reaped reward

33. Incidentally, the story points to the diverse expressions of what being a monk might mean.

34. *Desert Fathers*, 2.16, p. 11.

35. Brown, *Body and Society*, 215–17.

36. This is Brown's terminology.

37. The financial cost of the "liturgies," the honorary performance of civic offices, led to widespread flight (the original context of the word *anachōresis*)

from the economy of the Nile, life was harsh for most and poverty rife. The fertile Nile valley was no paradise. In Egypt it was possible to see all this, and see it against the desert, uninhabited, beyond the reach of civilization. The desert, says Brown, provided an "outside viewing point" where "the world" could be clearly seen.[38]

The "myth of the desert," as Brown observes, "was one of the most abiding creations of late antiquity."[39] City and desert became alternate imaginative spaces for human life. The abiding power of these alternate spaces is reflected in Western art. Schongauer's engraving simply hints at the desert, but most other visual representations of *The Temptation of Saint Anthony* (including those of Grünewald and Bosch) place Anthony in a desert landscape with the city in the distance. City *or* desert is the clear choice.

So the monks fled the city and established for themselves an alternate world, a counterculture. The desert was a place full of metaphorical possibility: a place of exile, resonant with the rich biblical traditions of wilderness, but it was also a new frontier, the fearful abode of the demonic, awaiting the proclamation of the Gospel.[40] To assert that the Anthonys among the Christian community had "made a city in the desert,"[41] to use Athanasius's now famous phrase, was not only to draw attention to the numbers that had taken up this way of life but also to declare audaciously that this new frontier had been conquered.

From the perspective of the city, however, the desert stripped away a person's former social identity. Mediterranean culture was still dominated by considerations of honor and shame, so that the renunciation of birth, wealth, and status—one's whole social narrative—was equivalent to giving up one's being in the world. In the desert, monks lived a physically marginal exis-

---

or absenteeism, particularly among small farmers. See Rubenson, *Letters of St. Antony*, 92–95.

38. Brown, *Body and Society*, 216. For the social background, see also Rubenson, *Letters of St. Antony*, 89–95; Harmless, *Desert Christians*, 3–11.

39. Brown, *Body and Society*, 216.

40. See Stewart, "Anthony of the Desert," in Esler, 1092–95.

41. Brown, *Late Antiquity*, 101; Athanasius, *Life of Antony*, chap. 14, pp. 42–43.

tence, dependent on manual work (and the volatility of a market economy to exchange their products for bread) and at the mercy of an unforgiving physical environment. They consistently repudiated anything that could be construed as honor in worldly terms, often even ecclesiastical honor. (There are, for instance, a number of stories of monks who flee rather than accept ordination, including that of Ammonius, a disciple of Pambo, who sliced off his left ear to avoid being made a bishop.[42])

All this looks very like the social inferiority and lowliness that is often denoted as humility (Lat *humilis*; Gk *tapeinos*) in the Greco-Roman texts I have already examined.[43] Lucian, for example, condemns the lowly, animal-like existence of a stonemason: "You will be a groundling, with groundling ambitions, altogether humble [*tapeinos*]; you will never lift your head, or conceive a single manly or liberal thought."[44] The desert here is that sort of ground, a ground for "groundlings," a place of humility.

2.2.2 Abba Arsenius: The Downward Journey of the Desert

Abba Arsenius, in the *Sayings of the Fathers*, rather than Anthony, is the most vivid exemplar of this movement from city to desert and the accompanying physical and social manifestation of humility.[45] Arsenius (ca. 360–449), born in Rome, classically educated and of senatorial rank, had been tutor to the sons of Emperor Theodosius I. In 394 he left the imperial palace for Alexandria and soon after became a disciple of John the Little at Scetis.[46] Arsenius comes across as a somewhat difficult character, austere, solitary.

---

42. Palladius, *The Lausiac History*, trans. Robert T. Meyer (Westminster, MD: Newman Press, 1965), chap. 11, pp. 46–47.

43. See chap. 1, section 1.2.2, 15–17.

44. Quoted in Klaus Wengst, *Humility: Solidarity of the Humiliated: The Transformation of an Attitude and Its Social Relevance in Graeco-Roman, Old Testament-Jewish and Early Christian Tradition*, trans. John Bowden (London: SCM Press, 1988), 8.

45. Much of the material about Arsenius can be found in *Desert Fathers*, bk. 15, "Humility," and under his name in the *Alphabetical Collection*.

46. Also known as John the Dwarf.

He seems to have attracted few disciples (only Alexander, Daniel, and Zoïlus are known), and indeed his self-confessed difficulty with human company was the cause of distress to many who tried to visit him.[47] But for all the challenges of his character, Arsenius shows most starkly what it meant to leave the city, its wealth, its comforts, and especially its intricate systems of privilege and honor. And he reveals the continued struggle involved in this renunciation.

Arsenius's journey begins with the same two-stage journey seen in the *Life of Antony*—away from the city, and then further and further into the desert:

> While still living in the palace, Abba Arsenius prayed to God in these words, "Lord, lead me in the way of salvation." And a voice came saying to him, "Arsenius, flee from men and you will be saved." Having withdrawn to the solitary life he made the same prayer again and he heard a voice saying to him, "Arsenius, flee, be silent, pray always, for these are the sources of sinlessness."[48]

For Arsenius, finding "the way of salvation" meant giving up the highly privileged life of a Roman courtier. To "flee from men" in this context is shorthand for the renunciation of the whole system of honor, privilege, and wealth. What he is fleeing is a particular means of defining the human person represented, in his case, by the emperor and the palace: like Anthony, he is renouncing the world.

It is important to note here that Arsenius is a Roman, not an Egyptian: his social displacement is different, indeed significantly more extreme, from that experienced by locally born monks. The

47. His behavior was a struggle even for fellow monks. See *Sayings*, 3, 17–18 (Arsenius 13, 38). In the latter text an *abba* shares with one of the disaffected visitors the vision that had helped him see that there were different paths for different people: "Two large boats were shown to him on a river and he saw Abba Arsenius and the Spirit of God sailing in the one, in perfect peace; and in the other was Abba Moses with the angels of God, and they were all eating honey cakes."
48. *Sayings*, 9 (Arsenius 1, 2).

contrast between his way of life in the palace and his way of life in the desert is vividly painted in the *Sayings of the Fathers*: "It was said of him that, just as none in the palace had worn more splendid garments than he when he lived there, so no-one in the Church wore such poor clothing."[49] One imagines him here meeting Abba Pambo's stringent dress code: "The monk should wear a garment of such a kind that he could throw it out of his cell and no-one would steal it from him for three days."[50] Arsenius's cell stank. He refused to change the water used for weaving his palm leaves more than once a year, saying, "Instead of the perfumes and aromatics which I used in the world I must bear this bad smell."[51]

Arsenius no longer clings to his privileged classical education, marveling instead at the "Egyptian peasants," his fellow monks, who "acquire virtues by hard work [*ponōn*]."[52] It was a noticeable wonder that someone as well educated as Arsenius sought the advice of an old Egyptian monk, his social inferior: " 'Abba Arsenius, how is it that you with such a good Latin and Greek education, ask this peasant about your thoughts?' He replied, 'I have indeed been taught Latin and Greek, but I do not know even the alphabet of this peasant.' "[53]

Arsenius's renunciation of wealth and all that it implies is radical. When a magistrate turns up with the will of one of his relatives, a senator, bequeathing him a large fortune, he goes to destroy the will: "I was dead long before this senator who has just died."[54] During an illness Arsenius finds himself completely destitute and, with thanks to God, receives charity from another.[55] This seemingly innocuous gesture is in fact a sign of how far Arsenius

49. *Sayings*, 9 (Arsenius 4).
50. *Sayings*, 197 (Pambo 6).
51. *Sayings*, 11 (Arsenius 18).
52. *Sayings*, 10 (Arsenius 5); PG 65:89.
53. *Sayings*, 10 (Arsenius 6). There may be an element of Coptic pride in the preservation of this saying—but other sayings also note Arsenius's reluctance to write. The traditional picture of the Egyptian monks as "destitute and illiterate farmers" has been challenged: for example, Rubenson argues for a high level of biblical and theological literacy (Rubenson, *Letters of St. Antony*, 89–125).
54. *Sayings*, 14 (Arsenius 29).
55. *Sayings*, 12 (Arsenius 20).

has traveled from Rome, from the city and its social transactions. In the city, the giving and receiving of charity were embedded in systems of patronage and power. To be in receipt of charity signaled dependence and powerlessness. And conversely, to be the giver of alms was a sign of self-sufficiency and power.[56] Aristotle's magnanimous man could never be the recipient of charity. Indeed receiving charity would have been considered humiliating.

Here already is a signal that humility and humiliation are related in the desert tradition. Certainly the fact that the sharp distinction made in English is rarely so clear in these texts provides a challenge for translators. Is the dependence that resulted from the radical renunciation of social position and material wealth experienced negatively as humiliation, or positively as humility? A saying of Cassian in Greek describes the renunciation of wealth as *tapeinophrosyne*, here translated by Ward as "humiliation":[57] "There was a distinguished official who had renounced everything and distributed his goods to the poor. He kept a little bit for his personal use because he did not want to accept the humiliation [*tapeinophrosynēn*] that comes from total renunciation, nor did he sincerely want to submit to the rule of the monastery. Saint Basil said to him, 'You have lost your senatorial rank without becoming a monk.'"[58]

When this same saying appears in the *Verba Seniorum*, Ward avoids both *humility* and *humiliation*, translating the Latin *ex omnibus renuntiantium humilitatem* as "the poverty of those who renounce everything."[59] While *humilitas* can connote poverty, this translation loses the resonance of the relationship between mate-

---

56. The giving of alms was also a potential source of vanity. See, for example, *Desert Fathers*, 6.17, p. 57.

57. PG 65:245. Walter Grundmann notes a mental or dispositional component in *tapeinophrosyne* in its use in texts from the apostolic era (Walter Grundmann, "Ταπεινος," in *Theological Dictionary of the New Testament*, ed. Gerhard Friedrich, trans. Geoffrey W. Bromiley [Grand Rapids, MI: Eerdmans, 1972]. This sense may be operative in this saying of Cassian, but the material resonances are still strong.

58. *Sayings*, 114 (Cassian 7).

59. *Desert Fathers*, 6.10, p. 56; PL 73:890.

rial poverty and humility. Renunciation is humiliating from the perspective of the dominant culture. But from the countercultural perspective of the desert, such humiliation is regarded positively, since it is a signal of a total change in allegiance: from the world (as a senator) to God (as a monk). Renunciation offered a freedom from attachment that enabled the monk (the *monachos*) to seek God single-mindedly because, simultaneously, it revealed the monk's utter dependence on God. The only attachment is to God.[60]

The desert tradition recognizes, however, the relativity of both poverty and wealth, making no simplistic equation of humility and material poverty.[61] A story found in two places with minor variations in the Greek *Alphabetical Collection* tells of the outrage of a fellow monk at finding Abba Arsenius, who was ill, lying on a bed with a pillow.[62] A priest defends this provision by comparing the social origin of Arsenius (the emperor's court) with that of his fellow monk (a shepherd). It is in fact Arsenius who has traveled the greater social distance; the former shepherd is now living a life of greater comfort. It is Arsenius who is now "afflicted," the former shepherd who is "comforted."[63] The great reversals of the Gospel echo here. The monk repents, prostrating himself before the priest: "Father, forgive me, for I have sinned. Truly the way this man follows is the way of truth, for it leads to humility, while mine leads to comfort."[64]

But while wealth and poverty are relative, the way one lives materially is not irrelevant. The desert tradition sees renunciation, giving up, and letting go of material comfort as the sure, downward road to humility. This road is costly: Arsenius is described as

60. When Affy becomes a bishop he is unable to sustain his rigorous ascetical practices and wonders if God's grace has left him. He receives this reply to his question: "No, but in the desert you had no man to help you, and God alone sustained you. Now you are in the world, and have men to help you" (*Desert Fathers*, 15.13, p. 52; see also *Sayings*, 35–36 [Apphy 1]). Also *Sayings* 156–57 [Netras 1]). Note that *Apphy* is the Greek rendering of *Affy*, found in the *Alphabetical Collection*.

61. Burton-Christie, *Word in the Desert*, 245–47.

62. *Sayings*, 208–10 (An *abba* of Rome 1), and *Sayings*, 16–17 (Arsenius 36).

63. *Sayings*, 17 (Arsenius 36).

64. *Sayings*, 17 (Arsenius 36).

"afflicted," implying that his embrace of standard ascetical practices, including the embrace of relative material poverty, leads to
both exterior and interior suffering. His physical life is a universe
away from the imperial palace: he now experiences extremes of
hunger and thirst, heat and cold, the challenge of all-night vigils,
the strain and tedium of manual work, the roughness of monastic
clothing, and dirt with no prospect of a bath. Interiorly, dealing
with the memory of his previous life would be an early if not
ongoing challenge: a source of nostalgic longing or of (dangerous) pride at its abandonment. Interiorly it is very different for
the (upwardly mobile) shepherd turned monk.[65]

Arsenius does not easily dispense with his former life: it is not
completed with the physical acts of leaving the palace or even by
living in solitude. It continues to have an impact on his social relations. Those who live near him are clearly conscious of his former
status and the luxurious life of the palace that he once enjoyed.
The slightly curious story of Arsenius excluding himself from
worship (the *synaxis*) when his fellow monks fail to share some
small dried figs with him gives an indication of their difficulty.
You can feel them tiptoeing around him. They think he will be
offended by such a paltry offering. One should imagine here, by
contrast, plates loaded with succulent *fresh* figs gracing a palace
dining table. But Arsenius feels excluded: "You have cast me out
by not giving me a share of the blessing which God had given the
brethren and which I was not worthy to receive." The brothers
are "edified at the old man's humility," and the priest takes him a
share of the figs and brings him to the *synaxis*.[66] The protest about
his unworthiness feels somewhat forced, but what is clear is that
Arsenius does not want to be treated differently from his brothers.
He is willing to and indeed wants to share their (humble) way
of life. When the brothers marvel at Arsenius's "humility" they

65. Burton-Christie, commenting on this story in its extended form, suggests that "Arsenius's way of life has . . . little to commend it when measured
against the accepted ascetical standards of the desert" (*Word in the Desert*,
247). This statement may be an exaggeration. He is, however, correct in noting
that the key "contrast [is] in the *directions* of their lives."

66. *Sayings*, 11 (Arsenius 16); see *Desert Fathers*, 15.8, p. 149.

are astonished by the distance he has come: he has given up life in the imperial court to live among Egyptian peasants. His is a story of the embrace of downward social mobility, an intentional embrace of solidarity with the lowly.

Arsenius seems similarly "afflicted" when he endeavors to live out the renunciation of social status. Multiple stories tell of his difficulties with visitors. He asks Archbishop Theophilus not to visit, because if he offers hospitality to him he will have to open his door to all: he does not want to privilege a person of rank, even of ecclesiastical rank.[67] When a woman of senatorial rank visits he prays to forget her visit.[68] The core issue for Arsenius is the corrosive effect of being honored; the flattered self can easily succumb to pride. Only God is to be honored. In the words of John the Little, "Let us honour only one and everyone will honour us; for if we despise one, that is God, everyone will despise us, and we will be lost."[69] In the desert, the monks endeavored to live from a radically different foundation, a particular challenge for those whose lives had been formed in Roman, worldly, power structures: "It was said of Abba Arsenius and Abba Theodore of Pherme that, more than any of the others, they hated the esteem [*doxan*] of other men. Abba Arsenius would not readily meet people, while Abba Theodore was like steel when he met anyone."[70]

Arsenius, like all solitaries, discovers that one inevitably takes oneself into the cell. It is the interior work that takes a lifetime. For Arsenius, the road to humility involves a "great reversal" of his previous existence, a radical "process of unselfing," to use Rowan Williams's resonant phrase.[71] This stripping of the social self is expressed concisely in the only preserved saying by Abba Andrew: "Three things are appropriate for a monk: exile, poverty,

67. *Sayings*, 10 (Arsenius 8).

68. *Sayings*, 13 (Arsenius 28). Arsenius is rude, and she is highly offended. This story, though, is partly about the dangerous presence of a woman.

69. *Sayings*, 90 (John the Little 24).

70. *Sayings*, 14–15 (Arsenius 31).

71. Rowan Williams, *The Wound of Knowledge: Christian Spirituality from the New Testament to St. John of the Cross*, 2nd ed. (Cambridge, MA: Cowley Publications, 1991), 27.

and endurance in silence."[72] In the cluster of stories about Arsenius, his city self is disassembled in the desert, reassembled according to a new design rooted in the gospels ("the humble way of Christ"[73]), and reimagined in the context of the desert monastic experiments.

The contemporary orthodox scholar Stelios Ramfos helpfully expresses this process of unselfing, this way of humility: "The definitive form of ascetic withdrawal, I would say, is a withdrawal from every kind of self-assertion, that is, holy humility. My life acquires value through my being something, or thinking that I am something. Humility is voluntary withdrawal precisely from this 'being something.'"[74] In choosing this path one finds no arrival at a settled sense of self—and perhaps this reality is what makes Arsenius a particular icon of humility.

Later in his life, when Arsenius decides to leave his cell to escape interruptions, his own disciples are left wondering how they have offended him. When he becomes seriously ill in Alexandria, none of them visits. When he finally returns "to the mountain," his disciples fall at his feet, and Arsenius joins them, weeping. He is, he says, the dove who, finding nowhere to rest, has returned to the ark.[75] Abba Daniel paints this picture of Arsenius toward the end of his life:

> When from time to time he came to church he would sit behind a pillar, so that no-one should see his face and so that he himself would not notice others. His appearance was angelic, like that of Jacob. His body was graceful and slender; his long beard reached down to his waist. Through much weeping his eye-lashes had fallen out. Tall of stature, he was bent with old age. He was ninety-five when he died.[76]

72. *Sayings*, 37 (Andrew 1).
73. This phrase is used by Arsenius in *Sayings*, 15–16 (Arsenius 33).
74. Quoted in David G. R. Keller, *Oasis of Wisdom: The Worlds of the Desert Fathers and Mothers* (Collegeville, MN: Liturgical Press, 2005), 140.
75. *Sayings*, 15 (Arsenius 32).
76. *Sayings*, 18–19 (Arsenius 42); see also *Desert Fathers*, 15.10, p. 151.

Arsenius is, by now, no one in particular, and yet, through this very process of self-emptying, or unselfing, he has become "like an angel."

2.3 Between Heaven and Earth: Locating the Self in Eternity

If the desert is the setting for the remaking of identity, what is it for? What is the goal of this process of unselfing? And why is humility the way? The focus now moves more explicitly to the purpose of the monastic project, discovering the eschatological orientation that is at the heart of both the *Life of Antony* and the *Sayings of the Fathers*.

2.3.1 Anthony and the Open Heavens

Athanasius's *Life* depicts Anthony as one who endures repeated contests with the demonic.[77] In Schongauer's engraving he is encircled by fantastic demons: while he seems to be suspended between heaven and earth, the demons are energetically beating and pulling him downward. What is he doing here? Where is he going?

The *Life* contains a number of stories that depict temptation and the demonic as having some sort of bodily appearance. While Anthony is living in the tombs adjacent to his village, demons seem to crash noisily through the walls and are "changed into the forms of beasts and reptiles." Anthony finds himself wrestling with "the shapes of irrational beasts," with "lions, bears, leopards, bulls, and serpents, asps, scorpions and wolves," each moving "in accordance with its form."[78] During his long period of withdrawal to the abandoned fortress, Anthony explains to visitors, who have

---

77. For an analysis of the functioning of demonology in early Egyptian monasticism, see David Brakke, "The Making of Monastic Demonology: Three Ascetic Teachers on Withdrawal and Resistance," *Church History* 70, no. 1 (2001): 19–48. Brakke argues that the way in which demonology functions in the thought of the desert monastic practitioners is different from that in Athanasius, who has a broader audience and the larger Christian narrative in mind.

78. Athanasius, *Life of Antony*, chap. 9, p. 38.

overheard the sounds of "clamouring mobs," that "the demons
create apparitions and set them loose on those who are cowardly."[79]
In his instructions to his disciples,[80] Anthony warns that when the
strategy of implanting "evil thoughts" fails, demons attack the
heart "by fabricating phantasms, transforming themselves, and
imitating women, beasts, reptiles, and huge bodies and thousands
of soldiers."[81] Schongauer's engraving undoubtedly draws on all
of this tradition, but a further story, told much later in the *Life*,
places this contest with the demonic in the air:

> Once when [Anthony] was about to eat, rising to pray around
> the ninth hour, he felt himself being carried off in thought,
> and the wonder was that while standing there he saw himself,
> as if he were outside himself, and as if he were being led
> through the air by certain beings. Next he saw some foul and
> terrible figures standing in the air, intent on holding him back
> so he could not pass by. When his guides combated them, they
> demanded to know the reason, if he was not answerable to
> them. And when they sought an accounting of his life from
> the time of his birth, Antony's guides prevented it, saying to
> them, "The Lord has wiped clean the items dating from his
> birth, but from the time he became a monk, and devoted him-
> self to God, you can take an account." Then, as they levelled
> accusations and failed to prove them, the passage opened
> before him free and unobstructed. And just then he saw him-
> self appear to come and stand with himself, and once more
> he was Antony, as before.[82]

Where was Anthony being led in this vision? What is the "open
passage" that Athanasius speaks of here?

The story needs to be placed, initially, in the context of pre-
Christian philosophical traditions, both Jewish and Greek, that
imaged spiritual progress in terms of an ascent from earth to
heaven. Behind Athanasius's narrative is the complex history of

79. Athanasius, *Life of Antony*, chap. 13, p. 41.
80. Athanasius, *Life of Antony*, chaps. 16–43, pp. 43–64.
81. Athanasius, *Life of Antony*, chap. 23, p. 48.
82. Athanasius, *Life of Antony*, chap. 65, pp. 78–79.

theological engagement with classical philosophy, particularly with Platonism in its various forms.[83]

In echoing this philosophical vocabulary of spiritual ascent,[84] Athanasius signals to his audience the changed status of the Christian religion: the Christian ascetics, not their pagan counterparts, are now the custodians of spiritual vision. There is no need "to cross the sea for virtue [Gk *aretē*]" like the Greeks, says Athanasius: "Do not be afraid to hear about virtue, and do not be a stranger to the term . . . *the Kingdom of God is within you*. . . . All virtue needs . . . is our willing, since it is in us, and arises from us."[85] The virtuous self is the self that remains or recovers how "we were made" by God.[86] The rediscovery of this nature requires entering a struggle or contest (*agōn*) with the "principalities" and "powers," the demonic forces that constantly threaten to pull us off course: "The mob of them is great in the air around us."[87]

Anthony has undertaken such combat and emerges transformed. For Athanasius, Anthony is the paradigm of humanity renewed in the image of God.[88] When Anthony emerges from the desert fortress, after twenty years of combat, Athanasius paints him as a fully integrated human being:

83. This context has been mapped by two seminal studies: Andrew Louth, *The Origins of the Christian Mystical Tradition: From Plato to Denys* (Oxford: Clarendon Press, 1981), esp. 1–51, and Bernard McGinn, *The Foundations of Mysticism: Origins to the Fifth Century* (New York: Crossroad Publishing, 1991), esp. 23–61.

84. In time this vocabulary of spiritual ascent comes to dominate the Christian mystical tradition. In Schongauer's engraving of Anthony, the craggy rock in the right-hand corner, as well as signifying the desert, draws on the iconography of the steep mountain to represent the difficulty of spiritual progress.

85. Athanasius, *Life of Antony*, chap. 20, p. 46; PG 26:873. The biblical quotation is Luke 17:21. Italics indicating quotation are retained from Gregg's translation.

86. Athanasius, *Life of Antony*, chap. 20, p. 46.

87. Athanasius, *Life of Antony*, chap. 21, p. 47; PG 26:875.

88. The restoration of humanity in the image of God is a central theme in Athanasius's theology. For example, *De Incarnatione*, chaps. 13–14, in Athanasius, Contra Gentes *and* De Incarnatione, trans. Robert W. Thomson (Oxford: Clarendon Press, 1971). See Harmless, *Desert Christians*, 90–93.

> Anthony came forth as though from some shrine, having been
> led into divine mysteries and inspired by God. . . . And when
> [those who came to him] beheld him, they were amazed to
> see that his body had maintained its former condition, neither
> fat from lack of exercise nor emaciated from fasting and com-
> bat with demons, but was just as they had known him prior
> to his withdrawal. The state of his soul was one of purity, for
> it was not constricted by grief, nor relaxed by pleasure, nor
> affected by either laughter or dejection. . . . He maintained
> utter equilibrium, like one guided by reason and steadfast in
> that which accords with nature.[89]

If Anthony emerges as the transformed or perfected human
being here, the understanding of this transformation is quite different from that offered by the Platonic tradition. While Platonism
understood the spiritual task as a return or "ascent" to God, a
realization of one's true, that is divine, nature, Athanasius stresses
the ontological distance between God and creation. This distance,
as Andrew Louth notes, can be bridged only by God, by an act
of grace.[90] This act of grace is the coming of God to us in Christ.[91]

Christology is central to Athanasius's understanding of human
destiny. Indeed, as Harmless points out, the vision of Anthony
moving through the air echoes precisely Athanasius's understanding of the crucifixion in his treatise *On the Incarnation*. Christ
is raised up on the cross in order that the air, the abode of the
demonic, may be purified and a way cleared to heaven.[92]

When Anthony speaks to those gathered outside the fortress,
he puts his transformation in a christological frame, urging them
"to prefer nothing in the world above the love of Christ" and "to
keep in mind the future goods and the affection in which we are
held by God, who *did not spare his own Son but gave him up for us
all.*"[93] Paradoxically, as Louth explains, for Athanasius ascent is

---

89. Athanasius, *Life of Antony*, chap. 14, p. 42.

90. Louth, *Christian Mystical Tradition*, 99.

91. Athanasius, *De Incarnatione*, chap. 13.

92. Harmless, *Desert Christians*, 87; Athanasius, *De Incarnatione*, chap. 25.

93. Athanasius, *Life of Antony*, chap. 14, p. 42. The biblical quotation is
Rom 8:32.

dependent on descent, the descent of God: "Man can only know God if God comes to him, comes *down* into the realm of corruption and death that man inhabits."[94] The incarnation is precisely this descent of God. Here too incarnation and monastic asceticism are linked. Louth again: "In the light of the Incarnation, those who desire to identify themselves with this God who comes down must follow the same movement."[95] Just as the *Sayings of the Fathers* tradition affirms Arsenius's renunciation of status, Athanasius affirms Anthony's way of life as an exemplary vehicle for living out this paradoxical way of descent that leads to graced ascent. In Anthony's vision his heavenly guides offer the same affirmation of monastic life.

Above all, though, in this episode in the *Life of Antony* Athanasius is painting an eschatological vision. The reader is invited to view human existence from an eternal perspective. The picture of Anthony moving through the air, ascending toward the heavens, offers a preview of the judgment of his soul. The "foul and terrible figures," the demons intent on obstructing his progress, are defeated, as Anthony's guides act as his advocates. The way ahead (to heaven), "the open passage," is cleared by the operation of grace ("the Lord has wiped clean the items dating from his birth") and by the faithfulness of his devotion to God since becoming a monk.

Anthony's ascent is no ecstasy; it is not an experience of bliss, or even "mystical union."[96] Rather this episode affords a view of the self placed in an eternal frame. It offers an eschatological view of the self, where the soul is measured, outside time and space, on God's terms. Nevertheless, there is a partly realized quality to this eschatological perspective: it bears fruit in the present. Anthony emerges after the contest with a soul characterized by "purity."[97]

94. Louth, *Christian Mystical Tradition*, 99.

95. Louth, *Christian Mystical Tradition*, 99.

96. Nor is there an emphasis on *theoria* or contemplation in the *Life* (Louth, *Christian Mystical Tradition*, 100). There is a well-articulated caution around visionary experience in the literature of the desert. Spiritual *experience* is not the goal of monastic life: as Abba Sisoes says, "Seek God, and do not seek where he dwells" (Sisoes 40; *Sayings*, 220).

97. Athanasius, *Life of Antony*, chap. 14, p. 42.

2.3.2 Judgment and Humility

The *Sayings of the Fathers* have a similar, intense concern with this eschatological frame, particularly with judgment. This subject can present difficulties for the modern reader. The preoccupation with death and judgment is the complete antithesis of contemporary Western culture's denial of death and resounding rejection of any notion of divine accountability. But the literature of the desert shows a tight relationship between ultimate destiny, judgment, and the lived life. Human life is lived toward its ultimate end, toward God, and this orientation motivates the monk: it is both the source of hope and the occasion for sorrow or compunction.[98]

Amma Sarah beautifully expresses the double-sided nature of this eschatological vision: "I put out my foot to ascend the ladder, and I place death before my eyes before going up it."[99] The goal is ascent, the movement toward God, but ascent simultaneously requires that one place oneself before God, for judgment, aware of the infinite distance between the human and divine. One is humbled before God.

While a significant number of sayings urge remembrance of God's judgment after one's physical death, the primary concern of these sayings is to bring this awareness into the present. This awareness is often expressed as "the fear of God":

> A brother asked a hermit, "Why is my heart hard, and why do I not fear God?" He said to him, "I think that if you have reproach in your heart, you will know fear." The brother said to him, "What is that reproach?" The hermit said, "To reprove your soul in all things, saying to it, 'Remember that you have to meet God.' Say also to your soul, 'What do I want with

---

98. See, for example, Theophilus the Archbishop 4 (*Sayings*, 81), a lengthy saying that describes the process of weighing the soul after physical death and its consequent motivating power in living a worthy life. For an extended treatment of eschatology and compunction, see Burton-Christie, *Word in the Desert*, chap. 6.

99. *Sayings*, 230 (Sarah 6). I examine the metaphor of the ladder in later chapters.

people?' I think that if anyone tries to do this, the fear of God
will come to him."[100]

Having an eschatological vision of life means living with a
sense of the immediacy of God, and this awareness in turn leads
to a sense of one's unworthiness. In the words of Abba Matoes,
"The nearer a man draws to God, the more he sees himself a
sinner."[101] An interaction between Abba Poemen and a disciple
makes the same point but takes it further:

> A brother asked Abba Poemen, "What ought I to do?" The old
> man said to him, "When God is watching over us, what have
> we got to worry about?" The brother said to him, "Our sins."
> Then the old man said, "Let us enter into our cell, and sitting
> there, remember our sins, and the Lord will come and help us
> in everything."[102]

The intended outcome of an increasing awareness of one's sin
is not despair but an acknowledgment of one's dependence on the
mercy of God. Another saying by Poemen makes a similar point:
"A brother questioned Abba Poemen, 'What ought I to do about
the turmoils that trouble me?' The old man said to him, 'In all our
afflictions let us weep in the presence of the goodness of God, until
he shows mercy on us.' "[103] This painful opening of the heart before
God is experienced by the monk as undergoing a sort of death,
the death of the self: "Poemen said that a brother asked Moses,
'How does someone die to self? Is it through his neighbour?' He
answered, 'Unless you think in your heart that you have been
shut in a tomb for three years, you cannot attain to self-loss.' "[104]

---

100. *Desert Fathers*, 3.22, p. 17. "What do I want with people?" is a reminder,
I suggest, that the opinions of other people are irrelevant: only God's judgment counts. See also *Desert Fathers*, 3.21, pp. 16–17.

101. *Sayings*, 143 (Matoes 2); see *Desert Fathers*, 15.28, p. 157.

102. *Sayings*, 189 (Poemen 162).

103. *Sayings*, 185 (Poemen 122). Similarly, *Desert Fathers*, 3.17, p. 15.

104. *Desert Fathers*, 10.63, p. 103; see *Sayings*, 141 (Moses 12). Here Abba
Moses is asked "how someone could consider himself as dead towards his
neighbour."

The tomb, Poemen says elsewhere, is the "place of tears and compunction."[105] The resonance with stories of Jesus dead and buried in a tomb is deliberate. There is here, as Douglas Burton-Christie observes, a "profound appropriation of the paschal mystery."[106] The experience of the tomb unites the monk with the suffering and death of Jesus. Likewise, the tomb becomes the place of transformation, the place from which renewed life springs. Abba Cronius expresses this idea in intimate terms: "If the soul is vigilant and withdraws from all distraction and abandons its own will, then the spirit of God invades it and it can conceive because it is free to do so."[107]

The fundamental way of being or orientation that enables such a reception of the divine is humility, understood here as the emptied self. This understanding is expressed starkly by Abba Alonius: "If I had not destroyed myself completely, I should not have been able to rebuild and shape myself again."[108] Underlying this advocacy of self-emptying is the desire to follow the pattern of Jesus's own self-emptying, his kenosis even to death (Phil 2:7). What does this rebuilt self look like? Abba Alonius again: "If only a man desired it for a single day from morning till night, he would be able to come to the measure of God."[109] The end of this process of self-emptying is not death but a renewal in the image of God. The goal is Christlikeness.

In Athanasius's telling of Anthony's story, this goal is realized. When Anthony emerges from the desert fortress after twenty years of interior combat, he is a Christlike figure: he heals, exorcises demons, consoles, reconciles, and teaches wisely. And he shares with his hearers the eschatological hope that lies behind his inner, and outer, transformation: "the affection in which we are held by God" and the promise of "future goods." As the "desert

105. *Sayings*, 173 (Poemen 50).

106. Burton-Christie, *Word in the Desert*, 244.

107. *Sayings*, 115 (Cronius 1). Cronius's words resonate here with Mary's receptivity to being a God-bearer; the Greek word *tekein*, which has the sense of "bringing forth," is also used in the gospels (Matt 1:23, Luke 2:6).

108. *Sayings*, 35 (Alonius 2).

109. *Sayings*, 35 (Alonius 3).

was made a city" by all those "who left their own people and registered themselves for the citizenship in the heavens,"[110] the notions of ascent and humility are tied decisively together. In the words of Abba Hyperichius: "The tree of life is high, and humility climbs it."[111]

The same hope-filled eschatological vision underpins the simple humility of Arsenius's weekly practice: "On Saturday evenings, preparing for the glory of Sunday, he would turn his back on the sun and stretch out his hands in prayer towards the heavens, till once again the sun shone on his face. Then he would sit down."[112]

2.4 Habits of the Desert: The Practice of Humility

In Schongauer's etching, Anthony is wearing a monastic habit. The habit could be read as a code for a whole way of life. The practice of taking or being vested in distinctive clothing had signaled, from the earliest development of Christian monasticism, the act of renouncing secular life and becoming a monk.[113] Indeed, it was not long before each element of the habit resonated with symbolic meaning.[114] The English word *habit*, from the Latin *habitus*, has retained among its primary connotations the idea of a "settled tendency or practice."[115] To take the habit in a monastic setting came to mean embracing a way of life, a set of customs or practices designed to establish patterns of behavior and create an inner disposition that would enable one to pursue the goal of single-mindedly seeking God. It is, as the desert monks found, no easy task to "keep your thoughts pointed straight to God" (Evagrius).[116] The habit symbolizes commitment to the *practice* of monasticism.

---

110. Athanasius, *Life of Antony*, chap. 14, pp. 42–43.

111. *Desert Fathers*, 15.49, p. 161.

112. *Sayings*, 14 (Arsenius 30).

113. *RB 1980*, app. 5, pp. 439–40.

114. See Evagrius, *Praktikos*, Prol. 12–14; and John Cassian, *The Institutes*, trans. Boniface Ramsey (New York: Newman Press, 2000), bk. 1.

115. *Concise Oxford Dictionary*, 5th ed., s.v. "habit."

116. This phrase is attributed to Evagrius Ponticus in the Coptic *Life of Evagrius*, 24. See Tim Vivian, "Coptic Palladiana 2: *The Life of Evagrius (Lausiac*

So what are the habits or practices that support the monk's search for God, and how are these related to humility? Is it possible to *practice* humility?

While renunciation of one's previous existence marks the entry to monastic life, there is a realistic recognition in the desert literature that the imaginative power of one's former life will still be active. As in the case of Arsenius, the monk takes his former self with him to the desert. In the *Life of Antony*, Athanasius reveals that Anthony's first phase of temptations primarily consisted of the tug of the life he had physically left behind.[117] The process of "destroying" and "rebuilding" the self, to use Alonius's words, takes time and requires *askēsis* or training.[118]

In his *Life of Antony*, Athanasius sets out to demonstrate how this process can be undertaken. The Prologue is explicit: Anthony's way of life is intended to provide a pattern for other monks. Indeed Gregory of Nazianzus (ca. 326–390) suggests that the *Life* was "a rule for monastic life in the form of a narrative."[119]

Anthony took the first steps in his monastic journey while he was living on the fringes of his village. The pattern of *askēsis* or discipline that he undertook had already been established by other solitaries, and while Athanasius moves over this quickly in order to give his attention to Anthony's withdrawal further into the desert, these disciplines remain core to the emerging monastic ways of life. Withdrawal from the ordinary business of

---

History 38)," *Coptic Church Review* 21, no. 1 (2000): 8–23, here 19. Macarius of Alexandria sets himself the task of keeping "my mind fixed upon God without distractions for the space of but five days" but flees his cell in fear after only two days and nights (Palladius, *Lausiac History*, chap. 18.17–18).

117. "First [the devil] attempted to lead him away from the discipline, suggesting memories of his possessions, the guardianship of his sister, the bonds of kinship, love of money and of glory, the manifold pleasure of food, the relaxations of life" (Athanasius, *Life of Antony*, chap. 5).

118. The Greek term *askēsis* originally referred to training, discipline, or practice and came to be particularly associated with the training of the body by athletes (*A Greek-English Lexicon*, compiled by Henry George Liddell and Robert Scott, 9th ed. [Oxford: Oxford University Press, 1925], s.v. "*askēsis*").

119. Quoted in Harmless, *Desert Christians*, 69; Grégoire de Nazianze, *Discours 20–23*, SCh 270 (Paris: Éditions du Cerf, 1980), 21, 25.

life and some experience of solitude is a given.[120] Anthony then learns how to practice the solitary life by carefully observing and conversing with those who have already traveled this path: the "old man" from a neighboring village "who had practiced from his youth," and those who had a reputation for "zeal." From these elders he receives "supplies for traveling the road to virtue." He learns to orient his thoughts and energies away from the memory of his past and in the service of his training ("he weighed . . . his thoughts"). He undertakes manual work to support himself and, after buying his bread, gives away any excess earnings to those in need. He practices unceasing prayer when he is alone. He listens intently to the words of Scripture (the unstated assumption here is that Anthony is attending the public liturgy of his local church) and commits it to memory.[121] To this suite of practices Anthony, in the face of temptation (his "contest against the devil"), adds what are often called the "bodily disciplines" of vigils and fasting.[122]

These practices—withdrawal into solitude, immersion in Scripture, eldership, the "weighing of thoughts," work, prayer, fasting, vigils—continued to form the basic training regime for desert monks. The *Sayings of the Fathers* contain many sayings concerning the practice of these disciplines. A sample gives the flavor. On fasting: "How can we acquire the fear of God when our belly is full of cheese and preserved foods?"[123] On withdrawal and silence: "If the soul keeps far away from all discourse in words, from all disorder and human disturbance, the Spirit of God will come in to her and she who was barren will be fruitful."[124] On Scripture: "The nature of water is soft, that of a stone is hard; but if a bottle is hung above the stone, allowing water to fall drop by drop, it wears away the stone. So it is with the word of God; it is soft and

---

120. Athanasius is a clear advocate of an anchoritic or solitary model of monasticism.

121. Athanasius, *Life of Antony*, chaps. 3–4, pp. 31–33.

122. Athanasius, *Life of Antony*, chap. 7, pp. 35–37.

123. *Sayings*, 192 (Poemen 181).

124. *Sayings*, 195 (Poemen 205).

our heart is hard, but the man who hears the word of God often, opens his heart to the fear of God."[125]

Anthony is saved from *akēdia* (Gk and Lat *acedia*), a sort of spiritual despondency, by learning to practice an alternate rhythm of work and prayer.[126] For Apollo, who had become a monk after killing a pregnant woman and her unborn child, work was salvific: "I am going to work with Christ today, for the salvation of my soul, for that is the reward he gives."[127]

Many sayings are concerned with ensuring that the practice or training is actually serving the goal of monastic life. The texts make it clear that the fathers saw an ever-present danger of confusing means and ends. The desert tradition is clear: practices in themselves do not make a monk.[128] As one monk says: "Even if our mouths stink from fasting, and we have learnt all the Scriptures, and memorized the whole Psalter, we may still lack what God wants, humility and love."[129]

In discussing the pitfalls and perversions of monastic practice, the monks continually call their hearers back to their deeper purpose. An eschatological view of the self as humble before God underpins their thinking. Practices are meaningless if one is not oriented toward God, and "what God wants" is "humility and love." Humility, not practice, is the basis of progress: "The

---

125. *Sayings*, 192–93 (Poemen 183).

126. *Sayings*, 1–2 (Anthony 1). The term *akēdia* is difficult to translate. Ward suggests "despondency, depression, listlessness, a distaste for life without any specific reason" (*Alphabetical Collection*, Glossary, 249). See also Harmless, *Desert Christians*, 324–27. In Evagrius's *Praktikos*, *akēdia* is famously described as "the noonday demon" (18).

127. *Sayings*, 36 (Apollo 1).

128. *Desert Fathers*, 10.65, pp. 103–4 (see *Sayings*, 196 [Pambo 2]). Two brothers come to Pambo, each with his differing practices around food, fasting, and almsgiving, and each asks whether he will be "saved or lost." After several days of silence, Pambo imagines himself in their place: " 'Pambo fasts for two days and then eats two large buns; do you think that makes him a monk? No, it does not.' Then he said, 'Pambo makes two vegetable stews every day and gives them away to the poor: do you think this makes him a monk? Not at all.' "

129. *Desert Fathers*, 10.94, p. 111.

more we bend ourselves to humility, the more we are lifted up to make progress."[130] Humility is the opposite of self-will, believing that one is able to save oneself.[131] The error of self-sufficiency can cause beginners to rely on their own efforts to achieve their goal: "If you see a young man climbing up to heaven by his own will, catch him by the foot and pull him down to earth for it is not good for him."[132]

Humility seems to critique or relativize practice. So, for example, a monk who normally eats on alternate days breaks his fast to welcome visitors: "A fast has its own reward, but whoever eats because of love, obeys two commandments: he loses his self-will, and he refreshes his brothers."[133] Again, humility, understood as loss of self-will, and love (of neighbor) are the overriding principles.

Similarly, humility seems to guard the operation of the freedom and grace of God. Ascetic practice cannot be used to manipulate God. A monk who fasts for seventy weeks is still unable to exegete a piece of Scripture. When he finally leaves his cell to seek the assistance of a brother, an angel is sent to tell him, "The seventy weeks of your fast have not brought you near to God but now you are humbled and going to your brother, I have been sent to show you the meaning of the text."[134] The interior condition of the monk is exposed: fasting itself had not led to the inner state that would allow him to hear a word of God. He finds that place of humility, the place of selfless receptivity, not through his ascetical practice but through dependence on another brother. He places his humbled self humbly before another. The practice of "manifestation of thoughts," in which monks shared their thoughts with their *abba*, entailed a similar lowering of the self before another. This was a key discipline in enabling the desert monks to understand

130. *Desert Fathers*, 15.77, p. 167.

131. For a discussion of self-will, self-direction, and self-deception, see Columba Stewart, "Radical Honesty about the Self: The Practice of the Desert Fathers," *Sobornost* 12, no. 1 (1990): 25–39, here 32–33.

132. *Desert Fathers*, 10.114, p. 116.

133. *Desert Fathers*, 13.10, p. 136.

134. *Desert Fathers*, 15.72, p. 166.

the workings of the inner life, as Columba Stewart suggests, "to learn about the topography and inhabitants of their hearts."[135]

The *Sayings of the Fathers* recognizes the complex relationship between external practices and interior dispositions. Mastery of a particular practice is merely the first step; only when a practice is interiorized can it begin to be fruitful. Even silence is not seen as intrinsically virtuous: "Even if you have succeeded in the habit of keeping silent, you should not have that in you as though it was a kind of virtue, but say: 'I am not worthy to speak.'"[136] Again, humility is the underlying discipline.

Concern with exterior practices could be a distraction, could even be ridiculous, as a story of an old man who wore a mat demonstrates.[137] When Abba Ammonas sees him, he says: "This is no use to you." But the man doesn't listen and instead asks for advice regarding which asceticism to take on next: a retreat to the desert, anonymity in a foreign land, or entombment in his own cell with a more rigorous regime of fasting. These "thoughts occupy me," the man says, as he lays his options out. Ammonas replies: "It is not right for you to do any of these three things. Rather, sit in your cell and eat a little every day, keeping the [word] of the publican always in your heart, and you may be saved."[138] The man is described as "hard-working," but his obsession with exterior practice had distracted him from the real work of the monk and endangered his salvation. His mind is consumed with thoughts of ascetic feats, and perhaps honors, instead of his own unworthiness.

The allusion to the gospel story of the Pharisee and the publican (Luke 18:9-14) helps to draw the contrast sharply: pride in one's religious practice versus profound humility before God.[139] In the Gospel of Luke it is the heartfelt prayer of the publican,

---

135. Stewart, "Radical Honesty," 26.

136. *Desert Fathers*, 15.79, p. 167.

137. *Sayings*, 26 (Ammonas 4).

138. Ward's translation has "world" instead of "word." Perhaps a typographical error. See PG 65:120.

139. The two figures of Pharisee and publican are often used as a shorthand way of referring to pride and humility.

"God, be merciful to me, a sinner," that receives divine approval, rather than the self-justifying practices of the Pharisee. A saying variously attributed to Amma Syncletica in the Greek *Alphabetical Collection*[140] or Abba Hyperichius in the *Verba Seniorum*[141] makes the same point: "Imitate the publican, and you will not be condemned with the Pharisee. Choose the meekness of Moses and you will find your heart which is a rock changed into a spring of water."[142]

Ammonas not only advocates a modest ascetical regime but also highlights the centrality of a humble interior disposition. Indeed this interior work should be the focus, not the wearing of mats. Anthony, Ammonas's teacher, agrees. This way of embracing "the word of the publican" is also reflected in a saying by Anthony: "Our great work is to lay the blame for our sins upon ourselves before God, and to expect to be tempted to our last breath."[143]

Humility offers a secure foundation for practice. Only the presence of humility ensures that practices are oriented toward rather than away from God. As Amma Theodora notes, the demons are masters of ascetic practice:

> Neither asceticism, nor vigils nor any kind of suffering are [*sic*] able to save, only true humility can do that. There was an anchorite who was able to banish the demons; and he asked them, "What makes you go away? Is it fasting?" They replied, "We do not eat or drink." "Is it vigils?" They replied, "We do not sleep." "Is it separation from the world?" "We live in the deserts." "What power sends you away then?" They said, "Nothing can overcome us, but only humility." "Do you see how humility is victorious over the demons?"[144]

140. *Sayings*, 233 (Syncletica 11).

141. *Desert Fathers*, 15.50, p. 161.

142. *Sayings*, 233 (Syncletica 11). Ward's translation of the Latin version attributed to Hyperichius reads, "Imitate the publican, to prevent yourself being condemned with the Pharisee. Follow the gentleness of Moses, and hollow out the rocky places of your heart, so that you turn them into springs of water" (*Desert Fathers*, 15.50, p. 161).

143. *Desert Fathers*, 15.2, p. 148; see *Sayings*, 185 (Poemen 125).

144. *Sayings*, 84 (Theodora 6). Similarly, *Sayings*, 233 (Syncletica 15).

Humility, then, is the only ground or foundation for the spiritual life and for fruitful practice. That it should be the foundation for living a Christian life is not, of course, surprising, since this is the foundation of the incarnate life of Christ. While the christological basis of the *Sayings of the Fathers* is rarely explicitly stated, the kenotic or self-emptying nature of the life and death of Jesus clearly underlies this somewhat cryptic saying: "Humility is the ground on which the Lord ordered the sacrifice to be offered."[145] Just as humility is the ground on which Jesus offered his life, so it is the only productive ground on which the monk can offer his or her life.

Yet exterior disciplines, visible actions, are not unimportant. When asked, "Which is better, bodily asceticism or interior vigilance?" Abba Agathon replies: "Man is like a tree, bodily asceticism is the foliage, interior vigilance the fruit. According to that which is written, 'Every tree that bringeth not forth good fruit shall be cut down and cast into the fire' (Matt 3:10) it is clear that all our care should be directed towards the fruit, that is to say, guard of the spirit; but it needs the protection and the embellishment of the foliage, which is bodily asceticism."[146]

There is a dialogical relationship between inner and outer being. Abba Ammonas patiently awaits the departure of a public ferry in order to cross the river, weaving a handful of palm leaves, refusing the offer of a lift in another boat. When he is asked why he had done this, he replies, "So as to walk without any anxiety of spirit."[147] Choosing an exteriorly lowly action, waiting for the public ferry to depart rather than accepting a lift on a private boat, is consonant with the interior humility that Ammonas wishes to cultivate. Embracing privilege would lead to interior disturbance. The aim is consonance between the interior and exterior life, an integrity that enables the monk to experience inner peace or wholeness. This is a picture of the self in action. Ammonas protects his inner self (the fruit) by carefully choosing his actions (the foliage).

145. *Desert Fathers*, 15.37, p. 158.
146. *Sayings*, 21 (Agathon 8).
147. *Sayings*, 26–27 (Ammonas 6).

Similarly, Abba Motius offers practical advice for preempting the sin of pride:

> If you live somewhere, do not seek to be known for anything special; do not say, for example, I do not go to the *synaxis*; or perhaps, I do not eat at the *agape*. For these things make an empty reputation and later you will be troubled because of this. For men rush there where they find these practices. . . . Wherever you live, follow the same manner of life as everyone else and if you see devout men, whom you trust doing something, do the same and you will be at peace. For this is humility: to see yourself to be the same as the rest.[148]

These sayings highlight the value of mapping the interior consequences of exterior actions. This sort of self-knowledge will enable the monk to make wise choices and experience peace.

There is, then, a delicate, even paradoxical, relationship between humility and practice. The efficacy of one's practice is dependent on the prior presence of humility, yet, paradoxically, one's receptivity to humility can be deepened through the practice of the monastic disciplines. Humility is not the direct product of external practices. Viewed as the ground or basis of practice, however, humility seems able to be *cultivated*, as one might cultivate soil: encouraging the conditions that will enable growth toward wholeness and eliminating those that impede it.

Abba Motius's saying, though, marks a crucial point in this exploration of humility in desert monasticism. Many sayings regarding humility concern the relationship of the self to others as well as that most difficult of monastic practices, obedience. But how does eschatological humility, that is, humility before God, play out in human relations?

2.5 Turning the Other Cheek: The Humiliated Self

A number of sayings highlight the importance of obedience and its relationship to humility. Abba Pambo, one of the early

---

148. *Sayings*, 148 (Motius 1); see *Desert Fathers*, 8.11, p. 80.

monks of Nitria, received a visit from four monks of Scetis. As each one talked to Pambo, he spoke of the others' virtues. One had fasted, another had lived in poverty, the third was known for his charity. The fourth monk, who "had lived for twenty-two years in obedience to an old man," was praised as the greatest. Pambo said, "Each of the others has obtained the virtue he wished to acquire; but the last one, restraining his own will, does the will of another. Now it is of such men that the martyrs are made, if they persevere to the end."[149]

Another saying describes a vision of various ranks in heaven. The obedient occupy the fourth rank but outshine those above them, wearing "necklaces and crowns of gold," because "the obedient have gone beyond their self-will, and depend only on God and the word of their spiritual guides." So, the saying concludes, practice of obedience is considered the gateway to virtue: "It is the salvation of the faithful, the mother of all virtue, the entry into the kingdom; it raises us from earth to heaven."[150]

These stories help to clarify a number of points. First, there is a clear connection between obedience and humility. The backdrop, again, is an emphasis on self-emptying and dependence on God. Obedience in this context can be seen as a form of humility, indeed a form of social humility: putting oneself below another, abasing or submitting oneself to the other, humbling or lowering oneself.

Second, there is a link between obedience in the monastic setting and martyrdom. In the literature of martyrdom the heavenly crown is the reward for faithful endurance of suffering and death in the name of Christ. Martyrdom is the ultimate form of self-

149. *Sayings*, 196 (Pambo 3); see *Desert Fathers*, 14.7, pp. 142–43. Gk *homologētai*; Lat *confessores*. A more accurate translation here would be *confessors* rather than *martyrs*, a distinction that was common in the patristic period. Confessors were willing to declare their faith publicly "to the end," but not all became martyrs. See John Anthony McGuckin, *The Westminister Handbook to Patristic Theology* (Louisville, KY: Westminster John Knox Press, 2004), s.v. "Confession-Confessor."

150. *Desert Fathers*, 14.19, p. 147.

emptying. In the desert literature, the crown of the martyrs is being transferred to the self-denying, obedient monk.[151]

This shift can be seen, for example, in a story told by Macarius the Great (the Egyptian) of two "delicate" and very young men who come wishing to live at Scetis. Seeing that they have been "brought up in comfort," he tries to send them away. When they will not be dissuaded, Macarius tells himself, "Suffering will make them go away of their own accord," and proceeds to instruct them in the practices of the monastic way of life: how to make themselves a cell, how to make ropes in order to earn their bread. After three years Macarius wonders why they have not sought further guidance from him; they never come to share their "thoughts" (*logismoi*) like other monks; he just sees them silently attending church to receive "the oblation." When he visits and observes their "way of life," Macarius finds that they have (jointly) found the way to God through faithfully following his rather harsh (and somewhat cynical) initial instructions. When they die, Macarius takes others to see their cell, saying, "Come and see the place of martyrdom of the young strangers."[152] Through the renunciation of their previous lives of comfort (a physical and social humbling) and their simple faith in and obedience to Macarius's initial "word," the two young men achieve the status of martyrs.

If the crown is the ultimate heavenly reward, it is also used as an image for the burden of suffering. A monk suffers for nine years under the weight of his "thoughts." In despair he says, "I have ruined myself, I have perished already, I will go back to the world." But as he journeys he hears a voice saying, "Those temptations which you endured for nine years were your crowns. Go back to your cell, and I will take these evil thoughts from you." The monk then realizes that temptations in himself should

151. Crowns also descend on the monks killed by barbarians at Scetis. See *Sayings*, 140 (Moses 10), *Desert Fathers*, 18.14, p. 191. The idea that monasticism was a form of martyrdom (white martyrdom rather than red) is found early in its development (Louth, *Christian Mystical Tradition*, 98–99). The vocabulary of martyrdom—*agōn*, and images of beasts and wild animals arising from the context of the arena or circus—is also found in Athanasius's *Life of Antony*.

152. *Sayings*, 134–36 (Macarius the Great 33).

not cause him to despair of (or judge) himself, since "if we use these thoughts well they will give us a crown."[153] Depending on what monks do with their "bad thoughts," they can either "suffer shipwreck" or "earn a crown."[154]

Bearing the crown of suffering is a form of solidarity with Christ. Like Jesus, the monk bears a crown of thorns. Obedience and suffering and self-denial are connected to the "way of the cross." Hyperichius states this clearly: "The monk's service is obedience. He who has this shall have his prayers answered, and shall stand by the Crucified in confident faith. For that was how the Lord went to his cross, being made obedient even unto death."[155] The reference to Philippians 2:8 is evident here ("he humbled himself and became obedient to the point of death—even death on a cross"). Obedience is a form of self-emptying or kenosis. Thus Abba Or can say, "The crown of the monk is humility."[156]

If then obedience, in imitation of Christ, is a radical form of self-emptying, the monastic way of life offers training to enable it: "Just as young shoots are easily trained back and bent, so it is with beginners who live in submission."[157] In the words of Amma Syncletica, "Obedience has the promise of humility."[158]

The story of the monk's being directed by his *abba* to plant and water a bare stick is the classic illustration of the valuing of training in obedience. The *Sayings of the Fathers* tells this story of John the Little, who obediently walks a lengthy distance each day to collect water for the stick until, after three years, it "came to life

---

153. *Desert Fathers*, 7.42, p. 73.

154. *Desert Fathers*, 10.89, p. 110. See also 7.43, pp. 73–75, where a disciple becomes the unknowing recipient of crowns when he resists the temptation to sleep rather than remain waiting for his *abba's* instruction (the *abba* himself has fallen asleep!): "God can bestow crowns upon us even for resisting little temptations."

155. *Desert Fathers*, 14.11, p. 143; see *Sayings*, 239 (Hyperichius 8).

156. *Sayings*, 247 (Or 9).

157. *Sayings*, 69 (Isaiah 2).

158. *Desert Fathers*, 14.9, p. 143.

and bore fruit."[159] The exaggeration to a point of absurdity here is undoubtedly designed for resistant beginners.

The humility that comes from submission, however, is often not far from what might be understood as "humiliation."[160] A hermit tells himself that he is "perfectly virtuous." God humbles him by telling him to submit to the instructions of an archimandrite.[161] The hermit asks, "What must I do to be saved?" The archimandrite tells him to "take a whip and go and herd . . . swine." He does so, and people think he has gone mad. "But God looked on his humility, and saw how he bore these insults with patience, and told him to go back to his cell."[162] Herding swine was considered to be "humiliating" work.

The fruitfulness of some acts of obedience is, however, less clear. Sometimes obedience is deemed to be foolish. John, the disciple of Abba Paul, is told to collect some dung from a hyena's den.[163] John is concerned about meeting the hyena. Abba Paul tells him, jokingly, to tie her up and bring her to him. John takes him literally and returns with the hyena on a rope. Abba Paul is amazed but "wanted to humiliate him" and so strikes his disciple, telling him he is a fool, and sets the hyena free.[164] This is an uncomfortable story, though beating was an accepted part of the monastic regime.[165] Abba Paul, it seems, is equally impressed and appalled by John's obedience. Is the beating an attempt to stave

159. *Sayings*, 85–86 (John the Little [the Dwarf] 1), *Desert Fathers*, 14.3, p. 141. For a comparison with the version found in Cassian's *Institutes*, see Harmless, *Desert Christians*, 222–23.

160. Indeed, the English translators of these texts again struggle here.

161. *Archimandrite* is a Greek term, perhaps referring here to the leader or abbot (to use later terminology) of a large monastic community or of several communities.

162. *Desert Fathers*, 15.52, pp. 161–62.

163. The den of a lioness in the *Desert Fathers* version.

164. *Sayings* 109 (John, disciple of Abba Paul, 1); see *Desert Fathers*, 14.4, p. 141: "humble him."

165. Palladius, *Lausiac History*, chap. 7.3, p. 40.

off any pride that John might feel in regard to his foolish feat? Is it a sign of parental-style frustration at the stupidity of the action?[166] Similarly, verbal abuse is commended as a form of training: "Nothing is so useful to the beginner as insults. The beginner who bears insults is like a tree that is watered every day."[167] An enacted parable reveals the intention of exposure to insults. After the destruction of Scetis by barbarians (407–408), Abba Anoub and his seven brothers set up a temporary camp in an old temple at Terenuthis. There is a stone statue in the temple, and each morning, on rising, Anoub throws stones at its face. Each evening, he kneels before it, begging for forgiveness. At the end of the week, when the brothers come together as usual on Saturday, his brother Poemen asks why he did this. Anoub says,

> "When you saw me throwing stones at the face of the statue, did it speak, or did it become angry?" Abba Poemen said, "No." "Or again, when I bent down in penitence, was it moved, and did it say, 'I will not forgive you'?" Again Abba Poemen answered, "No." Then the old man resumed, "Now we are seven brethren; if you wish us to live together, let us be like this statue, which is not moved whether one beats it or whether one flatters it."[168]

The aim here is an interior stability that is not threatened by insults or dependent on praise. Anthony says of a monk who is unable to bear insults, "You are like a village magnificently decorated on the outside, but destroyed from within by robbers."[169] Anthony uses a similar "beating the stone" enacted parable in the training of Ammonas. The fruit of this training in interior stability is "goodness," so Ammonas "took no notice of wickedness":

---

166. One might also ask questions regarding the motivation behind the order. *Desert Fathers*, 15.73, warns that orders should themselves be given "in humility and the fear of God" and not from "self-will and desire for power."
167. *Sayings*, 69 (Isaiah 1).
168. *Sayings*, 32–33 (Anoub 1); *Desert Fathers*, 15.11, pp. 151–52.
169. *Sayings*, 4 (Anthony 15).

instead of giving a young pregnant girl a penance, he blesses her womb and gives her an extravagant gift of linen.[170]

Ammonas has, the saying explains, made "progress in the fear of God." This fear of God, eschatological humility, gives him the interior stability that enables him to withdraw the normal projections that damage human capacity to be fully open to the other. He does not need the approval of others for his actions; he enjoys a freedom that enables him to respond with compassion to someone who has been labeled an "unhappy wretch." His radical dependence on God gives birth to humility and love.

A similar pattern is evident in the stories of monks defeating demonic forces by turning the other cheek. Underlying this phrase is a gospel imperative outlined in a saying by Anthony:

> The brethren came to the Abba Anthony and said to him, "Speak a word; how are we to be saved?" The old man said to them, "You have heard the Scriptures. That should teach you how." But they said, "We want to hear from you too, Father." Then the old man said to them, "The Gospel says, 'if anyone strikes you on one cheek, turn to him the other also [Matt 5:39].'" They said, "We cannot do that." The old man said, "If you cannot offer the other cheek, at least allow one cheek to be struck." "We cannot do that either," they said. So he said, "If you are not able to do that, then do not return evil for evil," and they said, "We cannot do that either." Then the old man said to his disciple, "Prepare a little brew of corn for these invalids. If you cannot do this, or that, what can I do for you? What you need is prayers."[171]

The capacity to bear insults is a sign of obedience to the gospel command and a sign of one's obedience to the humble way of Jesus.

This way of humility enables the monk to exercise the same power over the demonic that is seen in Jesus' ministry. So, for example, Abba Daniel tells the story of the healing of a nobleman's

170. *Sayings*, 27 (Ammonas 8). Ammonas perceives that the girl is "near to death": giving birth was dangerous and often resulted in mortality for either mother or child, or both. The linen was intended for a potential burial.
171. *Sayings*, 5 (Anthony 19).

daughter. Faced with a case of demonic possession, the nobleman is advised to seek the help of some anchorites (hermits), but the very capacity that enables them to bring healing (their humility) would also prevent them from willingly coming to cure the girl (because of their fear of vainglory or pride). A disciple of the anchorites is consequently tricked into visiting the nobleman's house. On entering the house the possessed girl slaps the disciple. He immediately turns the other cheek, an action that forces the demon out: "Violence! The commandment of Jesus Christ is driving me out." On hearing what has happened, the anchorites explain: "The pride of devils must fall before humble obedience to the commandments of Jesus Christ."[172]

It is notable that the demon calls the disciple's action "violence": turning the other cheek is, paradoxically, a powerful act. In his discussion of Jesus's instruction to turn the other cheek Walter Wink suggests that the gospel imperative is actually a way of refusing to accept humiliation. The slap, he argues, is intended "not to injure but to humiliate, to put someone in his or her place." It was a way of "admonishing inferiors" used by masters to rebuke slaves, husbands their wives, parents their children, and so on: it signaled unequal (social) relations, where the expected response was submission, not retaliation. Jesus, Wink argues, advocates not a weak form of submission to being humiliated but a nonviolent response that shifts the balance of power. By turning the other cheek the humiliated person gives a message that robs the oppressor of further power over him or her. In Wink's words, this action says, "Try again. Your first blow failed to achieve its intended effect. I deny you the power to humiliate me. I am a human being just like you. Your status does not alter that fact. You cannot demean me."[173]

---

172. *Desert Fathers*, 15.14, p. 153; see *Sayings*, 51–52 (Dan 3): "This is how the pride of the devil is brought low, through the humility of the commandment of Christ." *Desert Fathers*, 15.53, p. 162, makes a similar connection. Turning the other cheek is enacted humility that results in the immediate exorcism of a demon.

173. Walter Wink, *Engaging the Powers: Discernment and Resistance in a World of Domination* (Minneapolis, MN: Fortress Press, 1992), 176.

Perhaps a similar power dynamic is operating in the desert monastic story. In the case of the possessed girl, the demon is claiming superiority (power) over human life. When the disciple offers the other cheek, he is refusing to acknowledge this power. His obedience to the command of Christ signals that there is only one power that he will acknowledge: the power of Jesus, which, paradoxically, is characterized by humility. The disciple's non-violent action turns out to be a powerful form of resistance. He stands secure in his identity as an obedient follower of Christ, and this identity cannot be overturned by the demonic. Indeed in the presence of this secure identity the power of the demonic is itself overturned. When Abba Anthony asks, "What can get through the snares of the enemy?" the answer he receives is "Humility."[174]

Humility similarly underpins the understanding of forgiveness: "If anyone says 'Forgive me', and humbles himself, he burns up the demons that tempt him."[175] What might these tempting demons be? Arrogance, self-justification, self-righteousness, perhaps. To admit that one is wrong certainly lowers the self in front of another. The capacity to offer unilateral forgiveness is seen as a sign of humility. Indeed, one saying shows it as definitive: "What is humility? . . . It is if you forgive a brother who has wronged you before he is sorry."[176] Both asking for and offering forgiveness involve a lowering of the self before another. The act of forgiveness alters power relationships. The "brother who has wronged you" is the offender or debtor, who has caused suffering and, perhaps, humiliation. Forgiveness frees both parties from the tangled web of debt: it gives the one who has been damaged freedom from the power of the debt or offense, and it frees the debtor.

A vivid story told by Arsenius illustrates this point well. Two men on horseback (representing pride) are carrying a long plank of wood between them. They are trying to take the wood into a temple, but neither of them will give way to the other to enable

174. *Sayings*, 2 (Anthony 7).

175. *Desert Fathers*, 15.78, p. 167.

176. *Desert Fathers*, 15.60, p. 163. For a related saying, see *Desert Fathers*, 15.63, p. 163.

them to fit the wood through the door endwise. Arsenius then interprets the story: "These are the men who bear the yoke of righteousness with boasting, and they will not be humble enough to correct themselves and go in by the humble way of Christ, and therefore they remain outside the kingdom of God."[177]

Righteousness is damaged by pride and so, paradoxically, becomes an impediment to entry into the kingdom of God. Humility allows one to see one's own need for correction. The basis for asking for, and offering, forgiveness is then an awareness of one's own sinfulness before God (eschatological humility); human judgment is relativized by divine judgment. When a wronged brother wishes to seek revenge, Abba Sisoes prays with him: "God, we no longer need you to care for us, since we do justice for ourselves."[178] The reality is, of course, that we do need God's care. When the monk places himself in "the presence of the goodness of God," he finds both that he is a sinner and that God is merciful.[179] And he finds himself in solidarity with other sinners equally in need of mercy. Humility here, to pick up Wengst's suggestive phrase, is indeed "the solidarity of the humiliated."[180]

2.6 Conclusion

Schongauer's engraving of Anthony can now be read in the light of this study. To the modern eye Anthony looks like a humiliated self, but the literature of desert monasticism signals that the relationship between humility and humiliation needs to be understood in a more nuanced way. It is now possible to read the

177. *Desert Fathers*, 18.2, pp. 184–85; see *Sayings*, 15–16 (Arsenius 33).

178. *Sayings*, 212 (Sisoes 1).

179. *Sayings*, 185 (Poemen 122).

180. Wengst, *Humility*, 58. This solidarity is vividly enacted in the story of Abba Moses' refusing to attend a council called to judge a brother who had committed a fault. When he finally comes, he carries with him a leaky jug of water, saying, "My sins run out behind me, and I do not see them, and today I am coming to judge the errors of others" (*Sayings*, 138–39 [Moses 2]). Similarly, Macarius the Great was called "a god upon earth" because he "would cover the faults" of others (*Sayings*, 134 [Macarius the Great 32]).

image of Anthony positively, as a humble, and even humbled, self. The move from city to desert destabilizes the self, stripping away one's former socially constructed identity and exposing the monk to radical dependence on God. Sustained by an eschatological vision, the hope of the kingdom of heaven, the monk stands in humility before God, aware both of his or her own limits and of God's loving mercy. So, as Abba Alonius says, "In the world there is only myself and God." This understanding is the source of interior peace.[181] This eschatological humility allows one to be both realistic about oneself (the demons will still tug at one's being) and hopeful regarding human destiny (renewal in the image of God, Christlikeness, heaven).

This vision finds its ground and power not crudely, in the very real distance between God and humanity, between Creator and creature: this reading would be to see humility as simply forced on us by our relative powerlessness. Rather, and paradoxically, it locates humility in God's own self-emptying, in the humility of Christ. Hope has a christological basis: human beings are not simply "worthless servants" but are created to be Christlike, invited to walk in the same humble, self-emptying way as Christ. Humility here is the way of love. So, when he is securely grounded in this way, Anthony is able to say, "I no longer fear God, but I love Him. For love casts out fear."[182]

Where is God in Schongauer's etching of Anthony? It does not seem too big a leap to see Anthony here as a Christlike figure, lifted before the viewer, his suffering, his humiliation, visible for all to see, but simultaneously vindicated as he ascends toward the open heavens.

Still, one cannot but be struck by the solitariness of Anthony in Schongauer's engraving. It is not surprising that, as monasticism developed, communal expressions became the norm.

---

181. *Sayings*, 35 (Alonius 1).
182. *Sayings*, 8 (Anthony 32); *Desert Fathers*, 17.1, p. 177.

Interlude

From the Desert to the Cloister

The desert is a dangerous place. A destabilized self, vulnerable and open, might easily fall into self-deception. In the *Lausiac History*, written some fifty or sixty years after the *Life of Anthony*, Palladius (ca. 363–ca. 431) relates a number of salutary tales of ascetic practice gone wrong. Valens, who had come to the Egyptian desert from Palestine, became increasingly arrogant, believing that he had been visited by angels so that "he felt he was too good to partake of the Mysteries," that is, the communal sharing of the Eucharist. Finally he claimed to have seen Christ himself and announced to the brothers gathered in the church, "I have no use for Communion, for I saw Christ this very day." Hearing this, the *abbas* "bound him and put him in irons for a year," and through "their prayers and the living of an ordinary, unbusied life" he was cured of the disease of conceit.[1] The remedy, while sounding harsh, involved a reconnection with the monastic community.

A similar story, found only in the Syriac recension of the *Lausiac History*, is told of Eucarpius at Scete. He too removed himself more and more "from communion and association with the brothers." While his motivation was to devote "himself entirely to constant prayer," he succumbed to pride and, like Valens, believed he had seen Christ. Imagining that he had found a shortcut to "purity

1. Palladius, *The Lausiac History*, trans. Robert T. Meyer (Westminster, MD: Newman Press, 1965), 25.

of heart," he challenged the spiritual leadership of the *abbas* and advocated abandonment of the "lesser" disciplines of physical asceticism, intercessory prayer, and contemplation of Scripture. Again, Eucarpius was healed of what was deemed to be pride through reconnection with community. His spiritual health was secured by the command of the *abbas* "to minister to the sick and wash the feet of strangers."[2] Eucarpius had to take up the towel.

Here the practice of service to others was intended to facilitate an inner transformation, from pride to humility. This is precisely the line of thinking present in Basil of Caesarea's strong advocacy of communal life as essential for healthy monasticism. Basil (ca. 330–379) made a crucial contribution to the development of monasticism in both the East and, via the Rule of Saint Benedict, the West.

Experiments in communal religious life are not, of course, unique to Christianity, and the historical growth of cenobitic (Gk *koinos bios;* "common life") monasticism is as complex as the emergence of anchoritic forms. Nonetheless, the two figures of Pachomius and Basil loom large in the history of the development of the communal forms of Christian monasticism that have dominated the West. In Upper Egypt, Pachomius (ca. 292–346) developed *koinonia* (communities) that were highly organized and increasingly regulated. The physical layout of the Pachomian *koinonia* shared many elements found in later Benedictine monasteries. The monastery was separated from the outside world by a high wall; entry was via a gatehouse, complete with gatekeeper. Nearby was a guesthouse, for postulants and visitors. Within the enclosure were a church, a meeting place, an infirmary for the sick, group houses for the monks, a dining hall, a kitchen, a bakery, stores, and, increasingly, provisions for carrying out various

---

2. Syriac Lausiac History 73, in Tim Vivian and Rowan A. Greer, *Four Desert Fathers: Pambo, Evagrius, Macarius of Egypt, and Macarius of Alexandria: Coptic Texts Relating to the "Lausiac History" of Palladius* (Crestwood, NY: St. Vladimir's Seminary Press, 2004), 170–72. My attention was drawn to these stories through the work of Demetrios S. Katos, "Humility as the Harbinger of Imageless Prayer in the Lausiac History," *St. Vladimir's Theological Quarterly* 51, no. 1 (2007): 107–21.

skilled crafts. Over time, more formal arrangements began to order the life of the *koinonia* and, indeed, Pachomius is credited with the composition of the first known set of monastic rules.[3]

Alongside the Pachomian experiments, the writings of Basil of Caesarea, particularly the *Longer* and *Shorter Rules* (or *Longer* and *Shorter Responses*, LR and SR), had a decisive impact on the theological underpinnings of cenobitic monasticism.[4] In the penultimate chapter of the sixth-century Rule of Saint Benedict, Benedict specifically commends Basil's "Rule" to his monks (RB 73.5), and its influence is pervasive.[5] In his home territory of Cappadocia, Basil

---

3. For an overview of Pachomian monasticism, see Marilyn Dunn, *The Emergence of Monasticism: From the Desert Fathers to the Early Middle Ages* (Malden, MA: Blackwell Publishing, 2000), 25–32; William Harmless, *Desert Christians: An Introduction to the Literature of Early Monasticism* (Oxford: Oxford University Press, 2004), 115–41.

4. Rowan Williams, *The Wound of Knowledge: Christian Spirituality from the New Testament to St. John of the Cross*, 2nd ed. (Cambridge, MA: Cowley Publications, 1991), 109; Timothy Fry, ed., *RB 1980: The Rule of St. Benedict in Latin and English with Notes* (Collegeville, MN: Liturgical Press, 1981), 30–34. The terms *Longer* and *Shorter Rules*, though commonly used, are a somewhat misleading way of referring to the two divisions within Basil's *Great Asketikon*, his collected teaching and responses to questions regarding ascetic life. Anna Silvas, in her new English translation, uses the terms *Shorter Responses* and *Longer Responses* for these two forms, which seems more faithful to Basil's project: Basil himself never used the term "rule" in relation to the *Asketikon*. I use Silvas's translations unless otherwise noted. Silvas provides a thorough analysis of the possible editions and the complex transmission of the *Asketikon*. Several collections or editions were made during Basil's lifetime, reflecting, Silvas argues, different phases of Basil's life and the different contexts for which the collections were prepared. For a summary of her findings, see Anna Silvas, *The Asketikon of St Basil the Great*, Oxford Early Christian Studies (Oxford: Oxford University Press, 2005), 143–45. The earliest stage of development, known as the *Small Asketikon*, survives via the Latin version of Rufinus of Aquileia (ca. 345–411) and is known as the *Instituta Basili* or *Regula Basili*. As a translator, Rufinus is, as Silvas notes, better styled as a "sub-author," as he undertakes the task of bringing Greek texts to his Latin audience (Silvas, *Asketikon*, 129). On the transmission of the *Small Asketikon* to the West, see Anna Silvas, "Edessa to Cassino: The Passage of Basil's Asketikon to the West," *Vigiliae Christianae* 56, no. 3 (2002): 247–59.

5. The extent and significance of the influence of the *Regula Basili* on the Rule of Saint Benedict has been the subject of debate. See Silvas, "Edessa to Cassino," 256–57.

had encountered the radical ascetic movement that had clashed with church authorities at the Council of Gangra (ca. 340) and had been deeply influenced by one of its proponents, Eustathius of Sebaste, a family friend. On his return home following an education in classical rhetoric, inspired by the spiritual leadership of his sister Macrina and the transformation of his family household into an ascetic community, Basil abandoned the pursuit of a secular career and embraced the ascetic life. He visited monastic centers in Egypt, Palestine, Syria, and Mesopotamia and experimented with disciplined ascetic life alongside his family and, for a time, with his friend and contemporary, Gregory of Nazianzus.[6] By the time he was appointed bishop of Caesarea in 370, Basil was able to articulate and promote a vision of monasticism that, as Gregory observed, "reconciled . . . and united the solitary and community life" so that "the contemplative spirit might not be cut off from society nor should the active life be unaffected by the contemplative."[7] Basil's vision of a "charitable monastic life"[8] is grounded securely in the gospel imperative to love God and neighbor.[9] Basil commends withdrawal as "of great assistance in keeping the soul from distraction" and in avoiding becoming disoriented by worldly entanglements (LR 6), but for Basil, such withdrawal is not primarily a solitary project. Monasticism is simply a Christian life, and a Christian life cannot be lived without the neighbor.

In chapter 7 of his *Longer Rules*, Basil sets out his rationale for preferring life with "those of the same mind" to a solitary life lived "privately by himself."[10] For Basil, the solitary life exposes the monk to the danger of "self-pleasing" (LR 7.9), an egocentric ori-

---

6. Dunn, *Emergence of Monasticism*, 35; Fry, *RB 1980*, 31.

7. Gregory of Nazianzus, "Oration 43 or The Panegyric on S. Basil," in *Select Orations of Saint Gregory Nazianzen, Sometime Archbishop of Constantinople; S. Cyril of Jerusalem, S. Gregory Nazianzen*, trans. Charles Gordon Brown and James Edward Swallow, Nicene and Post-Nicene Fathers second series (Grand Rapids, MI: Eerdmans, 1955), 7:395–422, here 415–16.

8. Dunn, *Emergence of Monasticism*, 37.

9. Basil quotes Matt 22:36-39. Fry, *RB 1980*, 32.

10. Silvas notes that the text of the Greek *Asketikon* here refers to the "philosophic" life (Silvas, *Asketikon*, 180n146).

entation that could result in pride. Our need for others is clear, he argues, at the most basic level: "not one of us suffices for himself alone"; we are not self-sufficient, even for bodily needs. Indeed, Basil explains, God has created us for interdependence: to "have need of each other . . . so that we associate with one another" (LR 7.2, 4). We are unable to see ourselves without the help of the other. Reproof, ideally given with compassion, helps one see one's defects, but even from an enemy, it can inspire "a desire to be cured" (LR 7.6). Without someone "to test his work," the "individualist" will think he has "arrived at the highest perfection of the commandment" (LR 7.26).

Equally, Basil argues, it is not possible to fulfill the "commandment" in the absence of others. The "commandment" here is living out the self-giving love of Christ, the "law of love," seen most clearly in love of neighbor: "The very character of Christ's love does not permit an individual to seek his own interest, for Love . . . seeks not its own" (LR 7.5). So the danger for the solitary is that "having shut away his character without (any) training he will neither recognize his defects . . . nor (be able to) ascertain his progress in works, because he is stripped of all material for the accomplishment of the commandments" (LR 7.27–28).[11] The neighbor here both offers and receives the gift of service. Basil uses Pauline body imagery to expresses this interdependence:

> If we are not fitted together through our harmony into the solidarity of one body in the Holy Spirit, and each of us chooses the solitary life, not serving the common good in that dispensation which accords with God's good pleasure, but satisfying one's private passion of self-pleasing—how could we, thus split off and divided, preserve (and apply to ourselves) that (harmonious) relation and service of the members towards each other, or the subjection to our head, which is Christ? (LR 7.9–12)

If one is deprived of the presence of others, it is impossible, Basil suggests, to practice a Christian, that is, a Christlike, way of

---

11. Insertions by translator.

life: "If anyone says that he has enough for the amendment (and betterment) of his ways in the teaching of divine scriptures (and the apostolic precepts), then he . . . is like one who learns how to build but never builds anything, or like one being taught the smith's craft but who will not put the lessons into practice" (LR 7.31–33). By contrast, Basil points to the enacted teaching of Jesus:

> For behold how the Lord in his exceeding love for men did not deem sufficient the mere teaching of the word, but in order to hand on to us accurately and in very deed *an example of humility in the perfection of love*, having girded himself with a linen cloth, washed the feet of his own disciples. Whose feet then will you wash? For whom will you perform the duties of care? In comparison with whom shall you be (lower or even) the last, if you live by yourself? (LR 7.34–35; italics mine)

Humility here is both christologically centered and strongly social in orientation. The Christian life is, for Basil, the imitation of Christ (LR 43). And in this imitation, love and humility are fundamentally connected. Love is demonstrated paradigmatically by Jesus through the humble action of lowering himself before another: the master becomes the slave of the disciple. For Basil, neither humility nor love can be understood, or practiced, in the absence of others: "For in what way shall he put his humility to the proof if he has no one before whom he must show himself humble? In what way shall he show compassion who is cut off from the communion (and society) of the many?" (LR 7.29).

Humility and love are similarly connected and similarly at the center of Benedict of Nursia's monastic vision. Saint Benedict's Rule, rather than Basil's, ultimately shapes the Western monastic tradition.

Figure 2. Giovanni di Consalvo, *Benedict and the Poisoned Bread*, from the fresco cycle of the *Life of Saint Benedict*, Chiostro degli Aranci (Cloister of the Oranges), Badia Fiorentina, ca. 1430s.

Chapter 3

Humility and Community

The Rule of Saint Benedict

The workshop where we are to toil faithfully at all these tasks is the enclosure of the monastery and stability in the community.

—*The Rule of Saint Benedict*

The Badia Fiorentina, founded as a Benedictine monastery in 978 by a wealthy Tuscan widow, is now the home of a contemporary monastic community, the Fraternités de Jérusalem.[1] Within the Badia, on the walls of the Cloister of the Oranges, there is a series of frescoes depicting the life of the sixth-century founder of Benedictine monasticism, Benedict of Nursia. The paintings were probably produced between 1436 and 1438 by Giovanni di Consalvo, an otherwise unknown Portuguese disciple of Fra Angelico. The cycle, a series of events from Gregory the Great's *Life of Saint Benedict*, was well established by the fifteenth century. Many illuminated copies of

---

1. Responding to the religious and cultural upheavals of the 1960s and 1970s, the Fraternités de Jérusalem was founded in 1975 by Pierre-Marie Delfieux to live monastic life in the heart of modern cities. The initial foundation was in Paris, attached to the parish church of Saint Gervais. Monastic houses are now located in a number of European cities, including Vézelay, Strasbourg, Mont-Saint-Michel, Florence, Brussels, Rome, and Cologne, and in Montreal, Canada (http://jerusalem.cef.fr/monastiques/fraternites-monastiques).

the *Life* had been produced during the medieval period, as had other *Lives* of Benedict, Maurus, and Scholastica, the founding saints of the Benedictine order. So when cloister frescoes developed in fourteenth-century Italy and the lives of the founders of monasticism, including Anthony and Benedict, were among the chosen subjects, the iconography was already largely fixed. These frescoes were designed not for decoration but for meditation, as monks moved around the cloister, from oratory to refectory, from dormitory to kitchen.[2]

One of the scenes depicted in the Cloister of the Oranges concerns the story told in Gregory's *Life* of Benedict and the poisoned bread. According to this story, the presence of Benedict's thriving monastic community had become a source of intense resentment for Florentius, the priest of the local parish. Driven by wildly destructive envy, he sent Benedict bread that was both blessed and poisoned. Benedict received the bread with thanks but also discerned "what harm hid in that bread" (8.2).[3] Gregory continues:

> Now at dinner time a [raven] used to come from the adjoining woods and accept food from [Benedict's] hand. When it had come at the usual hour, the man of God threw the bread the priest had sent before the [raven]. And he commanded it: "In the name of the Lord Jesus Christ, take this bread, and throw it in a place where no one can find it." Then the [raven], with its beak open and its wings expanded, began to run in a circle around the bread and croak. It was as if it were saying that it wanted to obey, but could not carry out the orders. But the man of God urged it again and again: "Take it away! Do not

---

2. Anne Frances Dawtry, "Benedictine Order," in Grove Art Online; Oxford Art Online, http://www.oxfordartonline.com/subscriber/article/grove/art/T007854; Marco Chiarini, "Giovanni di Consalvo," in Grove Art Online, Oxford Art Online, http://www.oxfordartonline.com/subscriber/article/grove/art/T032524; Marjorie Jean Hall and John N. Lupia, "Cloister," in Grove Art Online; Oxford Art Online, http://www.oxfordartonline.com/subscriber/article/grove/art/T018230.

3. Quotations are from Gregory the Great, *The Life of Saint Benedict*, trans. Terrence G. Kardong (Collegeville, MN: Liturgical Press, 2009). Kardong's numbering follows the critical Latin text of Vogüé but omits the reference to Gregory's *Dialogues*, the original context of the *Life*.

be afraid! Throw it where no one can find it." After long hesi-
tation, the [raven] took the loaf in its beak and departed. After
three hours it returned minus the bread; and it received its
daily ration from the hand of the man of God. (*Life* 8.3)[4]

In the Badia fresco, Benedict, seated between two monks, leans
over the table, having placed the bread before the raven. The
raven dominates the foreground, bent over the poisoned bread,
midnight-black feathers mirrored in the habit of the monks seated
around the refectory table. Above this scene, draped over a rafter,
almost swinging before the viewer's eyes, is a towel. This is a story
about humility and community. How is this so?

This chapter explores the relationship between humility and
community in the most influential text for cenobitic monasticism
in the West, the Rule of Saint Benedict (RB).

3.1 The Rule of Saint Benedict in Context

The Rule of Saint Benedict has had an inestimable impact on
the development of Western monasticism.[5] When it was compiled
in Italy in the mid-sixth century by Benedict of Nursia, however,
it was simply one rule among many.[6] In the century following

4. I have altered Kardong's translation of the Latin *corvus* from *crow* to
raven: it is likely that the bird associated with Benedict is the common raven.
5. Claude Peifer, in his essay "The Rule of St. Benedict," in the Introduction
to *RB 1980*, marking the fifteen-hundredth anniversary of Benedict's birth,
suggested that the Rule is "the most influential document in the entire history of Western monasticism" (Claude Peifer, "The Rule of St. Benedict," in
RB 1980: The Rule of St. Benedict in Latin and English with Notes, ed. Timothy
Fry [Collegeville, MN: Liturgical Press, 1981], 65–112, here 65). *RB 1980* was
a landmark publication, bringing much twentieth-century European scholarship to the English-speaking world. I rely substantially on its introductory
essays for the background to the RB. See also Marilyn Dunn, *The Emergence
of Monasticism: From the Desert Fathers to the Early Middle Ages* (Malden, MA:
Blackwell Publishing, 2000), chap. 6; Columba Stewart, *Prayer and Community:
The Benedictine Tradition* (London: Darton, Longman, and Todd, 1998), chap. 1.
6. Dunn suggests a date of 546 or after 554 on the basis of internal evidence.
See Dunn, *Emergence of Monasticism*, 127. The traditional attribution of the
Rule to Benedict of Nursia, founder of the monastery of Monte Cassino, is

Pachomius and Basil, cenobitic monasticism had spread through an increasingly fragile Roman Empire. By the early sixth century, monasticism was both more diverse and more institutionalized than it had been in the fourth century. Monastic foundations ranged from large "basilical" monasteries, attached to significant churches, increasingly focused on the performance of liturgy, to monasteries with attached hospices, to federations of related houses, to small private households.[7] Amid this diversity, and in the face of political and social decay, there was an increasing trend toward cenobitic forms of monastic life.[8] The Council of Chalcedon (451) had brought monasteries under the authority of the local bishop, and an increasing number of written rules evolved that ordered the life of monastic communities.[9] Amid the range of expressions of monasticism, however, there was also a growing tradition of wisdom, shared orally and via written texts, which gave coherence to the monastic movement.[10] The Rule of Saint Benedict builds on this tradition. It is, as Stewart has observed, both "an original work" and "deeply traditional," as Benedict offers "an interpretation and application of previous monastic experience."[11]

The Rule of Saint Benedict, following an emerging pattern for monastic rules, comprises two basic parts: spiritual doctrine (Prologue and chapters 1–7) and practical regulations (chapters 8–73). As Claude Peifer observes in his essay in the introduction to *RB 1980*, one of "the most notable features of the RB is its brevity."[12] The Rule gives a comprehensive yet succinct coverage of the key elements of cenobitic spirituality and sufficient detail regarding the practical ordering of the monastery to guide, but not constrict,

---

relatively secure. See Hubertus R. Drobner, *The Fathers of the Church: A Comprehensive Introduction*, trans. Siegfried S. Schatzmann, with bibliographies updated and expanded for the English edition by William Harmless and Hubertus R. Drobner (Peabody, MA: Hendrickson Publishers, 2007), 508. For transmission and editions of the text, see Peifer, "The Rule," 102–12.

7. Dunn, *Emergence of Monasticism*, 97–98.
8. Peifer, "The Rule," 67.
9. Dunn, *Emergence of Monasticism*, 97–98.
10. Peifer, "The Rule," 67–68, 85–86.
11. Stewart, *Prayer and Community*, 20.
12. Peifer, "The Rule," 91.

the operation of real communities. It is worth having the shape and scope of the Rule in view:[13]

Monastic Doctrine		
Prologue	Call to monastic life	
Chaps. 1–3	Cenobitic framework of Rule and abbot	
Chaps. 4–7	Primer of monastic spirituality	4 Tools of Good Works 5 Obedience 6 Silence 7 Humility
Monastic Regulations		
Chaps. 8–20	Structure and content of liturgical prayer	
Chaps. 21–67	Structures and practice of common life	23–30 Penitential code 43–46 Code of satisfaction 58–63 Acceptance of new members and order in the community 21–22 Deans and the dormitory 31–34 Material goods 35–42 Food and sleep 47–52 Work, prayer, exterior relationships 64–65 Selection of abbot and prior 66 Porter
Chaps. 68–73	"Appendix" revisits theology of monastic life	Fraternal relationships

13. This table has been developed using the overviews of Peifer and Stewart. Peifer, "The Rule," 91–92; Stewart, *Prayer and Community*, 20–21. The division between doctrine (Prologue–chap. 7) and regulation (chaps. 8–73) was proposed by Vogüé. See Adalbert de Vogüé, *La Règle de saint Benoît*, vol. 1, SCh 181 (Paris: Cerf, 1971), 206, and vol. 5, SCh 185 (Paris: Cerf, 1971), 384. Mary Forman, by contrast, argues that an examination of the scriptural sources and their exegisis in RB reveals "complex interrelationships of various chapters of the whole Rule," so that this twofold division is somewhat arbitrary (Mary Forman, "Benedict's Use of Scripture in the Rule: Introductory Understandings," ABR 52, no. 3 [2001]: 324–45, here 341). The schema is offered here as a simple overview with this caveat in mind.

Apart from the authorship of the rule bearing his name, nothing is known with certainty about Benedict himself.[14] The *Life* contained in book 2 of the *Dialogues* of (Pope) Gregory the Great (590–604) is virtually the only source offering biographical information.[15] According to the *Life*, Benedict was born into a free family in the region of Nursia and sent as a youth to Rome for a classical education. He abandoned his education, remaining "learnedly ignorant and wisely uninstructed," and his family and inheritance in order to "please God alone" (Introduction 1). He initially withdrew to Effide (modern-day Affile), accompanied by his childhood housekeeper, and then to deeper solitude in a cave near Sublacus (Subiaco), assisted by a monk named Romanus.

Called to be the leader of a group of monks, Benedict found his first experience of cenobitic life to be, according to the *Life*, disastrous: the monks found him too demanding and tried to poison him. Indeed, poisoning features several times in the *Life*. Benedict fled back to his cave but later established a cluster of small monasteries (twelve monasteries, each with twelve monks) in the same region. Again in response to conflict, Benedict relocated to Mons Casinus (Monte Cassino), displacing a pagan temple and engaging with the local population.[16] Here he spent the remainder of his life. The closing section of the *Life* notes that Benedict wrote a rule for monks "outstanding for its discretion and limpid in its diction" and that his life and the Rule were in harmony, "for the holy man could in no way teach other than he lived" (*Life* 36.1).

While historically the *Life* has found a treasured place in the Benedictine tradition, its reliability, authorship, and historical impact have been questioned.[17] The traditional account suggested that Gregory wrote book 2 of the *Dialogues* in 593–594, drawing

14. The traditional dates for Benedict are ca. 480–ca. 547. Drobner suggests dates of 480/490–555/560 (Drobner, *Fathers of the Church*, 504–7).

15. Drobner, *Fathers of the Church*, 505.

16. Through correlation of internal historical references, the move to Monte Cassino is generally dated to 529/530. See Drobner, *Fathers of the Church*, 506–7.

17. For an outline of the issues, see Terrence G. Kardong, "Who Wrote the Dialogues of Saint Gregory? A Report on a Controversy," CSQ 39, no. 1 (2004): 31–39.

on the witness of Benedict's disciples, and that his commendation of Saint Benedict's Rule ensured its immediate propagation and long-term primacy in Western monasticism. The twentieth century saw this neat picture crumble. The relationship between the *Dialogues* and the Rule has been the subject of much scholarly debate. Doubt was cast as to whether the Rule of Saint Benedict was used in sixth- or seventh-century Rome, and discrepancies between Gregory's monastic ideas and the Rule were noted. The current consensus is that the Rule of Saint Benedict did not become normative until the Carolingian reform of the ninth century.

The contrasting styles, and intentions, of the two texts offer a significant challenge: the *Life* is hagiography, full of visions and miracles, painting Benedict as a spiritual hero; the Rule, by contrast, is a rule, a *regula*, relentlessly practical and grounded in ordinary life. In the *Life*, Benedict's early experience is as an anchorite, yet the Rule demonstrates a practical grasp of emerging traditions of cenobitic monasticism. The two texts cannot be easily wedded; they are, as Terrence Kardong suggests, "apples and oranges" and best considered separately.[18]

Over the past twenty years, a challenge regarding the authorship of the *Dialogues* has further complicated the picture. Francis Clark argues that the *Dialogues* are actually a late seventh-century fabrication, compiled from materials in the papal archives, to advance a political agenda. This view has been vigorously contested.[19] Nonetheless, it is no longer possible simply to rehearse biographical details from the *Dialogues* without caution, nor to assume the immediate ascendency of the Rule of Saint Benedict from the existence of this text.

The way in which the Rule of Saint Benedict is understood has similarly undergone a revolution. While Benedict had traditionally been viewed as the "gifted inventor" of the Rule, the contemporary scholarly consensus is that his Rule is substantially

18. Terrence G. Kardong, Preface, in *The Life of Saint Benedict, by Gregory the Great: Translation and Commentary* (Collegeville, MN: Liturgical Press, 2009), ix–xii, here ix.

19. Gregorian authorship has been recently reasserted by Michaela Zelzer, "Gregory's *Life of Benedict*: Its Historico-Literary Field," CSQ 43 (2008): 327–37.

copied from the longer Rule of the Master (RM) so that Benedict has been recast from "creative genius" to "a good selector and editor."[20] The Prologue and first seven chapters of the Rule of Saint Benedict are very close to the text of the Rule of the Master. The structure of the remaining chapters follows a similar order, but as Benedict progresses, Aquinata Böckmann notes, "he diverges more and more." Indeed the divergences have allowed scholars to identify more clearly Benedict's particular contribution to the evolution of monastic life. As Böckmann says, "We can see what he accepted, what he omitted, what he corrected and what he added from other traditions or from his own experience."[21] Attending to the results of this scholarly work is important to this study as it particularly sharpens our appreciation of Benedict's valuing of community and his positive estimation of monastic life as "essentially joyful and dynamic."[22]

The Rule of the Master was not the only source for the Rule of Saint Benedict, moreover, and the RM itself was built from other sources. All compilers of monastic rules have been editors who have gleaned wisdom from written and oral traditions and

20. Aquinata Böckmann, *Perspectives on the Rule of St. Benedict: Expanding Our Hearts in Christ*, trans. Matilda Handl and Marianne Burkhard (Collegeville, MN: Liturgical Press, 2005), 3, 6. Traditionally it was believed that the RM drew on and expanded RB. This theory was challenged in the 1930s by Augustine Genestout, who argued that the RB was, on the contrary, dependent on RM. Vigorous debate ensued and, by the 1960s, the consensus had shifted. For a brief introduction to the debate and a discussion of the relationship of the RB to the RM, see Claude Peifer, "The Rule," 69–73, 79–83. More recently, Marilyn Dunn reignited the debate, contending that RM shows signs of Irish influence and is therefore more likely to have been associated with Columbanian monasticism in seventh-century northern Italy. This view has been vigorously contested. See Marilyn Dunn, "Mastering Benedict: Monastic Rules and Their Authors in the Early Medieval West," *English Historical Review* 105, no. 416 (1990): 567–94; Adalbert de Vogüé, "The Master and St. Benedict: A Reply to Marilyn Dunn," *English Historical Review* 107, no. 422 (1992): 95–103; Marilyn Dunn, "The Master and St Benedict: A Rejoinder," *English Historical Review* 107, no. 422 (1992): 104–11.

21. Böckmann, *Perspectives*, 6.

22. Terrence G. Kardong, *Benedict's Rule: A Translation and Commentary* (Collegeville, MN: Liturgical Press, 1996), 33.

placed it in the context of their own and their community's experience. And, in practice, monastic rules operate in the same way, in the dynamic context of a tradition and community. The most significant source, the ground from which everything else stems, is, however, the Bible; the Rule of Saint Benedict and the traditions around it are simply, as Böckmann says, "an aid to living the Gospel."[23] The Rule of Saint Benedict is packed with biblical quotations and allusions, as is the Rule of the Master. It also incorporates and responds to the inheritance of the fathers: Cassian (and behind him Evagrius), Basil, Pachomius, and the desert fathers, Augustine, and Cyprian. In the final chapter of his Rule, Benedict—and this is pure Benedict—makes the priority of the Scriptures and the richness of his inherited tradition visible:

> For anyone hastening on to the perfection of monastic life, there are the teachings of the holy Fathers, the observance of which will lead him to the very heights of perfection. What page, what passage of the inspired books of the Old and New Testaments is not the truest of guides for human life? What book of the holy catholic Fathers does not resoundingly summon us along the true way to reach the Creator? Then, besides the *Conferences* of the Fathers, their *Institutes* and their *Lives*, there is also the rule of our holy father Basil. (RB 73.2-5)[24]

How then does one approach the RB? Historically, as Lorenza Sena argues, there have been two basic approaches. A "spiritual" or existential approach, interested in "the edification and practical life of the community," was the dominant approach until the sixteenth century. And a "scientific" approach, which focuses on the "archaeological, historical, and literary" features of the Rule, began to be adopted in the seventeenth century and

---

23. Böckmann, *Perspectives*, 8.

24. Quotations from the Rule of Saint Benedict use the translation provided by *RB 1980* unless otherwise stated. The weight given to the influence of Benedict's various sources is a matter of considerable debate, as is the significance of his list in RB 73. For an overview, see Kardong, *Benedict's Rule*, 612–15. Kardong's commentary is of particular significance in consciously bringing the considerable body of European scholarship to the English-speaking world.

dominated the twentieth.[25] Contemporary monastic commentators have sometimes sensed a tension between objective or scientific approaches to scholarship and their existential engagement with monastic life.[26] Böckmann sensibly reminds her readers that "no totally objective interpretation" is possible.[27] In addition, her "principles for a maximally objective interpretation of the RB" emphasize the importance of reading the Rule against its historical context and its known literary sources, and with an awareness of our own context, interpretive choices, attitudes, and agendas.[28] She also reminds us that diversity of interpretation is part of the RB story and that the Rule in fact points away from itself to the Bible and to Christ: "Absolutizing the Rule is not the aim of RB."[29] Perhaps this openness, one might even say its humility, gives the Rule continued energy.

In this chapter, I endeavor to attend to the literary processes behind the text, especially where these affect the interpretation of notions of humility and community. Such attention is particularly important, as Michael Casey notes, in relation to RB 7, the focused discourse on humility, since this chapter of the Rule is substantially reliant on the Rule of the Master (RM 10), which is in turn dependent on a section of Cassian's *Institutes* (4.39).[30] Both existential and scientific approaches will assist in exploring the very practical questions raised by living in human community.

Finally, as one would expect from a tradition that stretches back for sixteen centuries, the literature on the RB is vast. This chapter relies substantially on the work of contemporary monastic scholars writing in English, especially Terrence Kardong and

---

25. Lorenzo Sena, "The History of the Interpretation of the Rule of Saint Benedict," ABR 56, no. 4 (2005): 394–417, here 394.

26. See, for example, Adalbert de Vogüé, *The Rule of Saint Benedict: A Doctrinal and Spiritual Commentary*, trans. John Baptist Hasbrouck, CS 54 (Kalamazoo, MI: Cistercian Publications, 1983), 4–5; Kardong, *Benedict's Rule*, xiii.

27. Böckmann, *Perspectives*, 8.

28. Böckmann, *Perspectives*, 8–9.

29. Böckmann, *Perspectives*, 9.

30. Michael Casey, *Truthful Living: Saint Benedict's Teaching on Humility* (Leominster, UK: Gracewing, 2001), 43–45.

Michael Casey, together with Adalbert de Vogüé and Aquinata Böckmann in translation.

3.2 Communal Eschatology: "All Together to Everlasting Life" (RB 72.12)

The desert *abbas*, as I have argued in chapter 2, understand humility in an eschatological frame. Standing before God they are aware both of their own frailty and human limits, and of God's mercy and love, experienced in God's own self-emptying in Christ. This ground is not simply a place where one remembers one's creatureliness. It is a place of transformation and hope: through imitation of the humble Christ, the monk walks humbly toward the open heavens. What difference does it make when this ground is walked in a community? If, as Basil argues, the growth of self-forgetful love and humility requires the presence of the neighbor, does this fact alter the monastic vision, and if so, how?[31]

In his introductory book on the Benedictine tradition, Columba Stewart asserts, "The genius of Benedict was to situate the individual search for God within a communal context that shaped as well as supported the quest. For him community was not simply the place where one seeks God but its vital means."[32] This is an important claim, one that is well substantiated by contemporary scholarship. But it is not self-evident. What is the purpose of Benedict's monastery? Is it primarily for the individual, a vehicle for individual salvation, so that the community is simply incidental, or is it at best the means to an end? Or does the community in

---

31. The tradition sometimes seems to pull in two directions. So, for example, Abba Alonius says, "If a man does not say in his heart, in the world there is only myself and God, he will not gain peace" (*The Sayings of the Desert Fathers: The Alphabetical Collection*, trans. Benedicta Ward, rev. ed., CS 59 [Kalamazoo, MI: Cistercian Publications, 1984], 35 [Alonius 1]). One's God-orientation informs other relationships: "vertical" first, "horizontal" second. On the other hand, Anthony says, "Our life and our death is with our neighbour. If we gain our brother, we have gained God, but if we scandalise our brother, we have sinned against Christ" (*Sayings*, 3 [Anthony 9]). Here the orientation appears to be horizontal, though there is actually a fusion, as God appears as neighbor.

32. Stewart, *Prayer and Community*, 15.

Benedictine monasticism, as Stewart suggests, have a more fundamental significance?

The first chapter of the Rule of Saint Benedict, "The Kinds of
Monks," implies an essentially instrumental view of cenobitic monastic life. Cenobites are defined as those who "belong to a monastery, where they serve under a rule and an abbot" (RB 1.2). Two
aberrant types of monks are summarily dismissed: sarabaites, who
live without rule or abbot to guide them, and gyrovagues, who
drift from place to place motivated entirely by self-will. But the
text also implies that the anchoritic or hermit life is a stage beyond
cenobitic monasticism: trained in "the battle line" of fraternal community, anchorites are now able to embark on "the single combat of
the desert" (RB 1.5). This inference is problematic since, as Kardong
notes with some passion, it tends to render community a means to
an (individual) end:[33] "To relegate common life to the ancillary task
of forming anchorites cuts at the very heart of community. When
people make cenobitic vows, they commit themselves to the other
members of the community (as well as to God). To say *in principle*
that this covenantal relation is merely instrumental means that
one can simply use others for personal growth—and leave them
behind when convenient."[34] Böckmann agrees, suggesting, "no
real community can exist in this situation."[35]

Benedict in this chapter is entirely dependent on his major
source, the Rule of the Master. The view that training in a monastic community is preparation for anchoritic life in turn rests
on Cassian and Jerome.[36] But elsewhere both Benedict and the
Master, in parallel passages (RM Ths 46 and RB Prol. 50), assume

33. Kardong, *Benedict's Rule*, 37.
34. Kardong, *Benedict's Rule*, 43.
35. Böckmann, *Perspectives*, 34.
36. Kardong, *Benedict's Rule*, 37. Cassian, having observed cenobitic monasticism in Palestine, speaks of the "still more excellent" way of the anchorites:
"These latter, dwelling first for a long time in cenobia, having been carefully
and thoroughly instructed in the rule of patience and discretion, having mastered the virtues of both humility and poverty and having totally destroyed
every vice, penetrate the deep recesses of the desert in order to engage in
terrible combat with the demons" (Cassian, *Institutes*, 5.36.1). It is noteworthy,
however, that Cassian suggests that humility is "mastered" in community.

that the monk will stay in the monastery until death. Indeed RB 1, as Kardong suggests, sits rather uneasily with the rest of Saint Benedict's Rule.[37]

How does Benedict regard monastic community? The contours of his thoroughly communal vision can be best detected by viewing Benedict against the Rule of the Master. In his divergences from the Master, as we have already noted, Benedict's voice is most clearly heard. The Master and Benedict have quite distinctive views on the nature and purpose of monastic community. These differences can be seen at the very beginning of the Rule in Benedict's somewhat tentative addition to the Prologue but confidently in the penultimate chapter of the Rule (RB 72). An examination of these two sections of the Rule gives a clear picture of Benedict's communal eschatology.

3.2.1 From a School of Suffering to a School of Love: Prologue 45–50

The final part of the Prologue (45-50) begins with a declaration taken straight from the Rule of the Master: "Therefore we intend to establish a school [*schola*] for the Lord's service."[38] The phrase "school of the Lord's service" has become, as Kardong observes, a commonplace for the Benedictine monastic project, but its sense is not straightforward.[39] In the Latin of Late Antiquity, *schola* could have a range of meanings: a place where "one practices, learns or does a specific service,"[40] a group "gathered for a common purpose," often under a master,[41] or a time of learning

---

37. Kardong, *Benedict's Rule*, 43.

38. Latin: *Constituenda est ergo nobis dominici schola servitii* (RM Ths 4). For the Latin text of RM, I use the critical edition by Adalbert de Vogüé, ed., *La règle du Maître*, 2 vols., SCh 105, 106 (Paris: Cerf, 1964–1965), hereafter SCh 105 and SCh 106.

39. Kardong, *Benedict's Rule*, 31. For extended treatments of *schola* in the RB, see Böckmann, *Perspectives*, 33–35; Kardong, *Benedict's Rule*, 31–33; Vogüé, *Rule of Saint Benedict*, 13–36.

40. Böckmann, *Perspectives*, 34.

41. Kardong, *Benedict's Rule*, 31.

in preparation for the future.[42] The Rule of the Master places an emphasis on the preparatory and master-pupil understandings of *schola*. Indeed, the monastery as school, Böckmann suggests, is central to the Master's vision and program; the monk enters "to learn under the abbot as teacher, the art of spiritual warfare, of fighting self-will and the devil."[43] The purpose is not "fraternal community," but individual mastery. Indeed the Master actually encourages a culture of shaming and rivalry among the brothers, which Böckmann calls "a pedagogy of ambition."[44]

For the Master, the school of the monastery is primarily a way of preparing for judgment. Earthly life is seen negatively, with temptation always at hand and human life a constant battle against sin and the devil. While, as Vogüé observes, there is nothing original about the Master's anthropology, or his soteriology, what is noticeable is its pessimistic intensity; in the Master's monastery both "the individual and the collective conscience are . . . haunted" by thoughts of sin and the judgment.[45] So the motivation for a myriad of practices is the avoidance of sin:

> Does the monk happen to be on his way to the oratory to celebrate one of the little hours? The avowed motive for the celebration is to render thanks to God for the last three hours passed free of sin. Is he organizing the use of time? The primary end assigned to work is so to occupy the spirit as to dispel evil thoughts. Do the monks pray before beginning any work? They do so to implore divine assistance not to commit sin or displease the Lord at any moment.[46]

42. Kardong, *Benedict's Rule*, 31.
43. Böckmann, *Perspectives*, 6.
44. Böckmann, *Perspectives*, 6.
45. Adalbert de Vogüé, Introduction, in *The Rule of the Master*, trans. Luke Eberle, CS 6 (Kalamazoo, MI: Cistercian Publications, 1977), 44. All quotations from the *Rule of the Master* (henceforth designated as RM) use Eberle's translation unless otherwise stated.
46. Vogüé is drawing on RM 50.16–17, 50.3–5, 37–38, and 50.47–50, respectively.

Human life is extended simply so that we will have time to "amend our evil ways" (RM Ths 36), but while it is a battle to the finish line, this path is salvific because it is linked to the suffering of Christ. The Master's monastery, as Kardong says, is "a school of suffering."[47] The closing words of the Master's Prologue make this reality plain:

> Therefore our hearts and our bodies must be prepared for the battle of holy obedience to the precepts. And as to what nature in us finds impossible, let us ask the Lord to ordain that his grace come to our assistance. And if we desire to escape the punishment of hell and attain eternal life, it is now, while there is still time, while we are yet in the body and while we have the chance to put all these things into effect by the light of this life, that we must hurry and do what will profit us forever. We must therefore establish a school of the Lord's service, so that, never rejecting his guidance but persevering in his teaching in the monastery until death, we may by patience merit to share in the sufferings of Christ so that the Lord may make us coheirs [*coheredes*] of his kingdom. Amen. (RM Ths 40-46)[48]

Benedict replicates the Master word for word until he reaches the *schola*. At this point Benedict departs from the Master, substantially modifying the notion of *schola* with words of encouragement and hope:

> Therefore we intend to establish a school for the Lord's service. *In drawing up its regulations, we hope to set down nothing harsh, nothing burdensome. The good of all concerned, however, may prompt us to a little strictness in order to amend faults and to safeguard love. Do not be daunted immediately by fear and run away from the road that leads to salvation. It is bound to be narrow at the outset. But as we progress in this way of life and in faith, we shall run on the path of God's commandments, our hearts overflowing with the inexpressible delight of love. Never swerving from his instructions, then, but faithfully observing his teaching in the*

47. Kardong, *Benedict's Rule*, 32.
48. *La Règle du Maître*, SCh 105:324–26.

monastery until death, we shall through patience share in the
sufferings of Christ that we may deserve also to share in his
kingdom. Amen. (RB Prol. 45-50)[49]

The tone of Benedict's additions and alterations softens the
Master's school of suffering. While Benedict affirms the value of
monastic discipline and order, he does so in the context of love. Discipline is not only for the correction of vice but also to "safeguard
love" (*caritatis*).[50] The end is not simply the attainment of heaven,
but the present experience of the heart enlarged (*dilitato corde*) with
the inexpressible delight or sweetness of love (*inenarrabili dilectionis dulcedine*), a taste of heaven on earth.[51] Instead of being made
"coheirs" (*coheredes*) of the kingdom, Benedict's monks become
"companions" (*consortes*).[52] His Rule has a participatory flavor.

Crucially, and in contrast to the Master, Benedict embraces
Cassian's realized eschatology.[53] Benedict is optimistic about this
life; if the monastic path is initially tough, as the monk progresses
he will be able to "race along the way of God's commandments
[*mandatorum*]."[54] This is a joyful path. Oriented toward eternal
life, the mature monk enjoys, even in this life, the fruits of inner
transformation. The same essentially optimistic and partly realized eschatology underpins desert monasticism. So, for example,
the desert Amma Syncletica says, "In the beginning there are a
great many battles and a good deal of suffering for those who

49. Italics indicate Benedict's additions.
50. Benedict uses *caritas* here, and throughout the Rule, to express brotherly
love or love for the community or for the abbot (Böckmann, *Perspectives*, 38).
51. This is the only occurrence of the phrase *inenarrabili dilectionis dulcedine*
in RB. The phrase has been identified as an "epexegetical genitive," in which
the terms *dilectio* and *dulcedo* enhance each other while referring to the same
reality (Böckmann, *Perspectives*, 41, 48n32; Kardong, *Benedict's Rule*, 24).
52. This is clearer in Kardong's translation (RB Prologue 50: "Then we will
never depart from his teaching and we will persevere in his doctrine in the
monastery until death. Likewise, we will participate in the passion of Christ
through patience so as to deserve to be *companions* [*consortes*] in his kingdom.
Amen." My emphasis).
53. Kardong, *Benedict's Rule*, 24.
54. Trans. Kardong, *Benedict's Rule*, 24.

are advancing towards God and afterwards, ineffable joy. It is like those who wish to light a fire; at first they are choked by the smoke and cry, and by this means obtain what they seek."[55]

3.2.2 Together, with Ardent Love: RB 72

If Benedict's monastic path is a hopeful and joyful one, it is so because it is trod together with others. Inner work is carried out in a communal context.[56] Inner transformation stems from the practices of communal life. This communal focus is particularly evident in RB 72, the penultimate, perhaps originally the last, chapter of the Rule, where one senses Benedict confidently, even rhetorically, summing up his monastic vision. This is an enunciation *par excellence* of Benedict's communal eschatology.

RB 72, "The Good Zeal of Monks," is considered the "finale"[57] or even "climax"[58] of the Rule. Indeed, Böckmann likens it "to the hymn of love in 1 Corinthians 13," giving us "the perspective for reading the entire Rule."[59] Manning similarly argues that the communal emphasis of RB 72 provides the hermeneutical key for the whole of the Rule.[60] It is worth quoting the chapter in full:

> Just as there is a wicked zeal of bitterness which separates from God and leads to hell, so there is a good zeal which separates from evil and leads to God and everlasting life. This, then, is the good zeal which monks must foster with fervent love [*ferventissimo amore*]: They should each try to be the first to show respect to the other (Rom 12:10), supporting with the greatest patience

55. *Sayings*, 230–31 (Syncletica 1). This connection is made by Böckmann, *Perspectives*, 42.

56. Andrew Marr, *Tools for Peace: The Spiritual Craft of St. Benedict and René Girard* (Lincoln, NE: iUniverse, 2007), 7.

57. Kardong, *Benedict's Rule*, 598.

58. Böckmann, *Perspectives*, 52.

59. Böckmann, *Perspectives*, 53.

60. Kardong, *Benedict's Rule*, 599. I rely on Kardong's reading of Manning here. As Kardong says, though, "A problem, of course, is that RB 72 only occurs at the end of the document, so we must virtually learn to read the Rule backwards!"

one another's weaknesses of body or behavior, and earnestly competing in obedience to one another. No one is to pursue what he judges better for himself, but instead, what he judges better for someone else. To their fellow monks they show the pure love of brothers [*caritatem fraternitatis caste*]; to God, loving fear; to their abbot, unfeigned and humble love [*humili caritate diligant*]. Let them prefer nothing whatever to Christ, and may he bring us all together to everlasting life. (RB 72.1-12)

This is, Böckmann suggests, "one of the most intense" chapters of the Rule.[61] The language is both carefully crafted and passionate, perhaps daringly so. The word *zelus* (zeal) was a Greek loan word meaning "exceptional fervor and enthusiasm"[62] and refers to "the power of motivation in a person."[63] It is a word that could have negative connotations, but here Benedict uses it positively.[64] As Kardong says, "Benedict is willing to use this risky word to make an important point: religion is by and large a matter of the heart."[65] Zeal, the heart, can be oriented in different ways. Benedict's monks are exhorted to practice their (good) zeal "with fervent love" (*ferventissimo amore*, RB 72.3). Kardong translates this phrase as "with the warmest love" in an attempt to capture the sense of the intentional superlative *ferventissimo*.[66] Böckmann (in translation from German) is far bolder with "most ardent love."[67] Indeed the sort of fraternal love that Benedict is advocating among his monks here, as Kardong observes, may well make readers uneasy.[68]

61. Böckmann, *Perspectives*, 51.
62. Kardong, *Benedict's Rule*, 588.
63. Böckmann, *Perspectives*, 55.
64. For negative uses in RB see, for example, 4.66, 65.22.
65. Kardong, *Benedict's Rule*, 588.
66. Kardong, *Benedict's Rule*, 590.
67. Böckmann, *Perspectives*, 51. Böckmann also draws attention to the fact that Benedict uses all three Latin words for love in this chapter: *caritas, amor*, and *diligere*. While *amor* "connotes a vital love that takes hold of a person's entire being and implies passionate love," she notes that, by Benedict's time, *caritas* and *amor* had become virtually synonymous, perhaps because of the influence of Augustine's christianization of the term *amor* (Böckmann, *Perspectives*, 57, 74n17).
68. Kardong, *Benedict's Rule*, 590.

The rest of the chapter sketches the shape of this "ardent love," beginning with a quotation from the letter to the Romans exhorting the monks to compete in showing respect, or honor, to each other (*honore se invicem praeveniant*, RB 72.4). Kardong notes that while honor "seems to be a rather flat and cold type of love," it might also be that Benedict sees "basic human respect" as a "very high form of love."[69] He misses, however, the connection with humility. As Böckmann reminds us, the basis of Christian community is equality before God, not social class or rank. When we honor others, she suggests, "we place ourselves below them, look up to them," and "realize that we can learn much from others."[70] In Benedict's exhortation here, Böckmann suggests, the practice of RB 7 ("On Humility") "is presupposed": "If we realize we are the least and believe in it in our hearts (7.51), we will truly give honor to others."[71]

This honoring of the other is not, however, about creating a different hierarchy, with ourselves at the bottom. Mutuality (*invicem*: "in turns, alternately, mutually, each other, one another") is stressed. This emphasis becomes clear as Benedict continues. Monks are to support "one another's weakness" with "the greatest patience" (*patientissime*—another superlative, RB 72.5). They are to compete "in obedience with one another" (RB 72.6). It is important to note the horizontal, mutual form obedience takes here.[72] Monks are to work for the advantage (*utile*) of the others (RB 72.7). They are, Benedict summarizes, to offer the pure, selfless love of brotherhood (*caritatem fraternitatis caste*, RB 72.8).

Böckmann argues that Benedict deliberately chooses the language of brotherhood rather than the language of family.[73] Indeed, his favorite word for cenobites is *frater*.[74] Again the emphasis is on mutuality, as Kardong points out: "One cannot be a brother

69. Kardong, *Benedict's Rule*, 591.
70. The issue of rank in the monastery is considered in more detail below (section 3.5), 136–43.
71. Böckmann, *Perspectives*, 59.
72. Böckmann, *Perspectives*, 62–63; Kardong, *Benedict's Rule*, 592–93.
73. Böckmann, *Perspectives*, 65–66.
74. Kardong, *Benedict's Rule*, 35. *Frater* is used 102 times in the Rule.

Reclaiming Humility

without another."[75] Even the exhortation to love their abbot has a communal flavor: he is *their* abbot (*abbatem suum*), he is part of the community, and the love (*caritate diligant*) that they are to show him is to be of no different quality (*sincera et humili*, "unfeigned and humble") from that expressed in the whole brotherhood (RB 72.10). In this chapter, as Böckmann notes, community, the fraternity, comes first. The abbot is "the abbot of the brothers."[76]

Benedict places all of these instructions regarding fraternal relationships in the context of the *telos*, the goal, of not just the monastic but also the Christian journey:[77] "Let them prefer nothing whatever to Christ, and may he bring us all together [*pariter*] to everlasting life" (RB 72.12). Of course Christian love, Christlike love, is the theme of the whole chapter: this last verse brings this into the foreground and stresses once again the *shared* nature of this journey. Both the word "order" and the use of the Latin adverb *pariter* here make the communal nature of the enterprise plain: *nos pariter ad vitam aeternam perducat.*[78]

With their placement at this crucial climax of the Rule, these words can be read as a clear signal of Benedict's deep valuing of cenobitic life. There is no suggestion here that community life is a mere preparation for withdrawal to eremitic life. Cenobitic life is intended to lead directly to eternity. Christopher Jamison, speaking from his experience as a contemporary Benedictine abbot, expresses this understanding with vivid accuracy: "We get to heaven together or not at all: there are no private compartments on the Benedictine journey to everlasting life."[79]

---

75. Kardong, *Benedict's Rule*, 594.

76. Böckmann, *Perspectives*, 69.

77. Böckmann, *Perspectives*, 73.

78. Böckmann, *Perspectives*, 71–72; Kardong, *Benedict's Rule*, 597. The significance of *pariter* in highlighting the communal emphases of monastic practices in RB was first noted by Marian Larmann, "The Meaning of *omnes pariter* in RB 49.3," ABR 29, no. 2 (1978): 153–65.

79. Christopher Jamison, *Finding Sanctuary: Monastic Steps for Everyday Life* (London: Weidenfeld and Nicolson, 2006), 118. This trajectory in the Rule is consistent with that of the *Life of St. Benedict*. As Stewart observes, in the *Life* Benedict begins as "a solitary and zealot" and becomes a "thoroughly social monk" (Stewart, *Prayer and Community*, 27).

The Rule of Saint Benedict, then, offers an optimistic vision of the human journey, oriented toward eternity and lived communally, with the expectation of the experience of "the sweetness of love" along the way. This communal eschatology underpins Benedict's thinking about the theology and practice of the monastic life.

3.3 The Ladder of Humility

How, then, does this communal eschatology interact with notions of humility in the Rule? Indeed, how does Benedict understand humility?

The obvious starting point for such an enquiry is RB 7, in which Benedict uses the image of a ladder with twelve steps to describe the journey toward "the highest summit of humility" (*summae humilitatis*, RB 7.5). Certainly "the ladder of humility" is among the most abiding and influential constructs that accompany the spread of the Rule.[80] RB 7 is the longest chapter in the Rule, signaling the significance of humility in Benedict's vision of the monastic journey. But mapping Benedict's understanding and intentions is not a straightforward task. The chapter exhibits a surprising lack of clarity concerning the notion of humility itself, resulting in problems both for Benedict's text and for contemporary interpreters of the Rule. A cluster of interrelated questions arises. While Benedict never calls humility a virtue, he nonetheless regards it as a desirable quality.[81] Can humility, therefore, be directly cultivated? The construct of the ladder seems to imply that it can. Is humility a work or a grace? Can one possess humility, or is there a necessary self-forgetfulness involved in its emergence?

---

80. So, for example, Bernard of Clairvaux takes it up in *The Steps of Humility and Pride* (see chap. 4), and Thomas Aquinas does so in his *Summa Theologiae*; see Paul Delatte, *The Rule of St. Benedict: A Commentary*, trans. Justin McCann (London: Burns, Oates, and Washbourne, 1921), 103. Its influence persists in much contemporary popular literature. For example, Carol Bonomo, *Humble Pie: St. Benedict's Ladder of Humility* (Harrisburg, PA: Morehouse Publishing, 2003); Joan D. Chittister, *Twelve Steps to Inner Freedom: Humility Revisited* (Erie, PA: Benetvision, 2003).

81. Casey, *Truthful Living*, 57.

The nature of the relationship between humility and humiliation also resurfaces. The text of the Rule offers no easy path through these questions.

A number of issues shed light on these questions: the complexities that arise from the reworking of the textual sources that lie behind RB 7, the problems created by the use of the metaphor of the ladder, and the danger of reading humility from a narrowly individual perspective rather than in the context of the communal orientation of the Rule.

3.3.1 RB 7 and Its Pedigree: Cassian, the Master, and Benedict

It is not easy to hear Benedict's voice in chapter 7 of the Rule. There is a complex layering of texts: Benedict is substantially dependent on the Master, who in turn is reworking Cassian, but Benedict also brings his own perspective. The interrelationship of these texts has been the subject of much fruitful scholarly attention, particularly by Vogüé. The end result is, however, a certain ambivalence regarding the once-unquestioned assumption of the centrality of RB 7 to Benedict's monastic theology. For Paul Delatte, writing at the beginning of the twentieth century, "The seventh chapter is justly regarded as the finished expression of monastic spirituality."[82] By contrast, Kardong, at the end of the same century, concludes, after his careful exegesis of the chapter, that "RB 7 is somewhat unwieldy and confusing in its present state."[83] It is worth taking time to unpack some of this complex layering of texts in RB 7. The journey from Cassian to the Master to Benedict helps to explain some of the muddiness that continues to accumulate around the understanding of humility, and it helps us to read Benedict himself with a little more clarity.

The foundational source for RB 7 is a discourse attributed to Abba Pinufius at the end of book 4 of Cassian's *Institutes* (4.39).[84]

---

82. Delatte, *Rule of St. Benedict*, 104.
83. Kardong, *Benedict's Rule*, 168.
84. Unless otherwise indicated, all quotations from Cassian's *Institutes* and *Conferences* use the translations by Boniface Ramsey. For the Latin text

Pinufius, an Egyptian monk whom Cassian knew from his time in Bethlehem, is in Cassian's writing an icon of humility. In this discourse, Pinufius gives instruction to a newly received brother, outlining the expected course of monastic life. As the life of the monk unfolds, Pinufius teaches, the manifestation of humility is a sign of progress in the spiritual journey, a journey that moves from fear to love. Indeed, Pinufius says, "When [humility] is possessed in truth, it will at once bring you a step higher to love [*caritatem*]" (*Institutes* 4.39.3).[85]

For Cassian, the spiritual journey begins with "the fear of the Lord," understood not as a psychological state but as a life-changing recognition of the reality of God. Such recognition inspires a process of conversion, a turning away from worldly concerns, including, for the monk, the complete renunciation of family and possessions. This "deprivation" (*priuatione*), which, it should be noted, is deeply social, gives birth to humility.[86] The monk then embarks on the much more difficult inner work: the stripping away of desires, or of self-will. This process results in the elimination of vices and the growth of virtues, but the ultimate goal is "purity of heart" and "apostolic," or perfect, love. Cassian summarizes the overall movement (again styled as a precept of Pinufius):

> According to the Scriptures, "the beginning" of our salvation and "of wisdom is the fear of the Lord." From the fear of the Lord is born a salutary compunction. From compunction of heart there proceeds renunciation—that is, the being deprived of and the contempt of all possessions. From this deprivation humility is begotten. From humility is generated the dying of desire. When desire has died all the vices are uprooted and wither away. Once the vices have been expelled the virtues bear fruit and grow. When virtue abounds purity of heart is acquired. With purity of heart the perfection of apostolic love [*caritatis*] is possessed. (*Institutes* 4.43)[87]

---

of the *Institutes*, I use *Jean Cassien: institutions cénobitiques*, ed. Jean-Claude Guy, SCh 109 (Paris: Cerf, 1965), hereafter SCh 109.

85. *Jean Cassien*, SCh 109:180.

86. *Jean Cassien*, SCh 109:184. Section 3.5 below returns to this theme.

87. *Jean Cassien*, SCh 109:184.

The pattern outlined here accords with that found in fourth-century desert monasticism. For Cassian, as for the desert *abbas* and *ammas* before him, humility stands at the center of the monastic project. Humility is the fruit of the renunciation of self-will and the foundation of "apostolic love."

In 4.39 Cassian gathers the received, lived wisdom to offer a brief phenomenology of humility, detailing the ten "indications" (*indiciis*) of its presence.[88] These indicators are later incorporated and transformed into the Master's (and then Benedict's) twelve steps. The ten indicators are:

1. a person has put to death in himself all his desires [Lat *voluntates*, self-will];[89]
2. he conceals from his elder not only none of his deeds but also none of his thoughts;
3. he commits nothing to his own discretion but everything to his [elder's] judgment and listens eagerly and willingly to his admonitions;
4. he maintains a gracious obedience and a steadfast patience;
5. he neither brings injury on anyone else nor is saddened or sorrowful if anyone else inflicts it on him;
6. he does nothing and presumes nothing that neither the general rule nor the example of our forebears encourages;
7. he is satisfied with utter simplicity and, as being an unfit laborer, considers himself unworthy of everything that is offered him;
8. he does not declare with his lips alone that he is inferior to everyone else but believes it in the depths of his heart;
9. he holds his tongue and is not loudmouthed;
10. he is not ready and quick to laugh.

(*Institutes* 4.39.2, adapted)

At the end of this list Cassian emphasizes again that these are simply indicators and that the list is not exhaustive: "By such in-

88. *Jean Cassien*, SCh 109:180.
89. *Jean Cassien*, SCh 109:180.

dications, and by others like them, true humility is recognized" (*Institutes* 4.39.3). Neither is this, as Kardong points out, a list of tasks.[90] Cassian is not setting out a program: rather some signposts on a journey, the journey of monastic life itself.[91] Importantly, Cassian offers signs of the presence of humility, not a definition of humility.

In Cassian's *Conferences* the reason for this approach becomes clear. For Cassian humility, or humble love, is the essential nature of Christ. Christ is "the Teacher of humility" (*Conferences* 15.7.3). And while Cassian urges his readers to "learn" and "practice" the humble way of Christ, he also recognizes its graced nature: "Humility . . . is the teacher of all the virtues; it is the most firm foundation of the heavenly edifice; it is the Savior's own magnificent gift" (*Conferences* 15.7.2). To walk in the way of humility is to walk in the way of Christ. To walk in the way of Christ is to walk in the way of humility.

What happens to Cassian's understanding of humility at the hands of the Master and Benedict? What began as indicators of humility become the rungs of an elaborate metaphorical ladder, stretched between earth and heaven. Indeed the whole of Cassian's monastic journey, from fear of God and renunciation to the growth of humility and love, is forced into the somewhat rigid schema of the ladder. Admittedly, as Vogüé points out, Cassian himself introduces the idea of steps (*gradibus*) and sequence (*ordine*),[92] but Cassian is careful to ensure that humility is recognized as a fruit of the monastic journey, not as a program or as its primary object.

The Master is less careful in this regard. In the shift from what Cassian declares to be an incomplete list of ten indicators to the Master's twelve[93] steps (*gradus*), it takes effort not to see a

---

90. Kardong, *Benedict's Rule*, 162.

91. Casey uses *milestones* (Casey, *Truthful Living*, 57).

92. Adalbert de Vogüé, *Community and Abbot in the Rule of St. Benedict*, CS 5 (Kalamazoo, MI: Cistercian Publications, 1979), 1:187; Cassian, *Institutes* 4.38; *Jean Cassien*, SCh 109:178: *Ad quem perfectionis statum his gradibus atque hoc ordine peruenitur*: "This state of perfection is arrived at by these steps and following this order."

93. Twelve, of course, is a biblically significant number.

program. As Vogüé observes, what begins as a "simple description" is given "a false air of being a gradated method."[94] Grace is severely at risk here: as Kardong suggests, "intended or not, such a ladder is vulnerable to the charge of self-salvation."[95]

Similarly, while Cassian does not use the term *humility* or cognates in his description of its possible indicators, thus carefully avoiding the possibility of tautology, RM 10, and subsequently RB 7, are awash with various Latin forms of *humilis*.[96] The Master adds a plethora of biblical proof texts, somewhat trimmed by Benedict in RB 7, and various steps (5, 7, 11) include exhortations to behave humbly. So, for example, in the fifth step the monk is urged to make humble confession to his abbot (*humilem confessionem abbatem*) of his sinful thoughts or actions.[97] This practice becomes, as Vogüé notes, "an exercise of humility which consists in testifying to one's own wickedness."[98] Vogüé is particularly concerned to point out the very real loss to the Master's scheme of the tradition of spiritual discernment (*discretio*) that underpins Cassian's second mark, to serve the Master's emphasis on obedience to the abbot;[99] however, we might also note a loss of clarity around the understanding of humility itself. Humility here appears to be imposed or required rather than a graced fruit of spiritual progress. Confession to another of one's dark secrets and of one's impurity of heart and hidden destructive acts is in itself humiliating, in the sense that one is lowering oneself in front of another.[100] Openness, or truthfulness, about the inevitably

94. Vogüé, *Rule of Saint Benedict*, 118.

95. Kardong, *Benedict's Rule*, 163.

96. Vogüé, *Community and Abbot*, 1:214. RM 10 has six instances in biblical quotations and twenty-three in the remainder of the text; RB 7 has six and twenty-two, respectively.

97. RM 10.61; SCh 105:432. Benedict omits the Master's instruction that this be vocal (*linguae*) confession.

98. Vogüé, *Community and Abbot*, 1:215.

99. For a thorough analysis of Cassian's understanding of *discretio*, see Antony D. Rich, *Discernment in the Desert Fathers:* Diakrisis *in the Life and Thought of Early Egyptian Monasticism* (Bletchley, Milton Keynes, UK: Paternoster, 2007), 75–119.

100. In fact, as Casey observes, the Master often utilizes the verb *humiliare* to indicate a physical lowering or bowing of the head or body. Benedict does

divided self is a sign of the presence of humility. To speak of humble confession here verges on tautology.

Two further aspects of the Master's reworking of Cassian are significant for the evolution of the ladder in the Rule of Saint Benedict. First, RM has strong emphasis on entry into heaven as the goal of monastic life. The Master includes a long description of the nature of heaven (RM 10.91-120), and each of his steps is accompanied by the words "the disciple mounts the first rung of humility on the ladder of heaven," etc. Second, with its necessary focus on the ordering of cenobitic life—the Master is not talking of desert anchorites—the Master adds an "overlay of authority" to almost every step.[101] So, for example, Cassian's relatively gentle reference to obedience, in the context of the discernment of thoughts by one's spiritual *abba* (indication 3), becomes in step 3 unhesitating obedience to one's superior (RM 10.45-51). The order of the community, and particularly the authority of the abbot, becomes the critical issue.

Benedict pulls back from both of these changes. With his embrace of a more realized eschatology, Benedict omits much of the Master's material on heaven, including the repetitious introduction to each step. Benedict is interested, as I have already noted, in *participation* in the kingdom of God in the present, not simply in future reward. Similarly, while the stress on obedience is still present in Benedict, he seems to have softened some of the harsher edges of the Master. Significantly, in the RB the much-reduced step 3, on obedience, begins with a crucial rationale: "for the love of God" (*pro Dei amore*, RB 7.34) the monk is to "submit to his superior in all obedience." Again significantly, the only biblical rationale that Benedict retains in his redaction of this step is Philippians 2:8: we are "imitating the Lord," who "became obedient even to death" (RB 7.34).[102] On this occasion, Benedict omits the

---

not continue this usage, consolidating the shift in understanding humility as an interior quality (*Truthful Living*, 57, 75n10). See, for example, RM 8.19–20; 13.61; 14.21; 23.50; 53.14.

101. Kardong, *Benedict's Rule*, 164.

102. Kardong provides a fuller summary of Benedict's changes to the Master's text (Kardong, *Benedict's Rule*, 165–67).

Master's insistence that the obedience to the abbot demonstrates obedience to the Lord (RM 10.51).[103] Benedict seems to be turning down the Master's heavy-handed identification of abbot and God.

In listening for Benedict's voice in RB 7, though, it is important to consider not simply his departures from the Master but also his decision to retain a substantial portion of the Master's text.[104] Benedict does not go back to Cassian and start again but rather takes the Master's elaboration, forged in a similar cenobitic context, and, consistent with his overall vision, modifies it in the direction of a more realized eschatology.

3.3.2 The Ladder of Humility: Metaphor and Theology

Turning now to an examination of the text of RB 7, we find the theological and metaphorical parameters of the chapter signaled in the opening lines:

> Brothers, divine Scripture calls to us saying: *Whoever exalts himself shall be humbled, and whoever humbles himself shall be exalted* (Luke 14:11; 18:14). In saying this, therefore, it shows us that every exaltation is a kind of pride, which the Prophet indicates he has shunned, saying: *O Lord, my heart is not exalted; my eyes are not lifted up and I have not walked in the ways of the great nor gone after marvels beyond me* (Ps 130 [131]:1). And why? *If I had not a humble spirit, but were exalted instead, then you would treat me like a weaned child on its mother's lap* (Ps 130 [131]:2).
>
> Accordingly, brothers, if we want to reach the highest summit of humility, if we desire to attain speedily that exaltation in heaven to which we climb by the humility of this present

103. "The Lord as well shows that we obey him when we are subject to the abbot, for he says to our teachers: 'Anyone who listens to you listens to me, and anyone who rejects you rejects me'" (RM 10.51). But in RB 2.2, 5.15, and 7.44–48, Benedict retains the idea of the abbot's standing in the place of Christ/God.

104. Benedict excises RM 10.20–28 (trimming the series of biblical quotations used to support step 1) together with RM 10.92–122 (the Master's long description of heaven, which ends his chapter) and substantially trims step 3 (RM 10.45–51). The rest of the text of RB 7 is, with a few exceptions, identical to RM 10.

life, then by our ascending actions we must set up that ladder
on which Jacob in a dream saw *angels descending and ascending*
(Gen 28:12). Without doubt, this descent and ascent can signify
only that we descend by exaltation and ascend by humility.
Now the ladder erected is our life on earth, and if we humble
our hearts the Lord will raise it to heaven. We may call our
body and soul the sides of this ladder, into which our divine
vocation has fitted the various steps of humility and discipline
as we ascend. (RB 7.1-9)

The chapter begins with the very strong Latin verb *clamat*,
meaning "to cry out." The cry is to the *fratres*, the brothers, urging them to listen to the Scriptures, and as Kardong suggests,
the tone is "exhortatory and highly personal."[105] Here Benedict
is highlighting an important, perhaps central, piece of teaching.
The brothers are to pay attention to the words of Jesus: "Whoever
exalts himself shall be humbled, and whoever humbles himself
shall be exalted" (Luke 14:11, 18:14). This scriptural quotation
supplies the rationale for the whole chapter.[106]

By beginning with the Lucan proclamation of the "great reversal," the chapter establishes the framework for a new set of values
and relations, a new way of living. What was once lowly or poor
is now considered exalted. What was ranked low is now ranked

105. Kardong, *Benedict's Rule*, 135.
106. In his overview of RB 7, Kardong suggests that the use of Scripture
in this chapter is "disappointing": texts are misused, or used carelessly, and
other key texts are entirely absent. In particular he bemoans the absence of
any reference to Matt 11:28-30, with its emphasis on Christ as the model of
humility (Kardong, *Benedict's Rule*, 167). What is the reason for the omission of such an obvious text? First, Benedict is simply following the Master
here. Second, it is possible that this omission also reflects Benedict's (and
the Master's) high Christology. The humility of Christ is not something that
can be simply assumed or taken on. Benedict does not emphasize the christological foundation of humility until step 3, which makes use of Phil 2:8,
exhorting the monk to "all obedience for the love of God" in imitation of
Christ, who "became obedient even to death" (RB 7.34). The way to follow
Christ is through obedience. One cannot simply decide to be humble. One
cannot simply be Christlike. One becomes Christlike. Humility is the fruit
of a different way of living.

high. Human measurements of honor are thus overturned. In the Gospel of Luke these texts have very strong social resonances,[107] and it may be that these are not entirely absent from RB 7.[108] RB 7.5 suggests that heavenly exaltation is attained *per praesentis vitae humilitatem*, best translated "by [or through] the humility of this present life" (*RB 1980*), not "by humility in this present life," as Kardong suggests.[109] The lowly (monastic) way of life provides the vehicle. Read in this way these opening lines offer a rationale for the embrace of monastic life. If the Rule is indeed a little rule for beginners (RB 73.8), it is important to remind the novice that there is a reason for the radical renunciation that is foundational to monastic life: the way up is down. This is on a par with Cassian's summary monastic scheme (*Institutes* 4.43): humility begins with renunciation, the deprivation of and contempt of all possessions (goods, rank, honor, and so on).

---

107. The saying in Luke 14:11 concludes a parable told by Jesus regarding honor and rank. Speaking to those who "chose the places of honor" at a meal in a Pharisee's house, Jesus' parable suggests, by contrast, that guests at a wedding feast should take not the place of honor but the lowest place. The argument here is about "self-promotion" (Kardong's translation of *exaltationem*; see Kardong, *Benedict's Rule*, 136): if one places oneself too high, one may well be humiliated by being asked to sit further down the table, thereby accepting a lower place in the social pecking order. By starting low, one may well be honored with a place further up. The motivation here is difficult, even suspect, of course. In Luke 18:14 Jesus' saying concludes the story of the Pharisee and the tax collector (or publican), which overturns the accepted order of religious righteousness. In the desert monastic literature, of course, the Pharisee and publican are used as a shorthand for pride and humility.

108. Kardong takes a contrary view: "By and large, they [the Master and Benedict] find ascetical and interior meanings for texts that are social and external in scope" (Kardong, *Benedict's Rule*, 167). There is a danger of social resonances being underread in the Rule. Casey warns against reading humility with an anachronistic subjectivity, suggesting that for Bernard of Clairvaux "humility would have seemed to have been [more] a matter of objective lifestyle than of psychological stance. A monk was humble in so far as he embraced 'hard work, a hidden life and voluntary poverty'" (Casey, *Truthful Living*, 23–24). The same could be said generally in relation to RB. Section 3.5 picks up this theme again.

109. Eberle concurs with his translation of the parallel text in RM 10.5: "one rises by the humility of the present life."

The internalization of this countercultural dynamic, the transformation of the heart, is the central task of the monastic life; here Benedict, following the Master, offers the metaphor of the ladder, which frames the rest of his chapter.[110] This image is problematic from a number of perspectives: the coherence of Benedict's use of the metaphor of the ladder, the danger that the ladder implies a program for the achievement of humility, the risk of minimizing the length of the journey, and its tendency to emphasize the individual over the community.[111] All of these require exploration.

First, the metaphor is not entirely coherent (even less so in Benedict than in the Master). The ladder, the text says, is our earthly life. The ladder here, though, is not simply a path or vehicle but is somehow conceived as a picture of the self, with the sides of the ladder representing body and soul. The rungs of the ladder are steps of humility and discipline along the divine ascending vocation. Later in the chapter, however, as one mounts the steps of humility, it feels, imaginatively, as if the self is detached from the ladder, giving the unfortunate impression that the "ascent" to the "summit of humility" is a work rather than the result of grace. This conclusion is certainly not intended, as RB 7.8 makes clear: the ladder is raised to heaven by God (*quae humiliato corde a Domino erigatur ad caelum*).

Benedict's redaction of the Master at RB 7.8 contributes to the confusion of imagery here. In this instance the Master's thinking seems clearer:

110. The image of the ladder is not, of course, new to Christian discourse. The ladder of Jacob's dream (Gen 28:12) had become an image of spiritual ascent in patristic writings. In the seventh century it provided the primary metaphor for John Climacus's *Ladder of Divine Ascent*, perhaps the most influential treatise on the spiritual life in the East. As was already noted, the fourth-century Desert Mother, Amma Sarah, connected spiritual ascent with humility before God: "I put out my foot to ascend the ladder, and I place death before my eyes before going up it" (*Sayings*, 230 [Sarah 6]).

111. The hierarchical overtones of the image of the ladder also make it vulnerable to a feminist critique. Interestingly, in her rehabilitation of humility for "a feminist spirituality," Chittister avoids the image completely and speaks of "principles or degrees of development" rather than steps (Joan D. Chittister, *Heart of Flesh: A Feminist Spirituality* [Grand Rapids, MI: Eerdmans, 1998], 98).

Scala uero ipsa erecta nostra est uita in saeculo, quae humiliato corde et capite suo in praesenti hoc tempore, exaltatum a Domino mortis exitum erigat ad caelum.

Now, this ladder set up is our life in the world, and with heart and head made humble in this, its present time, it lifts up to heaven its last end, death, exalted by the Lord. (RM 10.8, trans. Eberle)

While the train of thought seems awkward, certainly in translation, the Master makes it clear that humility, being humbled, is part of the experience of this life, but that God uses this vehicle—the ladder, the humility of the present life—to lift us to heaven.

Benedict is more succinct, and while RB 7.8 makes it clear that God does the raising, the image of the ladder is even less coherent.

Scala vero ipsa erecta nostra est vita in saeculo, quae humiliato corde a Domino erigatur ad caelum.

Now the ladder erected is our life on earth, and if we humble our hearts the Lord will raise it to heaven. (RB 7.8; trans. *RB 1980*)

The towering ladder is, of course, our earthly life. When the heart is humble, God raises it up to heaven. (trans. Kardong)

The *RB 1980* translation here is misleading: it makes the monk the primary actor, the owner or maker of his or her own humility. Kardong initially suggests another rendering, "when the heart is humiliated," but immediately rejects this translation.[112] Elsewhere he claims, "[*Humiliato*] never means 'humiliate' in RB. That is a degradation that does not enter into Benedict's thinking. The only spiritually useful form of humility is that which is fully accepted

---

112. Kardong, *Benedict's Rule*, 137. Kardong also abandons the ladder image completely here and makes the heart the object of elevation.

and internalized by the subject, and not imposed by authority on a resisting object."[113]

Certainly Benedict never advocates degradation. But where does humility come from? It can't be self-generated: the probable result of such an enterprise would be a false humility. Is there an authority imposing humility here, albeit on an accepting subject? It may be that the much-contested image of the weaned child (RB 7.4), which sits at the beginning of the chapter, holds a clue.

RB 7.4 continues a quotation from Psalm 130 (131) begun in RB 7.3. What if, the psalmist asks, my thinking is not humble? What if I raised my own spirit? This situation is, of course, the norm for human beings. We are experts at self-promotion. If this is our situation—and it is—the text continues, in RB 7.4 (RM 10.4):

> *sicut ablactatum super matrem suam, ita retribues in animam meam.*

> then you would treat me like a weaned child on its mother's lap. (trans. *RB 1980*)

> Then you will refuse me like a mother does a weaned child. (trans. Kardong)

> Like a weaned child on its mother's lap, so will you requite my soul. (trans. Eberle)

The sense of the Latin here is difficult, as the variety of translations indicate and as many commentators have noted.

Unlike the Hebrew text of the Psalms, where the picture of the weaned child is a picture of contentment, here the Latin seems to have the opposite sense. Kardong suggests that the weaned child is now "a symbol of frustration."[114] *RB 1980* comments, "If the weaned child were humble, it would accept without a fuss the substitute for its mother's breast. If it does not have a humble

---

113. Kardong, *Benedict's Rule*, 459. Cf. Casey, who recognizes that "there remains an ambiguity throughout the literature . . . about whether *humilitas* is an objective state of lowliness or humiliation or an inner disposition" (Casey, *Truthful Living*, 75n10).

114. Kardong, *Benedict's Rule*, 136.

spirit, it will reach for the now forbidden breast, and so incur retribution."[115] Both *RB 1980* and Kardong interpret *retribues* (*retribuo*: "restore," "give back," "repay," "requite"[116]) negatively here, but this need not be the case. I offer an alternate suggestion: the weaned child (the *ablactatum*), with newly found independence, is in danger of feeling superior to (or above) the mother and so must be corrected. While *super matrem* refers to the mother's lap, it seems no coincidence that the word *super* occurs here among a cluster of words expressing ideas of elevating and lowering. In the same way, then, God will put the spirit of the self-promoter back in its correct place. That is, God will remind us that we are still, always, children of God. In a sense this is a humiliating realization: so the picture becomes one of *positive* humiliation. The mother (God) gently reminds the weaned child (the spirit/soul) that he or she is still a child.[117]

Returning, then, to RB 7.8, the picture becomes clearer. When "the heart is humiliated," that is, back in its place, it is paradoxically raised to heaven. We do not own or control "our" humility, but the reality is that when the heart is (brought) low, then and only then is it opened to heaven. There is a continuity between the notions of the *humiliato corde*, the humiliated heart, the *dilato corde*, the opened heart, and the goal of *puritate corde*, purity of heart.

A second difficulty with the ladder image is that in RB 7 the ladder not only signifies the direction of spiritual progress but also begins to look like a program.[118] They are "*steps* of humility and discipline."[119] This programmatic feel seems particularly obvious in the Rule of the Master, which prefaces each step by the words,

115. *RB 1980*, 192n7.4.

116. Lewis and Short, *A Latin Dictionary*, s.v. "retribuo."

117. Patrick Barry's recent translation comes close to this sense: "If I failed to keep a modest spirit and raised my ambitions too high, then your correction would come down on me as though I were nothing but a newly weaned child on its mother's lap" (*The Benedictine Handbook* [Norwich, UK: Canterbury Press, 2003], 28).

118. The grace-versus-works issue in the debate between Augustine and Cassian is discussed in chap. 1.4.

119. *RB 1980* notes, "Gradus means both 'step' and 'degree,' but the image of the ladder determines the question here" (*RB 1980*, 193n7.10).

"The disciple mounts the *second* rung of humility on the ladder of heaven if . . . ," etc. Benedict, with his more realized eschatology, omits the reference to the "ladder of heaven" and simply refers to "the first step of humility," etc. Kardong suggests that Benedict is pulling back from the Master's elaboration of the ladder image, in part to lighten the weighty and repetitive reminder of one's status as a disciple.[120] This may be so, but Benedict does retain the steps (*gradus*) rather than return to Cassian's signs (*indiciis*), so he still gives an impression of a sequence or program. Again, the understanding of humility is itself at risk. In Benedict at this point *humilitatis* begins to look like a commodity. Paradoxically, the Master's repetitious lengthier wording actually retains a sense of humility as being a way or path.

A third difficulty—and this may well simply be a modern problem—is that the image of the ladder masks the length of this journey toward humility. For a contemporary, achievement-focused culture, there is a danger that the ladder of humility might be read as a step machine, where one sweats out a prescribed program to achieve spiritual fitness—or, worse, an escalator bringing one speedily and effortlessly to the top floor, so that there is a sort of inevitability regarding the outcome. Outside the monastic cloister, it is easy to romanticize or minimize the difficulty and length of the project. Indeed, one might gasp at Casey's declaration that "the ladder of humility gives us a sequential account of the way in which humility manifests itself over forty or fifty years of monastic living."[121] This is not the sort of time frame for human transformation that we have come to expect in the modern world, where even a three-year psychotherapeutic commitment is considered extravagant. And in communities that are so transient, how can anyone expect to grow, or indeed flourish?

Contemporary Cistercian Francis Kline gives a sense of the complexity and length of the monastic project in his imaginative

---

120. Kardong, *Benedict's Rule*, 165.
121. Casey, *Truthful Living*, 57. Note here that Casey is clear that the ladder is not a program but rather the fruit of monastic life. Monastic life is the program.

reflections on "how monastic observances work in a person's life."[122] So, for instance, he describes the early battles of the novice monk:

> Vigilance over all behavior is recommended to the novice under the law of obedience, silence and humility. These are easy enough to understand in the mind, and one may wholeheartedly agree with them in principle. But they begin to enter the heart when the first howls of loneliness and emptiness are heard from a harried novice. For the Rule allows companionship, food, diversion in work, etc., only at fixed times. Hands that reach out for support and camaraderie get slapped back. Hunger comes hard to one who is used to eating immediately when hungry. The Rule stands firm. The novice, like a pricked snail gone back to its shell, must learn to feed in solitude on deeper springs discovered in the Scriptures and monastic tradition if bitterness is not to drive one from monastic spirituality. What can one do but close the door on the screams, praying that some better life will awaken? No easy mitigations can be allowed to blunt the starkness of the landscape. Otherwise, it would not be a desert.[123]

Kline too finds the ladder image restrictive. It would be helpful, he suggests, to imagine each rung of the ladder as "a room opening onto a larger room, whose windows, showing a different landscape, compel us to explore the door and pass through it." Kline, like Benedict, wants to focus on a realized eschatology: "The comparison is not between this world of skewed values and the pure, airy world at the top of the ladder, but between a diminished sense of self glued to the floor of untruth, and the height of the ladder which expands the person to take in more and more reality, a reality redeemed and revealed by Christ as the Truth."[124] To find and live in that expansive, spacious reality is costly.

122. Francis Kline, *Lovers of the Place: Monasticism Loose in the Church* (Collegeville, MN: Liturgical Press, 1997), 50.
123. Kline, *Lovers of the Place*, 57–58.
124. Kline, *Lovers of the Place*, 50.

Finally, as a metaphorical construct the ladder is not particularly helpful in thinking about humility in a communal setting. It works well enough for the Master, with his primary focus on vertical rather than horizontal relationships. So it is possible to imagine monks on various rungs of the ladder, as vividly depicted in the famous twelfth-century icon of the Ladder of Divine Ascent from Saint Catherine's Monastery, Sinai. But in the Master too, the monks often seem to be pitted against each other, rivals in humility. The climate here is not far from the darker edge of contemporary individualism. For Benedict, by contrast, mutuality, the shared journey, is of primary importance. But on the ladder there is room for only one individual on any rung. So here, having the ladder as the primary image of humility seems unhelpful. There is a danger of losing sight of the fundamentally communal character of the Rule.

3.3.3 *The Ladder of Humility in Community*

While the construct of the ladder sits rather uncomfortably with the communal nature of the Rule, it is nevertheless true that the cenobitic context significantly shapes the content of the steps. Conversely, the steps now make sense only in the context of community life. It is, despite the metaphorical difficulty, a communal ladder.

There is a significant shift in emphasis from Cassian to the Master and Benedict in the direction of communal life. Behind Cassian one can still sense the desert anchorite, but by the time of Benedict there was a maturing of the marriage between the desert's heart wisdom and its outworking in monastic community. How one lives, day by day, with one's neighbor became the critical spiritual and practical question. Put differently, how power operates in cenobitic monasticism is a critical issue. So the Master and Benedict are both intensely concerned with authority, with the abbot and obedience. Less obviously, though, they are also concerned with honor and its counterparts, dishonor, shame, and even humiliation. Humility here has a social context and social implications.

A summary of the steps according to the Rule of Saint Benedict will be helpful here:

1. keep the fear of God always before one's eyes;
2. do not delight in satisfying one's desires out of love for one's own way;
3. submit to the superior in all obedience for love of God;
4. when obedience involves harsh, hostile things or even injustice of some sort, embrace them patiently with no outcry;
5. reveal through humble confession to one's abbot all evil thoughts that enter one's heart, as well as the evils secretly committed;
6. be content with low and dishonorable treatment;
7. confess with one's tongue, but also believe with all one's heart that one is lower and less honorable than all the rest;
8. do nothing except what is encouraged by the common rule of the monastery and the example of the veteran members of the community;
9. hold back one's tongue from speaking, and out of love for silence do not speak until someone asks one a question;
10. do not be quick to laugh at the slightest provocation;
11. when one speaks at all, do so gently and without laughter, humbly and seriously, with few and careful words;
12. one's humility is not only in one's heart, but is apparent in one's very body. (RB 7.10-62, trans. Kardong, adapted)

Communal concerns are clearly evident in these steps. While step 1 sets in place the monk's eschatological orientation, the remaining steps are concerned with how the individual monk relates to others. Love of neighbor is interpreted for the cenobitic monastery.

Step 3 places the abbot firmly in authority, though with the "common rule" and wisdom of the elders (step 8) as the larger frame. If the self is to be emptied, through an obedience to one's superior that imitates Christ's obedience "even to death" (Phil 2:8), it is emptied in front of others. There is a nakedness about life in this community: even one's secret sins and evil thoughts are to be bared to the abbot (step 5), who here represents "the Lord" (RB 7.45-48).

Step 4 has a particular weight in a communal context: it is inevitable that the monk will sometimes feel aggrieved by others' actions. Admittedly, the broader objective must always be kept in view: the submission of self-will to the divine will (step 2). But for the cenobitic monk, unlike the desert anchorite, there is no escape to one's cell, nor can one simply find another *abba*. Nonmonastic moderns are understandably horrified by the suggestion that one should respond with patient obedience to authority when that authority, the abbot, is dealing out harsh, hostile, or even unjust treatment (step 4). This proposition looks terrible in theory, but perhaps within the actual practice of monastic community it is simply the particular burden and cost of cenobitic life. Injustices are bound to occur in the community. How will the monk, seeking the path of love, deal with this inevitability?

Certainly, step 6 must be read against the pragmatic background of the monastery; certain tasks must be done, many of them menial, even humiliating. The Latin *vilitas* in this step (*omni vilitate vel extremitate*) has the sense of "being treated like a slave."[125] The question then becomes how the monk thinks about this. What does it do to his or her sense of self? A sign of growth in humility will be not simply one's acceptance of this situation and a sense of one's (perpetual) unworthiness, but an embrace of the status of slave that resonates with Christ's own "taking on the form of a slave" (Phil 2:7). Benedict does not make this christological link explicit, but it certainly sits in the wings.

Even the exhortations regarding silence and speech in steps 9, 10, and 11 have a particular relevance to communal life: speech, and indeed even silence, can be used for either good or ill in human community.

What is beginning to emerge here is that RB 7 must be read alongside the practices of the monastery. It is important to recall that the Rule is not primarily a theological treatise but a practical handbook. And regardless of the difficulties posed by the ladder and steps of RB 7, humility is centrally important to the Rule, even if one might wish for greater theological coherence

125. *RB 1980*, 199n7.49; Kardong, *Benedict's Rule*, 153.

in its explication. The primary focus of the Rule is building the communal way of life that will lead, through humility, to "the sweetness of love." So while RB 7 looms large in the Rule, it must be read in the context of the whole. Paradoxically, RB 7 may not be the best way into an understanding of humility in the Rule of Benedict at all. It may be that an examination of humility in the context of practice is potentially a more fruitful route. The rest of this chapter considers this possibility.

3.4 Practicing Humility in the Monastic Workshop

What practices support the journey toward humility and love? How does the Rule construct a community that both supports and shapes this journey? After the hopeful heights of "perfect love" described at the end of RB 7, that is, at the completion of the Rule's discourse on monastic spirituality, Benedict immediately plunges into the tough mechanics of monastic life: RB 8 takes us straight to the oratory and a discussion of the practice of Vigils. While the rest of the world sleeps, the monks rise in the dark of the night to pray watchfully for the dawn. The Office of Vigils is a distinctive feature of monastic life, a hidden offering of attentiveness when most humans are unconscious. In this reversal of the usual order of life we are already on the way down.

Monastic life prioritizes the integration of inner and outer worlds. It understands the complex relationship between inner motivations and external actions, and our need for ongoing conversion. Purity of heart enables one to love truly: when inner motivation is free from ambiguity, rivalry, and self-will (or, we might say, self-obsession), one is able to act from love—for the other. The Rule provides a framework designed to encourage the process of integration and the goal of purity of heart. Nothing in the outer world is deemed irrelevant to this project. In this regard, the content of the Rule comes as a surprise to casual readers. Imagining they are opening a "spiritual" guidebook, they may be puzzled to find, for example, chapters on "Qualifications of the Monastery Cellarer" or "Kitchen Servers of the Week."

This dynamic relationship between interior and exterior worlds intersects with "the interplay of individual and community" that is at the core of cenobitic monastic life.[126] Again, community life is the intentional vehicle for the journey toward humility and love. As Stewart says: "The common life becomes the very language and texture of growth into Christ, as the call is tested and refocused in the myriad interactions, formal and informal, that create monastic community."[127] Inner transformation occurs in and because of communal life.

How does one "practice" humility in this context? The answer lies, in fact, in the whole way of life. Benedictine cenobitic monasticism offers a particular *way of humility*. Here it is important to acknowledge, of course, that the growth of humility is ultimately a divine grace beyond our capacity to analyze or manipulate. It may be possible, however, to bring to the foreground some of the key elements of Benedict's monastic program that conspire toward its growth.

The fundamental shape of Benedictine monasticism is captured by Benedict's definition of cenobites as those who "belong to a monastery, where they serve under a rule and an abbot" (RB 1.2). The same threefold framework is apparent in the reception of a novice: in the presence of the whole community gathered in the oratory, the new brother promises "stability, fidelity to monastic life, and obedience" (RB 58.17). It is in this context that the journey toward humility is encouraged. In what follows, then, the growth of humility in community is viewed from three perspectives. First, the monastery as *the place* where the monk commits to this journey (section 3.5), then *service* as the fundamental underpinning of monastic community (section 3.6), and finally *obedience*, the costly practice of humility in community (section 3.7). These three perspectives by no means exhaust the question but are one way of framing and limiting consideration of the relationship between humility and community.

126. Columba Stewart, "In Community," in *The Benedictine Handbook* (Norwich, UK: Canterbury Press, 2003), 279.
127. Stewart, "In Community," 279.

3.5 The Monastic *Polis*: A Place of Humility

Benedict's monks do not merely live in the monastery: they are "monastery men." This, as Basil Pennington points out, is a more accurate rendering of the Latin *hoc est monasteriale* (RB 1.2).[128] The monastery is not simply a location in space but a place that forges identity. To enter the monastery is to embrace a whole way of being, the monastic way of being.

The monastery has become, one might say, an alternate *polis*. If the monks of fourth-century Egypt had, as Athanasius declared, made the desert a city (*polis*) by the time of Benedict, there was a growing body of wisdom regarding how that *polis* should be ordered in order to achieve its particular end.[129] How would this *polis* facilitate the growth of humility and love?

As we have seen in the literature of desert monasticism and in Cassian, to enter the monastery means the renunciation of one's previous life, including material possessions and one's social identity, family, and status. But this primary renunciation has continued expression inside the monastery walls as well. The monastic life is to be a humble, lowly way of life: the social implications are inescapable. Monks take on a materially lowly way of life. They are allowed no private possessions but receive basic simple clothing and a moderate amount of food (no red meat) and drink (RB 39, 40, 55).[130]

128. M. Basil Pennington, *Listen with Your Heart: Spiritual Living with the Rule of Saint Benedict* (Brewster, MA: Paraclete Press, 2007), 103.

129. By the ninth century the monastic *polis* in Western Europe had taken on a recognizable shape, and this shape to a large extent reflects the Rule of Saint Benedict. The Plan of St. Gall, the earliest known medieval architectural plan of a large-scale building complex, is a case in point. The drawing includes ground plans for over forty buildings as well as a road, gardens, walls, an orchard, and a cemetery. The plan envisaged a large, elaborate church; accommodation for the abbot, monks, novices, the sick, pilgrims, and guests; a school; facilities for the storage and preparation of food, including brewing and baking, and for the practice of various crafts; a blacksmith shop, saddlery, and so on; housing for livestock and poultry, and, it must be said, for servants. This was a plan for a monastic *polis* (http://www.stgallplan.org/en/index.html).

130. Where the monastic standard of living sat in relation to the rest of the culture undoubtedly varied over time and place. Poverty is always relative,

And if novices believe that their renunciation of secular life is to embrace a life exclusively devoted to prayer, they have a further shock in store. As the classic Benedictine formula says, the life is characterized by *ora et labora*, by prayer and work.[131] While the work of the oratory (the *opus Dei*)—the liturgical life of the monastery—orders the monastic day, Benedict also prescribes daily manual labor (*labore manuum*) alongside prayerful reading (*lectione divina*) (RB 48). For Benedict, manual labor could even extend to working in the monastery fields: "[The brothers] must not become distressed if local conditions or their poverty should force them to do the harvesting themselves" (RB 48.7). Clearly the communities that Benedict had in mind were not poor, but hardship was nonetheless a possibility. Manual labor, a sign of social humility, is not above Benedict's monks. Indeed, Benedict holds up the practice of manual labor as a positive, if somewhat distant, ideal: "When they live by the labor of their hands, as our fathers and the apostles did, then they are really monks" (RB 48.8). Alongside Peter's fishing and Paul's tent making, the basket-weaving desert *abbas* are surely in Benedict's mind here.[132]

While there are changes in the material aspects of life, it was the social ordering of the monastery that particularly set it apart from the surrounding secular culture. Benedict's monastery embraced a truly diverse collection of people: nobles, government officials,

---

and there is no vow of poverty in RB. As was the case in fourth-century desert monasticism, for some monks, entry into the monastery meant a higher standard of living than they had enjoyed in secular life.

131. The formula is not itself found in the Rule, and some scholars have noted the dangers in using the abbreviated slogan. Understood broadly, however, it remains a helpful summary. See Drobner, *Fathers of the Church*, 507. Marie-Benoît Meeuws argues that work and prayer are related (and often debated) throughout monastic history, not just in the Benedictine tradition. She identifies the first use of the maxim *ora et labora* as occurring in the foundation documents of the German Beuronese Congregation, established by Maurus and Placid Wolter in the 1860s (Marie-Benoît Meeuws, " 'Ora et Labora': Devise Bénédictine?" *Coll* 54 [1992–1993]: 193–219).

132. Historically, Benedictine monasticism has struggled with this ideal. Monastic reforms inevitably included material simplification. Cistercian reform is a case in point.

craftsmen, laborers, rich and poor, educated and illiterate, free-men and former slaves, old and young, Romans and barbarians.[133] Within the monastery walls, however, distinctions are intention-ally eliminated: one deliberately renounces secular ways of defin-ing oneself in relation to others, one's social construction, and the Rule implements an agenda of social leveling.[134]

Early on, the Rule clearly states the theological imperative for this social leveling: *"whether slave or free, we are all one in Christ* (Gal 3:28) and share alike in bearing arms in the service of the one Lord; for *God shows no partiality among persons* (Rom 2:11)" (RB 2.20). The monastery aims to live out this oneness by building what is basically an egalitarian brotherhood.[135] As John Fortin demonstrates, the consequent program can be seen in practice in the way Benedict deals with named social classes in the Rule.[136] So, for example, RB 59 carefully specifies that when the sons of nobility are offered to the monastery they must give up their inheritance rights and must not be given any means to acquire personal possessions.[137] Similarly, Benedict is adamant that in the monastery private ownership is a vice (*vitium*, RB 33.1). The monk is to "give, receive or retain" nothing, "not a book, writing tablets or stylus—in short, not a single item" "as his own" (RB 33.3). Material gifts here symbolize social transactions that, in turn, imply power relationships. The giver has power over the receiver; the receiver is indebted to the giver. There is no room for such transactions in the monastery.

Again, the initial renunciation of status is merely a signal of what is to come. Sustaining this program of social leveling is by

---

133. Böckmann, *Perspectives*, 50. This list is found in the *Life of Saint Benedict* as well as the Rule.

134. The following discussion draws on John R. Fortin, "Social Class in Saint Benedict's Monastery," CSQ 43, no. 2 (2008): 199–215, here 207–15.

135. I use the word "egalitarian" here with some caution. This is not, it should be noted, a democracy.

136. Fortin, "Social Class," 201–6.

137. RB 59.7 notes that the same instruction holds for the poor (*pauperi-ores*), but it is clearly a bigger issue for the nobility. For a discussion of the problematic practice of child oblation, see Kardong, *Benedict's Rule*, 491–92.

no means straightforward, of course, and its implementation raises other questions. In secular society, where order and status, one's place in a finely structured hierarchy, were critical to identity formation, what did it mean to have a place in this radically reordered society of the monastic *polis*?[138] Order, or rank, in the community becomes a critical matter: who am I in *this* society? In addition, there are practical matters: Where do we sit in the oratory or at the table? Who takes Communion first? In what order do we process? Who leads the psalms? Order is necessary for both the formation of identity and the functioning of the group. How can it be achieved in what is intended to be an egalitarian brotherhood? How can the cultivation of humility be protected while ensuring that monastic society can function?

Benedict and the Master propose distinct solutions to the question of order. Again, viewing Benedict against the Master yields some helpful insights.

The Master is aware of the inverse relationship between rank and humility and outlines a radical strategy to safeguard humility.[139] In the Master's monastery there are no ranks whatsoever below the abbot:

> The abbot must take care never to appoint anyone second to himself, nor to assign anyone to third place. Why? So that by not causing anyone to become proud of the honor and by promising the honor of being his successor to someone who lives a holy life, he may make all eager to rival one another in doing what is good and in humility, just as the Lord judged the apostles quarreling over first place when "he brought a child into their midst and said: 'Let anyone who wants to be great among you be like this, and let anyone who wants to be first among you be your servant.'" (RM 92.1-5)

138. Kardong raises the question of whether a discussion of rank is meaningful for contemporary life: "In today's culture, the whole idea of personal place is so weakened that it might be questioned whether this whole discussion [RB 60, etc.] has any real meaning" (Kardong, *Benedict's Rule*, 496).

139. For the following discussion I draw on Kardong's analysis of rank (Terrence G. Kardong, "Benedict's Insistence on Rank in the Monastic Community: RB 63.1-9 in Context," CSQ 42, no. 3 [2007]: 243–65).

The Master's way of dealing with rank, supported by its gospel rationale, might initially strike us as profoundly egalitarian, but in fact, as Kardong has demonstrated, it is a recipe for the creation of poisonous rivalry. The Master avoids completely the permanent designation of rank. Instead, the abbot is instructed to "constantly change the order of precedence" (RM 92.33). Everyone has a turn at sitting next to the abbot at table or standing next to him in the oratory, so "that no one may then be made proud of the honor of ranking second, and no one give way to despair because of ranking last" (RM 92.37). But even if pride and despair are avoided, the Master's system openly encourages rivalry. In the Master's monastery, there is only one rank that the brother should aspire to, the rank of abbot. Indeed, in the Rule of the Master the goal of monastic life is becoming like the abbot rather than becoming Christlike. The Master's abbot is set over and against the brothers: not only does the abbot represent God in the monastery but he also wields godlike powers.[140] This is dangerous ground indeed.

In practice, such a regime is more likely to result in displays of false humility and destructive rivalry than "holy competition."[141] The Master's regime of constant change, of second guessing, is intended to be a "prescription for becoming humble" (RB 92.7) and to make the brothers compete for honors. But humility here is impoverished and almost incomprehensible, a matter of superficially observable behaviors and perverse and obsessive competition. The fueling of this desire for honor, albeit "holy" honor (RB 92.50), is inimical to the growth of the sort of self-forgetfulness or self-loss that leads to genuine humility. Kardong suspects that the Master's motivation is actually to prevent challenges to the authority of the abbot: "If no one has any status, no one has a power base from which to make trouble."[142] This may be so, but the impact of competition here, with brothers being encouraged to outdo each other in humility in front of the abbot, would have

---

140. Kardong, "Benedict's Insistence on Rank," 262. Kardong thinks "the Master raises the abbot too high" and "pegs the rest of the monks too low."
141. "Holy competition" is Kardong's phrase (Kardong, "Benedict's Insistence on Rank," 258).
142. Kardong, "Benedict's Insistence on Rank," 264.

been poisonous to the whole community. There is nothing here of the mutuality that Benedict speaks of in the penultimate chapter of his Rule.[143]

Benedict sets out his approach to community rank in RB 63, stating both the norm and the principles for making exceptions:

> In the monastery, they should keep to their ranks [*ordines*] as established by the time of entry, merit of life [*vitae meritum*] or the abbot's arrangement. The abbot should not disturb the flock committed to him, nor should he arrange anything unjustly as if he had unlimited power. But he should always keep in mind that he will have to answer to God for his decisions and deeds. Therefore the brothers should approach for the kiss of peace and for Holy Communion, to intone a psalm and to stand in choir, according to the rank [*ordines*] the abbot has given them or which they themselves have. In no situation at all shall chronological age have any part in determining or influencing the ordering of the community. . . . Therefore, with the exception of those whom, as we have said, the abbot promotes after careful reflection or demotes for certain reasons, the rest must maintain their rank according to time of entry. So, for example, one who arrives at the monastery at the second hour should realize that he is junior to one who came at the first hour, no matter what his age or status [*aetatis aut dignitatis*]. (RB 63.1-8; trans. Kardong)

Benedict's approach to rank, as Stewart suggests, "achieves order but abolishes privilege."[144] Benedict does not follow the Master but returns to what Kardong suggests is the mainstream cenobitic tradition, rejecting hierarchical rank but utilizing date of entry as the norm for monastic ordering.[145] This tradition understood the paradoxical risk in seeking to be humble. In the Rule

---

143. Elsewhere Kardong has analyzed the question of power and authority in the monastery, fruitfully using the mimetic conflict theory of René Girard (Terrence G. Kardong, "Benedict's Prior: RB 65," CSQ 40, no. 2 [2005]: 117–34). See also Marr, *Tools for Peace.*

144. Stewart, *Prayer and Community,* 66.

145. Kardong, "Benedict's Insistence on Rank," 257.

of Basil, for example, rule 10 answers the question "How should we behave when it is time to be seated?" with the directive to sit where instructed by the superior. Jesus' teaching (particularly Luke 14:7-11) must have inspired an undignified rush for the lowest place at the table. As Kardong says, "evangelical humility" could easily turn into "unholy competition."[146]

If date of entry (*conversationis tempus*, RB 63.1) is the starting point, Benedict also wants a certain flexibility in ordering the monastery. He gives the abbot power to determine rank but not in the arbitrary manner seen in the Master. The consistent criterion that the abbot must consider in determining rank is "merit of life" (*vitae meritum*, RB 63.1), and a consistent indicator of its absence is pride.[147] While Benedict is adamant that chronological age should never be a determinant of rank, there is nonetheless an ordering of the community that relates to experience and growth in monastic life.

It is important here to remember that the underlying principle of community for Benedict is mutuality (RB 63.17), including respect for those who are further ahead in the monastic journey. He specifies the ways of addressing both "juniors," those new to the monastic life regardless of chronological age, and "seniors," those further along the journey, again regardless of age: "The seniors are to call their juniors by the title 'brother,' but the juniors should call their seniors '*nonnus*,' which means 'reverend father'" (RB 63.12, trans. Kardong). Monastic order is intended not only to provide a means for arranging the mechanics of community life but also to encourage perseverance in the monastic journey. Ahead of the newcomers are the *nonnus*, who, like the desert *abbas* before them, provide an encouraging example of the fruitfulness of fidelity to monastic life. The ordering of the community serves the purpose of monastic life, the growth of humility and love. Indeed, on the same basis Benedict allows for God to see difference

---

146. Kardong, "Benedict's Insistence on Rank," 256–57.
147. See, for example, the way in which Benedict carefully deals with clergy in the monastery. He recognizes the dangers of ecclesiastical as well as secular rank and the risk that ordination can lead to pride. See RB 60 and 62.

in the community of Christ: "Only in this are we distinguished in his sight: if we are found better than others in good works and in humility" (RB 2.21).[148]

Benedict's exceptional cases confirm this principle. So, for example, Benedict instructs that the abbot should be willing to listen to the criticism of a visiting monk offered with love and humility (*cum humilitate caritatis*) and that the community should urge such a monk to stay so that "others can learn from his example" (RB 61.4, 9). In this case, this monk's place (*locum*, RB 61.11) could be raised above date of entry. Conversely, if a brother who leaves the monastery, abandoning the vow of stability, returns, he must be given the last place (*in ultimo gradu*, literally, "the last step") "as a test of his humility" (*ex hoc eius humilitas comprobetur*, RB 29.2). So while the ordering of the community proceeds on a different basis from secular (and ecclesiastical) standards, there is still an "up and down" inside the monastery, an order that in fact resonates with the order implied by the ladder of humility in RB 7. Up is down and down is up: "we descend by exaltation and ascend by humility" (RB 7.7).

In the monastic *polis*, then, the monk is given a place in the community. This gift, as Kardong suggests, is "an important corollary of the virtue of stability . . . not only does one commit oneself unconditionally to the community, but one is given a place in the group."[149] This place, however, is designed to form a new, countercultural identity, one characterized by humility. For the *monasteriale*, the monastery man, the monastic *polis* offers a place that encourages the growth of humility. In the context of this place, the practice of humble service is intended to increase love, or *caritas*.

---

148. *Solummodo in hac parte apud ipsum discernimur, si meliores ab aliis in operibus bonis et humiles inveniamur.* The Latin verb *discerno* means "to separate," "set apart," "distinguish between," or "discern." See Kardong: "The only way we count more with God is if we are found superior to others in good works and still humble."

149. Kardong, *Benedict's Rule*, 355.

3.6 The Yoke of Service: Humble Love and the Monastery Kitchen

Benedict seems fully aware that the ordering of monastic community is a delicate matter. Motivation is all. So, for example, he draws attention to the reasons for the acceptance of the visiting monk: "because wherever we may be, we are in the service [*servitur*] of the same Lord and doing battle for the same King" (RB 61.10). It is worth listening to the outsider because all share the same goal. The community, including the abbot, is oriented toward Christ; indeed it is a community constituted in the service of Christ. Everything is tested against this fundamental standard, the *telos* of the monastery. In Benedict's monastery, the monks are "to prefer nothing whatever to Christ" (RB 72.11).

It is worth noting RB 2.20 again, with its stress on equality under Christ. Common service to Christ ultimately relativizes rank in the monastery. All are "under one Lord" (*sub uno Domino*), and all are equal (*aequalem*) in carrying the burden (*baiulamus*) of service (*servitutis militiam*).[150] Service to the one Lord (RB 61.10) is both the ultimate determinant of rank in the community and the critical motivator of action. The life of the monastery is arranged so that this service can be practiced. What do these arrangements look like?

When the novice is received as a brother he promises "fidelity to monastic life" (*conversatio morum*, RB 58.17), that is, the "external and physical disciplines" that "establish parameters and space for the transformation of mind and heart."[151] The Latin word *conversatio*, "way of life," often translates the Greek *askēsis*,

---

150. Kardong suggests that the verb *baiulo* (to bear) gives the use of *militiam* (obligation) military overtones. See Kardong, *Benedict's Rule*, 56. *RB 1980* observes that "in the Vulgate *baiulamus* is used of Jesus carrying the cross in John 19.17" (*RB 1980*, 175n2.20). For Benedict, service is always understood as the imitation of Christ.

151. Stewart, *Prayer and Community*, 88. There has been considerable debate over the translation and interpretation of the phrase *conversatio morum suorum*, particularly regarding its status as a separate vow (see Claude Peifer, "5. Monastic Formation and Profession," in *RB 1980*, 437–66, here 459–63).

"training."[152] The novice makes a commitment to the monastic regime, which includes prayer, *lectio*, work, renunciation of private property, chastity, prescriptions on food, drink, rest, fasting, and vigils. What is distinctive about this training regime in cenobitic monasticism is, however, its communal nature. The brothers eat, sleep, pray, and work together. While there is significant provision for silence in Benedict's monastery, the monks are rarely alone. The self, in a sense, is spectacularly and permanently on view.[153]

If, then, this monastic environment results in a certain transparency, how does the training regime actually help? There is potential for this environment to be experienced negatively, as a nightmare; certainly, as Kline suggests, as a harsh desert.[154] What are the communal practices that actually help to build consonance between interior (motivation) and exterior (actions)? What practices lead to positive rather than negative results, in the growth of humility and love? Significantly, the opportunities for mutual service most clearly offer this prospect. As a number of scholars have noted, RB 35, Benedict's instructions regarding kitchen servers, is a case in point.[155]

It is possible to miss the significance of this chapter, imagining that it is simply about the mechanics of getting food on the table. In many ways RB 35 summarizes Benedict's vision of cenobitic monasticism, certainly in its practical outworking. Again, the contrast with the Master is instructive. RM 18 and 19 are devoted to the same subject, but the Master's treatment is focused on mechanics and, typically, on what can go wrong, on the prospect of

152. Peifer, "5. Monastic Formation," 459.

153. In contemporary nonmonastic life, intensive communal experiences in situations removed from everyday life are sometimes used both to expose and transform (or heal) the self in the context of a small community. A recent reality TV series, *Brat Camp*, for families experiencing difficulties managing their teenage children, is a case in point.

154. Kline, *Lovers of the Place*, 58.

155. Fortin, "Social Class," 212–13; Mary M. Keys, "Humility in the Monastic Polis: The Rule of St. Benedict," *Conference Papers—Midwestern Political Science Association* (2007): 1–42, here 34–36.

"negligence" (RM 18.7), and on the necessity of watching for the "faults and vices" of the brothers (RM 18.5).

By contrast, RB 35 is concerned with ensuring that kitchen service is understood as part of the spiritual program of the monastery. Benedict therefore begins by emphasizing the spiritual principle that informs all that follows: "The brothers should serve one another" (*Fratres sibi invicem serviant*, RB 35.1). Here, as Böckmann points out, Benedict again addresses the community as brothers, not monks.[156] The consequences of abolishing secular order become very real here. All will take a share in the considerable labor required to put food on the table. Böckmann paints a picture: "Concretely we may think of monks coming from richer families or the nobility who, before entering the monastery, had never done such work! Perhaps they had even brought their slaves to the monastery in the hope that by doing so they would be freed from such service (as happened in later centuries)."[157]

But in Benedict's monastery, no one is excused from kitchen service unless sick or engaged with an essential task (*gravis utilitatis*) that similarly serves the community (RB 35.1). All carry the burden of the work of the kitchen equally. Mutuality (*invicem*) is stressed: all serve, all are served (cf. RB 72.4). In the kitchen, the commitment to common service to Christ is enfleshed in a practical way in the life of the community. And in line with Benedict's optimistic communal eschatology, the objective, and indeed the outcome, of such service, is the increase of love (*caritas*) (RB 35.2). Not only is love the objective, but it also constitutes the motivation and the milieu for carrying out this often difficult work: the brothers are to serve one another, literally, *under* love (*sub caritate*, RB 35.6).[158]

---

156. Aquinata Böckmann, *Around the Monastic Table—RB 31–42: Growing in Mutual Service and Love*, trans. Matilda Handl and Marianne Burkhard (Collegeville, MN: Liturgical Press, 2009), 110.

157. Böckmann, *Around the Monastic Table*, 110. In the Cistercian reform, for example, the creation of the lay brothers was, in part, a means of regularizing the growth of a separate laboring class in monastic communities.

158. Kardong, following Lentini, notes that in late Latin *sub caritate* could mean "because of love." This would strengthen this sense of love as the motivating force (Kardong, *Benedict's Rule*, 292).

Benedict does not use the word *humility* in this chapter. By contrast, the Master names kitchen service as an opportunity for "practicing humility" (*humilitatem exerceant serviendi*, RM 18.8).[159] Böckmann offers an explanation for the difference. She notes that later in the Rule, Benedict requires artisans or craftsmen to "practice their craft with all humility" (*cum omni humilitate*). In this case, the danger is a form of pride, a raising of the self, imagining that in the skillful practice of the craft, the artisan-monk is bestowing something special on the monastery (RB 57.1-2). There is no such danger inherent in kitchen service, Böckmann argues, since no special skill is required and "because it was usually seen as humiliating and difficult, and thus it was more necessary to emphasize love as its basic attitude."[160]

Perhaps so, but it is precisely because kitchen service is humiliating, lowly work that it becomes *par excellence* a practice of humility, that is, a practice that encourages the internalization of humility. Humility is not an attitude to be put on: it is a way of being. Indeed, humility cannot be practiced directly but is more the fruit of looking away from achievement of any kind, even the achievement of humility. Kardong, following Böckmann, similarly suggests that in kitchen service "humility might upset the egalitarian principle" and that this is why Benedict "prefers to see love as the basic motivation."[161] But this chapter is precisely about enacted humility: the whole community serves, the whole community is lowered, they are all *under* love.

So what is happening here? Is Benedict avoiding tautology, as Cassian does in his account of the signs of humility? Perhaps he is implicitly commending a way of humility but avoiding confusing terminology. Has Benedict failed to see a connection between service and humility, between humility and love? There is substantial evidence to the contrary. RB 35 outlines a practice of enacted humility: humble (humiliating) kitchen service is

159. Similarly, RM 25.4, where the week of kitchen service is described as a week of humble service (*ministerio humilitatis*).
160. Böckmann, *Around the Monastic Table*, 116.
161. Kardong, *Benedict's Rule*, 292.

placed in a liturgical frame that is unmistakably modeled on Jesus' washing of his own disciples' feet (John 13). Christ is the model of humility. Service, humility, and love are bound firmly together.

In fact, placing RB 35 against RB 7 reveals key elements of the steps of humility enacted in a communal context but with the emphasis on mutuality strengthened. This is very much Benedict's voice in RB 35: he substantially recrafts the Master. For example, he leaves no place for self-will in kitchen service (step 2): it is not an optional activity but an act of communal obedience. But it is obedience "for the love of God," as Benedict says in his significant addition to step 3 (RB 7.34). Benedict's sincere belief is that mutual service builds love in the monastic community. Kitchen service is a form of mutual submission; each brother takes a turn in lowering himself before the other in the performance of what are considered socially demeaning tasks.

Here, the taking on of lowly, even humiliating, work resonates with step 6: "that a monk is content with the lowest and most menial treatment, and regards himself as a poor and worthless workman in whatever task he is given" (RB 7.49). This lowering, this self-humiliation, has a specific end in view: the monk lowers himself in the same way that Christ humbled himself; he serves in imitation of Christ's service; he renounces or puts aside self-will in the same way that Christ emptied himself.

There is ample evidence that it is this imitation of Christ that Benedict has in mind. At the heart of RB 35 he places a highly significant ritual: foot washing. Benedict is not the first to connect kitchen service with foot washing. Cassian's *Institutes* (4.19) describes a similar commitment to the servile labor of the kitchen and a weekly ritual of foot washing. In the Rule of the Master, it is a daily task completed at the end of Compline (RM 30.1-7). In Benedict (as in Cassian) a weekly ritual takes what is an ordinary, if menial, task and emphasizes its symbolic meaning. (The Master has a fascinatingly different closing ritual for his kitchen servers that will be discussed later.)

Böckmann suggests that chapter 35 of the Rule is carefully crafted by Benedict into a number of ring compositions, where elements are mirrored around a core idea.[162] At the center of Benedict's composition are the feet of the brothers. Verses 7 to 11 of Böckmann's literal translation and analysis make this structure clear:

A: 7 The one completing his week is to do the cleaning on Saturday.

B: 8 The towels used by the brothers to dry hands and feet, they are to wash.

C: 9 The feet of all, however, are to be washed by the one completing his week and the one beginning his.

B[1]: 10 The utensils of his service he is to return clean and in good repair to the cellarer.

A[1]: 11 The cellarer is to give them to the one beginning so that he knows what he gives and receives back.[163]

Here is the answer to Basil's sharp question, "Whose feet will you wash?"[164] The brothers wash each others' feet in precise imitation of Christ's washing of his disciples' feet and his command (*mandatum*) that they also should wash one another's feet (John 13:14).

So what looks like a simple but orderly regime for getting the domestic tasks completed is, in fact, replete with theological significance. This is a richly resonant text.[165] Three things are worth noting. First, the cleaning is carried out on Saturday, in preparation for the weekly celebration of the Resurrection on Sunday. Second, this is the only use in the Rule of the Latin word for towels (*lintea*), a term used twice in the Vulgate rendering of John's account of Jesus washing his disciples' feet (John 13:4-5), again a

---

162. Böckmann, *Around the Monastic Table*, 104–8. Kardong discusses the contribution of Borias to the discovery of chiastic structures in RB in Terrence G. Kardong, "The Achievement of André Borias, Exegete of Benedict's Rule," ABR 44, no. 2 (1993): 179–220, here 194–97.

163. Böckmann, *Around the Monastic Table*, 104.

164. LR 7.35.

165. For the following discussion I draw on Böckmann's helpful analysis (Böckmann, *Around the Monastic Table*, 102–29).

signal that the gospel imperative is what Benedict has in mind.[166] Finally, in Benedict (unlike Cassian) the foot washing is carried out by both the one who has served and the one who will serve. Just as Jesus subverts the recognized order of master and servant (the master becomes servant), so the foot-washing ritual deliberately subverts the order of served and server. Mutuality is stressed as the served and server share common ground. As Böckmann observes, "At the end of each week we could also say each side received Christ. The servers imitated Christ in their service and were allowed to serve him and to wash his feet; the others were served by Christ; both sides received his mercy."[167] This same emphasis on service is evident in RB 53.13, where the whole community, including the abbot, washes the feet of the guest. In this case, however, the christological significance is articulated: "guests . . . are to be welcomed as Christ" (RB 53.1).[168]

Foot washing is, as Böckmann observes, a concrete demonstration of the meaning of service. Indeed one could hardly think of a more literal enactment. Service lowers one before another. In RB 35.9, she notes, the word *feet* (*pedes*) is "placed at the beginning of the sentence and thus emphasizes that one bends down to the other rather than standing over the other."[169] Feet, bared for washing, signify humility.

This chapter also demonstrates Benedict's concern with interior and exterior consonance, with the relationship between external actions and what might be happening in the mind and heart. While no one is exempt from kitchen service (with the exceptions already noted), Benedict allows the weak to be given help so that "they may serve without distress" (RB 35.3). Similarly, on fast days, where only one meal is taken in the late afternoon or early

---

166. Böckmann, *Around the Monastic Table*, 118. Böckmann notes that *lintea* is also used in the Rule of Basil in connection with Jesus' footwashing (n17). The more common Latin word for towel would have been *mantele*.

167. Böckmann, *Around the Monastic Table*, 118.

168. By contrast, and with characteristic suspicion, the Master requires that guests be put to work after two days and spied on to ensure that they are not thieves (RM 78 and 79).

169. Böckmann, *Around the Monastic Table*, 118.

evening, Benedict provides the weekly servers with additional food and drink "so that at mealtime, they may serve their brothers without grumbling or hardship" (RB 35.13).[170] These sorts of provisions give Saint Benedict's Rule the moderate, humane tone that contributed to its widespread adoption, but it has a deeper purpose.

Benedict sees that if love is to be increased as a result of this service, he needs to pay attention to the emotional environment around kitchen and table. So the weak are not driven to despair by being given tasks beyond their capacity, nor are they excluded from receiving the benefits of service; instead they are given the gentle help that will allow participation. Similarly, table service on an empty stomach is not likely to result in interior peace. The before-dinner snack enables the waiters to put aside their own hunger and to carry out their service of the other brothers with generosity rather than grumbling (*murmuratione*, RB 35.13). Benedict is less interested in getting the job done—there are any number of ways that getting food on the table can be achieved—than in the transformation of ordinary, even humiliating, work into an opportunity for the cultivation of humble love.

Finally, and significantly, Benedict frames the whole conduct of table service with liturgical prayer, that is, in the context of an intentional evocation or remembering of God's presence. Table and oratory, the twin foci of communal life, are intentionally brought together. Kitchen service begins and ends with prayer in the oratory at the close of Sunday Lauds. The outgoing and ingoing kitchen servers "make a profound bow in the oratory before all and ask for their prayers" (RB 35.15). This action in itself is unusual for a Sunday, when in recognition of the day of Resurrection prostration is not normally performed. The action is a ritual reminder of the foot-washing ritual performed on the previous day.[171] The liturgy continues: "Let the server completing his week recite this verse: *Blessed are you, Lord God, who have helped me and comforted me* (Dan 3:52; Ps 85 [86]:17). After this

170. Similar provisions are made for the weekly reader: RB 38.10.
171. Böckmann, *Around the Monastic Table*, 124.

verse has been said three times, he receives a blessing. Then the one beginning his service follows and says: *God, come to my assistance; Lord, make haste to help me* (Ps 69 [70]:2). And all repeat this verse three times. When he has received a blessing, he begins his service" (RB 35.16-18).

The whole community joins in the repetition of the versicles. As Kardong observes, "The significance of this triple antiphonal chant is to symbolize the communal nature of all monastic roles and offices."[172] Kitchen service is both of and for the whole community. Here the whole monastic community bears the yoke of humble service with and for the Christ they seek.

3.7 The Bread of Obedience: The Difficult Heart of Humility

In the Master's monastery, the end of the week of kitchen service is marked not with foot washing but with a different ritual, set in the refectory. At the end of the daily meal the weekly servers gather and store the crumbs of bread that remain on the table. On the seventh day these crumbs are combined with eggs or flour to make a "small cooked dish" that is shared after Compline before "the drinking of the last warm beverage." First, the dish is placed on the abbot's table; then the kitchen servers make their request for prayer: "Please, lords [*domini*], pray for us, for we have finished our week of humble service." The whole community kneels with the abbot to pray for the servers, and when the prayers have concluded the servers, quoting Psalm 85 (86):17, say: "Let those who hate us see, to their confusion, that you, O Lord, have helped us and comforted us" (RM 25.1-6).

At this point, there is an opportunity for the abbot to speak, or pray, and then the servers "give the sign of peace" to the abbot, their deans, and brothers (RM 25.7). When all are again seated at the table, the abbot blesses the dish of cooked crumbs and presides over their ritual eating:

172. Kardong, *Benedict's Rule*, 296.

The abbot makes a sign of the cross over the little dish; with a spoon he first serves himself from what he has just blessed, then places a spoonful into the mouth of each of those who are sitting with him at his table. And when he has made the round of his table companions he calls up the waiters and puts some into their mouths also. Then the waiters hand the abbot as many dishes as there are tables and into them he dishes out whatever number of spoonfuls corresponds to the number of brothers at each of the tables. Their deans do the distributing into the mouth of each of the brothers, so that everyone receives some of what has been blessed. When this is finished, they take the last warm beverage, then rise, saying, "Thanks be to God." (RM 25.8-11)

This ritual eating of crumbs is obligatory. If the kitchen servers fail to prepare and present this dish "through negligence," the abbot withdraws a portion of their bread ration until "they make satisfaction and promise to amend" (RM 25.12). What is the meaning of this ritual, and why is it important to the Master? Why is it connected with kitchen service?

First, the eucharistic resonances are clear: as Bynum has observed, this "prototypical meal" "hover[s] in the background of any banquet," indeed, we might add, any Christian communal eating.[173] Böckmann suggests that the Master's highly ritualized meal, which takes place after Communion has been received in the oratory, sits in the tradition of the Christian agape meal.[174]

173. Caroline Walker Bynum, *Holy Feast and Holy Fast: The Religious Significance of Food to Medieval Women* (Berkeley: University of California, 1987), 3. Bynum argues that eating and its renunciation are central to "religious world denial" in late medieval Europe. While the focus of her study is significantly later, eating is a similarly highly charged, theologically thick activity in the monastic rules examined here.

174. It is worth recalling here also that there are no priests in the Master's community, so the Eucharist is not (generally) celebrated in the monastery. The sharing of Communion is "by extension." So the Master's highly ritualized meal seems to function as a monastic virtual Eucharist. This, of course, is an observation made from a considerable historical distance. As Vogüé points out, Communion *extra missam* was common in this period, with "the faithful" giving themselves Communion at home during the week with

The bread is blessed by the abbot, so that the remaining crumbs are handled with great care: this is considered to be holy bread.[175]

This crumb-eating ritual has a number of biblical resonances that are worth exploring. In the gospel stories of the miraculous feeding of the crowds, Jesus' disciples gather the leftover bread (Vulgate *fragmentum*[176]) into baskets (Mark 6:43, 8:8; Matt 14:20; Luke 9:17; John 6:12-13). The Latin word for crumbs (*mica*) used by the Master is found, however, in the Vulgate translation of the Christian Scriptures in only two stories: the story of Jesus' encounter with the Canaanite or Syrophoenician woman and the story of Lazarus and the rich man (or Dives). In the latter story, the poor man, Lazarus, longs to satisfy his hunger with crumbs that have fallen from the rich man's table (Luke 16:20-21).

Jesus' interchange with the Canaanite woman similarly uses the metaphor of crumbs and the table. Rejecting her initial request for help for her demon-possessed daughter, Jesus says: "It is not fair to take the children's food [*panis* 'bread'] and throw it to the dogs [*canis*]." She responds, "Yes, Lord, yet even the dogs [*catelli* 'puppies,' 'whelps,'] eat the crumbs [*micis*] that fall from their masters' table" (Matt 15:26-28). In both of these stories eating the crumbs that fall from the table is a sign of lowness or baseness: humiliating poverty in the case of Lazarus and, for the Canaanite woman, religious otherness. She is, in the eyes of the Jewish Jesus, metaphorically speaking, a dog (*canis*). In the gospel story, the woman subverts this humiliating designation by a surprising move. She acknowledges her humiliating position and simultaneously claims her entitlement to inclusion. She metaphorically eats the crumbs from the table.

---

bread received on Sundays. Similarly, highly ritualized meals with multiple blessings are not unique to Christian communities but reflect the ceremonial of the Roman world. See Vogüé, "Introduction," *Rule of the Master*, 31–38.

175. Böckmann, *Around the Monastic Table*, 218. The Master carefully excludes other food and drink from this status by prescribing a provisional blessing: "Bless, O Lord, whatever we are to consume of this" (RM 23.18).

176. All references to the Vulgate use the Stuttgart edition: *Biblia Sacra: iuxta Vulgatam versionem*, ed. Bonifatius Fisher, Robert Weber, and Rober Gryson (Stuttgart: Deutsche Bibelgesellschaft, 1994).

Is this, in part, what is happening in the Master's crumb-eating ritual? Böckmann, while acknowledging that "one might smile" at this strange-sounding ceremony, suggests that the ritual simply demonstrates "that for the Master everything was sacred just like Holy Communion."[177] Its association with lowly kitchen service, however, seems to invite further connections. Indeed, Vogüé proposes that the crumbs "symbolized the entire week's service and showed that the servers had seen to it that nothing went to waste."[178] The connection between humility and the crumbs could, perhaps, be pushed further.

The bread in the Master's refectory is lowered from a basket hanging above the abbot's table "to give the impression that the provisions of God's workmen [*operariis*] are coming down from heaven" (RM 23.2).[179] The metaphors of lowering are already operative here. The kitchen servers similarly sense their lowly, even humiliating, position. Are the monks here, perhaps, eating their own humiliation, the bread of affliction (Deut 16:3)? Are they remembering Christ's own "kitchen service"—as the distributor of bread at the miraculous feeding and at the Last Supper—and receiving the now visibly humble Christ?

Certainly, the atmosphere here seems very different from the foot-washing ritual in RB. When requesting the prayer of the community, the Master's kitchen servers address the community as lords (*domini*) (RM 25.4).[180] There is a clear acknowledgment that this is lowly service (*ministerio humilitatis*, RM 25.4), not so different from Benedict's understanding, but here there is an assumption that because the server is involved in lowly, humiliating work, he will be hated. The one who performs the humiliating work is humiliated or shamed by it; his person is soiled by his contact with what is considered low. But ironically, the server is able to proclaim that even if he is necessarily humiliated by the performance of this base service, God has been helping and

177. Böckmann, *Around the Monastic Table*, 218.
178. RM 181n1.
179. Vogüé, *Règle*, SCh 106:110.
180. Vogüé, *Règle*, SCh 106:132.

consoling him ("Let those who hate us see, to their confusion, that you, O Lord, have helped us and comforted us," RM 25.6, citing Ps 85 [86]:17).

Significantly, in his foot-washing ritual, Benedict omits the first half of this quotation from Psalm 85 (86):17 (RB 35.16). How can kitchen service be the object of hatred, when one serves in imitation of Christ? What happened to the Master's crumb-eating ceremony? Was it a widely practiced ritual? Was it still practiced in Benedict's monastery? And, more important for our purposes, what are the implications of the differing choices of ritual to begin and end kitchen service? What different understandings of humility underpin these differing practices?

One possibility is that the differing emphases of the Master and Benedict reveal differing emphases regarding the grounding of humility. From one perspective humility is simply the condition of being a creature rather than being the Creator. Here the stress is on our dependence and the enormous distance between God and humanity. We are the "unworthy servants." This seems to be the Master's primary emphasis. While Benedict shares this basic understanding (for example, in RB 7.49), he also wants to hold the humility of Christ as his primary model and essential motivation: we are to "prefer nothing whatever to Christ" (RB 72.11), and Christ washes our feet. We serve because Christ served. We bend down because Christ bent down.

There is a tension, of course, between these two emphases: we are not Christ. We are limited and fallen creatures, but our God-given desire is to become Christlike. And to become Christlike means walking a humiliating, self-emptying path. It means lowering oneself before the other, giving way to the other. We eat the bread of humiliation *and* wash the others' feet.

This is why obedience becomes the irreducible and difficult core of humility in community. Obedience means precisely giving way to the other, placing oneself below another; it means relinquishing power. The Rule of Saint Benedict is uncompromising on this and returns to this theme again and again. The cenobite serves *under* a rule and an abbot (RB 1.2). Obedience is the *modus operandi* of the monastery, and it has a theological rationale. The abbot is "believed to hold the place of Christ in the monastery"

(RB 2.2), and to offer obedience to one's superior is to offer obedience to God (RB 5.15). It is a sign that one has indeed heard the Gospel call to follow Christ and abandon self-will: "Such people as these immediately put aside their own concerns, abandon their own will [*voluntatem propriam deserentes*], and lay down whatever they have in hand, leaving it unfinished" (RB 5.7-8).[181] Obedience is to the call and way of the obedient Christ. It is an imitation of Christ, as both the second and third steps of humility make clear:

> The second step of humility is that a man loves not his own will nor takes pleasure in the satisfaction of his desires; rather he shall imitate by his actions that saying of the Lord: *I have come not to do my own will, but the will of him who sent me* (John 6:38). . . . The third step of humility is that a man submits to his superior in all obedience for the love of God, imitating the Lord of whom the Apostle says: *He became obedient even to death* (Phil 2:8). (RB 7.31-34)

Obedience is all very well when the terms are agreeable, but often they are not. Step 4 recognizes this fact but continues to exhort the monk to embrace obedience: "The fourth step of humility is that in this obedience under difficult, unfavorable, or even unjust conditions, his heart quietly embraces suffering and endures it without weakening or seeking escape" (RB 7.35-36).

As for the desert *abbas*, the command of Christ to "turn the other cheek" is given as the underlying rationale: "In truth, those who are patient amid hardships and unjust treatment are fulfilling the Lord's command: *When struck on one cheek, they turn the other; when deprived of their coat, they offer their cloak also; when pressed into service for one mile, they go two* (Matt 5:39-41)" (RB 7.42).

How do the dynamics of power work when such acts of self-denial are practiced within a monastic community? In the desert, the nonviolent strategy of turning the other cheek could function as a powerful form of resistance to the demonic.[182] The dynamic seems

---

181. The fishing nets of Jesus' first disciples are in sight here (Matt 4:22) (*RB 1980*, 187n5.7).

182. See above, chap. 2.5, 81–83.

much more dangerous within a closed community. Are there any practices that offer a clue to Benedict's thinking here? A glimpse can perhaps be found in RB 71, which approaches obedience from a communal perspective. It does not make for comfortable reading, since, as Kardong points out, while Benedict embarks with an optimistic statement regarding the benefits of mutual obedience, he quickly resorts to a hierarchical picture, where junior monks appear to be required to bear the burden of conflict in the community.[183]

> If a monk is reproved in any way by his abbot or by one of his seniors, even for some very small matter, or if he gets the impression that one of his seniors is angry or disturbed with him, however slightly, he must, then and there without delay, cast himself on the ground at the other's feet [*prostrates in terra ante pedes eius*] to make satisfaction, and lie there until the disturbance is calmed by a blessing [*dum benedictione sanetur illa commotio*]. Anyone who refuses to do this should be subjected to corporal punishment or, if he is stubborn, should be expelled from the monastery. (RB 71.6-9)

Certainly the final provisions are harsh. As Kardong says, "No system that requires underlings to solve all conflict by capitulation and self-accusation can be said to be healthy."[184] But is this picture entirely negative? Is there a paradoxical "turn the other cheek" style of power in throwing oneself at the feet of the accuser and, indeed, in staying put until a blessing is wrested from the one who believes that he has been wronged? Here potential resentment or bitterness is drawn out rather than hidden. Is this, in fact, a healthier response to the often hidden and festering resentment that characterizes much communal life? Is this a form of eating the bread of one's humiliation, absorbing the bitterness that threatens mutuality (*invicem*) and the *blessing* of obedience (*oboedientiae bonum*)? This is dangerous ground, of course, and open to all sorts of abuse. But the clear intention is healing and

183. Kardong, *Benedict's Rule*, 581–86.
184. Kardong, *Benedict's Rule*, 586.

restoration of community. If—and of course this is a big if—the seniors are themselves making progress in monastic life, then they should be able to facilitate for the junior, less experienced members, this way of healing.

3.8 The Raven at the Table: Benedict Practices Humility

And now to return to Giovanni di Consalvo's fresco, *Benedict and the Poisoned Bread*, in the Cloister of Oranges. The setting is the refectory. There is a sense of enclosure here—the room (read *monastery*) is separated from the external world. In fact, the rest of this panel shows the well-dressed servant of the priest delivering the poisoned bread—the violent intrusion of the secular world. This interior space is marked by simplicity: the walls in this refectory are not decorated with frescos. This simplicity gives weight to each of the elements of the composition: table, monks, Benedict, raven, bread, towel. The artist has also chosen a simple palette—white, black, and the pale ochre tones of bread or flesh.

Within the walls, the communal nature of this gathering is clear. There are no distinctions in dress: each wears a black habit. Yet each monk is carefully drawn as an individual: this one with a straight nose, that one with a beak, this one young, that one old and bearded. Each has a place at the table, a place in the monastic community. The monks are positioned in the same plane with the white-clothed table linking them horizontally, stressing their mutuality.

The table, of course, carries with it eucharistic overtones; in other pictorial versions of this Benedictine story, the whole scene could be mistaken for the Last Supper. Christlike, Benedict sits at the head of the table. The white tablecloth signals the hope of resurrection. The towel, not white but flesh-colored, swings over the whole scene: not only does it hang above the table, but its shadow strikes the bare wall. The towel gives the whole scene its *telos*: "prefer nothing whatever to Christ" (RB 72.11). This story is about love (*caritas*), about the self-emptying service exemplified by Jesus' washing the feet of his disciples. The towel is a symbol of humility.

This is the setting, the stage for a drama: the story of Benedict and the poisoned bread. All eyes are focused on the interaction between Benedict and the raven.

In human imagination the raven has had a checkered, primarily negative history. A bird of prey, feeding off dead and rotting flesh, neglectful even of its own offspring, the raven often represents the rapacious and merciless, the darker side of human nature. In Gregory's *Life of Saint Benedict*, however, the raven has already been partly tamed: Benedict's raven appears each day at meal-time to receive bread from the hand of his friend and master. The raven must also here represent the once unruly monk, tamed by the monastic regime of obedience to "rule and abbot," so that his unruly nature is also transformed. He too becomes a friend and disciple of Benedict and thereby a friend and disciple of Christ.

In Gregory's story of Benedict and the poisoned bread, how-ever, the raven struggles with obedience. The poison that has been brought into the community, delivered in the form of the blessed bread, is the corrosive consequence of envy: the local priest, Flo-rentius, has become so enraged with his hatred of Benedict and his community that he endeavors to eliminate his rival. Benedict commands the raven, "In the name of the Lord Jesus Christ, take this bread, and throw it in a place where no one can find it" (*Life* 8.3). This command must feel like an "impossible task" (RB 68.1), even, perhaps, a call to obedience under "difficult, unfavorable or even unjust conditions" (step 4, RB 7.35). When a priest sends a gift of blessed bread to a monastery it would normally be re-ceived with gracious thanks (see RM 76). But this bread is deeply ambiguous: it is blessed *and* poisoned. Benedict is able to perceive this ambiguity—highlighting the central importance of discern-ment—and decides that the bread must be removed from the community and disposed of where it can do no harm.

But the raven is unconvinced by Benedict's intended remedy. So, struggling with obedience, the raven makes a show of its con-cerns by flapping its wings, running around the bread in circles, and croaking. Why not publicly expose the treachery of the priest and seek revenge? Wouldn't the raven just love to pick over his carcass? (And, in fact, Benedict's disciple Maurus does precisely that a little later in the story when Florentius meets his divinely appointed death. By contrast, Benedict grieves over the death of his enemy and the glee of his disciple.[185]) Benedict is advocating mercy here, a costly mercy: the raven will need to fly a long distance—before even being fed!—in order safely to rid the community of this poison.

Finally, after considerable encouragement and being told not to fear, the raven obeys and flies off with the bread. The raven has become the conduit of grace, taking away the poison from the community. Sadly, this is not the end of Florentius's jealous rage, so when the poisoning fails, he tries to discredit the brothers' choice of monastic life by sending naked dancing girls to tempt them to lust. This time, Benedict's response is to remove himself—the prime object of the priest's envy—in order to preserve the community. So, Gregory says, "he decided to give way before envy," to "humbly cede" (*humiliter declinauit*) to the priest's hatred (8.5, 6).[186] Benedict bends himself to this vicious other, carrying Florentius's hatred and bitterness away from the community. Under Benedict's tutelage, the raven has already done the same.

In the Badia fresco, the Christlike figure of Benedict leans over the table, lowering himself before both the raven-disciple and his off-stage betrayer, Florentius, present in the form of the poisoned bread. Benedict is in essence washing the feet of his enemy. Benedict here embodies humility, the costly relinquishment of ego, of self-will, which bends even to hatred. In a word, his action is *kenotic*. Between the raven's flapping and Benedict's gracious bending is a long and costly journey.

185. The final scene is ripe with bathos: as Benedict departs, Florentius looks on with glee from his balcony. But then "God struck Florentius a terrible blow": he is accidently crushed to death by the collapse of his balcony. Benedict, though, takes no delight in the destruction of his enemy. Instead, he grieves deeply over his death, in the same way that David grieves over the death of Saul (*Life* 8.6-9).

186. For the Latin text, see Adalbert de Vogüé, ed., *Gregoire le Grand: Dialogues*, SCh 260 (Paris: Éditions du Cerf, 1978), 2:164.

3.9 Conclusion

Several themes emerge or are reinforced through this exploration of the Rule of Saint Benedict. First, when speaking of humility, it is impossible to avoid the material and the social. The monastic journey begins with renunciation of one's material possessions and familial relationships. But the rest of the journey, which is focused on the renunciation of self-will, is built on material lowliness and humility in one's dealings with the other members of the monastic community. It is hard to imagine a manifestation of humility that does not involve something quite material, or that does not have implications for one's social relations. Humility is always about lowering. It is about an equal place at the table where everyone takes up the towel.

Second, monastic community, the *cenobium*, offers a particular environment for the cultivation of humility: it offers the presence of another before whom one lowers oneself. The permanent presence of others tests what is happening interiorly and simultaneously offers opportunities for reshaping the self. This reshaping takes a very long time, a lifetime in fact. Benedict bends over graciously; the raven flaps around. What is happening within the hearts of the rest of the community? Many things, no doubt, and not all of them holy. The whole question of whom one lives before is important: in the monastery, oratory and table give the monk a two-way view. We live in view of God and each other. The eschatological perspective has significant consequences for daily life. The monk lives with the long view, under the judgment of God, but lives this long view in the present, in view of the abbot and the brothers. Benedict is optimistic: this project offers the prospect of "the sweetness of love." The raven can be tamed.

Finally, the tradition holds continuing difficulties regarding the nature of humility itself. The ubiquitous ladder of humility, in the form given by Benedict, potentially mediates the dangerous idea that humility is a work rather than a grace, something that can be possessed rather than a fruit that is paradoxically manifested by self-forgetfulness. By refocusing on practice, however, it is possible to discern in Saint Benedict's Rule a more nuanced theology of humility, founded in his understanding of Christ as the humble judge who leaves his throne to wash our feet. It is this commitment to the way of Christ, the way of humble love, that motivates both the individual and the community. Humility grows naturally in an environment of self-giving, mutual service.

A place at the table, a towel, and an unruly raven: here, then, is the challenging shape of humility in monastic community. A demanding call within the monastic enclosure; is it possible at all outside the monastery wall?

Figure 3. Filippino Lippi, *Apparition of the Virgin to Saint Bernard*, ca. 1480–1486, Church of the Badia, Florence. © SCALA, Florence.

Chapter 4

Humility and Public Life

Bernard of Clairvaux

The way is humility, the goal is truth.

—*Bernard of Clairvaux*, On the Steps of Humility and Pride[1]

In 1115, at the age of twenty-five and just two years after entering the New Monastery of Cîteaux,[2] Bernard of Fontaines was selected

---

1. For the Latin texts of Bernard's works I use the most recent critical edition: *Sancti Bernardi opera*, ed. Jean Leclercq, C. H. Talbot, and Henri M. Rochais, 8 vols. (Rome: Editiones Cistercienses, 1957–1977), hereafter abbreviated SBOp. English translations are generally from the Cistercian Fathers Series unless otherwise noted. I use the standard Cistercian Publications abbreviations for Bernard's writings. In-text references are generally to section numbers, not page numbers. For the letters I have used the traditional number (as in SBOp) followed by the number in Bruno Scott James's translation (prefaced with J): (Bernard of Clairvaux, *The Letters of St. Bernard of Clairvaux*, trans. Bruno Scott James [Stroud, UK: Sutton Publishing, 1953; repr. 1998], with a table correlating James's numbering with the traditional scheme on 538–52). English translations of the letters are those of James unless otherwise noted. I have followed Leclercq's dating of the texts.

2. Cîteaux was founded in 1098 by a small group of monks led by Robert of Molesme. It was initially known as the *novuum monasterium*, the New

165

as leader of a group of twelve monks sent to establish a foundation at Clairvaux. In the same year, Bernard was formally elected abbot, a position he held for the rest of his life. Regardless of his talent and passion, and indeed perhaps because of them, this early elevation to leadership was a recipe for disaster. He was young and inexperienced. Within a few years his health had completely broken down. His body was weakened by excessive fasting and the physical and mental toll of establishing a new monastery. Further, his intellect and idealism separated him from his fellow monks. According to his first biographer, William of Saint-Thierry, it was only through the humility of the monks in his charge—their "self-abasement" when "accused"—that Bernard began to mistrust his own zeal: "He realized that he was demanding of simple monks a degree of perfection that he had not yet attained." Slowly and painfully he learned to live among his fellow monks "on their level."[3] In the

----

Monastery. The beginnings of what became the Cistercian Order were apparently difficult. According to the founding documents of the order (compiled over twenty years after the event), Robert returned to the Benedictine monastery of Molesme after only a year. Only under the third abbot, Stephen (commonly, if erroneously, known as Stephen Harding), did Cîteaux begin to attract significant numbers of adult converts, Bernard among them. The aim of the founders, like many other new monastic foundations of the period, was, again according to the later founding documents, to live out the Rule of Saint Benedict authentically.

3. William of Saint-Thierry, et al., *Vita Prima Sancti Bernardi Claraevallis Abbatis, Liber primus* 29, 30, ed. Paul Verdeyen, CCCM 89B (Turnhout: Brepols, 2011), 29–85, here 55–56. Fr. Hilary Costello's English translation of Recension B of the entire *Vita Prima*, based on a manuscript at Mount Saint Bernard Abbey (UK), is forthcoming in 2015 from Cistercian Publications (*The First Life of Bernard of Clairvaux*, trans. Hilary Costello, CF 76 [Collegeville, MN: Cistercian Publications, forthcoming 2015]). Chapter numbers of the translation correspond to those in the CCCM edition. I use the Life, or *Vita Prima* as it is generally known, with a sense of caution. It presents a number of complex, interrelated problematic issues: its preparation to support Bernard's canonization, its multiple authors (and the varying relationships among Bernard and these authors), and the complex history of redactions (at least two separate streams). The degree of textual complexity here, as Bredero indicates, is greater than that of most lives of saints (Adriaan H. Bredero, *Bernard of Clairvaux: Between Cult and History*, trans. Reinder Bruinsma [Grand Rapids,

modern world one would probably surmise that Bernard had experienced a nervous breakdown.[4]

Bernard was effectively stood down and placed under obedience to his local bishop. A small hut was built outside the monastery enclosure, similar, William tells us, to "such as lepers often have near public crossroads," where, removed from the burden of day-to-day administration, Bernard could recover physically and spiritually.[5] This obedience was for a period of twelve months.[6] When Bernard returned to the community, though, he simply "returned to his accustomed former ways, like a bow under tension, and again took up his original rigorous life, like a cascade of water that has been held back and suddenly released."[7] Bernard's presence in the community became increasingly intolerable: his constant vomiting was disturbing, especially during the offices (to manage it he "had a receptacle dug into the earth by the place where he was standing"). Finally, "he was forced to leave the common life and live by himself alone," joining his brother monks only "for the sake of conferences or consoling

MI: Eerdmans, 1996], 20). For a summary of Bredero's discussion of textual problems, see his appendix 2, pp. 288–90.

4. Michael Casey, "Bernard of Clairvaux: The Man Behind the Image," *Pacifica* 3, no. 3 (1990): 269–87, here 274. There are a number of resonances between Bernard and the twentieth-century Cistercian monk and writer Thomas Merton. In Merton's account of this early phase of Bernard's life, one senses Merton's own story of early, damaging enthusiasm: "The young abbot is already cracking up under the burden of life in which Cistercian austerity is intensified twentyfold by indigence, lack of food, and by his own implacable asceticism. . . . Part of his 'formation' has been his training in the knowledge of human nature. First, he has had to learn that man is not an angel, that monks still have bodies, and that although he himself has tried not only to mortify his desires but also to put to death the senses themselves, it is better to remember that man is human and that his human nature is supposed to be divinized by grace, not destroyed by it" (Thomas Merton, *The Last of the Fathers: Saint Bernard of Clairvaux and the Encyclical Letter* Doctor Mellifluus [London: Catholic Book Club, 1954], 29–30, 32).

5. William of Saint-Thierry, et al., *Vita Prima* 33, CCCM 89B:58.

6. According to Bredero's chronology, this period can be dated to 1119. See Bredero, *Between Cult and History*, appendix 1, pp. 282–87.

7. William of Saint-Thierry, et al., *Vita Prima* 38, CCCM 89B:62.

them or the need for monastic discipline."[8] The hut became a more permanent home.

In this hut, outside the monastery enclosure, in the mid-1120s, Bernard wrote the drafts of three homilies that, with revision and the addition of a fourth, became one of his most widely circulated works, *In Praise of the Blessed Virgin Mary* (*Homilia in laudibus virginis matris*).[9] Bernard refers to his chronic ill health and separation from the monastic community in the prologue to the collection. Still driven "not to waste what little bit of leisure I can snatch during the night by depriving myself of sleep," he determined to use Vigils to say, in writing, "something in praise of the Virgin Mother" from Luke's account of the annunciation. Unlike the majority of his writings, which respond to particular invitations or pastoral or even political situations, this project, Bernard says, is for himself: to "satisfy my own devotion."[10] Here, to a greater degree than is perhaps the case in other writings, Bernard speaks to himself.

Filippino Lippi's lyric painting *Apparition of the Virgin to Saint Bernard* (ca. 1480–1486), reproduced at the beginning of this chapter, pinpoints this moment in Bernard's life. In the open book propped in front of the rocky outcrop, Lippi has painted, in the script common to Italian Bibles of the fifteenth century, the beginning of the story of the annunciation to Mary: *Missus est angelus Gabriel a Deo in civitatem Galilaeae* (Luke 1:26, "The angel Gabriel was sent by God to the town of Galilee"). Lippi (ca. 1457–1502) is equally careful to specify the precise text that Bernard is writing. The text, written in the fifteenth-century

---

8. William of Saint-Thierry, et al., *Vita Prima* 39, CCCM 89B:63.

9. Bernard of Clairvaux, *Homilies in Praise of the Blessed Virgin Mary*, trans. Marie-Bernard Saïd, CF 18 A (Kalamazoo, MI: Cistercian Publications, 1993). For the Latin text see SBOp 4:13–58. These homilies are sometimes referred to as *Missus est* (abbreviated Miss), from the beginning of the passage from Luke 1:26-27 at the start of Homily 1, SBOp 4:13.

10. Bernard makes this statement at the end of his preface to Homily 1 (CF 18:3).

humanistica hand, is from the end of Homily 2.[11] In translation, it says of Mary,

> Surely she is very fittingly likened to a star. The star sends forth its ray without harm to itself. In the same way the Virgin brought forth her son with no injury to herself. The ray no more diminishes the star's brightness than does the Son his mother's integrity. She is indeed that noble star risen out of Jacob whose beam enlightens this earthly globe. She it is whose brightness both twinkles in the highest heaven and pierces the pit of hell, and is shed upon earth, warming our hearts far more than our bodies, fostering virtue and cauterizing vice.[12]

Only fragments of this text are visible of course, but the reference to one of Bernard's most famous passages, known as *respice stellam, voca Mariam* ("look to the star, call upon Mary"), is unmistakable. And for those who needed a summary, the frame of the painting bears the inscription "IN REBVS DVBIIS MARIAM COGITA MARIAM INVOCA": "In matters of doubt, think of Mary, invoke Mary."[13]

Lippi's painting hangs in the church of the Badia Fiorentina, not far from the cloister fresco depicting Benedict and the Raven. It was originally commissioned for the del Pugliese family chapel attached to the monastery church of Santa Maria alle Campora, near the southwestern gate of the city of Florence, but during the siege of 1529–1530 it was moved for its protection to the Badia, the Campora's mother church.

The painting, its content and its location, tells a richly layered story about the spiritual and cultural milieu and the politics of

---

11. David L. Clark, "Filippino Lippi's *The Virgin Inspiring St. Bernard* and Florentine Humanism," *Studies in Iconography* 7–8 (1981–1982): 175–87, here 177–78.

12. Miss 2.17; SBOp 4:34; CF 18A:30. It is worth noting here Bernard's use of the terms *virtue* and *vice* simply as part of the vocabulary of the Christian life.

13. Jill Burke, *Changing Patrons: Social Identity and the Visual Arts in Renaissance Florence* (University Park, PA: Pennsylvania State University Press, 2004), 147.

Renaissance Florence. It also reflects the aspirations of its donor, the wealthy merchant Piero del Pugliese (1428–1498).[14] And it tells, among other things, a story (perhaps not entirely believable) about humility and public life. For Bernard, Mary is an icon of humility. For Piero del Pugliese, and in the Florentine imagination, Bernard is a model of the contemplative in action, a saint who spoke about Christian life in the public square. This chapter explores the intersection of these ideas.

4.1 The Problem with Bernard

4.1.1 Life and Work[15]

Bernard of Clairvaux (1090–1153) was born at Fontaine, near Dijon in Burgundy, the third child of a knight, Tescelin Sorus, and his wife, Aleth of Montbard.[16] He was educated by the canons of Saint Vorles de Châtillon. Though it is likely that he had been designated by his family for a religious vocation,[17] he was raised in a "chivalrous milieu," where he saw his brothers engaged in

14. The cultural layers of this story are explored by Burke. See especially *Changing Patrons*, chap. 7.

15. For a concise overview of Bernard's life and work, see Michael Casey, "Bernard of Clairvaux, St., 1090–1153," in *Encyclopedia of Monasticism*, ed. William M. Johnson (Chicago: Fitzroy Dearborn Publishers, 2000). The "Introduzione Generale" to the Italian edition of *Opere di San Bernardo*, recently translated into English by Elias Dietz, provides an excellent overview of Bernard's life, work, and theology, summarizing much of Leclercq's massive contribution to Bernardine studies: Jean Leclercq, "General Introduction to the Works of Saint Bernard (1)," CSQ 40, no. 1 (2005): 3–25; Jean Leclercq, "General Introduction to the Works of Saint Bernard (2)," CSQ 40, no. 3 (2005): 243–51; Jean Leclercq, "General Introduction to the Works of Saint Bernard (3)," CSQ 40, no. 4 (2005): 365–93.

16. Bredero has challenged the birth date of 1090 (calculated on the basis of Bernard's entering Cîteaux in 1112), arguing on the basis of manuscript alterations and the internal evidence of the *Vita Prima* for Bernard's entry to Cîteaux in 1113 and his birth in 1091. See Bredero, *Between Cult and History*, 203. Leclercq and Casey retain 1090 as Bernard's year of birth while adopting 1113 as the year of entry to Cîteaux. See Leclercq, "General Introduction (1)," 5–6.

17. G. R. Evans, *Bernard of Clairvaux* (New York: Oxford University Press, 2000), 7.

the knightly pursuit of war. Awareness of this context, as Jean Leclercq notes, helps to make sense of some of the more difficult aspects of his character, particularly "his combative ardor and a certain taste for taking command."[18] At about the age of twenty Bernard decided to become a monk but delayed acting on this decision until 1113, when he and a substantial group of relatives and friends, including five of his brothers and an uncle, entered the New Monastery of Cîteaux. In 1115 he became abbot of Clairvaux, the third new foundation made by Cîteaux. The young order grew so rapidly that by the middle of the century there were more than 350 Cistercian monasteries across Europe. To become a Cistercian, as G. R. Evans has suggested, became the most fashionable monastic choice of the day.[19] By the end of Bernard's life, Clairvaux itself had made nearly seventy foundations and another hundred affiliations.[20]

While Bernard spent the early years of his abbacy at Clairvaux, his sphere of influence widened alongside the expansion of the order. His treatise *Apologia* (ca. 1124–1125) responded to the tensions between the old monastic orders, particularly the Benedictine, or "Black Monks," of Cluny and the Cistercians. Bernard's influence extended beyond monastic institutions: so, for example, he wrote a rule of life for the Knights Templar, *In Praise of the New Knighthood* (1128–1136), and a short treatise (or long letter) *On the Conduct and Office of Bishops* (ca. 1127).

The papal schism of 1130–1138 thrust Bernard even further onto the European political stage. Aligning himself with Innocent II, Bernard traveled widely to advocate his acceptance. Bernard was a persuasive speaker as well as a gifted writer, and he was called on, and chose, to use these powers in a variety of situations. Bernard emerged as a statesman and diplomat; indeed he is commonly recognized as one of the most influential figures in

18. Leclercq, "General Introduction (1)," 6.

19. Evans, *Bernard of Clairvaux*, 8.

20. Traditionally, under the influence of Bernard's early biographers, the growth of the order was widely attributed to the role and influence of Bernard. For a more nuanced reading, see Bredero, *Between Cult and History*, 201–5, 248–63.

twelfth-century Europe.[21] In the early 1140s, he was a key player in the condemnation of the theology of Peter Abelard. He traveled through Languedoc preaching to counter the dualist Cathar heresy. In 1146 and 1147 he traveled around Europe to promote what became known as the Second Crusade; he bore much of the blame for its terrible failure.

This is only a sample of Bernard's extensive activities. Alongside this increasingly active life Bernard continued to write, not only in support of the varied causes that won his attention but also about the contemplative life, the life of the Spirit. He began his *magnum opus*[22] and most celebrated contribution to the development of mystical theology, the *Sermons on the Song of Songs*, in the 1130s and continued working on this sequence until his death, leaving Sermon 86 unfinished. In his last years his political activity contracted. His literary output continued, however, resulting in some of his most mature work, including *On Consideration* (ca. 1148–1153), written for the Cistercian Pope Eugenius III. Bernard left a significant body of writing, including treatises, sermons, and over five hundred letters.[23]

Bernard was aware of the tension between his monastic vocation and his public role. Writing to a colleague, the Carthusian prior of Portes, Bernard expressed the tension between his monastic vocation and his public role in his own now-famous words:

> It is time for me to remember myself. May my monstrous life, my bitter conscience, move you to pity. I am the chimæra of my age, neither cleric nor layman. I have kept the habit of a

21. A verdict repeated as recently as 2009. See Brian Patrick McGuire, "Writing about the Difficult Saint: Bernard of Clairvaux and Biography," CSQ 44, no. 4 (2009): 447–61, here 448. Bredero, by contrast, argues that the evaluation of Bernard's role in his own day may have been "somewhat exaggerated," a distortion inspired by the need to defend his external activities in the *Vita* being prepared for his canonization (Bredero, *Between Cult and History*, 8).

22. This is Pranger's designation; see M. B. Pranger, *Bernard of Clairvaux and the Shape of Monastic Thought: Broken Dreams* (Leiden: E. J. Brill, 1994), 22.

23. Casey notes that Leclercq has estimated that about half of the extant manuscripts of Bernard's work are contemporaneous (Casey, "Bernard of Clairvaux, St.," 146, 148).

monk, but I have long ago abandoned the life. I do not wish to tell you what I dare say you have heard from others: what I am doing, what are my purposes, through what dangers I pass in the world, or rather down what precipices I am hurled. If you have not heard, enquire and then, according to what you hear, give your advice and the support of your prayers.[24]

These words were written in about 1150 in the shadow of the failure of the Second Crusade, but the tension ran through Bernard's whole life.[25] While allowing for the possibility of rhetorical flourish, Brian McGuire suggests that Bernard was internally conflicted with regard to his involvement with the world.[26] Adriaan Bredero stresses the need to read this text in its historical context. Bernard, at the time of writing this letter, found himself in "an impossible position" politically: with the failure of the Second Crusade still stinging, he had been chosen to lead a new campaign, a task for which he felt himself ill equipped.[27] If he was internally or psychologically divided, the pressure on him was external, the consequence of his very public life, a life he had, in fact, chosen. Nonetheless the chimæra tag has persisted through history.

4.1.2 Character and Cult

Writing to Goethe in 1802, German philosopher and writer Friedrich Schiller (1759–1805) judged that this self-confessed

24. Letter 250; J326, trans. James and Bredero; SBOp 8:147: *Ego enim quaedam Chimaera mei saeculi, nec clericum gero nec laicum.* James renders *Chimaera mei saeculi* as "a sort of modern chimæra." Bredero's rendering here seems preferable (Bredero, *Between Cult and History*, 188). A chimæra is a monster with a lion's head, goat's body, and serpent's tail.

25. In about 1133, for example, he wrote to Guigo the Carthusian, "Happy are those who during evil times are hidden in the house of the Lord, who under the shadow of his wings are able to await in hope their passing. As for me, unhappy man, naked and poor, it is my lot of labor. An unfledged nestling, I am obliged to spend most of my time out of my nest exposed to the tempests and troubles of the world" (Letter 12; James 13).

26. McGuire, "Writing about the Difficult Saint," 448.

27. For Bredero's discussion of the interpretation of this text, see Bredero, *Between Cult and History*, 186–93.

contradiction between Bernard the monk and Bernard the politician made him simply a charlatan:

> Recently I occupied myself with Saint Bernard and this encounter gave me much pleasure. It might be difficult to find another figure in history who was so wise in worldly ways and yet, at the same time, such a spiritual crook, who through his elevated position, however, could play his role with such dignity. He was the oracle of his days, and dominated these, in spite of the fact—or rather: because of the fact—that he remained a private person and let other persons be in positions of leadership. Popes were his students and kings his creatures. He hated and suppressed all progress as much as he could and favored the greatest stupidity of monks. He himself had only the intellect of a monk and had no other qualities than shrewdness and hypocrisy.[28]

Schiller's judgment is harsh, and he is clearly simply wrong about Bernard's intellectual capacities. But what he has pinpointed is the inherent, pervasive contradiction in Bernard's life between monk and politician.[29]

If the shape of Bernard's life seems contradictory, his character poses a greater challenge. So, for example, Rowan Williams styles Bernard "a maddeningly paradoxical man": "Intolerant and unjust, sometimes politically unscrupulous, with an astonishing confidence in his own authority, and yet also loving and compassionate, reconciling, humble, bitterly aware of the oddity of his own position as a monk wielding vast influence in the world."[30]

28. Translated and quoted in Bredero, *Between Cult and History*, 179.

29. Bredero, *Between Cult and History*, 179. It is worth noting that Schiller talks of a contrast between private and public space, a theme touched on a number of times in the course of this study.

30. Rowan Williams, *The Wound of Knowledge: Christian Spirituality from the New Testament to St. John of the Cross*, 2nd ed. (Cambridge, MA: Cowley Publications, 1991), 118. Jean Leclercq (1911–1993), Bernard's most significant promoter and twentieth-century scholar, reflecting in 1973 on his own journey with Bernard, admitted that "twenty-five years of friendship" had been followed by "a period of distrust" inspired by the negative judgment of

The "problem of Bernard" is one that even predated his death. Bernard was marked for sainthood: the material that would be required for his canonization was being prepared during his lifetime. William of Saint-Thierry began writing material for the *Vita* about 1145, at a time when Bernard's health was poor and his death seemed imminent. William himself died in 1148 with the work unfinished. Ultimately the compilation of this first *Vita* involved another three key players: Geoffrey of Auxerre, Bernard's secretary and the key driver of the project, Raynaud of Foigny, a former secretary, and Arnaud de Bonneval, a Benedictine abbot who knew something of Bernard's work during the papal schism. As Bredero has carefully demonstrated, the context for this work—preparing a case for Bernard's canonization—gave the enterprise a distinctive shape. The *Vita* emphasized Bernard's involvement with church and society (and probably overemphasized his influence), countered criticism, and smoothed out the flaws in his character. Here is, to use Bredero's phrase, the first "cultic evaluation."[31] While the hope of early canonization was thwarted by the death of Pope Eugenius III in 1153, Bernard was canonized in 1174. His cult bloomed vigorously until the Enlightenment.

Thomas Merton began his short introduction to the life of Bernard with a warning: "The enigma of sanctity is the temptation and often the ruin of historians."[32] The reality is, however, that in the post-Enlightenment period, while Roman Catholic apologists clung to his sanctity, historians increasingly dealt harshly with Bernard, particularly in relation to his dealings with Abelard and heretics, and because of his involvement in the Second Crusade. Fortunately, the current situation is quite different. More than half a century of solid critical scholarship has led to a place where

---

historians, then "a time of enthusiasm which was indubitably excessive" (Jean Leclercq, *Bernard of Clairvaux and the Cistercian Spirit*, trans. Claire Lavoie, CS 16 [Kalamazoo, MI: Cistercian Publications, 1976], 5).

31. Bredero, *Between Cult and History*, 18.

32. Merton, *Last of the Fathers*, 23. This short introduction was written to accompany the encyclical letter *Doctor Mellifluous*, issued by Pope Pius XII in 1953 to mark the eight hundredth anniversary of Bernard's death.

there is more fruitful engagement between historians and theologians.[33] The production of a critical edition of Bernard's works (which both included new works and excluded nonauthentic work), together with substantial work on the social, cultural, and intellectual history of the twelfth century itself, underpins a growing corpus of historically sensitive and textually critical studies.[34]

From a theological perspective, as Michael Casey counsels, it is no longer possible to consider Bernard's thinking outside its twelfth-century intellectual and cultural frame.[35] In relation to the subject of humility and public life, historical context is critically important to the interpretation of Bernard's theology. It is, as Bredero points out, a two-way street: if Bernard was politically influential, his own thinking must also have been shaped by his involvement in political affairs.[36]

4.1.3 *Writing and Rhetoric*

Bernard was a writer. In fact, as Wim Verbaal notes, Bernard was "the first Cistercian to make a deliberate choice to write and to publish his writings and not to limit himself to the internal, institutional regulations of the young Order."[37] The fact that he wrote with a personal flavor and that his work circulated widely under his own name does not necessarily sit comfortably with

33. The annual face-to-face meeting of historians and theologians in the context of the Medieval Congress in Kalamazoo, Michigan, has undoubtedly been a major contributor.

34. For an overview of scholarship from 1950 to 1991, see Michael Casey, "Bernard of Clairvaux: Forty Years of Scholarship," in *Saint Bernard of Clairvaux: The Man*, ed. John Stanley Martin (Melbourne: Dept. of Germanic Studies and Russian, University of Melbourne, 1991), 31–45. For a recent summary of biographical issues, see McGuire, "Writing about the Difficult Saint."

35. Casey, "Bernard of Clairvaux, St.," 144; Casey, "Bernard . . . Forty Years of Scholarship," 34.

36. Bredero, *Between Cult and History*, 17.

37. Wim Verbaal, "The Sermon Collection: Its Creation and Edition," in Bernard of Clairvaux, *Sermons for Advent and the Christmas Season*, trans. Irene Edmonds, et al., ed. John Leinenweber, CF 51 (Kalamazoo, MI: Cistercian Publications, 2007), vi–lxiv, here viii.

early Cistercian practice: the earliest documents of the order were all published anonymously, and the founders left no personal writings. Indeed, in the preface to his first published work, *On the Steps of Humility and Pride*, Bernard appears to struggle with the costliness of broader exposure for his writing. There is a particular and obvious risk in going public on the subject of humility, although in this case the broader exposure is initially limited to other Cistercian houses: the work was written in response to the request of a relative, Godfrey of Langres, who was then the abbot of Fontenay, Clairvaux's second foundation. Nonetheless, Bernard makes the leap: "Finally I decided it was better to send you this cargo of words than to seek safety by lying snug in the harbor of silence" (Hum, preface).[38] Bernard has made a choice: he has rewritten the sermons he had already given to his community, extended them, and sent them out to the larger, albeit monastic, world. He has chosen speech over silence, a public presence over anonymity. Verbaal suggests that the question that Bernard faced was fundamental to the monastic vocation: "Does a monk strive only for his personal salvation or does he have obligations towards the world outside the monastery?"[39] There is a further question, however. Is the writer also being called into existence here, the writer who longs, however ambivalently, for an audience?

Bernard was a prolific author, and his works were widely circulated even in his day. And, as McGuire observes, it was "Bernard's talent for writing that brought him out of the monastery."[40] His literary activity made him a public figure. What did this do

---

38. SBOp 3:19; Bernard of Clairvaux, *The Steps of Humility and Pride*, trans. M. Ambrose Conway, CF 13A (Kalamazoo, MI: Cistercian Publications, 1973), 28. Hereafter CF 13A. English translations are also available in *Bernard of Clairvaux: Selected Works*, trans. G. R. Evans (New York: Paulist Press, 1987); and Bernard of Clairvaux, *The Steps of Humility*, trans. George Bosworth Burch (Notre Dame, IN: University of Notre Dame Press, 1963). Ambrose Conway's translation is used unless otherwise noted.

39. In speaking of "personal salvation" Verbaal is, perhaps, neglecting the Benedictine emphasis on the communal nature of the journey toward salvation. The contrast, however, between a focus on the vocation of the cloister and engagement with the world remains (Verbaal, "Sermon Collection," ix).

40. McGuire, "Writing about the Difficult Saint," 449.

to Bernard, and especially to his sense of self? Does his writing reveal the development of a public, literary persona that became Bernard's primary way of being?

In his provocative literary analysis of Bernard's work, M. B. Pranger also notes the astonishingly personal nature of Bernard's writings but claims to observe another contradictory current as well: a growing distance from himself, arising from rhetorical performance:

> I know of no author after Augustine and before Petrarch who has been so unashamedly personal when writing about spiritual matters. But it would be even harder to think of someone whose personal revelations have taken on so ritualized and theatrical a performance as to become increasingly remote in the process.[41]

This is a bold and controversial claim that cannot be settled here. Pranger's fundamental thesis is that Bernard's writing is both subject to and plays against a monastic script. So the iterative, journey-like, woven nature of Bernard's writing mirrors the open, unfinished nature of the monastic project—though this is hardly a new insight. In fact, Pranger's suggestion that monastic life is best characterized by the metaphor of "broken dream" echoes the experience of the desert. Thus for example the preservation of Abba Pambo's deathbed declaration—"I am going to God as one who has not yet begun to serve him"—does indeed signal a celebration of the "broken dream," of failure, in the monastic tradition.[42] From a literary perspective Abba Pambo's speech may well be read as a performance that lacks authenticity, as "ritual complaint,"[43] but theologically the reverse is true. Theologically, it reflects the growth of a profound existential and eschatological humility: the realization that spiritual growth is paradoxically

---

41. Pranger, *Bernard of Clairvaux*, xi.
42. *The Sayings of the Desert Fathers: The Alphabetical Collection*, trans. Benedicta Ward, rev. ed., CS 59 (Kalamazoo, MI: Cistercian Publications, 1984), 197 (Pambo 8).
43. Pranger, *Bernard of Clairvaux*, 23.

marked by an increased sense of the distance between the human and the divine.[44]

What does one make of Bernard's repeated *trepidatio* before his audiences, volubly expressed in the introduction to almost every piece of his writing?[45] Is it rhetorical performance or authentic humility? The question is important here because for Bernard, humility is fundamentally about truthfulness, about authenticity. If he himself was caught, therefore, in a web of rhetorical self-deception, his authority to speak on humility and public life—or indeed any matter—is compromised. There is no doubt, as Leclercq indicates, that Bernard wrote with an eye to style. He utilized his various literary genres—letter, treatise, satire, sermon, etc.—with a learned mastery. His Latin was at once accomplished and imaginative. Leclercq calls Bernard a juggler![46] But Bernard's style, Leclercq argues, was always in the service of his deeper purpose: the persuasive communication of his spiritual experience.[47]

Perhaps so, but the dangers posed by the creation of a literary persona cannot be easily dismissed.[48] How much was Bernard a product of his own discourse? This is an unanswerable question, of course. Pranger's view is that Bernard became precisely this, a product of his own speech. Pranger, however, misunderstands,

---

44. Pranger's literary approach is difficult to engage from a theological perspective. Where does one ground the conversation? Pranger uses the spatial metaphor of the Cistercian monastery (simple austerity set against wild nature) as a sort of controlling idea, but, as one of his reviewers suggests, Pranger has (deliberately) taken on the style of his subject and "has given us what amounts to stream-of-consciousness commentary on stream-of-consciousness commentary" (Alexander Murray, Review of *Bernard of Clairvaux and the Shape of Monastic Thought: Broken Dreams*, by M. B. Pranger, *Journal of Ecclesiastical History* 47, no. 1 [1996]: 149–51, here 151).

45. Leclercq, "General Introduction (2)," 246. From a literary perspective Leclercq suggests that Bernard successfully avoids "the usual commonplaces" and monotony so that each of his prologues is "a little masterpiece."

46. Leclercq, "General Introduction (2)," 249.

47. Leclercq, "General Introduction (2)," 243.

48. Pranger is critical of the Leclercq "school" for "a tendency prematurely to separate feelings and devotion from their rhetorical setting." He wants to retain a tighter relationship between literary form and self-expression, between medium and message (Pranger, *Bernard of Clairvaux*, 9n11).

I think, the significance of text in monastic formation: much of Bernard's writing has the character of *lectio divina*—extended, albeit written, meditations drawing deeply on the Holy Scriptures. This textuality is not necessarily incompatible with authenticity.[49]

The resonances with the equally prolific twentieth-century Cistercian Thomas Merton are instructive here. The publication of Merton's journals, with their highly personal flavor, has not been met with universal acclaim, especially in monastic circles. "Let them write spiritual journals as frank as mine," Merton said to Leclercq in 1966, revealing that one of the things at stake was indeed the whole question of what publication does to the self: is it possible to be truthful (humble) in public?[50] Merton was himself well aware of this risk. In a number of his letters to Leclercq he correlated the renunciation of writing with his desire to deepen his experience of "solitude and obscurity and the humility proper to a true monk."[51] It is hard, perhaps impossible, to be a writer and simultaneously stand naked before God:

> I have stopped writing, and that is a big relief. I intend to renounce it for good if I can live in solitude. I realize that I have

49. Indeed, Leclercq suggests, this immersion in text and the way in which it shapes writing is characteristic of monastic culture. The monastic practice of *lectio*, which includes verbalizing and "ruminating" on the words of Scripture, results in the text being "inscribed" or "digested" into the monk's whole being. This method had a direct influence on the production of new writing through the "phenomenon of reminiscence whereby the verbal echoes so excite the memory that a mere allusion will spontaneously evoke whole quotations and, in turn, a scriptural phrase will suggest quite naturally allusions elsewhere in the sacred books." Leclercq describes these as "hooks" that catch and hold other hooks, thereby creating "the fabric of the whole exposé" (Jean Leclercq, *The Love of Learning and the Desire for God: A Study of Monastic Culture*, trans. Catherine Misrahi, 2nd ed. [New York: Fordham University Press, 1974], 72–74).

50. Thomas Merton to Jean Leclercq, November 18, 1966, in *Survival or Prophecy? The Correspondence of Jean Leclercq and Thomas Merton*, ed. Patrick Hart, MW 17 (Collegeville, MN: Cistercian Publications, 2008), 106.

51. Merton to Leclercq, August 21, 1953, in *Survival or Prophecy?* 28. See also Merton to Leclercq, May 18, 1953; June 3, 1955; November 19, 1959, in *Survival or Prophecy?* 25, 49, 64.

perhaps suffered more than I know from this "writing career." Writing is deep in my nature, and I cannot deceive myself that it will be very easy for me to do without it. At least I can get along without the public and without my reputation! Those are not essentially connected with the writing instinct. But the whole business tends to corrupt the purity of one's spirit of faith. It obscures the clarity of one's view of God and of divine things. It vitiates one's sense of spiritual reality, for as long as one imagines himself to be accomplishing something he tends to become rich in his own eyes. But we must be poor, and live by God alone—whether we write or whatever else we may do. The time has come for me to enter more deeply into that poverty.[52]

Ironically, Merton immediately went on to offer Leclercq a manuscript, material that was later published as *Thoughts in Solitude*. One could imagine Bernard doing likewise.

There is no easy route through this maze of rhetoric and authenticity. In a parallel way, this difficulty reflects the elusive nature of humility itself. Humility, as I have already noted, is a fruit that arises from self-forgetfulness and is never an achievement. Neither, indeed, is authenticity. Bernard is aware of human limits and our capacity for self-deception. If he is a juggler, he is aware that he often drops the balls.

Bernard's corpus is large and diverse. For the purposes of this chapter, an exploration of humility and public life, I have chosen to focus on two key texts: Bernard's treatise *On the Steps of Humility and Pride*, his earliest exposition of a theology of humility, and his letter-treatise *On the Conduct and Office of Bishops*, which takes this theology into the public square. One limitation of this approach is that both are relatively youthful works. I hope to ameliorate this limitation by extending the conversation into a selection of other texts. First, I turn to *On the Steps of Humility and Pride* in order to map Bernard's foundational understanding of humility.

---

52. Merton to Leclercq, August 11, 1955, in *Survival or Prophecy?* 50.

4.2 Bernard and Humility: *On the Steps of Humility and Pride*

On the Steps of Humility and Pride (*Liber de gradibus humilitatis et superbiae*[53]) was Bernard's first published work. He wrote the treatise in the mid-1120s, when he had a solid decade of monastic experience behind him. He had already had to face his own weaknesses and had had sufficient experience of monastic community to have developed a nuanced understanding of the purpose and practice of monastic life. The treatise outlines that understanding by building on the seventh chapter of the Rule of Saint Benedict, the central chapter of what was for the Cistercians a, if not the, core monastic text. Here Bernard is drawing before his audience (initially the brothers of the growing Cistercian reform movement) the wisdom of the monastic tradition that stretches back to Anthony and the Egyptian desert. He assumes knowledge of the Rule; it is the backdrop against which his treatise is written. (It is possible that even his first readers failed to grasp its close relationship to the Rule—hence their complaints that Bernard had "described the steps not of humility but pride."[54])

Bernard's relationship with his source is, though, highly dynamic. The treatise can be divided into two parts.[55] The first (Hum 1.1–9.27) offers a theological framework for understanding both the goal and the nature of the steps of humility. It constitutes an early version of Bernard's theology of humility, one that builds on that offered by the Rule of Saint Benedict. In the second part of the treatise (Hum 10.28–22.56), Bernard intentionally turns Benedict's steps on their head: rather than giving an account of the steps of humility, the way that leads to God, Bernard describes, in vivid and often satirical detail, the steps of pride, the downward path that leads further and further from God. The rationale for this

---

53. SBOp 3:13–59.
54. Hum Retractatio; SBOp 3:15; CF 13A:25.
55. I follow Pennington's schematic outline of the treatise here (M. Basil Pennington, "Introduction," to Bernard of Clairvaux, *The Steps of Humility and Pride*, 1–24, here 15–17).

approach, Bernard says, is his own experience: "I could not very well describe the way up because I am more used to falling down than to climbing." Unlike Benedict, who had the steps of humility "in his heart," Bernard is able only to "tell you what I know myself, the downward path." Bernard claims that by studying this path, "you will find the way up."[56] Reversed, the path becomes the way of humility: it is the same road, says Bernard; only the direction has changed.

This claim is not self-evident. Indeed, one always wishes that there were a different road, one that did not expose one's weaknesses. But here Bernard is an experienced observer of and participant in the monastic project: monastic life is not lived in a different, holier space; the same chronic failures and limits that characterize secular life are found within the monastery walls. The only difference is that the monk has chosen intentionally to walk toward them.[57] There is no route toward God that does not entail a humiliating encounter with human weakness, with the broken or false self. The way of humility is a way of humiliation. Spiritual progress is painfully slow because there is always interplay between grace and nature, between grace and human freedom:[58]

> Your grace is sufficient for me when my own virtue fails. With the foot of grace firmly planted on the ladder of humility, painfully dragging the foot of my own weakness behind me, I should safely mount upward, until, holding fast to the truth, I attained the broad plain of charity [*caritatis*]. . . . Thus I warily enter on the narrow way, step by step safely ascend the steep ladder, and by a kind of miracle climb to the truth, behind the time perhaps, and limping, but still with confidence. . . . Why did I ever desert the truth! If I had not been so lightheaded and stupid as to come down from truth I would

56. Hum 22.57; SBOp 3:59; CF 13A:82.

57. André Louf, *The Way of Humility*, trans. Lawrence S. Cunningham, MW 11 (Kalamazoo, MI: Cistercian Publications, 2007), 11.

58. While Bernard does not use these terms in *The Steps of Humility and Pride*, he is clearly aware of this theological dialectic and the underlying issues. His theological treatise, *On Grace and Free Choice* (*De gratia et libero arbitrio*), dates from the same period of his life (ca. 1128).

not now be faced with the slow and hard climb back to it. Did
I say, "come down"? "Crash down" would be more like it.[59]

The way that leads to God is dependent on grace and subject to
human freedom—and therefore human weakness.

4.2.1 The Fall from Humility: A Phenomenology of Pride

In the well-known second half of the treatise (Hum 10.28–22.56)
Bernard offers a vivid picture of human weakness, a phenomenology of pride, which is psychologically astute.[60] Indeed the
continued popularity of the treatise probably rests on his engaging
and often playful description of the downward steps that characterize the fall from humility. The downward journey begins with
curiosity (*curiositas*), which Bernard describes vividly as a failure
or disorientation of attention:

> The first step of pride is curiosity. How does it show itself?
> You see one who up to this time had every appearance of being
> an excellent monk. Now you begin to notice that wherever he
> is, standing, walking or sitting, his eyes are wandering, his
> glance darts right and left, his ears are cocked. . . . These
> symptoms show his soul has caught some disease. He used
> to watch over his own conduct; now all his watchfulness is
> for others.[61]

Bernard then strengthens his case, using an image taken from the
Song of Songs. The curious man "does not know himself so he
must go forth to pasture his goats [Song 1:7]." The goats are his
"eyes and ears," "the windows through which death creeps into
the soul." With his attention elsewhere his soul begins to starve.[62]

---

59. Hum 9.26; SBOp 3:36; CF 13A:55.
60. I have chosen to examine the latter half of the treatise first, partly
because it is better known but also because it helpfully sets the scene for
Bernard's more theological discourse in the first half of the treatise.
61. Hum 10.28; SBOp 3:38; CF 13A:57.
62. Hum 10.28; SBOp 3:38; CF 13A:57.

This wandering of attention, away from the self, is in striking and deliberate contrast to the picture of the humble monk found at the twelfth step of humility in RB 7. The eyes tell the story. The truly humble monk, wherever he is found, has a bowed head and downcast eyes: he stands in solidarity with the publican before God, aware of his own sinfulness, "humbled in every way" (RB 7.62-66).[63] By contrast Bernard's falling monk begins to look like the Pharisee. It is precisely the wandering of the eyes, his superior "glance" in the direction of his fellow supplicant, that the gospel condemns.

The consequences of curiosity, of wandering eyes, become clearer when Bernard describes the second step of pride, levity of mind (*levitas mentis*):[64]

> The monk who observes others instead of attending to himself will begin before long to see some as his superiors and others as his inferiors; in some he will see things to envy, in others, things to despise. The eyes have wandered and the mind soon follows. It is no longer steadily fixed on its real concerns and is now carried up on the crest of the waves of pride, now down in the trough of envy. One minute the mind is full of envious sadness, the next childishly glad about some excellence he sees in himself. . . . One moment he is sulky and silent except for some bitter remarks; the next sees a full spate of silly chatter. Now he is laughing, now doleful; all without rhyme or reason.[65]

63. The trope of the "downcast eyes" is used in the *Vita Prima* in Arnold of Bonevaux's description of the visit of Pope Innocent II to the monastery at Clairvaux in 1131: "The bishops . . . marveled at the gravity of that congregation, which in this moment of such solemn joy had the eyes of all cast down to the ground [*oculi omnium humi defixi*], never darting around with vapid curiosity [*curiositate*] but with eyelids lowered in prayer, seeing no one yet seen by all" (William of Saint-Thierry, *Vita Prima* 2.6, CCCM 89B: 94). The Latin text is quoted in Ann W. Astell, *Eating Beauty: The Eucharist and the Spiritual Arts of the Middle Ages* (Ithaca, NY: Cornell University Press, 2006), 62n2. The *Vita* is almost certainly playing off Bernard's *The Steps of Humility and Pride* and RB 7 here.

64. SBOp 3:46. *Levitas* is a textual variant here for *levitate animi*. *Levitas* is opposed to the virtue of *gravitas*. Evans translates *levitas mentis* as "light-mindedness," rather than Conway's "levity of mind."

65. Hum 11.39; SBOp 3:46; CF 13A:66.

This passage is an accurate description of the corrosive and chaotic impact of rivalry: the self is completely disoriented, untethered from the secure and humble ground of self-awareness and self-knowledge. The further the monk moves from this ground, the more he travels both from God and from the true self and, indeed, from charity, a compassionate relationship with neighbor. So, step 3 (*inepta laetitia*, "giddiness," "foolish merriment") describes a false joyfulness: the monk who is overly cheerful, plays his audience for a laugh, sniggering and giggling in the silence—all signals of a disconnected self.[66] Step 4 (*iactantia*, "boasting") describes the dangerous path of self-promotion.[67] Step 5 (*singularitas*, "singularity"), identifies the consequential sense of being special, different from others.[68] Step 6 (*arrogantia*, "conceit") observes that others' praise confirms this self-assessment.[69] Step 7 (*praesumptione*, "presumption") recognizes that the self is now at center stage, putting oneself before others, taking first place.[70] Steps 8 (*defensione peccatorum*, "self-justification"[71]) and 9 (*simulata confessione*, "hypocritical confession"[72]) find the monk on the slippery ground of either excusing his own errors or magnifying them in a false pretense of humility. By the tenth step (*rebellione*, "revolt") the monk is in open conflict with his abbot and community.[73] Leaving the monastery is now inevitable. Outside the monastic framework, on step 11 (*libertate peccandi*, "freedom to sin"[74]) and step 12 (*consuetudine peccandi*, "the habit of sinning"[75]), sin—the fulfillment of one's own evil desires—can be freely embraced: God has receded totally from consciousness (as the psalmist says, "the fool says in his heart: There is no God": Ps 13:1).

66. Hum 11.39; SBOp 3:46; CF 13A:66–67.
67. Hum 13.41; SBOp 3:47–48; CF 13A:68–70.
68. Hum 14.42; SBOp 3:48–49; CF 13A:70–71.
69. Hum 15.43; SBOp 3:49–50; CF 13A:71–72.
70. Hum 16.44; SBOp 3:50; CF 13A:72.
71. Hum 17.45; SBOp 3:51; CF 13A:73.
72. Hum 18.46–47; SBOp 3:51–52; CF 13A:73–75.
73. Hum 19.48–49; SBOp 3:53; CF 13A:75–76.
74. Hum 20.50; SBOp 3:53–54; CF 13A:76.
75. Hum 21.51; SBOp 3:54–58; CF 13A:77–78.

Ironically, Bernard observes, freedom from fear is experienced most fully at both the top and bottom of the ladder of humility. One can either effortlessly sin or effortlessly love. Cupidity (*cupiditas*)[76] or desire, understood negatively, pulls from below, while love (*caritas*) energizes the journey to the top.[77] Those who find themselves midcourse, by contrast, experience the strain of being pulled in both directions (Hum 21.51). In accord with Bernard's original image, they climb or limp painfully up the ladder, nudged on by grace yet hampered by weakness. If only, they may now say with Bernard, echoing the second step of pride: "If [only] I had not been so lightheaded [*leviter*] and vain [*inaniter*] as to come down from truth I would not now be faced with the slow and hard climb back to it."[78] Look where *curiositas* leads.

4.2.2 Humility and Truth

This idea of walking either toward or away from truth is central to Bernard's thinking about humility (and pride), and it forms his primary contribution to a theology of humility.[79] This first treatise, however, offers a taste of Bernard's fluid style of doing theology, the way in which he builds on his chosen metaphors and schemes iteratively and flexibly rather than systematically.[80] Over the larger canvas of his whole literary corpus, Bernard continues to develop and refine his understanding of humility. *On the Steps of Humility and Pride*, however, signals Bernard's basic direction or orientation, which does not significantly change even as his theology becomes more nuanced.

The first part of the treatise (1.1–9.27) seeks to map a theology of humility. Bernard develops his theology in two fundamental

---

76. SBOp 3:55. *Cupiditas* here is a negative form of desire or passion, in contrast to *voluntas* (will, free-will, desire), which has a more neutral sense.

77. Hum 21.51; SBOp 3:55; CF 13A:77.

78. Hum 9.26; SBOp 3:36; CF 13A:55.

79. In fact this theme (walking toward or away from truth) connects the two seemingly disconnected parts of the treatise.

80. Leclercq, "General Introduction (2)," 248; Leclercq, "General Introduction (3)," 369.

stages. First (1.1–2.5), he contextualizes the steps of humility: the steps have a goal (truth). Without such a goal no one would be motivated to take this difficult path. This section addresses the question, why humility? Bernard wishes his readers to understand the very real attractiveness of this way. Second (3.6–9.27), Bernard endeavors to explain how it is that the steps of humility lead to "the promised reward of truth."[81] Here Bernard travels over the same ground again but at greater depth and with multiple diversions. In fact, Bernard is beginning to build what is known as his "mystical theology": he places humility in the context of his whole understanding of salvation. If his subject is a lowly one, Bernard's thinking is big.

A synthesis of this big picture assists in understanding Bernard's thinking on humility. His theological framework is both scriptural and trinitarian. He begins with a quotation from the Gospel of John: "I am the Way, the Truth, and the Life" (John 14:6). From this tripartite saying, he builds a structure that elaborates both the purpose and nature of monastic life. Climbing the steps of humility will lead to three steps or degrees[82] of truth: truth in ourselves, truth in our neighbors, and truth in itself.[83] These three degrees are also imaged as three dishes or foods at a banquet: humility as the bread of sorrow and wine of compunction, charity as the milk or oil of love, and contemplation as the solid bread of wisdom. Bernard correlates these three degrees or foods with the work of the three Persons of the Trinity: the Son brings reason to a place of humility, the Holy Spirit draws the will toward love, and the Father reveals and shares his glory through contemplative union.[84] Metaphor builds on metaphor, and the text is woven somewhat loosely, with detours and excursions along the way. But there is coherence, as the following table shows:[85]

---

81. Hum 3.6; SBOp 3:20; CF 13A:34.
82. Bernard uses both terms.
83. Hum 3.6; SBOp 3:20; CF 13A:34.
84. Hum 2.4–5; SBOp 3:19–20; CF 13A:32–33.
85. The table draws on that offered by Pennington, "Introduction," 11.

Person	Operates in	Way of	Metaphor	Degrees of Truth
Son	Intellect or reason (*ratio*)	Humility	Bread of sorrow/ wine of compunction	Knowledge of self/ truth about oneself
Holy Spirit	Will (*voluntas*)	Compassion Charity	Milk and oil of love	Knowledge of neighbor/ truth about others
Father	Soul (*animus*)	Contempla- tion	Solid bread of wisdom	Knowledge of God/ truth in itself

In the masterful opening of the treatise Bernard images humility as *a way* and sets this understanding in its christological foundations. Humility is certainly not the goal of the monastic journey, but it is the vehicle, the necessary instrument of our salvation:

> Before I speak of the different steps of humility—which indeed St Benedict does not ask us to count but to climb—I will try to show what we may expect to find at the top. The toil will be easier if we have the profit before our eyes. Our Lord shows us plainly both the difficulty and the reward of the work. "I am the Way, the Truth, and the Life" [John 14:6]. The way is humility, the goal is truth [*Viam dicit humilitatem, quae ducit ad veritatem*]. The first is the labor, the second the reward.[86]

Significantly, Bernard's starting point here is not ontological humility, creatureliness in view of the Creator. Rather, his concern is with the necessary correlation of humility and enlightenment (walking in "the light of life"). Bernard speaks positively of our highest calling; at the top of what will be an arduous climb, the

---

86. Hum 1.1; SBOp 3:16; CF 13A:1. See Burch: "He calls humility the way which leads to truth. The former is the toil; the latter, the fruit of the toil" (*Steps of Humility*, 123); Evans: "The way, he says, is humility, which leads to truth" (*Bernard of Clairvaux: Selected Works*, 102).

monk will find truth (*veritas*).[87] How can we know that humility is the way? Bernard immediately senses this question in his reader and establishes his case by quoting a further gospel text: "Learn of me for I am meek and humble of heart" (Matt 11:29).

Here Bernard establishes the Christocentric foundation for his whole understanding of humility and, indeed, of the monastic journey. We are humbly to follow the humble Christ.[88] This is the way to both truth and its end, (eternal) life: "He [the Lord] points to himself as an example of humility, a model of meekness. Imitate him and you will not walk in darkness but will have the light of life. What is the light of life but truth that enlightens every man that comes into this world and shows us where the true life is to be found."[89]

Bernard, as Emero Stiegman observes, works from a profoundly optimistic anthropology.[90] Created in the image of God (*imago Dei*), the human person never loses this imprint, the capacity to be "like God." Indeed it is the likeness that exists between creature and Creator that motivates the search or desire for God. In turning away from God, however, the creature falls into "the region of unlikeness": sin disfigures the likeness, pulling the crea-

---

87. Again, *truth*, for Bernard, is more than rational knowledge. As Casey suggests: "It signified the conformity of the created reality with the intention of its Maker" (Michael Casey, *Truthful Living: Saint Benedict's Teaching on Humility* [Leominster, UK: Gracewing, 2001], 29). From this perspective, *enlightenment* seems an appropriate term.

88. Bernard uses the precise text that Terrence Kardong laments is missing from the Rule of Saint Benedict (Terrence G. Kardong, *Benedict's Rule: A Translation and Commentary* [Collegeville, MN: Liturgical Press, 1996], 167).

89. Hum 1.1; SBOp 3:17; CF 13A:29.

90. Emero Stiegman, "Bernard of Clairvaux, William of St. Thierry, the Victorines," in *The Medieval Theologians*, ed. G. R. Evans (Oxford: Blackwell Publishing, 2001), 129–55, here 135. As Stiegman suggests (drawing on McGinn's insight), Bernard "represents what may be the fullest Western realization of 'the anthropological turn,' the conviction that the mystery of the human person is correlated to the mystery of God" (139). In this section I also draw substantially on the summaries of Bernard's anthropology by Charles Dumont, *Pathway of Peace: Cistercian Wisdom according to Saint Bernard*, trans. Elizabeth Connor, CS 187 (Kalamazoo, MI: Cistercian Publications, 1999), 33–35; and Leclercq, "General Introduction (3)," 379–82.

ture farther and farther away from his or her true nature. The spiritual journey then is a journey of intentional return, from unlikeness to likeness, to a place where "inalienable *image*" and "desired *likeness*" are fully reconciled.[91] The reality is, however, that this disjunction, the chasm between our true nature and what we have become, is deeply distressing and painful, and the return difficult. Monasticism is, for Bernard, the preeminent vehicle for this return and reform.[92]

The language of "image and likeness" is admittedly absent in Bernard's early work, including *On the Steps of Humility and Pride*, but his emerging thinking is evident.[93] The chasm between God and self, between grace and nature, truth and untruth, self-knowledge and self-deceit, life and death—or, using Bernard's later terminology, likeness and unlikeness—is real and painful, but it is bridged by a metaphorical ladder, the way of humility. At the top of the ladder, Bernard offers a vivid image of God "calling from his lofty station and crying to those who seek him," words not of harsh judgment but of encouragement:

> "Come to me all you who desire me and eat your fill of my fruits." "Come to me all you who labor and I will refresh you." He says: "Come!" Where? "To me, the Truth." How? "By humility." For what? "And I will refresh you." What is this refreshment which Truth promises to those who climb and gives when they gain the top? Is it perhaps love [*caritas*] itself?[94]

Here, of course, Bernard finds himself in full agreement with Benedict: by ascending the steps of humility the monk will "arrive at that perfect love of God [*caritatem Dei*] which casts out fear" (RB 7.67).

---

91. Leclercq, "General Introduction (3)," 381; Dumont, *Pathway of Peace*, 33–35. The late *Sermons on the Song of Songs* elucidate Bernard's theology of image and likeness in its mature form.

92. Dumont, *Pathway of Peace*, 36.

93. See Emero Stiegman, "An Analytical Commentary," in Bernard of Clairvaux, *On Loving God*, CF 13B (Kalamazoo, MI: Cistercian Publications, 1995), 45–195, here 63.

94. Hum 2.3; SBOp 3:18; CF 13A:31–32.

If Bernard's anthropology is optimistic, so is his eschatological vision. The language of judgment enunciated in the desert is certainly present in this treatise, but it has a gentler feel. For Bernard, judgment is the servant of a significant and positive goal: truth.[95] For Bernard, as for Benedict, this is at least a partly realized eschatology. Bernard is optimistic about the possibility of experiencing truth in this life, even if it is inevitably fleeting. In his tripartite scheme, the two parts of the human soul, reason (*ratio*) and will (*voluntas*), are perfected by the operations of or union with the Son and the Holy Spirit, thereby opening the soul up to the final step or degree: union with the Father, a form of contemplative "knowing" where "they are carried up to the hidden home of truth itself."[96]

In *On the Steps of Humility and Pride*, truth is the central hinge on which everything else hangs, with truth understood as originating in the very nature of God. Christ is indeed embodied truth: his is the voice of Truth that calls from the top of the ladder. In fact, as Bernard explains in Letter 18 (J19), which dates from the same period of his life, knowledge of the truth and therefore of God is only possible when the heart as well as the mind seeks to return to the source of our being. We are blind and ignorant "exiles" because we have failed to keep God (truth) in view. Without this God-orientation the objects of our love prove illusory ("nothing") and existence meaningless ("reduced to nothing"). The return begins "by faith in God and desire for him" and culminates in "understanding and love," which are for Bernard two aspects of truth or "two arms of the soul": "knowledge of and delight in truth."[97] For Bernard to find or to be found by truth is an ultimately joyful experience.

---

95. The final sections of the treatise (Hum 22.52–56) are an exhortation to pray for those who are lost or who have fallen along the monastic journey. Bernard never gives up hope in God's gracious mercy.

96. Hum 8.23; SBOp 3:35; CF 13A:53. Bernard's mystical thought is not separate from the rest of his theology. As Leclercq observes, Bernard never separates the "moral, ascetical, and mystical life." The tripartite scheme of the *Steps* in fact incorporates all three (see Leclercq, "General Introduction (3)," 384).

97. Letter 18.1–3; J19; SBOp 7:66–68. I am indebted to Dumont (and Merton behind him) for making the connection with Letter 19 (Dumont, *Pathway of Peace*, 74–75).

In *On the Steps of Humility and Pride*, Bernard writes that attaining the "knowledge of and delight in truth," or "understanding and love," requires cooperation between the human person and God. Both reason (*ratio*) and will (*voluntas*), the two parts of the human soul (*animus*), are involved in this process, which Bernard has worked into his trinitarian scheme. It is the incarnate Son, he argues, who enables right judgment (in the sense of truthful discernment):

> The Son of God, the Word and Wisdom of the Father, mercifully assumed to himself human reason [*ratio*], the first of our powers. He found it oppressed by the flesh, held captive by sin, blinded by ignorance, distracted by outward things. He raised it by his might, taught it by his wisdom, drew it to things interior. More wonderfully still, he delegated to it his own power of Judge. To judge is the proper act of Truth, and in this it shared when out of reverence for the Word to which it is joined, it became accuser, witness and judge against itself.[98]

The first fruit of this "union of the Word and reason" is humility—the truth about oneself. As John Sommerfeldt observes, humility, understood here as a form of knowledge (of the self), is accomplished by means of reason (*ratio*).[99] George Burch concurs, arguing from Letter 393 (J217) that for Bernard, humility "is a kind of consideration" and therefore "a function of the reason, not the will."[100] So Bernard says, "Humility has two feet: appreciation [*considerationem*] of divine power and consciousness of personal weakness."[101]

---

98. Hum 7.21; SBOp 3:32; CF 13A:48–49. "It is truth's task to judge. That is why, out of reverence for the Word to which it is united, human reason becomes its own accuser, witness, and judge" (Evans, *Bernard of Clairvaux: Selected Works*, 117).

99. John R. Sommerfeldt, *The Spiritual Teachings of Bernard of Clairvaux: An Intellectual History of the Early Cistercian Order*, CS 125 (Kalamazoo, MI: Cistercian Publications, 1991), 53–55.

100. George Bosworth Burch, "Introduction: An Analysis of Bernard's Epistemology," in Bernard of Clairvaux, *The Steps of Humility* (Notre Dame, IN: University of Notre Dame Press, 1963), 1–117, here 53.

101. Letter 393.3; J217.3; SBOp 8:367.

It is only reason transformed by grace, however, by "union with the Word," that is able to attain humility. Without the intervention of grace, reason is "oppressed," "captive," "blinded," and "distracted."[102] The incarnate Word, the Second Person of the Trinity, raises and teaches reason and draws it into himself (*introrsum trahens*[103]), so that reason is now able to judge with truth—that is, from the perspective of the Son, the embodiment of truth. It is Christ who enables us to see the truth about ourselves, that is, to judge rightly. The encounter with Christ offers a mirror to the self: "When in the light of Truth men know themselves and so think less of themselves it will certainly follow that what they loved before will now become bitter to them. They are brought face to face with themselves and blush at what they see. Their present state is no pleasure to them. They aspire to something better and at the same time realize how little they can rely on themselves to achieve it. It hurts them and they find some relief in judging themselves severely."[104] Here Bernard is in full agreement with the Augustinian definition of humility that he has quoted early in the treatise: "Humility is a virtue by which a man has a low opinion of himself because he knows himself well."[105] In Bernard's thinking, humility is a virtue that has arisen from taking a particular journey, the humiliating journey of facing the truth about the self.[106]

102. Hum 7.21; SBOp 3:32; CF 13A:49.
103. Hum 7.21; SBOp 3:32; CF 13A:49.
104. Hum 5.18; SBOp 3:29; CF 13A:45.
105. Hum 1.2; SBOp 3:17; CF 13A:30.
106. Bernard's use of the vocabulary of virtue reflects its embeddedness in the theological discourse of his time. As Evans indicates, and in line with medieval thought, Bernard understood virtue as a "power," a disposition that has become an ingrained habit (*habitus*). Evans, *Bernard of Clairvaux*, 135–36. While the source of this power or virtue is divine (see Bernard of Clairvaux, *Five Books on Consideration: Advice to a Pope* 5.10, trans. John D. Anderson and Elizabeth T. Kennan, CF 37 [Kalamazoo, MI: Cistercian Publications, 1976]), virtue requires the human cooperation of the will (see below, section 4.2.6) Bernard's most extensive discourse on virtue can be found in *On Consideration*. Book 1 includes an exposition of the classical virtues of prudence, fortitude, justice, and temperance. It is notable that Bernard never conflates humility and temperance; neither does he offer a definitive scheme of virtues.

4.2.3 The Birth of Compassion: Humility and Love

The journey does not stop here, however. If humility is seen only through the lens of Augustine's definition, there is a danger of settling for a primarily negative view: humility as essentially "self-loathing."[107] That is not Bernard's intention. For Bernard, the divine likeness is never totally eradicated, and indeed it is this understanding that drives the journey home from "unlikeness" to "likeness." In Bernard's three-stepped, trinitarian scheme, this truthful assessment of the self, if pursued to its end, gives birth to compassion:

> Love of truth makes [men] hunger and thirst after justice and conceive a deep contempt for themselves. They are anxious to exact from themselves full satisfaction and real amendment. They admit that to make satisfaction is beyond their own powers—when they have done all that is commanded them they acknowledge that they are still unprofitable servants. They fly from justice to mercy, by the road Truth shows them: "Blessed are the merciful for they shall obtain mercy." They look beyond their own needs to the needs of their neighbors and from the things they themselves have suffered they learn compassion [compati]: they have come to the second degree of truth.[108]

Compassion here, as Charles Dumont notes, should be understood as literally *cum-passio*, "to suffer with." Compassion in fact places one on the same ground as the other. As Dumont says, "Compassion is first and foremost a sign of the love which makes equal the persons who love one another."[109] One could think of

---

107. This is Kitchen's interpretation of Bernard (John Kitchen, "Bernard of Clairvaux's *De Gradibus Humilitatis et Superbiae* and the Postmodern Revisioning of Moral Philosophy," in *Virtue and Ethics in the Twelfth Century*, ed. István P. Bejczy and Richard G. Newhauser, Brill's Studies in Intellectual History [Leiden and Boston: Brill, 2005], 95–117, here 98).

108. Hum 5.18; SBOp 3:29–30; CF 13A:45–46. See Evans: "This is the second step of truth, to look beyond one's own needs to the needs of one's neighbors, and to know how to suffer with them in their troubles" (*Bernard of Clairvaux: Selected Works*, 115).

109. Dumont, *Pathway of Peace*, 70.

compassion here as arising from solidarity with the humiliated.[110] Humanly speaking this is impossible, Bernard observes: again it is a joint project dependent on grace, on the inpouring of divine love. This movement from justice to mercy, he argues, is the work of the Third Person of the Trinity:

> The Holy Spirit lovingly visited the second power, the will [*voluntas*]; he found it rotten with the infection of the flesh, but already judged by reason. Gently he cleansed it, made it burn with affection, made it merciful until, like a skin made pliable with oil it would spread abroad the heavenly oil of love even to its enemies. The union of the Holy Spirit with the human will give[s] birth to charity [*caritas*].[111]

It is worth noting here that this anointing of the Spirit, and the birth of *caritas*, have communal implications. Bernard's focus here is less on the individual, the transformation of the self, than on the transformation of the self-in-community, that is, the healing of relations with the other.

4.2.4 Two Types of Humility: Cold and Warm

In his later writings, Bernard understands these two movements, in the reason and the will, as different types of humility. The critical text here is a passage from Sermon 42 from *On the Song of Songs*.[112] Bernard begins by comparing the fragrance of nard with the fragrance of humility. He is reflecting on the words of

---

110. Kitchen views this identification negatively, arguing that the neighbor simply becomes "a kind of second self," so that otherness is dissolved. Taking up the criteria suggested by Wyschogrod's moral philosophy, this "denial of alterity," he argues, renders Bernard's thinking "inadequate" for the conduct of "moral discourse and practice" (Kitchen, "Bernard of Clairvaux's *De Gradibus Humilitatis et Superbiae*," 100–105). Chap. 5 considers the question of otherness and compassion and argues a contrary position.

111. Hum 7.21; SBOp 3:32; CF 13A:49.

112. Bernard of Clairvaux, *Sermons on the Song of Songs*, trans. Kilian Walsh and Irene Edmonds, 4 vols., CF 4, 7, 31, 40 (Kalamazoo, MI: Cistercian Publications, 1971–1980).

the bride, "While the king was on his couch, my nard gave forth its fragrance" (Song 1:12), which Bernard reads as an obedient and humble response to being reproved or rebuked:

> How good the fragrance of humility that ascends from the valley of tears, that permeates all places within reach, and perfumes even the royal couch with its sweet delight. The nard is an insignificant herb, said by those who specialize in the study of plants to be warm in nature. Hence it seems to be fittingly taken in this place for the virtue of humility, but aglow with the warmth of holy love [*sancti amoris*].[113]

Bernard proceeds to explain this refinement in his understanding of humility:

> I say this because there is a humility inspired and inflamed by charity [*caritas*], and a humility begotten in us by truth but devoid of warmth. This latter depends on our knowledge, the former on our affections. For if you sincerely examine your inward dispositions in the light of truth, and judge them unflatteringly for what they are, you will certainly be humiliated by the baseness that this true knowledge reveals to you, though you perhaps as yet cannot endure that others, too, should see this image.[114]

These two understandings have been variously called cognitive and conative humility,[115] or cognitive and affective humility.[116] It is the "inpouring of love" that allows the movement from a cold, rational understanding of the humiliating truth about oneself to a warm, affective, and ultimately liberating reality where one is no longer afraid to be known:

> So far it is truth that compels your humility, it is as yet untouched by the inpouring of love [*amoris infusione*]. But if you

---

113. SC 42.6; SBOp 2:36; CF 7:214.
114. SC 42.6; SBOp 2:36–37; CF 7:214.
115. Burch, "Bernard's Epistemology," 49.
116. Kitchen, "Bernard of Clairvaux's *De Gradibus Humilitatis et Superbiae*," 99.

were so moved by a love of that truth which, like a radiant light, so wholesomely discovered to you the reality of your condition, you would certainly desire, as far as in you lies, that the opinions of others about you should correspond with what you know of yourself. I say, as far as in you lies, because it is often inexpedient to make known to others all that we know about ourselves, and we are forbidden by the very love of truth and the truth of love to attempt to reveal what would injure another.[117]

Bernard's distinction between cognitive and affective humility ultimately derives from the development of his Christology. Bernard understands that at the foundation of a Christian understanding of humility is the humility of Christ. This is a humility motivated by love.

4.2.5 The Humility of God

Bernard first explores the relationship between humility and the incarnation in *On the Steps of Humility and Pride*. For Bernard, Christ offers the pattern for growth in compassion for neighbor. And he offers a daring idea: Christ "*learned* mercy."[118] For Bernard the incarnation involves a complete embrace of the human condition. The Son relinquished impassibility in order fully to experience human suffering:

> The blessed God, the blessed Son of God, in that form in which he did not think it robbery to be equal with the Father, was without doubt impassible before he emptied himself, taking on the form of a slave. Thus he had no experience of misery and subjection; he did not know by experience mercy and

---

117. SC 42.6; SBOp 2:37; CF 7:214–15. The phrase "by the very love of truth and the truth of love" is playful in Latin: *veritatis caritate et caritatis veritate*.
118. Hum 3.7; SBOp 3:23; CF 13A:38. Bernard understands that this is a contentious claim but makes a distinction between what Christ "knew from all eternity by his divine knowledge" and what "he now began in time to learn by human experience" (Hum 3.10). For a discussion of Bernard's theology of the incarnation, see Dumont, *Pathway of Peace*, 69–75.

obedience. He knew by the knowledge natural to him, but not by experience. He assumed a state that was not only less than what is his by right, but even a little less than that of the angels; for they too are impassible, but by grace, not by nature. Lower still he came to take our form, in which he could do what he could not do before, suffer and be subject to authority and learn by experience the mercy of a fellow-sufferer and the obedience of a fellow-subject.[119]

The consequence of this self-abasement is that we can now "go with confidence to the throne of grace" because we will meet there one who has suffered with us. Bernard knows that he is entering risky ground:[120]

When I say he became merciful I am not speaking of the mercy that was his in the happiness of eternity; but of the mercy that sprang from sharing in our misery. The work of his tender love had its beginning in his eternal mercy, its completion in the mercy shown in his humanity. All could have been done by the eternal mercy, but it would have failed somewhat in satisfying us. Both kinds of mercy were needed, but the latter is more in harmony with our condition. It was conceived with the delicacy of supreme tenderness. Could we have even imagined the infinite mercy if we had not seen it springing from one who shared our misery? In the impassibility of eternity he had an infinite compassion for us, but we could never have fully realized it except for the Passion we saw him suffering.[121]

The incarnation enables us to truly grasp God's mercy. By the time Bernard writes Sermon 42 in *On the Song of Songs* (sometime

---

119. Hum 3.9; SBOp 3:23; CF 13A:37–38.
120. Bernard's correction of a quotation in the *Retractatio*, while ostensibly about a misquotation of Scripture, is, perhaps, an indication that he knows he is on difficult theological ground. Bernard endeavors to distinguish the two natures of Christ, divine and human, carefully so that he can attribute the experience of misery to his earthly life: "His humanly acquired knowledge of the miseries of this life had its beginning in the experience of the limitations of human nature" (Hum 3.12; SBOp 3:25; CF 13A:40).
121. Hum 3.12; SBOp 3:25–26; CF 13A:40–41.

after 1138), he is more secure and confident, linking divine humility with divine freedom:

> Convicted by the light of truth then, a man may judge himself of little worth, but you know this is far from the equivalent of a spontaneous association with the lowly that springs from the gift of love [*caritatis*]. Necessity compels the former, the latter is of free choice [*voluntatis*]. "He emptied himself, taking the form of a servant," and so gave us the pattern of humility. He emptied himself, he humbled himself, not under constraint of an assessment of himself but inspired by love [*caritate*] for us.[122]

Bernard makes it clear that Christ is aware of the truth about himself: "Though he could appear abject and despicable in men's eyes, he could not judge himself to be so in reality, because he knew who he was. It was his will [*voluntate*], not his judgment, that moved him to adopt a humble guise that he knew did not represent him; though not unaware that he was the highest, he chose to be looked on as the least."[123] So Bernard is able to return, more securely this time, to the text from the Gospel of Matthew that he had used in *On the Steps of Humility and Pride*, this time with his distinction between reason and will assisting him to explain the troublesome differentiation between human and divine humility:

> And so we find him saying, "Learn from me, for I am gentle and humble in heart." He said "in heart"; in the affection of the heart, which signifies the will [*voluntate*], and a decision arising from the will excludes compulsion.[124] You and I truly know that we deserve disgrace and contempt, that we deserve the worst treatment and the lowest rank, that we deserve punishment, even the whip;[125] but not he. Yet he experienced all these things because he willed it; he was humble in heart,

122. SC 42.7; SBOp 2:37; CF 7:215.
123. SC 42.7; SBOp 2:37; CF 7:215.
124. Or necessity.
125. One might say that, unlike Christ, we deserve *humiliation*.

humble with that humility that springs from the heart's love, not that which is exacted by truthful reasoning.[126]

This is the only humility really worth the name, a humility that arises freely from love, humble love.

Bernard then holds up a picture of humility "aglow with love," which recalls the shape of humble love in the life of Christ, "who under love's inspiration emptied himself, under love's inspiration was made lower than the angels, under love's inspiration was obedient to his parents, under love's inspiration bowed down under the Baptist's hands, endured the weakness of the flesh, and became liable to death, even the ignominious death of the cross."[127] Bernard's direction is becoming clear here: humility "aglow with love" lowers itself, submits before another. Humility, in fact, is an attribute of love. So how does the monk imitate this pattern, this way of humility?

4.2.6 Assenting to Grace: The Practice of Obedience and the Conversion of the Will

For Bernard, this way of humility is a function of the will. One needs to face and accept the humiliating truth about oneself: "If you feel humiliated by that inescapable sense of unworthiness implanted by the Truth that examines both heart and mind in the very being of one who is attentive, try to use your will and make a virtue of necessity, because there is no virtue without the will's cooperation."[128]

Moreover, this embrace of the truth about oneself must be manifest. There should be integrity between one's interior and exterior life. It is all very well, Bernard says, to come, through the use of reason, to a sense of one's own unworthiness, but then to go

126. SC 42.7; SBOp 2:37; CF 7:215.
127. SC 42.8; SBOp 2:38; CF 7:216.
128. SC 42.8; SBOp 2:38; CF 7:216. Note here the relationship between virtue and human cooperation. Bernard's view of virtue here seems to be a combination of what is generally called grace and works. The primary work required, though, is simply the consent of the will.

about hiding this truthful assessment is another form of resistance to truth, indeed a form of disobedience to God. Integrity, truthfulness, requires that you not "appear externally in any way different from what you discover in your heart."[129] The challenge is to get the will to "cooperate," and for Bernard, as for the whole monastic tradition before him, the surest way is through obedience:

> You must rather submit to God and let your will be docile to the Truth; and more than docile, even dedicated. . . . It counts for little, however, that you are submissive to God, unless you be submissive to every human creature for God's sake, whether it be the abbot as first superior or to the other officers appointed by him. I go still further and say: be subject to your equals and inferiors. . . . If you seek an unblemished righteousness, take an interest in the man of little account, defer to those of lesser rank, be of service to the young.[130]

Obedience, submitting to the other, is the closest we can get to the pattern of Christ. If we wish to imitate his humility, the surest means is to lower ourselves, as he lowered himself.

This whole passage resonates with Bernard's description of monastic life in a letter he wrote (ca. 1138) to the monks of Saint Jean-d'Aulps:

> Our place is the bottom [*abiectio*], is humility, is voluntary poverty, obedience, and joy in the Holy Spirit. Our place is under a master, under an Abbot, under a rule, under discipline. Our place is to cultivate silence, to exert ourselves in fasts, vigils, prayers, manual work and, above all, to keep that "more excellent way" which is the way of charity; and furthermore to advance day by day in these things, and to persevere in them until the last day.[131]

Significantly, though, in Sermon 42, Bernard's understanding of submission extends beyond compliance with monastic hierarchi-

---

129. SC 42.8; SBOp 2:38; CF 7:216.
130. SC 42.8–9; SBOp 2:38; CF 7:217.
131. Letter 142.1; J151.1; SBOp 7:340.

cal order. It is not law but freedom that is the underlying motivation. It is the "more excellent way." So, like Christ, the monk will seek out "the man of little account," lower himself even before those of lesser rank, and serve even the young.[132]

Cold humility, arising from "truthful reasoning," is not the end, not the goal, but simply a step, and a limited one at that, in the journey toward warm humility, the humility infused with love. The journey from cold to warm humility requires the cooperation of will, which is what the practice of monastic obedience is intended to support and which in turn enables "the infusion of grace." God can work in us only with our permission. Paradoxically, freely chosen submission to God opens the way to a more expansive experience of freedom. Through it one takes on, as Bernard says, "the good odor of Christ." Humility is then experienced as free, spontaneous, fervent, warm, fruitful, and enduring.[133] Humble love flows. In the language Bernard uses elsewhere, the monk has journeyed from "unlikeness to likeness."

The humility that is inspired by love is characterized by stability: "The bride's humility is freely embraced, it is fruitful and it is forever. Its fragrance is destroyed neither by reprimand nor praise."[134] The self is interiorly secure, no longer tossed around by the opinions of others. The danger of crashing down the steps of pride has abated—momentarily. Humility here is a light, not a heavy, burden.[135]

132. SC 42.9; SBOp 2.39; CF 7:217.
133. SC 42.9; SBOp 2:39; CF 7:217.
134. SC 42.9; SBOp 2:39; CF 7:217.
135. As Rowan Williams observes, John the Short makes a similar point in distinguishing between the "light burden" of "self-accusation" and the "heavy burden" of "self-justification" (see *Sayings*, 90 [John the Dwarf, 21]). This distinction, Williams suggests, initially appears counterintuitive but is in fact entirely consonant with the understanding of the self in the desert tradition: "Self-justification is the heavy burden, because there is no end to carrying it; there will always be some new situation where we need to establish our position, dig the trench for the ego to defend. . . . Self-accusation, honesty about our failings, is a light burden because whatever we have to face in ourselves, however painful is the recognition, however hard it is to feel at times that we have to start all over again, we know that the burden is

Bernard thus offers a nuanced theology of humility. For him humility forms the very foundations of spiritual growth. Human flourishing is grounded paradoxically in the meeting of God and humility. This is in stark contrast to modern visions of the development of the self as being grounded in self-esteem. Since we are created in the image of God, the human vocation becomes a journey toward the recovery of the divine likeness imprinted in us. Humility is both the way of return to our divine source and a fruit of this journey. The humiliating encounter with our weakness, with our ontological limits, with the truth about ourselves, is a necessary part of this journey. God's self-identification with our weakness, through the incarnation of Christ, however, mediates the loving mercy that can transform this experience from a cold to a warm humility. When humiliation is met by love, humble love is born. Humble love, indeed, is the very nature of God.

What happens to this understanding of humility, forged initially in a monastic environment, when Bernard moves, or thinks, beyond the cloister?

4.3 Bernard and the World

Martha Newman notes that "some twenty-nine Cistercian monks were elected as bishops during Bernard's lifetime, seven more became cardinals, and one became pope."[136] No longer cloistered, these monks turned bishops were fully engaged in public life: caring for the laity within their dioceses, presiding at councils, judging ecclesiastical cases, managing property, collecting tithes, settling disputes, and maintaining relations with secular rulers. Bernard, as his correspondence shows, was often a key player in the promotion of Cistercian candidates to episcopal office. While he himself refused such appointment, he was deeply engaged in both ecclesiastical and secular politics, which were themselves

---

already known and accepted by God's mercy" (Rowan Williams, *Silence and Honey Cakes: The Wisdom of the Desert* [Oxford: Lion Publishing, 2003], 47–48).

136. Martha G. Newman, "Contemplative Virtues and the Active Life of Prelates," in Bernard of Clairvaux, *On Baptism and the Office of Bishops* (Kalamazoo, MI: Cistercian Publications, 2004), 11–36, here 19.

deeply entwined in this period. Even though Clairvaux remained his home, Bernard spent a great deal of his time outside his monastery participating in councils, mediating disputes, and promoting various people and causes. What was happening here? Why were monks so visibly active in public life?

4.3.1 The Virtuous Christian Community

To make sense of all this activity requires an understanding of the reforming drive of the Cistercian movement. While this movement began with the internal reform of monasticism, the Cistercian vision soon extended beyond the monastery wall.

The monastic reform movements of the eleventh and early twelfth centuries commonly stood against both "the world" and "the worldly church." Peter Damian (1007–1072), for example, was critical of both ecclesiastical corruption and the Gregorian reforms of the mid-eleventh century, which he considered "dangerously secular in character, coercive and violent."[137] As Williams suggests, with Peter Damian came a recovery of something of the original protest flavor of monasticism.[138] With the Cistercians, however, as Martha Newman has cogently argued, the traditional monastic act of social withdrawal functioned quite differently. It was, she argues, "less an attempt to avoid all social entanglements than an effort to differentiate the social role of monks from that of the secular clergy or the knightly aristocracy."[139]

In fact, Cistercian writers played with a range of different models and metaphors to conceptualize the place of the monk and monastery in society.[140] Following Gregory the Great, for example, Bernard used the triad of Noah, Daniel, and Job to signify

137. Williams, *Wound of Knowledge*, 117.
138. Williams, *Wound of Knowledge*, 117.
139. Martha G. Newman, *The Boundaries of Charity: Cistercian Culture and Ecclesiastical Reform, 1098–1180* (Stanford, CA: Stanford University Press, 1996), 2.
140. Newman, *Boundaries of Charity*, 109–15.

monastic, clerical, and lay orders of the church.[141] While ambiguities and tensions arose particularly in relation to the ranking of bishops, the critical point was that the monk had a place in the social order. Monastic withdrawal here was not primarily protest. Neither, it should be noted, did Cistercians view themselves as "society's professional penitents," as had been the case for a number of monastic communities in the tenth and eleventh centuries.[142] Like Gregory, the Cistercians viewed the monastery as a model Christian community and as a highly appropriate training ground for its leaders.[143]

There is no doubt, though, that Bernard considered that the monastery or cloister (*claustum*) offered the preeminent route to salvation. He imagined Clairvaux as a shortcut to the heavenly Jerusalem, an earthly paradise where, by the way of humility, the monk was able to experience both the unity of fraternal community (*caritas*) and union with God (contemplation).[144] Writing to the bishop of Lincoln about a young canon who had entered Clairvaux rather than continue his pilgrimage to Jerusalem, Bernard said,

> Your Philip has found a short cut to Jerusalem and has arrived there very quickly. . . . And this, if you want to know, is Clairvaux. She is the Jerusalem united to the one in heaven by whole-hearted devotion, by conformity of life, and by a certain spiritual affinity. . . . He has chosen to dwell here because he has found, not yet to be sure the fulness of vision, but certainly the hope of that true peace, "the peace of God which surpasses all our thinking."[145]

The monastery was a sort of spiritual hothouse, where spiritual progress might be made with greater focus and perhaps, despite

---

141. For an extended study of Bernard's tripartite scheme, see John R. Sommerfeldt, *Bernard of Clairvaux on the Spirituality of Relationship* (New York: Newman Press, 2004).

142. Newman, *Boundaries of Charity*, 2.

143. Newman, *Boundaries of Charity*, 113–15, 155–56.

144. Sommerfeldt, *Bernard of Clairvaux on the Spirituality of Relationship*, 13–16; Bredero, *Between Cult and History*, 267–75.

145. Letter 64; J67; SBOp 7:157–58.

its hardships, with greater ease, removed as it was from the "cares of the world." In fact, as Newman demonstrates, the Cistercians viewed themselves as a spiritual elite—a self-assessment that not surprisingly led to resentment among other monastic orders.[146] From this place of differentiation the Cistercians offered to both the broader church and to the world a model of virtuous Christian community intended to inspire both spiritual and social reformation. It is not surprising, then, that Bernard's writing often feels as though it is written with an eye to a large audience: there is a sense in which the monastery and its program is on view, its concerns thought about in the context of a wider frame. Bernard engaged with life beyond the monastery wall because salvation mattered; individuals, the church, society—all mattered to God.[147]

So, for example, while among Cistercian writers there is a resurgence in individual, interior interpretations of the bridal imagery of the Song of Songs, the understanding that had dominated the early medieval period of the bridegroom Christ and his bride the church was still used. Bernard, as Newman observes, often "slid" between bride as soul and bride as church, sometimes with no indication as to which he intended.[148] In Sermon 57, for instance, as he interprets the invitation of the lover or bridegroom, Bernard makes the case that the bride is both church and soul. He begins by urging the individual to be alert to the presence of God, to the

146. Newman, *Boundaries of Charity*, 136–39. The most famous tension in this regard was between Cistercians and Cluniacs. Peter the Venerable accused the Cistercians of pride: "But you, you alone in all the world are truly holy monks; all others are false and ruined. You alone are established following the interpretation of the Rule, yet you wear a habit of insolent color, and by displaying a splendor among the black, you distinguish yourself from all other monks" (quoted in Newman, *Boundaries of Charity*, 136). Singularity, step 5 of Bernard's ladder of pride, resonates here. The "insolent color" here is grey. Cistercian habits were made from undyed wool, so that they were often called "grey monks" and, later, "white monks." The Benedictines of the time were known as "black monks" because of the color of their habits.

147. For example, SC 46.1: "The better thing is to remain at ease and be with Christ; but necessity drives one forth to help those who are to be saved" (SBOp 2:56; CF 7:241).

148. Newman, *Boundaries of Charity*, 107–8.

bridegroom's knocking on the door. He then refers to the common understanding that the bride is an image of the church, drawing together the individual soul and the community of the church: "These words are not so applied to the Church as to exclude any one of us, who together are the Church, from a share in its blessings. For in this respect we are all, universally and without distinction, called to possess the blessings as our heritage."[149]

The call to divine union is for all persons, for every soul that constitutes the church. It is this "equation between the Church and the individual," Newman suggests, that explains the Cistercian vision of Christian (and social) unity: "If each Christian sought contact with the divine through *caritas*, then all Christians would be joined in a shared goal and by the shared virtues that led towards the love of God."[150] While this pattern was most evident in the monastery—indeed the monastery is the model—Bernard believed that all Christian society should strive toward this ideal.

The energy that motivates the movement from individual union to communal unity is in fact embedded in divine encounter. Tasting divine love, contemplative union, Bernard says later in the same sermon, actually inspires action, since the recipient of this grace is driven to seek the welfare of other souls:

> It is characteristic of true and pure contemplation that when the monk is ardently aglow with God's love, it is sometimes so filled with zeal and the desire to gather to God those who will love him with equal abandon that it gladly foregoes contemplative leisure for the endeavor of preaching. And then, with its desire at least partially satisfied, it returns to its leisure with an eagerness proportionate to its successful interruption, until, refreshed again with the food of contemplation, it hastens to add to its conquest with renewed strength and experienced zeal.[151]

This delicate alternation between contemplation and action is at the center of all Bernard's advice to those in public office.

149. SC 57.3; SBOp 2:120–21; CF 31:97–98.
150. Newman, *Boundaries of Charity*, 108.
151. SC 57.9; SBOp 2:124–25; CF 31:103.

If the taste of God inspires action, so does the taste of dissension, the absence of unity. Writing to the people of Rome, who have rebelled against their bishop, Pope Eugenius III, Bernard draws on Pauline body imagery to explain the impact of their actions on the church and each of its members:

> The trouble is in the head, and for this reason there is no member of the body so small or so insignificant as not to be affected by it, not even myself. This very great trouble affects even me although I am the least of all, because what affects the head cannot but affect the body of which I am a member. When the head is suffering does not the tongue cry out for all the members of the body that the head is in pain, and do not all the members of the body confess by means of the tongue that the head is theirs and the pain too?[152]

Sommerfeldt suggests that this passage represents "an accurate description of Bernard's role in the early twelfth-century Church and in the society of the time." He was a "tongue," Sommerfeldt claims, whose capacity for social analysis enabled him to articulate "the ideals and values of his society."[153] This passage is late Bernard (ca. 1146), so certainly by this time he has a very experienced, well-used tongue. The values that Bernard articulates, however, are those that have been particularly developed in the context of Cistercian life, values that Bernard hopes to spread in the broader society. Bernard longs for unity, for reconciliation in church and in society, because such unity is at the heart of his understanding of Christian life. He appeals to the Romans as their "friend" who, though physically distant ("over the mountains"), is wounded by their behavior:

> I entreat you for the love of Christ to be reconciled to God, to be reconciled to your rulers, I mean to Peter and Paul whom you have driven from your midst in the person of Eugenius, their vicar and successor. Be reconciled to the princes of the

152. Letter 243.2; J319; SBOp 8:131.
153. Sommerfeldt, *Bernard of Clairvaux on the Spirituality of Relationship*, 5–6.

earth. . . . Be reconciled at the same time to the thousands of martyrs who are in your midst. . . . Be reconciled also to all the Church of saints who everywhere are scandalized by what they hear of you.[154]

But Bernard's motivation does not stem only from the distress caused by dissension. Bernard acts from a double motivation: from the desire to share the fruits of contemplative, monastic life and from the desire to mend disunity and bring reconciliation to a broken world. This double goal accords with Newman's contention that the Cistercian monastery offered both social critique and a model for reform.[155]

There is consonance between Bernard's conception of individual conversion or reformation and his vision of ecclesiastical and social reform: in fact, they are of a piece.[156] The walls of the Cistercian monastery are, as Newman says, by no means "impermeable."[157] Indeed, as she eloquently concludes her study, "As long as Christian society continued to exist in pilgrimage on earth, the Cistercians extended their charity outside the boundary of their monastery."[158] Bernard's optimistic anthropology is matched by an equally optimistic ecclesial and social vision. If there is a partly realized quality in his eschatology, it is manifested not just in individual lives but in social relations.[159] Bernard's application of his program of monastic formation to nonmonastic

---

154. Letter 243.6; J319.6; SBOp 8:133.

155. Newman, *Boundaries of Charity*, 5.

156. Casey concurs: "[Bernard] projected the microspiritual world of individual conversion and spiritual growth onto the Church as a whole as well as onto many secular institutions that, in the 12th century, complemented ecclesiastical activities within a nominal Christendom" (Casey, "Bernard of Clairvaux, St.," 147).

157. Newman, *Boundaries of Charity*, 13.

158. Newman, *Boundaries of Charity*, 243. Newman argues that Cistercian political activity is neither out of character nor the result of degeneration or corruption in the Order, as has sometimes been assumed.

159. Evans makes a similar observation in relation to political life (Evans, *Bernard of Clairvaux*, 157).

contexts could, however, as Casey observes of Bernard's instructions to the crusaders, bring him to "the point of unreality."[160]

Where one might today make clear distinctions between private and public spheres, Bernard appears to have little interest in such a distinction. If twelfth-century Cistercian monasticism attended to and valued inner life with new or renewed emphasis, the notion of the individual should not be read anachronistically. Cistercian monastic life, resting on the Rule of Saint Benedict, is irreducibly communal.[161] Bernard's writings, especially works such as the *Sermons on the Song of Songs*, with their emphasis on the interior journey of the soul, make it actually easy to lose track of this reality. Community is always the setting. Social relations are never far from Bernard's thoughts, and certainly they are the practical and testing ground for his thinking.[162]

4.3.2 Contemplation and Action

If Bernard was convinced of the necessity of action in the world, he still experienced a tension between active and contemplative life. The preservation of a letter (ca. 1125–1130) from Hildebert, the archbishop of Tours, within Bernard's corpus, and particularly its unusual inclusion in Bernard's own register of letters, were perhaps, as Bredero suggests, inspired by an awareness of this tension.[163] Hildebert seeks Bernard's friendship and guidance because of what he perceives as the fruitfulness of Bernard's balanced, holy life. He says that Bernard has combined in an exemplary way both contemplative and active lives. Hildebert makes this point by using the Hebrew Bible image, common at the time, of Jacob's two wives, the beautiful, beloved Rachel and

---

160. Casey, "Bernard of Clairvaux, St.," 147.

161. Newman, *Boundaries of Charity*, 57–66.

162. Loving concern for others is, John R. Sommerfeldt argues, the key motivator for all activity (including Bernard's writing) that takes Bernard beyond the monastery (John R. Sommerfeldt, *Bernard of Clairvaux on the Life of the Mind* [New York: Newman Press, 2004], 112–19).

163. Bredero, *Between Cult and History*, 276–78.

the fruitful but less attractive Leah, as metaphors for contemplation and action:

> There are only few people who do not realize that you know
> a balm from its scent and a tree from its fruits. Similarly we,
> dear brother, have learned from what is current knowledge
> about you, how much you are focused on virtue and how
> impeccable you are in doctrine. For, although we are separated
> from you by too great a distance, we have heard what delight-
> ful nights you pass with your Rachel, and what abundant
> posterity is born to you from Leah, and how in all respects
> you live as one who pursues virtue and hates the flesh. None
> of those who have told us about you has spoken of you in any
> other way.[164]

The letter is highly flattering; in his response Bernard tries to
distance himself: "As for what you say of myself, I see in it not
what I am, but what I should like to be, and what I am ashamed
of not being."[165] But it must have struck a chord: the letter a person keeps for encouragement, perhaps, because it expresses, and
justifies, exactly what one is hoping (if failing) to achieve.

Bernard himself more often used the Mary-Martha dichotomy
to express the ongoing tension between contemplative and active
living. In *On the Song of Songs*, Sermon 57, he uses a triad—Mary,
Martha, and Lazarus—to represent contemplation, preaching,
and prayer. Mary enjoys contemplative repose and Martha serves,
while Lazarus seeks mercy ("groaning beneath the stone, beseech-
ing the grace of resurrection").[166] All three, Bernard says, are "the
Savior's intimate friends"; all live in the same house. Bernard has
been describing how "the mind is tossed to and fro" between the
refreshment of "contemplative leisure" and the desire to "add to
its conquests" through preaching, fearful "lest it cling more than

---

164. Letter 122, trans. Bredero; SBOp 7:302–3. Bredero, *Between Cult and
History*, 279. Bredero's translation retains the image of Rachel and Leah,
whereas James confines it to the footnotes (Bernard of Clairvaux, *Letters*, 185).
165. Letter 123; J126; SBOp 7:304.
166. SC 57.10; SBOp 2:125; CF 31:105.

is justified to one or the other of these rival attractions."[167] He describes the inner conflict using the experience of Job's suffering:

> Perhaps holy Job endured this when he said: "When I lie down I say, 'when shall I arise?' And then I look forward to the evening." That is, when at prayer I accuse myself of indifference at work; when at work of upsetting my prayer. You see here a holy man violently tossed between the fruit of action and the quiet of contemplation: [though] all the time involved in what is good he is ever repenting of imaginary sins, every moment seeking the will of God with tears. For this man the only remedy, the last resort, is prayer and frequent appeals to God that He would deign to show us unceasingly what he wishes us to do, at what time, and in what measure.[168]

In the midst of this interior turmoil Bernard is confident that, with "skill and vigilance," it is possible "that the soul of any one of us here" will "be seen to unite in due order and degree" the three different "endowments." Such a person will then "know how to mourn for his sins and to rejoice in God, and at the same time possess the power to assist his neighbors." Integration within each individual is the goal, but Bernard, both hopeful and realistic here, concedes that if "all three in each one" is a long-term vision, then at least it is possible to observe the different endowments "singly in different persons."[169]

For Bernard, then, it is never a question of active or contemplative life; it is always both, and always living in their tension.

---

167. SC 57.9–10; SBOp 2:124–25; CF 31:103–4.

168. SC 57.9; SBOp 2:125; CF 31:104.

169. SC 57.11; SBOp 2:125–26; CF 31:105. Within the monastery, then, Lazarus, "the mourning dove," represents the novices "just now dead to their sins"; Martha, "the Savior's friend," is "those who do the daily chores"; Mary, the contemplative, is "those who, co-operative with God's grace over a long period of time, have attained to a better and happier state" (SC 57.11; SBOp 2:126; CF 31:105–6). Bernard's schema could be read as a hierarchical one. For a discussion of this issue, see Sommerfeldt, *Bernard of Clairvaux on the Spirituality of Relationship*, chap. 8. Newman observes inconsistencies in Cistercian considerations of social ranking, which sometimes seem to be based on authority and sometimes on merit. See Newman, *Boundaries of Charity*, 106–15.

Human existence, whether inside or outside the monastery, makes this dialectic inevitable.

4.4 Humility and Public Life: *On the Conduct and Office of Bishops*

If there is an imperative to engage in public life, how is such engagement to be conducted? Bernard addresses this issue directly in two treatises: *On the Conduct and Office of Bishops* (*De moribus et officio episcoporum*)[170] and *On Consideration* (*De consideratione*). A third treatise, *In Praise of the New Knighthood* (*De laude novae militia*),[171] also deals with life beyond the monastery, specifically the vocation of knights. Bernard's large corpus of letters offers an important insight into his public engagement, but the treatises contain his most developed thinking. Further, while Bernard engages with secular rulers (as is evidenced by his extant letters), in his dealing with bishops he expresses his sharpest reflections on carrying the Christian vocation into the public square. Twelfth-century bishops held and exercised significant power (in areas that from a modern perspective might be deemed secular). Additionally, most bishops in that period came from the nobility, so the lines between secular and clerical leadership must often have become blurred. Bernard is deeply concerned with the way power is exercised, and his reforming agenda is evident not only in his advocacy of Cistercian candidates for episcopal appointments but also in his advice to both monastic and nonmonastic bishops. Indeed he addresses his treatise *On Bishops* to a nonmonastic bishop. In all of this literary activity, Bernard has the Christian conduct of public life clearly in view.

The treatise *On Bishops* was in fact originally an extended letter, written to Henry, archbishop of Sens, circa 1127, supposedly at

---

170. Henceforth *On Bishops* (SBOp 7:100–131). For an English translation, see Bernard of Clairvaux, *On Baptism and the Office of Bishops*, trans. Pauline Matarasso, CF 67 (Kalamazoo, MI: Cistercian Publications, 2004).

171. An English translation is in Bernard of Clairvaux, *In Praise of the New Knighthood: A Treatise on the Knights Templar and the Holy Places of Jerusalem*, trans. M. Conrad Greenia, CF 19B (Kalamazoo, MI: Cistercian Publications, 2000).

Henry's request.[172] It is centrally concerned with how the contemplative life of the monk can inform the very different life of the bishop. A significant part of the treatise focuses on how the foundational virtues of monastic life—chastity, *caritas*, and humility—can and should lay the foundations for the conduct of public life. *On Consideration* (ca. 1148–1153), which Bernard wrote for his former monk, now Pope Eugenius III, assumes these foundations and endeavors to deal with the complexities of "spiritual government."[173]

The salutation and opening of Bernard's letter-treatise *On Bishops* are worth noting. It begins: "To the Venerable Lord Henry, Archbishop of Sens, from Brother Bernard: if a sinner's prayer can be of any avail."[174] In the context of the rhetorical conventions of the time, there is nothing unusual about the form of this address. Bernard addresses his recipient formally, with his full title, styling himself simply as "Brother Bernard" and "a sinner." Bernard is highly sensitive to rank: Henry is the "holder of high office," "an eminence," as he says in the opening paragraph of the letter. Bernard, by contrast, protests that as a monk the task that he has been set is beyond him: "Who are we to write for bishops?" Bernard says he is able to fulfill the request only by an act of obedience, in recognition of the authority (power) of Henry's episcopal office. Should this protestation be read as rhetorical

172. For an introduction to the various editions of this letter-treatise, see Newman, "Contemplative Virtues," 22–23.

173. Elizabeth T. Kennan, "Introduction," in Bernard of Clairvaux, *Five Books on Consideration: Advice to a Pope,* CF 37 (Kalamazoo, MI: Cistercian Publications, 1976), 3–18, here 12. *On Consideration* has been read by subsequent popes into the present time, but it has historically also gained a wider readership among secular leaders. It was well known in late medieval and Renaissance Italy, contributing to the prominence of Bernard in the Florentine Republic. See Melinda Kay Lesher, "St. Bernard of Clairvaux and the Republic of Florence in the Late Middle Ages," *Citeaux* 35 (1984): 258–67, here 264. This text offers Bernard's mature view of public office and is the usual focus for the examination of his political thinking. See, for example, Evans, *Bernard of Clairvaux,* chap. 8. I have chosen to focus on *On the Conduct and Office of Bishops* because of its extensive discussion of humility. Its thinking remains foundational to the more pragmatic agenda of *On Consideration.*

174. SBOp 7:100; CF 67:37.

performance or authentic humility? Perhaps, though, that is a false dichotomy. Bernard, as is so often the case, begins his letter with rhetorical humility because he wishes to say hard things. He is, one might say, "speaking truth to power."[175] In Bernard's eyes, Henry has clearly made mistakes, and Bernard is clearing the way to name these.

Bernard's first response to Henry's failures is one of compassion, inspired by a train of thought that compares the hidden life of a monk to the very public life of a bishop:

> If I—skulking in my hole as it might be under a bushel, and giving out more smoke than light—am yet unable to avoid the wind's buffetings, but, plagued and pressured as I continually am by various temptations, am blown this way and that like a reed shaken by the wind, what of the man who finds himself set on a hilltop or on a lampstand?[176]

If Bernard finds himself "a burden and danger" to himself, how must it be for a bishop, who "even when his own problems let him be, has no respite from those of others"? Bernard imagines that as bishop he must be "harried and tormented."[177] At the beginning of *On Consideration*, Bernard similarly imagines Eugenius grieving under the burden of high office. In fact, Bernard says, if Eugenius is not grieving under its demands, he will grieve even more![178] Bernard assumes that Eugenius has relinquished the contemplative life unwillingly: he cannot imagine welcoming public office, and this assumption frames everything Bernard has to say. Public office is hardly to be desired because it is a difficult, if necessary, burden.

With this assessment in mind, Bernard begins to explore how bishops should carry that difficult but necessary burden. If Henry

---

175. This phrase has its origins in a pamphlet "Speak Truth to Power," published by American Quakers in 1955; it expresses the idea of nonviolent, prophetic truth-telling to those who hold political power.
176. Mor 1.1; SBOp 7:101; CF 67:38.
177. Mor 1.1; SBOp 7:101; CF 67:38–39.
178. Csi 1.1; SBOp 3:394; CF 37:25.

has made mistakes, he has taken one step that, in Bernard's eyes, is to be commended. He had taken counsel from two "prudent and well-intentioned" bishops.[179] Here, Bernard believes, Henry will find both sound advice and rare exemplars to guide not his rule (*dominium*) but his ministry (*ministerium*).[180] Drawing on the apostle Paul (Rom 11:13), Bernard here makes an important point. Honor is to be found in the work, not sought for oneself: "Honor your ministry: ministry, I repeat, not rule. You will in this way honor it, not yourself. For the man who looks after his own interests is bent on honoring himself, not the ministry."[181] Self-honoring—that is, pride—is for Bernard a core temptation of public office.

Next, Bernard draws attention to the material face of pride (and consequently the material face of humility). For Bernard, pride is inevitably signaled by the material trappings that commonly accompany "the grandeur of office." The honoring of ministry will not be achieved, Bernard says, "by *recherché* clothes, grand buildings and a parade of horseflesh."[182] Bernard mounts a vivid diatribe against prelates who indulge in a "positive cult of clothing." They are, he argues, looking in the wrong direction, modeling themselves on worldly people (and women at that!) rather than the martyrs who carry "the marks of Christ" in their bodies. On this occasion, Bernard also argues his case from the perspective of social inequality. It is the poor who protest most loudly: "What use to us, working in wretched conditions of cold and hunger, are all those spare clothes stretched over hangers or folded in travelling chests?" The poor, Bernard reminds his

179. Mor 1.2; SBOp 7:102; CF 67:39.
180. Mor 1.3; SBOp 7:103; CF 67:42.
181. Mor 1.3; SBOp 7:103; CF 67:42.
182. Mor 2.4; SBOp 7:104; CF 67:42. The translation beautifully captures the spirit of Bernard. His criticism here is reminiscent of his diatribe against Cluniac monastic practices in the *Apologia to Abbot William* (1125). For Bernard the physical, material aspects of monastic renunciation were nonnegotiable. Writing (ca. 1125) to his nephew Robert, who had fled the austerities of Clairvaux for the relative comfort of Cluny, Bernard exclaimed, "How could anyone amidst such vanities recognize the truth and achieve humility?" (Letter 1.5; J1.5).

readers, were equally created by God and redeemed by Christ: "We are therefore your brothers [*fratres*]."[183]

This self-identification with the poor is no accident. Bernard often describes Clairvaux as a community of *pauperes Christi*.[184] He is concerned here with the distance that high office potentially creates between ruler and ruled. As Newman has demonstrated, one of the outcomes of Cistercian monastic reform was a decrease in the distance between the abbot (the ruler of the monastery) and monks (the ruled). Historically, abbots had become distant from their monks, with lives dominated by administration and an accumulation of customs that specified differential treatment and rituals of honor. Cistercian abbots, by contrast, were given less discretion in the interpretation of the Rule than Benedict had actually allowed. Instead, customs and practices were established by the annual general chapter. There was a double effect here: the abbot's power was actually diminished, and the general chapter prevented the reemergence of customs that privileged the monastic ruler. The difference this system made in practice was noticeable: William of Malmesbury, writing circa 1124, observed that the Cistercian abbot "allows himself no indulgence beyond the others; he is everywhere present, everywhere attending to his flock, except that he does not eat with the rest because his table is always with the poor."[185] The abbot became once again one of the brothers, and mutuality or friendship a core value (RB 72 resonates here). Social distance is inimical to fraternal community. A form of social

183. Mor 2.7; SBOp 7:106; CF 67:45–46.

184. The foundational Cistercian documents, including the *Exordium Parvum*, consistently highlight the reformers' embrace of greater material poverty. The monks style themselves as "the new soldiers of Christ, poor with the poor Christ" (Bredero, *Between Cult and History*, 263). This self-understanding constitutes the Cistercian creation story, of course: the foundation myth, from which it is difficult if not impossible to retrieve either the original intentions or earliest practice. Poverty here is strictly relative. The Cistercians were not landless poor, and the growing Cistercian movement was soon well endowed. The language of poverty, as Bredero notes, gradually diminished. Nonetheless, the material aspects of renunciation were clearly of central importance (Bredero, *Between Cult and History*, 263–67).

185. Newman, *Boundaries of Charity*, 50.

humility is part of the Cistercian reform agenda. Both the material and social faces of humility are important to Bernard.

4.4.1 Monastic Virtues for Public Life: Chastity, Charity, Humility

The recognition of the burden of public office, the need for a small community of advisers, and the foundation of a materially humble life are Bernard's preliminaries. What he really wishes to highlight are the spiritual and moral ingredients of *honorable* episcopal *ministry* (as opposed to a *self-honoring* episcopal *rule*). Here Bernard goes straight to three foundational monastic virtues: chastity, charity, and humility.

The first, chastity, brings one closest to the "heavenly mode of life," closer to the intended divine "likeness," even though he is still living in the "land of unlikeness." The celibate or chaste priest offers the world a sample (a "fragrant balm") of heaven.[186] The paradise of the monastery has the same exemplary function.

Charity, the second monastic virtue, is the fruit of a pure heart. Again, Bernard emphasizes the proper location of honor. Purity of heart motivates the bishop to seek both the glory of God and the welfare of neighbor (not the glory of self): "The bishop in all he does and says seeks nothing of his own, but only the honor of God, his neighbors' salvation, or both together."[187] This way is one of costly self-offering, costly love that, Bernard warns, will be experienced as a sort of death: "He loses his life in this world that he may save it in the world to come."[188] This is the pattern learned from Christ himself. It is not possible to walk this path without self-knowledge. Love of neighbor is not possible, Bernard says, unless one has learned both to love oneself[189] and, perhaps most significant for a leader, carefully to examine one's conscience. It is always possible to drift away from love.[190]

---

186. Mor 3.8; SBOp 7:107; CF 67:48.
187. Mor 3.10; SBOp 7:108; CF 67:49.
188. Mor 3.11; SBOp 7:109; CF 67:50.
189. Mor 4.13; SBOp 7:110; CF 67:52.
190. Mor 4.14–16; SBOp 7:111–13; CF 67:53–56.

Humility, the third virtue, underpins both chastity and charity. There is nothing particularly new in Bernard's exposition here. Humility is described as the "bulwark and tower of all the virtues"[191] and is contrasted with the vice of pride, "a passionate desire for our own superiority."[192] Once again Bernard examines the shadow (pride) as a means of explicating humility. He celebrates humility as the primary virtue of Mary, the mother of Christ, and offers Christ as the model of humility. What is noticeable, however, is the space he gives to this subject. Humility is the direct subject of nearly half of the treatise (sixteen out of thirty-seven chapters).[193] In fact, humility, or its absence, is the underlying theme of the whole treatise. Further, the treatise exhibits particular emphases in its treatments of humility and pride: Bernard here has life beyond the cloister firmly in view.

With the same rationale that lay behind his long exposition on pride in *On the Steps of Humility and Pride*, Bernard spends considerable space mapping the shape of humility's "opposing vice." An understanding of pride will, he says, bring out "the beauty of the virtue."[194] This time, however, his eye is not on how pride is manifested in the context of monastic community but rather on its particular shape in the arena of public life. And he is especially concerned with the social consequences of pride. He distinguishes between two kinds of pride: blind pride (*caeca superbia*) and vain pride (*vana superbia*).[195] Bernard makes this distinction so that he can explore two dimensions of the operation of pride: how pride infects one's capacity to see oneself clearly and how it damages relationships with others. He focuses here on what threatens the public ministry of bishops.

The first kind of pride, blind pride, Bernard also calls *contumacia*, a defiant perseverance in one's own opinion.[196] This form

191. Mor 3.17; SBOp 7:113–14; CF 67:57.
192. Mor 3.19; SBOp 7:114; CF 67:58.
193. Newman, "Contemplative Virtues," 30.
194. Mor 5.19; SBOp 7:114; CF 67:58.
195. Mor 5.19; SBOp 7:114; CF 67:58.
196. SBOp 7:114. The Latin here could be translated as *arrogance*, but note that Bernard chooses to use *contumacia* here, not *arrogantia*—perhaps empha-

of pride, he argues, is a fault of the intellect or reason (*ratio*) that "leads a person either to see in himself some imaginary good or to believe he is the source of what he is, to glory in himself and not in God."[197] It is a form of self-sufficiency, which fails to recognize human dependence on God. The second dimension, vain pride, or vanity (*vanitas*), Bernard says, is a fault of the will (*voluntatis*), a "misdirection of the heart's desire."[198] Instead of giving thanks to God, as the source of all goodness, all gifts, the person is intently listening for, and delighting in, the praise of others. Glory is misdirected, self-directed; it becomes vainglory.

Both forms of pride are countered by humility. So the counter to blind pride is "the holding of our own superiority in contempt." Similarly, humility holds vain pride or misdirected desire in contempt, refusing to accept or even to seek a glory that actually belongs to God.[199] The journey from blind pride to humility is a journey from self-deception to self-knowledge, the truth about oneself. The journey from vain pride to humility is a journey from fear to love, from vainglory to charity—the same movement that Bernard maps in *On the Steps of Humility and Pride.*

Type of pride	Blind pride (*caeca superbia*) arrogance (*contumacia*)	Vain pride (*vana superbia*) vanity (*vanitas*)
Fault of . . .	Reason (*ratio*)	Will (*voluntatis*)
Looks for . . .	Glory in self (self-sufficiency)	Glory from others (vainglory)
Movement from . . .	Self-deception to self-knowledge	Vainglory to charity fear to love

Newman argues that these two types of pride are equivalent to steps 5 (*singularitas*, "singularity") and 6 (*arrogantia*, "conceit") in the descending ladder described in *On the Steps of Humility and*

---

sizing stubborn or willful defiance.
   197. Mor 5.19; SBOp 7:115; CF 67:58.
   198. Mor 5.19; SBOp 7:115; CF 67:58.
   199. Mor 5.19; SBOp 7:115; CF 67:59.

Pride, but the fit is by no means perfect.[200] If there is a correlation, and given Bernard's unsystematic style this can never be certain, then it may be with steps 6 (*arrogantia*, "conceit") and 7 (*praesumptio*, "presumption"). Nowhere in *On Bishops* does Bernard use the term *singularitas*, but *praesumptio* appears a number of times. At one point in the treatise he contrasts the humble person with "the arrogant and presumptuous man" (*arrogans et praesumptor*).[201] Nonetheless, Newman offers the helpful insight that in this treatise blind and vain pride correlate with the steps of pride in *On the Steps of Humility and Pride* that sit at the transition of rungs dealing with contempt for one's brothers and those dealing with contempt for superiors, that is, the interface between "submission and supervision."[202]

In public life, how the self sits in relation to others becomes even more critical. To use Bernard's earlier terminology, will the bishop rule or minister? Bernard's question is, how does pride endanger episcopal ministry? His response is, by damaging human relations. The "arrogant and presumptuous" man can see neither himself nor his neighbor clearly because he is preoccupied with honor (his own) and the accumulation of power (for himself). These two vices could be understood as arrogance and ambition, the commonly named temptations of all public leadership.

4.4.2 Pride: An Interior View

Bernard tries to imagine what pride looks like in the public square, what it might be like for a bishop. As abbot, with a significant public profile, he has some experience of how leadership can and does isolate one from the rest of one's community. He understands, therefore, the very real temptation to feed the self with the praise of others; he understands the human need for approval. And he also knows the fickleness of such approval. By contrast, the humble person will "examine his own actions

200. Newman, "Contemplative Virtues," 31.
201. Mor 5.21; SBOp 7:117; CF 67:61.
202. Newman, "Contemplative Virtues," 31.

so that his reputation may reside in himself alone and not in any one else." Bernard offers a pragmatic rationale for this approach: "He does not consider it safe to entrust his reputation to the lips of men—coffers with neither key nor bolt, wide open to anyone intent on harm. No safe place, that, to hide your treasure; downright silly, in fact, to put it where you cannot recover it at will. If you place it in my mouth, it is no longer in your power but in mine, because it is entirely up to me whether I speak well of you or run you down."[203]

Bernard gives this advice, one can well imagine, from his own experience. He understands the fleeting nature of reputation and the unreliability of its human custodians. Egos puffed up with pride can just as easily be deflated. The remedy for this hopeless round of seeking others' approval and being deflated by slander is to stand alone. Bernard names this place *conscience* (*conscientia*), which is "a good, sound pot designed for the keeping of secrets."[204] It is hard to know whether Bernard understands conscience here in a moral sense or simply as an interior consciousness (probably the latter). Nonetheless, and significantly, he admits that even the conscience is not a reliable guide: "I do not wholly trust myself, or even my own conscience, for, incapable as it is of grasping the whole of me, it cannot pass judgment on a whole of which it hears only part. *It is the Lord who is my judge.*"[205] There are limits to one's capacity for self-examination: this standing alone is not self-sufficiency, a form of blind pride, but a standing alone before God. Truth about the self, judgment, and humility coalesce again here, as they do in *On the Steps of Humility and Pride*. As Bernard reflects on God's more than intimate knowing of us in comparison with his own "minimal insight," he is overwhelmed with "trembling" before the majesty of his Lord, Jesus.[206] The only appropriate response is humility.

203. Mor 5.20; SBOp 7:116; CF 67:60–61.
204. Mor 6.21; SBOp 7:116; CF 67:61.
205. Mor 6.22; SBOp 7:118; CF 67:62–63. Emphasis in the original.
206. Mor 6.23; SBOp 7:118; CF 67:64.

The tone of the treatise at this point is personal and confessional. Perhaps Bernard is here modeling the remedy for pride, the journey one must take in order to break its hold. Certainly his point—about the limits of self-knowledge, our existential humility—could be summarized in a few words, but his extended self-examination takes the reader with him, so that we too cry out that we have "minimal insight." Bernard takes us by the hand, through the process of self-examination: this is the *way*, he seems to say, the way of humility. If, with Bernard, we have reached this point of trembling, which is perhaps close to humiliation—the self exposed, unable to know itself—Bernard calms us with the good news that judgment is to be administered by the Son, who in fact proclaims not judgment but mercy. But—returning to Bernard's nuanced theology of humility—this mercy does not arise from the distance between God and humanity but rather from nearness, from intimacy. The humble person, Bernard says,

> knows that God's nature is essentially kind; it did not shrink from the humility inherent in ours. Nor will that majesty which did not disdain to assume a lowly human body despise in us a humble, contrite heart. I do not know what induced the Godhead to associate ever more intimately with humility; at the last it clothed itself therein in order to appear to human beings. Substance, form, and bearing: all was humble that it took upon itself, commending to us thereby the excellence of the virtue which it wished to honor by this indwelling.[207]

Here is the warm humility that Bernard speaks of in Sermon 42, *On the Song of Songs*.

4.4.3 Pride: An Exterior View

Having dealt with what is essentially the interior climate of the self (combating blind pride with a humble assessment of the self), Bernard now turns to the exterior climate, to the ugly shape of *praesumptio* in the church. His description of ecclesiastical ambi-

---

207. Mor 6.24; SBOp 7:121; CF 67:67.

tion has a sadly timeless ring: "Clergy of every age and state, the learned as well as the ignorant, chase after ecclesiastical charges as though the reward for attaining them were a discharge from all care." Even the experience of the burden of office does not quench ambition. Men whose careers have already been privileged by birth and wealth are driven by ambition and greed to "widen their embrace and to extend their upward reach."[208] Higher honors, more honors. Made a dean or archdeacon, they seek to add "further preferments," all the time, of course, longing for that bishopric. Once that is attained, archbishop is the next stop, and then they begin to "frequent the court of Rome" in the hope of making "advantageous friendships."[209]

Bernard names this familiar pattern for what it is: a "passionate wish to rule the world," "unbridled lust for domination." Rule, not ministry; domination, not service. This pursuit of power inevitably results in rivalry, leaning into someone else's territory in order to extend one's influence.[210] Once again Bernard commends humility as the remedy: "An excellent thing is humility, which keeps the mind unruffled in the present against such carking cares and renders the conscience proof against the threat of punishment in the future. May it hold back your spirit, Father, from all such pernicious rivalry."[211]

Bernard's prescription for combating ambition has two prongs. Both are aspects of what one might style the way of humility. The first is the same as the remedy for blind pride: self-knowledge, which for Bernard is always knowledge of the self in relation to God. Here Bernard offers the apostle Paul as a model: "He compared himself to himself and measured himself by the standard which God had laid down for him."[212] He here reiterates the sense of standing alone in the presence of God. The second prong focuses on the relationship between self and others, and in particular on how one should hold authority. Bernard recognizes a

208. Mor 7.27; SBOp 7:123; CF 67:70.
209. Mor 7.27; SBOp 7:123; CF 67:70.
210. Mor 7.28–29; SBOp 7:123–24; CF 67:71–72.
211. Mor 8.30; SBOp 7:125; CF 67:73.
212. Mor 8.30; SBOp 7:125; CF 67:73.

very real tension between authority (power) and humility. Power, he says, should be held with a level of trepidation, certainly not with enjoyment ("the burden" again). Bernard dramatically pushes the spatial metaphor to its limits: "Once one has been raised to the heights, it is hard not to enjoy the elevation, and most unusual—but all the more admirable for being rare. A fear of heights will deter someone already on a pinnacle from any wish to venture higher. Do not think yourself fortunate in holding sway; consider yourself unfortunate if you are not of service. [*Non vos ergo felicem, quia praeestis, sed si non prodestis, infelicem putate.*]"[213]

Bernard uses the verb *prodesse* here (rather than *ministro* or *servio*), the same word that the Rule of Saint Benedict uses to describe the responsibility of the abbot: "His goal must be profit for the monks, not pre-eminence for himself" (RB 64.8). The emphasis here is less on servitude than on doing good or bringing benefit. But the final phrase, *infelicem putate* (*infelicem*: unfruitful, barren, unfortunate[214]), brings one back to earth. It might be translated, "If you are not bringing benefit to others, consider yourself barren." The self moves from the dizzying pinnacle of power back to its barren root. For Bernard, like the whole monastic tradition behind him, all relationships should be characterized by service. Bishops are not exempt. The remedy for combating self-serving ambition is to focus on benefiting others.

4.4.4 Obedience and Public Life

How then is a bishop meant to hold power? Bernard does not exempt bishops from obedience, from submission, and he believes that if a bishop is aware of his own dependence on others, submitting to those placed in authority over him, then he will be less likely to misuse his own power:

> So that you may safely hold sway over others, do not disdain to submit in turn to whomsoever you ought. The man who

213. Mor 8.30; SBOp 7:125; CF 67:73.
214. Charlton T. Lewis and Charles Short, eds., *A Latin Dictionary* (Oxford: Clarendon Press, 1879), s.v. "infelicem."

disdains submission is unfit to be a prelate. *The greater you are the more you should humble yourself* [Sir 3:20] is the counsel of a wise man. And this is the precept of Wisdom himself: *Let the greatest among you become as the least* [Luke 22:26]. For if it is proper to submit oneself even to the least, how can it be right to refuse the yoke of the greater? Better for your inferiors to see in you a model of the humble service that they owe you. [*Videant potius in vobis subditi quod vobis redhibeant.*][215]

Bernard illustrates this point using the story of the centurion who comes to Jesus seeking healing for his servant (Matt 8:5-13). This choice is significant. The centurion understands authority and its limits: "I too am a man under authority, with soldiers under me" (v. 9). Bernard commends the wisdom of this "pagan man," on the basis that he first "acknowledged himself a man, and only then a powerful one."[216] Acknowledgment of one's own limits makes it safer to exercise power over others: "Humility has been sent ahead to forestall the rush of pride. Indeed, where humility's bright banner goes before, arrogance can find no place at all. You admit you are weak, you confess to being dependent? Now you can say with all safety that you have soldiers under you. Indeed, it is because he was not embarrassed by his dependence that he justly deserved to have his rank honored."[217]

Further, Bernard suggests, the experience of being "under authority" oneself helps to moderate one's own use of power. As he says of the centurion, "The experience of his own subordination taught him to temper in turn his rule." Again, this passage is littered with the Latin prefix *sub*, "under":[218] it seems that Bernard is trying to tie down the exercise of authority. He wants his readers to associate authority with submission rather than elevation. This passage has strong resonances with Bernard's letter to the monks of Saint Jean-d'Aulps: "Our place is under a master, under

215. Mor 8.31; SBOp 7:125; CF 27:73–74.
216. Mor 8.32; SBOp 7:127; CF 27:75.
217. Mor 8.32; SBOp 7:127; CF 27:76.
218. SBOp 7:126–27.

an Abbot, under a rule, under discipline."[219] *Under (sub)* is the one word that sums up Bernard's thinking about power and authority.

Ultimately, Bernard argues, the centurion's understanding of authority reflects a larger pattern. All human authority is delegated (from God). Human authority, or dominion, therefore, is to be exercised from a stance of humility ("I too am a man under authority"). Power relations have, however, been disordered by human rebellion against divine order (they are captive to "the law of sin"). Order is restored to human relations once we have acknowledged our rebellion and our dependence on God. Humility must be recovered. So, in the case of the centurion, "it is because he was not embarrassed by his dependence that he justly deserved to have his rank honored."[220]

Public office is, then, a hard burden, which is to be carried with particular care and with a particular awareness of its pitfalls. The call to office is not to rule but to serve. The material expression of humility is not unimportant: material trappings of office can distance the ruler from the ruled and damage fraternal community. Material simplicity is an ideal Bernard wants to spread beyond the monastery walls. Similarly, in Bernard's vision for episcopal leadership, monastic values find a new place for expression, and the way of humility, in particular, is commended as the remedy for combating the manifestations of pride that haunt those who hold public office. The shape of this way of humility is consonant with that which Bernard first developed in the *Steps of Humility and Pride*: self-examination (before God), the movement from cold to warm humility, the necessity of obedience, and the fruit and priority of *caritas*. What Bernard emphasizes, however, is the careful way in which those in public office need to hold power: with trepidation, with constant awareness of the need to work for the benefit of others, and with an awareness of their own limits before God. Those who have been raised to higher office are still under authority.

219. Letter 142; J151.
220. Mor 8.32; SBOp 7:127; CF 27:76.

4.5 Practicing Humility in Public Life: *The Life of Saint Malachy*

In *On the Conduct and Office of Bishops* Bernard identifies a number of practices that, accompanied by God's grace, will enable bishops to hold their power with humility, to minister rather than rule. In *The Life of Saint Malachy* (1148) Bernard paints an even clearer picture of the way of life that supports his ideal bishop.[221] As Evans suggests, here Bernard offers a "theology of example."[222] Bernard knew Malachy, who had visited Clairvaux. More significantly, perhaps, Malachy was sufficiently removed from the Cistercian milieu to offer a model for the bishops in Bernard's more immediate environment.

Bernard summarizes the proper practical foundations of episcopal ministry: "Once Malachy was made bishop of Down he immediately concerned himself, as was his custom, with establishing a convent of regular clerics of his sons for his solace. Behold, he girds himself again for the spiritual contest like a new recruit of Christ. Once again he puts on the weapons so mighty with God, the humility of holy poverty, the rigor of monastic discipline, the leisure of contemplation and application to prayer."[223]

Bernard begins with the need for a community: Malachy takes some monks from his own monastery "for his solace" (the advisers, perhaps, of whom Bernard speaks at the beginning of *On Bishops*). Malachy also recognizes that in taking on a public office he will face a new environment, with new spiritual challenges, so he must prepare himself as if he were a young soldier, "a new recruit of Christ." Being a beginner again, after all, can in itself be an experience of humility. And the monastic disciplines and practices will provide the best tools, or "weapons," for this new environment. So Malachy gives monastic practices a life beyond the cloister. Significantly, Bernard names poverty, the material face

---

221. SBOp 3:307–78; Bernard of Clairvaux, *The Life and Death of Saint Malachy the Irishman*, trans. Robert T. Meyer, CF 10 (Kalamazoo, MI: Cistercian Publications, 1978). Henceforth V Mal.
222. Evans, *Bernard of Clairvaux*, 21.
223. V Mal 14.32; SBOp 3:339; CF 10:48.

of humility, as the first weapon. He then speaks of the "rigor of monastic discipline" (*disciplinae coenobialis*), alluding undoubtedly to the framework of prayer (the rhythm of offices), work, silence, vigils, and fasts.[224] This framework enables both "the leisure of contemplation" and "application to prayer." All these disciplines come from the cenobium, from a communal context, which is replicated in miniature outside the monastery in Malachy's "convent of regular clerics."

Not surprisingly, this is exactly the sort of model laid down in an early statute issued by the Cistercian general chapter of 1134:

> Bishops who have risen from our order shall hold to our customs in the quality of their food, in the form of their garments, in the observation of fasts, and in the office of regular hours, except that they can have a cloak of common cloth and sheepskin and a hat of similar materials or simply of wool, if they wish. With such things, however, they can only seldom enter our cloister and cannot take part in our chapters, because of their differences. For solace, they can be given someone from our houses, up to two monks and three lay brothers, if so many are necessary, as long as no secular business or cares are imposed on them.[225]

The material face of humility must be maintained, the monastic way of life sustained with the support of some "real" monks. Cistercian monks who became bishops held an anomalous position. They remained members of the order but were no longer monks. They had stepped out of the cloister but somehow took its life with them into the secular world to which they were now committed.

In the *Life of Malachy* Bernard links this way of life, monasticism in public, with its apostolic prototype. Bernard notes that Malachy has not been able to fulfill his ideal, an admission that undoubtedly mirrors Bernard's own frustrations regarding the tension between action and contemplation, a tension present even within the cloister. Nonetheless, Malachy's life shines in the public square:

224. SBOp 3:339; CF 10:48.
225. Quoted in Newman, *Boundaries of Charity*, 150.

Indeed everyone streamed to him in crowds, not only the common people, but noblemen and those in power. They rushed to put themselves under his wise direction and his holiness, to be taught and corrected and to submit to his rule. In the meanwhile he went here and there to sow his seeds, arranging and judging on ecclesiastical matters with complete authority like one of the Apostles.[226]

Bernard endorses this way of life because it has apostolic authority, an authority sealed by the presence of the Holy Spirit: "No one said to him: 'By what authority do you do these things?'—since they all saw the signs and wonders which he did and because where the Spirit is there is freedom."[227]

Historically, monasticism had long drawn on the apostolic witness, particularly the Acts of the Apostles, to validate the way of life. Here Bernard links this traditional validation with what one might call apostolic action. The monastic lifestyle undergirds Malachy's public actions. In a sense, all roads lead to Clairvaux here. Monks become bishops, and bishops are exhorted to become monk-like. For Bernard, humility and love (*caritas*), underpinned by monastic practices, are the foundations of Christian life, wherever it is lived.

4.6 Bernard the Juggler: Humility and Failure

I deliberately chose, at the beginning of this chapter, to present Bernard as a monk broken by excessive zeal rather than as the consummate statesman he became as he strutted the European political stage. It is the leper's hut, perhaps, that allows a glimpse of why, much later, Bernard says to Oger, "Humiliation is the . . . way to humility."[228] While Bernard is able to articulate a clear

---

226. V Mal 14.32; SBOp 3:339–40; CF 10:48.

227. V Mal 14.32; SBOp 3:340; CF 10:48. Bernard's stress on the apostolic character of Malachy's ministry can also be seen in Malachy's journey to Rome to seek the authority of the Apostolic See for his episcopate.

228. Letter 87.11; J90.11; SBOp 7:230: *Siquidem humiliatio via est ad humilitatem.* James adds *only*, which is not in the Latin, so "humiliation is the only way to humility."

vision for the exercise of leadership, he has also experienced its realities. So he reflects theologically on failure, not as a means of minimizing its seriousness but in order to embrace it as an inevitable part of leadership.

Oger was a canon regular who, after fourteen years, had resigned from the leadership of Saint-Nicolas-des-Prés, a community that he had been chosen to found. Bernard, writing circa 1139,[229] is responding to Oger's withdrawal from a position of authority. Bernard is hard on Oger, suggesting that in relinquishing his "pastoral charge" he may have "disburdened" himself, but in doing so he has "dishonored God." Bernard continues:

> Without doubt, you have, so far as you could, opposed his designs by casting yourself down from the post to which he had promoted you. If, by way of excuse, you allege the necessity of poverty, I reply that necessity wins a crown; if you allege the difficulty or impossibility of your position, I reply that all things are possible to one who believes. Better tell the truth and admit that your own quiet pleased you more than labouring for the benefit of others. I don't wonder at it, I admit that I feel the same way myself. . . . Either you should not have undertaken at all the care of souls or, having undertaken it, you should on no account have relinquished it, according to those words: "Are you married to a wife? Then do not go about to be free of her."[230]

It is, of course, too late for Oger to return to his "wife," but Bernard insists that Oger regard his decision with "fear": not the sort of fear that leads to despair but a fear that "engenders hope." There is, Bernard says, "a fruitless fear which is cruel and sad and which never obtains pardon because it never tries to; and there is a loving, humble, and fruitful fear which easily obtains mercy for anyone however great his sin." It is this sort of fear that "begets, fosters, and preserves humility." Warm humility again. Bernard is

229. Mabillon dates this letter ca. 1126, but, on the basis that this was written after Oger's resignation from Saint-Nicolas-des-Prés, ca. 1139 seems more secure. See Bernard of Clairvaux, *Letters*, 129.

230. Letter 87.3; J90.3; SBOp 7:226.

particularly concerned that Oger might be prey to false humility, an inverted pride gained from the act of relinquishing a position of power over others. While Bernard exhorts Oger to maintain a confidence in God's capacity to "use our disordered wishes and actions . . . to our advantage," he predicts a difficult path ahead: he commends Oger for his return to his motherhouse and for placing himself back under the obedience of his superior but warns that it is likely that Oger will be tempted with a nostalgic longing for what he gave up.[231]

Bernard concludes his letter with what begins as rhetorical humility but, characteristically, develops into something larger. Here he offers further insight into his own struggle with the relationship between humility and public life, the interplay between exterior and interior life. If he had remained silent, he says, he might have been mistaken for a wise man and, worse, his silence might have been interpreted as humility. By opening his mouth—by exposing his thoughts publicly—he risks humiliation: "As it is some will laugh at my stupidity, others will mock at me as a fool, and yet others will be indignant at my presumption."[232] Yet, he maintains, this public disclosure, making oneself vulnerable, is for the good; it is beneficial because "humiliations lead to humility and humility is the foundation of the spiritual life." He continues: "Humiliation is the only way to humility, just as patience is the only way to peace, and reading to knowledge. If you want the virtue of humility you must not shun humiliations. If you will not suffer yourself to be humbled, you can never achieve humility. It is an advantage for you that my foolishness should be made public, that I whose lot it has often been to receive undeserved praise from those who do not know me, should now be discomforted by those who have found me out."[233]

Bernard is not advocating humiliation for its own sake but for the sake of truth. His thinking here is consonant with that of *On the Steps of Humility and Pride*. The goal is always truth: "It is very

---

231. Letter 87.4–5; J90.4–5; SBOp 7:226–27.
232. Letter 87.11; J90.11; SBOp 7:230.
233. Letter 87.11; J90.11; SBOp 7:230.

dangerous for anyone to hear himself spoken of above what he knows he deserves. I pray that I may be humbled before men for the truth, just as much as it has been my lot to be undeservedly praised for what is not true."[234]

Bernard offers two quotations from Scripture to describe his experience of humiliation: "I rightly apply to myself those words of the Prophet: 'I have been lifted up only to be cast down and discomforted'; and again: 'Play the mountebank I will and humble myself in my own esteem,' for I shall play the mountebank that I may be mocked. [*LUDAM, ET VILIOR FIAM. Ludam scilicet ut illudar.*]"[235] In the first quotation, from Psalm 87 (88):16, the psalmist (or prophet) contrasts the experience of being raised (*exaltatus autem*) with that of being lowered, humbled, or humiliated (*humiliatus sum*). This is a passive experience.

But in Bernard's second quotation humiliation has also become a conscious choice. Bernard is referring to David's retort to Michal in 2 Samuel 6:22. David, the youthful king, has just danced naked through the streets of Jerusalem before the ark of God. Michal, the embittered daughter of Saul, ridicules his behavior, likening it to that of a naked idler (Vulgate: *nudetur unus de scurris* [2 Sam 6:20]). David's reply is simple: God has made him king in place of Saul; it is for God alone that he dances. So, David continues, "I will both play and make myself meaner [*vilior*: cheap, common[236]] than I have done: and I will be little in my own eyes" (Vulgate: *ludam et vilior fiam plus quam factus sum et ero humilis in oculis meis* [2 Sam 6.22]).[237]

James's translation of Bernard's letter tries to convey the paradoxical game that is being played here. As a mountebank is a hawker or charlatan, James uses the expression "to play the mountebank" to express the pretense involved in this bizarre behavior (David is a king, but he pretends to be a naked idler). The words *ludam, et vilior fiam* might, however, be more clearly translated as

234. Letter 87.12; J90.12; SBOp 7:231.
235. Letter 87.12; J90.12; SBOp 7:231.
236. Lewis and Short, *A Latin Dictionary*, s.v. "vilis."
237. *ludam* may also be operating as a word play in the Vulgate: in 2 Sam 6:2 David sets out from Judah (*Iuda*).

play the fool. Bernard embraces the image of play (*ludo*) to express this contradictory meeting of power and humility. This choice—to walk toward humiliation—is incomprehensible to the world: "What else do seculars think we are doing but playing when what they desire most on earth, we fly from; and what they fly from, we desire? Like acrobats and jugglers, who with heads down and feet up, stand or walk on their hands, and thus draw all eyes to themselves."[238]

It is, though, "not a game for children or the theatre," but a "pure and holy game," played to a heavenly audience, with an eschatological end in view: "We too play this game that we may be ridiculed, discomforted, humbled, until he comes who puts down the mighty from their seat and exalts the humble."[239] Like David, Bernard dances for God only.

Because this holy game is played by different rules, monastic life and monastically lived public life look (and often feel) like failure. The goal is truth, but our human capacity to speak truthfully is so limited that we will almost certainly get it wrong (and/or be judged as having gotten it wrong). What Bernard has discovered and continually rediscovers is the liberating experience of dancing naked before God. By exposing our limits, even our own duplicity, we paradoxically open ourselves to divine approval/heavenly admiration.

4.7 Bernard and the Florentine Republic

Returning finally to Filippino Lippi's painting in the Badia Fiorentina and to the question posed at the beginning of this chapter: does Bernard have something to say to Piero del Pugliese?

At the beginning of the fourteenth century, the figure of Bernard of Clairvaux was growing in importance in the Florentine commune, as is reflected in both literary and artistic production. His cult converged with the deeply embedded veneration of the Virgin Mary in the city, with Bernard celebrated as a model

238. Letter 87.12; J90.12; SBOp 7:231.
239. Letter 87.12; J90.12; SBOp 7:231.

devotee. So for example Dante, in the *Divine Comedy*, chooses Bernard as the pilgrim's guide for the last part of the journey in *Paradiso* as he contemplates Mary and the Trinity. This convergence of Bernard and Mary underpins a substantial iconographic tradition known as the *Doctrina* or *The Vision of Mary*, in which the Virgin appears to Bernard, who is seated or kneeling at his writing desk. David Clark suggests that Lippi's painting, the *Apparition of the Virgin to Saint Bernard*, is the "consummate expression of that tradition."[240]

The second of Bernard's *Homilies in Praise of the Blessed Virgin Mary*, among other texts, sits behind this tradition. In 1490 Piero del Pugliese donated to the monks of Campora, where Lippi's painting was originally located, a book containing selections of Bernard's works that included these sermons. Piero himself was a competent scribe, and it is not impossible that he had made this copy himself.[241] The painting draws on an already rich visual vocabulary, but in the joint hands of Lippi and his patron Piero, perhaps even under the latter's direction, its iconographic complexity is dizzying.[242]

Piero stands or perhaps kneels in prayer at the bottom right-hand corner of Lippi's painting. He is the donor, of course, but more too. He is the holder of public office, signaled by his costume, a black fur-edged robe and red *cappuccio*. His figure combines action and contemplation, as do the figures of the Cistercian monks in the top right-hand corner. Two brothers gaze toward the heavens in contemplation; two, in brotherly converse and clad in the black scapular designed to protect their monastic habits, have work in view, perhaps the scriptorium; and in the distance two others, living witnesses to *caritas*, carry a lame old man. It is possible to read an allusion to Anthony's tomb, or Benedict's cave,

240. Clark, "Filippino Lippi's *The Virgin Inspiring St. Bernard*," 175. For the place of Bernard in Florence and the development of the *Doctrina* tradition, see Lesher, "Republic of Florence," 258–67; James France, *Medieval Images of Saint Bernard of Clairvaux*, CS 210 (Kalamazoo, MI: Cistercian Publications, 2007), 239–63.
241. Burke, *Changing Patrons*, 149.
242. Burke, *Changing Patrons*, 149.

in the dark rocky recesses behind Bernard. Temptation's hard and barren desert is conquered; there the devil is chained, and wisdom, represented by an owl, is victorious. Virtue has triumphed over vice. And tacked to the rocks—above the piles of books, the gospel (all the texts that are informing this story) and the work in progress—is an epigram by the Stoic philosopher Epictetus, *Substine et abstine*, "bear and forebear." A revival of interest in Stoicism was part of the intellectual climate of Florence in the 1480s, but the motto also resonates with Bernard's thinking about the burden of public office. In Lippi's painting, Bernard becomes an honorary Florentine humanist.[243]

And perhaps Piero del Pugliese has become an honorary monk. Even though Piero sits at the periphery of this monastic world, at the edge of the painting, as a viewer, he is not separate. Permeable boundaries again. Lippi here shows Piero as the legitimate imitator of Bernard. Both men, of course, have exposed themselves to the charge of false humility. Bernard's noisy literary rhetoric and Piero's spatially realized lowly appearance alongside a saint and the Virgin make it hard to read them as paragons of humility. But this is hardly the point. Neither Bernard nor Piero is the ultimate focus of the painting. Both look to Mary—Mary, who is not a monk but who is an icon of humility and whose humble obedience in turn mirrors the humble obedience of the incarnate Son. In the painting only Mary has downcast eyes.

Lippi has caught Bernard midsentence. For a moment he sits in silent contemplation. Then he will write these, some of his most famous words:

> O you, whoever you are, who feel that in the tidal wave of this world you are nearer to being tossed about among the squalls and gales than treading on dry land, if you do not want to founder in the tempest do not avert your eyes from the brightness of this star. When the wind of temptation blows up within you, when you strike upon the rock of tribulation, gaze up at this star, call out to Mary. Whether you are being tossed

---

243. Burke, *Changing Patrons*, 146–49; Clark, "Filippino Lippi's *The Virgin Inspiring St. Bernard*," 178–80.

about by the waves of pride or ambition or slander or jealousy,
gaze up at this star, call out to Mary. When the immensity of
your sins weighs you down and you are bewildered by the
loathsomeness of your conscience, when the terrifying thought
of judgement appalls you and you begin to founder in the gulf
of sadness and despair, think of Mary. In dangers, in hardships, in every doubt, think of Mary, call out to Mary.[244]

It is not difficult here to imagine Piero del Pugliese pondering
these words in the context of his own turbulent world. Pride, ambition, slander, jealousy, and an uneasy conscience were natural
hazards for a merchant and holder of public office. Finally, and
significantly, Bernard's impassioned eloquence brings him to
silence: echoing the words of the apostle Peter, he says, " 'It is
good that we are here' sweetly to contemplate in silence what no
long-winded discourse could ever adequately explain."[245] Lippi
brings us this silence in his masterly painting: we see the pause
of Bernard's pen and the subject of his inner gaze. In fact, we
see the presence that meets his inner gaze: Mary. We see a pause
in Bernard's relentless stream of words, we see the moment of
transfiguring contemplation: his reference to the Synoptic Gospels
is a reference to the transfiguration and to a moment of mystical
awakening for Jesus' disciples. Here is Bernard, "that contemplative" (*quel contemplante*), in Dante's words.[246] The movement from
the "tidal wave of this world" (*saeculi profluvio magis*) to silent
contemplation (*contemplari in silentio*) is completed.[247] The theme
runs through the whole of Bernard's life and work: return with
humility to the source of virtue, and all will be well.

In Renaissance Florence, Bernard was revered for holding
together the world of action and the life of contemplation. In
his homilies *In Praise of the Blessed Virgin Mary*, Bernard names,
with passion and poetry, the stormy nature of human existence.

244. Miss 2.17; SBOp 4:34–35; CF 18A:30.
245. Miss 2.17; SBOp 4:35; CF 18A:31.
246. Bernard McGinn, *The Growth of Mysticism: Gregory the Great through the Twelfth Century* (New York: Crossroad Publishing, 1994), 162.
247. Miss 2.17; SBOp 4:35.

And he names it from his own humiliating experience, from his leper's hut at Clairvaux, when he was young and inexperienced. His words resonate equally with a fifteenth-century Florentine merchant bearing the weight of public office as they did with his original, monastic audience.

4.8 Conclusion

There is a sense in which one cannot help but feel defeated by Bernard, not simply because of the weight and complexity of his literary corpus, but because as a man he remains "maddeningly paradoxical."[248] In this chapter, I have endeavored to build a picture of how Bernard understood humility and how that understanding formed the foundations for his vision for the Christian conduct of public life. Against Bernard's ideal and, indeed, the whole Cistercian reform agenda, stand the realities of the public square. Bernard's own political actions often leave one aghast: his constant interventions in appointments, for example, as evidenced by his often vitriolic letters, and, of course, his prominent involvement in gathering support for the Second Crusade and then his deft distancing of himself from any responsibility for its failure.[249] Did Bernard ever admit to being wrong? Yet in *On Consideration* he does, finally, face the primary challenge of political engagement: discerning truth in an uncertain and complex world. Consideration, he says, is "thought searching for truth." By contrast, contemplation is the "apprehension of truth without doubt."[250]

There is a certain irony that Bernard is writing *On Consideration*, his most pragmatic contribution to living a public life, at the same time as he continues to expound his mystical theology in his long, never-to-be-finished series of sermons, *On the Song*

248. Williams, *Wound of Knowledge*, 118.
249. In *On Consideration* Bernard offers Pope Eugenius (and his broader readership) a theological interpretation of the failure. It is God's judgment on the unfaithfulness of the Crusaders: "How could they advance if they were continually turning back whenever they set out?" (Csi 2.2; SBOp 3:412; CF 37:49).
250. Csi 2.5; SBOp 3:414; CF 37:52.

of Songs. Perhaps his sharpened thinking regarding the discernment of truth emerged from this very juxtaposition. Was Bernard himself, in the last years of his life, entertaining doubts about the Cistercian program? Does his optimistic ecclesial and social vision collapse in the end? One thing is certain, however. In the late writing, humility remained for Bernard utterly foundational. It was perhaps the touchstone that continued to draw him back to the center of his faith, and even to his own limits. In the penultimate (in fact the last completed) sermon in *On the Song of Songs* Bernard expresses this understanding with a certain uncharacteristic modesty. So he may have the last word:

> Humility, my brothers, is a great virtue, great and sublime. It can attain to what it cannot learn; it is counted worthy to possess what it has not the power to possess; it is worthy to conceive by the Word and from the Word what it cannot itself explain in words. Why is this? Not because it deserves to do so, but because it pleases the Father of the Word, the Bridegroom of the soul, Jesus Christ our Lord, who is God above all, blessed for ever. Amen.[251]

There remain, however, very real questions about the place of humility in the public square. The next chapter considers the story of a contemporary Cistercian community that practiced the way of humility to its costly end. Despite a chronological leap of nearly nine centuries, the traditions already examined remain very much alive and tested in an arena of significance for religion in the contemporary world.

251. SC 85.14; SBOp 2:316; CF 40:210.

Figure 4. The Monks of Tibhirine. From left: Jean-Pierre, Paul, Amédée, Luc, Michel, Philippe, Christophe, and Christian.

Chapter 5

Humility and the Other

Christian de Chergé and the Monks of Tibhirine

Humility begins when I realize I have only this brief day, today, to give to him who calls me for all days [tout jour] and how can I tell him "yes" for always [toujours], if I don't give him this little day. . . . God has a thousand years to make a day; I have but one day to make eternity—today!

—*Christian de Chergé*

In the early hours of March 27, 1996, seven Cistercian monks from the Monastery of Notre-Dame-de-l'Atlas (Our Lady of Atlas), at Tibhirine in Algeria, were kidnapped by a group of armed men. A month later, extracts of a communiqué issued by the Groupe Islamic Armé (GIA) and dated April 18 were published in the Saudi newspaper *Al Hayat*, offering to free the monks in exchange for the release of GIA prisoners held by the Algerian and French governments. On April 30, tapes of the monks' voices, verifying that the monks were still alive, were delivered to the French embassy in Algeria, but, in a further communiqué dated May 21 and first broadcast on Moroccan radio on May 23, the GIA announced that in view of the French government's refusal to negotiate, they had

243

"cut the throats of the seven monks as we said we would do." The exact circumstances of their death, after fifty-six days of captivity, remain unclear.[1]

The seven monks were Fr. Christian de Chergé (fifty-nine years of age), prior of the monastery, Br. Luc Dochier (eighty-two), Fr. Christophe Lebreton (forty-five), Fr. Bruno Lemarchand (sixty-six), Fr. Michel Fleury (fifty-two), Fr. Célestin Ringeard (sixty-two), and Fr. Paul Favre-Miville (fifty-seven). The presence of this small monastic community, which had been at Tibhirine in the Atlas Mountains since 1938, was effectively removed. The only two surviving monks of the community, Fr. Amédée (Jean Noto) and Fr. Jean-Pierre Schumacher, moved to what had been an annex to the monastery in Fez, Morocco. Hopes of a return to Algeria have not been realized. Today the monastery that bears the name Notre-Dame-de-l'Atlas is located nearby in Midelt: it describes itself as a small remnant (*petit reste*) of the monastery of Tibhirine.[2] It is committed to continuing the distinctive monastic vocation that had emerged at Tibhirine. At the heart of this is a commitment to living and praying alongside its Muslim neighbors.

1. The monks' deaths are the subject of a French judicial inquiry begun in 2004. GIA involvement has been contested and claims made regarding Algerian government infiltration of the group. Others suggest that the monks died in crossfire during a military operation against the GIA. Remains of the monks were found on May 30, 1996. They were buried at Tibhirine on June 4. The events, as they are known, were carefully chronicled by Bernardo Olivera, then abbot general of the Order of Cistercians of the Strict Observance (OCSO) in a series of letters to members of the Order. They are published, with other documents, in Bernardo Olivera, *How Far to Follow: The Martyrs of Atlas*, CS 197 (Kalamazoo, MI: Cistercian Publications, 1997). For extracts of the GIA Communiqués 43 (April 18, 1996) and 44 (May 21, 1996), see Olivera, *How Far to Follow*, 21–22, 24–25. For a full English translation of Communiqué 43, see John W. Kiser, *The Monks of Tibhirine: Faith, Love, and Terror in Algeria* (New York: St Martin's Griffin, 2002), appendix A. Kiser's narrative account provides an invaluable introduction, in English, to the story of the Tibhirine monks and its setting within the complex politics of Algeria. A thorough, early account of events, also in English, was compiled by Donald McGlynn, abbot of the Cistercian community at Nunraw, Scotland; see Donald McGlynn, "Atlas Martyrs," CSQ 32, no. 2 (1997): 149–94.

2. www.notredameatlas.com, Sept. 30, 2010.

There is no one photograph that shows the Tibhirine community as it was constituted at the time of the kidnapping of the majority of its members on that night late in Lent 1996. Why would there be? It was hardly a monastic priority, and since late 1993 the community had been living in a situation of deteriorating security, following a GIA ultimatum warning foreigners to leave Algeria.[3] A few group photos have survived, however, including one from 1994 that includes most of the monks.[4] In this photograph, reproduced at the beginning of this chapter, what stands out immediately is the figure of Luc Dochier in the center. He is dressed, characteristically, in a grubby looking robe, cardigan, and a worn *taqiyah*, the round cap commonly worn by Muslim men. Indeed, when I first saw this photograph I imagined that he was an Algerian Muslim, standing among the Christian monks, "the other" in their midst.

But Luc was a monk, albeit different from the rest. Trained as a medical doctor in Lyon, France, during the 1930s, Luc Dochier (1914–1996) had joined the Trappist[5] community at Aiguebelle in the Rhône Valley in 1941 as a *frère convers*, a lay brother. Deeply marked by his wartime experience, having served as a medic in Morocco before the fall of France to the Germans and then as a volunteer in a German prisoner of war camp, his desire was to serve the poorest of the poor. In 1946 he moved to the small monastic community of Notre-Dame-de-l'Atlas at Tibhirine, where, for the next fifty years, he offered his services as a doctor to the people of the surrounding impoverished region of Médéa. He

3. In October 1993, three French consulate officers were taken hostage. Their release was accompanied by a message from the GIA giving all foreigners "one month to leave the country" (Olivera, *How Far to Follow*, 54). Olivera quotes from a chronology of events forwarded to him by Christian de Chergé, following the monastic community's own encounter with the GIA on Christmas Eve 1993.

4. Reproduced and dated in Christian Salenson, "Monastic Life, Interreligious Dialogue, and Openness to the Ultimate: A Reflection on the Tibhirine Monks' Experience," *The Way* 45, no. 3 (2006): 23–37, here 29.

5. Because of a seventheenth-century Cistercian reform movement centered at the French abbey of La Trappe, members of the OCSO were widely known as Trappists. In contemporary life members of this branch increasingly identify themselves simply as Cistercians or as members of the OCSO.

became the *toubib*, the doctor, respected and loved, trusted by both Muslim men and Muslim women, despite his brusque manner.[6] Luc lived out the distinctive vocation of a lay brother, a category that his Cistercian order eliminated in the wake of Vatican II. He was never a choir monk: even in his early days at Aiguebelle he "didn't like to be bothered by little details like going to the offices," preferring always "being of use to others."[7] Luc declined to sign the document on unification that would have changed his formal status from lay brother to monk. He was, perhaps, as Kiser suggests, stubborn in maintaining his position of humility.[8] Luc's presence at Tibhirine was a critical, if not central, element of the relationship between the monastery and the local Muslim community, and while his position was distinctive, his appearance in this late photograph of the monks somehow symbolizes the monastic journey of the Tibhirine community, its walk toward the other, a walk that ended in the deaths of seven monks.

This chapter explores the relationship between humility and the other by considering the life and writings of Christian de Chergé, the prior and primary theologian of this singular monastic community. At the core of Christian's vocation was a call to live alongside Algerian Muslims: "the other" (*les autres*). In the language of continental philosophy, *the other* connotes one radically different from oneself, one commonly perceived as a threat or even as an enemy.[9] From late 1988 until mid-1990, Christian

6. Olivera, *How Far to Follow*, 7; McGlynn, "Atlas Martyrs," 162–64; Kiser, *Monks of Tibhirine*, 160–63.

7. Kiser, *Monks of Tibhirine*, 162. Kiser quotes the recollections of Fr. Dominique, a monk of Aiguebelle.

8. Kiser, *Monks of Tibhirine*, 103. Kiser's source here is an interview with Bernardo Olivera. In his brief summation of Luc's life, Olivera remarks, "He was a laybrother by vocation and at heart. I still remember his question to me, 'What has happened to the laybrothers?'" (Olivera, *How Far to Follow*, 7).

9. See John D. Zizioulas, *Communion and Otherness: Further Studies in Personhood and the Church* (London: T. and T. Clark, 2006), 1–3. In this chapter I use *other* (lowercase) to denote humans and *Other* (uppercase) to denote God, with the exception of quotations, in which case I keep the rendering of the original. I occasionally use quotation marks for emphasis.

prepared and delivered a substantial series of talks to his monastic community on the subject of humility. During the same period, he wrote and delivered a significant paper on Christian-Muslim dialogue.

Christian's theology of humility, honed in the context of his monastic community, informed his understanding of otherness and his proposals regarding interfaith dialogue. Reading Christian's talks and his conference paper alongside the story of the Tibhirine community, one can clearly recognize the themes already enunciated in the course of this study. Theology and practice are inseparable. Humility, here as elsewhere, is embedded in eschatology and Christology. The practices of hospitality and community offer a locus for the cultivation of humility. In addition to taking humility into a more obviously ethical frame, this chapter, then, offers a further consolidation of a monastic theology of humility. It also considers where this theology leads when placed in the presence of the radically other.

5.1 Christian de Chergé: A Vocation to Algeria

5.1.1 Childhood and Education

Christian de Chergé (1937–1996) was born at Colmar, Haut-Rhin, into a family with an aristocratic and military pedigree. His father, Guy, himself from a military family, served in Algeria during World War II and was afterward promoted to the rank of general and appointed as director of studies in the War College, Paris. His mother, Monique, a devout Catholic with old French noble ancestry, encouraged the faith development of her large family of eight children. Christian was the third son. He grew up in a privileged environment. Apart from three war years spent in Algeria, his family lived in a fashionable quarter of Paris. Christian attended a Marianist school for boys, Sainte-Marie de Monceau, where he excelled academically. He sensed a priestly vocation early in his life, and in 1956, at the end of his schooling, he entered the Séminaire des Carmes in Paris, undertaking its rigorous six-year program of philosophy and theology. His entry was delayed by his surprising failure in the state baccalaureate exams, necessitating an additional year of study at a state school. This experience, Kiser suggests, gave the "star student . . . a dose of humility" and exposed him to greater social and intellectual diversity.[10]

5.1.2 Algeria: Formative Encounters

Christian's seminary program was interrupted by twenty-seven months of compulsory national service. In 1959, after completing officer training, he was posted to Algeria, where France had been waging an undeclared war since 1954.[11] This proved to be a decisive experience for his future: he was initiated, firsthand, into the politics of Algeria, he witnessed the emerging prophetic voice of the Algerian church against the backdrop of French colonial interests, he deepened his respect for Muslim Algerians, especially their commitment to God and to prayer, and he experienced the deep and costly hospitality of the other.

Christian was appointed to Tiaret as an officer with the Sectional Administrative Spéciale (SAS), to one of six hundred administrative districts designed to bring an already devastated rural Algeria more firmly under French control. The SAS soldiers worked alongside Algerian recruits, who were trained and paid to protect harvests and civilian infrastructure. Christian was returning to the country where he had already lived for three years as a child during the Second World War, a place where his parents had already taught him a respect for the Arab population. Writing to a friend in 1982, Christian recalled this formative experience and its consequence for his own faith:

> It was forty years ago this very year that I saw for the first time men praying in a way different from my fathers. I was five and was discovering Algeria during a first stay of three years. I remain profoundly grateful to my mother who taught

10. Kiser, *Monks of Tibhirine*, 23–25.
11. The war of decolonialization led to the independence of Algeria in 1962. Its history remains contested; it left both Algeria and France with significant scars that are yet to be healed.

my brothers and me respect for the integrity and the postures of this Muslim prayer. "They are praying to God," my mother said. Thus I have always known that the God of Islam and the God of Jesus Christ are not two gods.[12]

In Algeria in 1959 Christian found himself in a situation of considerable political and spiritual complexity. The fact that Algerian independence was firmly on the French political agenda led to a growing sense of betrayal among the European population. While the archbishop of Algiers, Léon-Étienne Duval, spoke in support of justice and self-determination for all Algerians, Christian's local parish priest vehemently opposed independence and showed little respect for Arabs or for Islam.[13]

In the course of his work, Christian had become friends with a village policeman, Mohammed, a Muslim family man. This friendship proved transformative: "He changed my life by liberating my faith in spite of the complexity of daily life and showed me how to live it simply as a response to what is natural and authentic in others."[14] One day, while walking together, the two were confronted by a group of *fells*, members of the Front de Libération Nationale (FLN). Mohammed put himself between their rifles and Christian, defending his friend as "a godly man

12. Quoted in Bernardo Olivera, "Monk, Martyr, and Mystic: Christian de Chergé (1937–1996)," CSQ 34, no. 3 (1999): 321–38, here 332. Olivera notes that the letter was later published as "To Pray as a Church Listening to Islam."

13. Kiser, *Monks of Tibhirine*, 9–10. The clergy were deeply divided over the role of the church in Algeria. Those who championed Algérie Française, keeping Algeria French, saw themselves as missionaries fighting for the survival of Christian civilization in North Africa against both Marxism and Islam. For Duval and his supporters, the Gospel message of radical inclusion required a different response, one of social justice and respect. Dubbed the "Muslims' bishop" by his opponents, Duval had a profound impact on Christian de Chergé (Kiser, *Monks of Tibhirine*, 12–21).

14. Trans. Kiser, *Monks of Tibhirine*, 10. See Marie-Christine Ray, *Christian de Chergé, prieur de Tibhirine*, 2nd ed. (Paris: Bayard, 1998), 47. Ray's source is "Témoignage de Christian de Chergé, Toussaint 1985, 'Prier en situation de conflit armé' ": "[Il] a aidé ma foi à se libérer en s'exprimant, au fil d'un quotidien difficile, comme une réponse tranquille, avec la simplicité de l'authenticité."

and a friend of Muslims."[15] The men withdrew, but the next day
Mohammed was found dead, his throat slit, outside the small village where he had lived with his family. This event, Mohammed's
offering of his own life for his friend, had a profound influence
on the rest of Christian's life:

> In the blood shed by this friend, who was assassinated because
> he would not practice hatred, I knew that my call to follow Christ
> would be lived sooner or later in the same country that gave me
> a tangible sign of the greatest love possible. . . . I knew also
> that this consecration of mine had to flow through [common]
> prayer in order to give true witness to the church's presence.[16]

5.1.3 Ordination and Monastic Vocation

On completing his military service, Christian returned to his
seminary studies and was ordained in 1964 as a priest of the
archdiocese of Paris. He then served as a chaplain for six years
at Sacré-Coeur in Montmartre, under the conservative Cardinal
Maurice Charles. The environment was at odds with Christian's
desire to serve among the "poor and *fraternelle*"[17] and with his own
emerging theology and practice as a priest, which was strongly
influenced by Vatican II (1962–1965). During this period he decided to join the Trappists, and on August 20, 1969, the feast day
of Bernard of Clairvaux, he began his novitiate at Aiguebelle. He
had returning to Algeria firmly in view, his choice of the Trappists motivated by their commitment to place, community, and
manual work (he deemed the Jesuits and the Benedictines too

---

15. Kiser, *Monks of Tibhirine*, 9.

16. Kiser, *Monks of Tibhirine*, 40; Ray, *Christian de Chergé*, 59. Ray's source is
"Témoignage de Christian de Chergé, Toussaint, 1985, 'Prier en situation de
conflit armé?' ": "Dans le sang de cet ami, assassiné pour n'avoir pas voulu
practiser avec la haine j'ai su que mon appel à suivre le Christ devrait trouver
à se vivre, tôt ou tard, dans le pays même où m'avait été donné ce gage de
l'amour le plus grand. . . . J'ai su, du même coup, que cette consécration
devait se couler dans une prière en commun pour être vraiment témoignage
d'Église."

17. Kiser, *Monks of Tibhirine*, 27, quoting Ray, *Christian de Chergé*, 67.

intellectual), but he chose this order above all because it had a community in Algeria, at Tibhirine near the Atlas Mountains.[18] He joined this community, Notre-Dame-de-l'Atlas, on January 15, 1971. In a letter to an old friend he expressed his sense of homecoming and hinted at the agenda that would become central to the Tibhirine community. The letter is filled too with Christian's idealism: "I have arrived in the Atlas Mountains surrounded by a population that is poor, but smiling, proud, and without bitterness. They are believers and respectful of all religious people, provided that what is in the back room corresponds with what is in the display windows."[19] To live out his faith with integrity, with "back room" and "display windows" matched, was Christian's passionate desire.

5.2 The Cistercians in Algeria

The Cistercians had been present in Algeria since 1843, when they had established a monastery at Staouëli with the support of the French government. Renowned for their agricultural enterprise, they were recruited both to assist in the colonization of rural Algeria and to provide a visible, yet modest—without too obvious a missionary element—spiritual presence that would improve the religious credibility of the French occupiers.[20] While the existence of the community at Staouëli, with 100 monks and 120 workers at its peak, clearly served colonial interests, it also gained the respect of the local inhabitants. Political changes in Europe and in the fortunes of its motherhouse, Aiguebelle, however, led to the monastery's closing in 1904 and the subsequent sale of the property. When the Cistercians returned to Algeria in 1934, they eventually settled in Tib-Hirine, "the gardens," a property at the foot of the Atlas Mountains that had once been an English colonial farm. This refoundation grew slowly, but by 1952, when

---

18. Kiser, *Monks of Tibhirine*, 30.

19. Quoted in translation: Kiser, *Monks of Tibhirine*, 39; Ray, *Christian de Chergé*, 90. Original source: Christian de Chergé, Lettre à Jacques et Majo Delage, August 4, 1973.

20. Kiser, *Monks of Tibhirine*, 35–37.

it was raised to the full status of an abbey, it had peaked at thirty-five members.[21]

During the Algerian War (1954–1962), the monastery remained largely sheltered from the conflict. In 1956 a group of refugee Muslim children was placed in a camp next to the abbey, and, with the subsequent arrival from the Tamesguida mountains of families fleeing the violence, the village of Tibhirine was born. The exception to this relative shelter was the 1959 kidnapping of Fr. Matthew and Br. Luc by the Armée de Libération Nationale (ALN): the two were quickly freed once Luc was identified as the local *toubib*. The situation after independence in 1962 was, however, quite different, and the monastery entered a long period of uncertainty and instability. The Algerian government redistributed most of the monastery's land to the local population (360 out of 374 hectares), and of the remaining fourteen acres only ten were capable of being cultivated. The monastery gave up further land to enable the construction of a local school. In the newly independent Algeria, Islam was now the state religion, and the church had to negotiate the continued presence of the monastery. The government permitted the community to have a maximum of only twelve members.

Ironically, a decision to close the community was made in 1963 not by the Algerian government but by the Cistercian general chapter meeting in Rome. The death of the then-abbot general Dom Gabriel Sortais and the intervention of Archbishop Duval gave the community a temporary reprieve. The abbot of Aiguebelle, Dom Jean-de-la-Croix, was commissioned to oversee the closing, but, persuaded by Duval of the importance of the community's continuation, in 1964 he secured eight volunteers from other European monastic houses to bolster the community.[22]

This method of recruitment—indeed, no other was possible in this environment[23]—meant that the community had both a fragil-

---

21. McGlynn, "Atlas Martyrs," 155–57.
22. McGlynn, "Atlas Martyrs," 157.
23. The Christian population was rapidly shrinking, and open conversion to Christianity was virtually impossible.

ity and a diversity that posed continued challenges. When Peter Gilmore, a member of the community for just one year, arrived at Tibhirine in 1965, there were twelve monks from four different monasteries, half of them under forty-five years old. When Christian arrived in 1971, there were thirteen monks from seven different monasteries.[24] In addition to the geographical isolation and changed political situation, this fluidity of the monastic community, in both its membership and its leadership, exacerbated the uncertainties. Behind all of this, however, stood a larger issue, as Gilmore observes: "It would appear that there were more than a few years of instability in the community and a long period of unanswered questioning as to what a Cistercian monastery was really called to do, or rather to be, in an exclusively Muslim environment."[25] The answer to this question emerged, over time, out of the particular, concrete situation in which this small monastic community found itself.

5.3 Tibhirine: An Emerging Vocation

A number of factors played a role in the continued existence of the monastery in the face of both internal fragility and the uncertainties of postindependence Algeria. First, the village of Tibhirine had grown around the monastery after its beginnings during the Algerian War with the settlement of refugees and families from the mountains adjacent to the monastery. The second factor was the presence of Br. Luc and the dispensary. The monks' developing ties to the villagers of Tibhirine and accompanying sense of responsibility for their welfare increased in the years that followed.

Beyond these local circumstances, the theology emerging from Vatican II began to have an impact on monastic communities generally, and specifically on interfaith dialogue. In 1978 Jean-de-la-Croix, already an experienced abbot, returned to the monastery as superior, a position he then held for six years. In 1979 he offered,

24. Peter Gilmore, "Atlas: Reawakened Memories and Present-Day Reflections," CSQ 35, no. 2 (2000): 231–38, here 232.
25. Gilmore, "Atlas," 232.

with the agreement of the monastic community, hospitality to the newly formed *Ribât es-Salêm* (Link of Peace). Founded by Claude Rault, the *Ribât* began as a group of Christian men and women, mainly Catholic religious, meeting to understand Islam better as a lived faith. The relationship between the monastery and the *Ribât* grew in significance over the years, offering mutual support and becoming a significant forum for interfaith dialogue.[26]

The decisive factor in the continuation of the monastery at Tibhirine was, however, the arrival of Christian de Chergé, with his specific vocation to Algeria and to Muslims and his subsequent election as prior. Not long after his arrival, Christian was granted leave for two years to study at the Pontifical Institute for Arabic and Islamic Studies under Fr. Maurice Borrmans. Here Christian learned Arabic, studied the Qur'an, and deepened his understanding of how religion in Algeria functioned.[27] When he was elected prior in 1984,[28] the community's vocation was finally clarified. As Gilmore suggests, "This event, together with the contact with the *Ribât*, was probably the real beginning of the community's stability and awareness of the role they were being called to play among the Muslims of Algeria."[29]

It is also worth noting the significant role that the Tibhirine monastery played in the Algerian church, which after 1962 found itself in an increasingly fragile place. For the Christian community in Algeria, the monastery provided a much-needed place of retreat, and the monastery's harmonious relationship with the villagers of Tibhirine offered hope that Muslims and Christians could live side by side. As Msgr. Henri Teissier, then archbishop of Algiers, said at a Mass held in Rome on October 10, 1996, after the deaths of the seven monks, "Tibhirine was for us an icon of our vocation as Christians seeking God in the land of Algeria, that

26. McGlynn, "Atlas Martyrs," 171–72.

27. Kiser, *Monks of Tibhirine*, 40–42.

28. The status of the monastery had been changed from abbey to priory, so Christian became prior rather than abbot. This change, McGlynn says, "corresponded better to reality and at the same time safeguarded their autonomy" (McGlynn, "Atlas Martyrs," 157).

29. Gilmore, "Atlas," 232.

is to say in a Muslim land. . . . I think there is no other monastery in the world which has such a general relationship with the
members of the local Church. Most of the priests, religious men
and women, as well as the laity living permanently in the diocese,
had a personal bond with the community."[30]

5.4 *Bribes d'humilité*: "Scraps of Humility"

As is common in both Benedictine and Cistercian monasteries,
Christian, as prior, regularly presented short talks (*chapitres* or
conferences) to the monks gathered as a community. These ses-
sions provided ongoing formation in the monastic tradition,
bringing its wisdom into the specific context in which the monastery found itself. At Tibhirine these talks were normally delivered three times a week in the morning. The notes that Christian
prepared for these talks between 1985 and 1996 have survived.[31]
These documents, it must be said, are notes from which Christian
spoke rather than full scripts, so they do not always offer fully
elaborated lines of argument. Nonetheless they provide, alongside his surviving homilies and other writing, a rich source for
exploring his evolving theology.[32]

For a period of almost eighteen months, from December
1988 until May 1990, Christian, working from the Rule of Saint
Benedict, presented a lengthy series of talks on the subject of

30. Quoted in McGlynn, "Atlas Martyrs," 149–50.

31. Published as Christian de Chergé, *Dieu pour tout jour: Chapitres de Père
Christian de Chergé à la communauté de Tibhirine (1985–1996)*, 2nd ed. (Montjoyer: Abbaye Notre-Dame d'Aiguebelle, 2006).

32. Christian de Chergé, *L'AUTRE que nous attendons: Homélies de Père
Christian de Chergé (1970–1996)* (Montjoyer: Abbaye Notre-Dame d'Aiguebelle,
2006). Bruno Chenu edited two important collections of the monks' writings.
The first, published soon after the death of the monks, contains a range of
documents, including some of the community's circular letters that document
the difficulties of their final years: Bruno Chenu, ed., *Sept vies pour Dieu et
L'Algérie*, 2nd ed. (Paris: Bayard, 1996). The second is dedicated wholly to the
writings of Christian: Christian de Chergé, *L'invincible espérance*, ed. Bruno
Chenu (Paris: Bayard, 2010). Like Bernard of Clairvaux, Christian was an
energetic writer.

humility.[33] Midway through this period, in September 1989, Christian delivered a lecture at the *Journées Romaines*, a conference focused on Christian-Muslim dialogue.[34] This paper, "L'échelle mystique du dialogue" ("The Mystical Ladder of Dialogue"), offers a theological rationale, perhaps his most developed, for the particular route taken by the Tibhirine community, a path that Christian typifies as *priants parmi d'autre priants* (praying among others who pray).[35] Taken together, this paper and the chapter talks reveal how Christian's understanding of humility underpins his theology of dialogue. For example, the fact that Christian chooses the ladder as his primary metaphor for interfaith dialogue, a metaphor that is central to the exposition of humility in chapter 7 of the Rule of Saint Benedict, is no coincidence.

Significantly, Christian shares with Bernard and other monastic theologians a fluid and metaphorical, rather than a systematic, approach. Edith Scholl notices Christian's close reading of the Rule of Saint Benedict and his method of following the trajectory of a particular word.[36] It is likely that this approach derives in part from the practice of *lectio divina*. Indeed Christian's writings often feel like an extended, shared *lectio* in which the various

---

33. I am indebted to the work of Edith Scholl in drawing attention to Christian de Chergé's writing on humility and draw substantially on her helpful English-language précis of this series of chapter talks (Edith Scholl, "Christian de Chergé on Humility," CSQ 41, no. 2 [2006]: 193–215). What I endeavor to add to her work is a reading of these talks against Christian's thinking about the other.

34. The conference was hosted by PISAI, The Pontifical Institute for Arabic and Islamic Studies. The full text of Christian's speech has been published as Christian de Chergé, "L'échelle mystique du dialogue," *Islamochristiana* 23 (1997): 1–26. Chenu offers a slightly revised version, which incorporates the additions to the third section of the paper as it was published in the *Lettre de Ligugé* 256 (1991–1992): 18–28. See Chergé, *L'invincible espérance*, 167–204.

35. There is no direct English translation for *priants*, "those who pray," but the verb *prier* "to pray," from which *priant* is derived, can also mean "to beg" or "implore." Perhaps this connotation also echoes in Christian's phrases, "Pray-ers among other pray-ers. Supplicants among other supplicants." The translation "Praying among other people who pray" is an attempt to capture the verbal, active emphasis of the French.

36. Scholl, "Christian de Chergé," 215.

resonances of a word or image are explored in turn, building a larger and more vivid picture along the way. He is also a story-teller who brings the experiences of his community to his theological reflection.

5.4.1 Humility: A Divine Climat

Christian's initial talks on humility show an immediate grasp of the critical issues concerning its nature and reflect a nuanced and mature reading of the monastic tradition. As he commences what became a lengthy series of talks, he acknowledges, like those writing before him, the impossibility of his subject and its hazards: the double danger of either daring to speak of humility and exposing one's lack of it or failing to speak of it and thereby giving an impression that one has "arrived." Such erroneous thinking, Christian says, has given rise to all the forms of "false humility" that we experience. The source of these difficulties, he suggests, is the tendency to treat humility as a moral virtue, something that can be acquired by effort, "one tool among others in the workshop of perfection."[37] (This tendency is, of course, the difficulty encountered at the commencement of this study.) In fact, he notes, the Rule of Saint Benedict never includes humility in the instruments of good works. By contrast, pride appears in the "catalogue of the moral life" and is listed among the capital sins. Is humility simply the opposite, or absence, of pride? he asks.[38] He endeavors to sort out this confusion. We know, he says, that pride is at the root of our damaged relationship with God. One senses that humility responds to this "story" (*histoire*): humility is *un comportement*, a response to this great sin (*le grand péché*), a way of standing truthfully in relationship to God.[39] For Christian, truth and humility are partners, as they are in Benedict and Bernard.

---

37. Chergé, *Dieu pour tout jour*, 259.
38. Chergé, *Dieu pour tout jour*, 259.
39. Chergé, *Dieu pour tout jour*, 259–60; December 5, 1988: "L'humilité est un comportement d'avant 'le grand péché', une qualité de relation entre l'homme et Dieu qui sonnerait JUSTE" (260) (Scholl, "Christian de Chergé,"

Christian here acknowledges the distance between the human and the divine and identifies humility as the key to the return from the original sin of pride to one's true place as a creature of the Creator. But he immediately moves further. In human life, he says, pride and humility "cohabit" like the weeds and wheat of Jesus' parable: "that which is of us and that which is not of us."[40] This is a helpful insight—and one that offers the possibility of liberation.[41] It is not about human effort. In this life we always bear our double nature: we are human beings stamped with the divine imprint. Humility is not a moral but a theological virtue, or, rather, in Christian's words here, humility is about *la vie théologale*, the action of God in us.[42] Christian is clearly drawing on the standard distinction in Catholic moral thought between theological and cardinal virtues, but, interestingly, he avoids the word *virtue* (Fr *vertu*) here.[43]

With this ground now cleared, Christian says, he is able to proceed to share some *bribes*—some scraps or fragments—on the subject of humility.[44] He can do this with a sense of "delight and freedom" because, he says, "Christian humility appears primarily to be a CLIMATE [*un climat*], which is not human, but upon which man is dependent if he wants to breathe freely."[45] Humility is simply part of the atmosphere, the given of the divine climate. When one breathes God, one breathes humility.

---

194). Scholl's page references are to the 1st edition of the *Chapitres* and do not correlate with the 2nd revised edition.

40. Chergé, *Dieu pour tout jour*, 260: "ce qui est de nous et ce qui n'est pas de nous."

41. Chergé, *Dieu pour tout jour*, 260.

42. Chergé, *Dieu pour tout jour*, 260.

43. In a later talk Christian does name humility as a theological virtue (Chergé, *Dieu pour tout jour*, 262).

44. A resonant phrase, perhaps suggestive of the fragments of leftover bread in the gospel stories of the miraculous feedings and the crumbs that have fallen from the table in Jesus' interchange with the Canaanite woman. I considered the significance of crumbs in relation to the Rule of the Master in chap. 3.

45. Chergé, *Dieu pour tout jour*, 260: "L'humilité chrétienne me paraît d'abord être un CLIMAT qui n'est pas de l'homme, mais auquel l'homme ne saurait échapper s'il veut respirer librement."

5.4.2 Humility and Obedience

In his second talk, Christian immediately tackles the relationship between humility and obedience. He takes his cue here from the Rule of Saint Benedict. Benedict, Christian notes, understands humility only in relation to submission or subordination. Not surprisingly, we find this connection difficult: we resile from dependence, wanting instead to be in control. But isn't this what is intended for us, Christian asks, when in the book of Genesis humans are given authority over creation? Are we not made in the image of "a God who creates and orders"?[46] The problem is that we tend to take power for ourselves; we make ourselves gods ("each takes himself for God the Father").[47] The result is anarchy. There would be anarchy in the Trinity too, Christian remarks with an exclamation, if such grasping of power were the case there.[48]

Returning to Benedict, Christian notes the Rule's insistence, stated in its strongest form in RB 5.1, that unhesitating obedience is the first step of humility. No humility without obedience; no obedience without humility: Christian emphasizes this double direction. That reality, Christian says, sends us back to the life of God (*la vie théologale*), and here he offers a significant shift in the usual understanding of obedience: "before being the attitude forced on a subject, it is first and eternally the disposition of the heart of the Son in his relation to the Father."[49] There is here, in Christian's reframing, a sense of freedom: obedience does not mean repression or violence. Rather, obedience, like humility, is part of the divine *climat*. This can be seen clearly, Christian continues, in the incarnation and in the cross: "The one who was obedient even to the humiliation of the incarnation and the cross, is for ever and ever the witness and joyful messenger of the YES to the Father.

46. Chergé, *Dieu pour tout jour*, 260; December 6, 1988: "Un Dieu qui creé et qui ordonne."
47. Chergé, *Dieu pour tout jour*, 260: "Chacun se prendrait pour Dieu le Père."
48. Chergé, *Dieu pour tout jour*, 260.
49. Chergé, *Dieu pour tout jour*, 260: "Avant d'être l'attitude contrainte du sujet, est d'abord et éternellement la disposition de coeur du Fils dans sa relation au Père" (translation draws on Scholl, "Christian de Chergé," 194).

'Unhesitating obedience' is his personal way of being in the bosom of the Trinity."[50] Humility and obedience are of a piece.

In his third talk, Christian continues this line of argument: "There is humility in God. It is CHRIST who tells us this by living it. Our way to God cannot be other than his: 'Have this mind in you that was in Christ Jesus' . . . [Phil 2:5]. We learn, to our astonishment, that it is by humility that we can be divinised, made like God, the old dream whispered by the serpent."[51]

This discovery that humility is part of the life of God takes us beyond definitions of humility that stop with the awareness of the distance between Creator and creature or awareness of sin (Christian still finds this emphasis in the twentieth-century monastic writing that he has been reading). The critical, indeed the particular Christian revelation is that humility is seen most clearly in the "kenosis of Christ as innate [*congénitale*] to the Son." That is, humility is who the Son is. This is "why to attach oneself to Christ and to attach oneself to humility, is all ONE."[52] Thus, as we follow Christ, the lost resemblance (the image of God) is restored in us, and, even better, humility becomes the *climat* of our relations with others.[53]

In his next talk, Christian summarizes the place he has reached: "Not being able to find humility among humans, we need to look

50. Chergé, *Dieu pour tout jour*, 260: "Celui qui s'est fait obéissant jusqu'à l'humiliation de l'incarnation et de la croix, est de toujours à toujours le témoin et le messager joyeux du OUI au Père. 'L'obéissance sans délai', c'est sa façon d'être personnel au sein de la Trinité" (translation draws on Scholl, "Christian de Chergé," 194–95). Christian often capitalizes words in his notes for emphasis, and these are reproduced in the printed edition of his chapter talks. I have retained these for the English translations.

51. Chergé, *Dieu pour tout jour*, 261; December 7, 1988: "Il y a de l'humilité en Dieu. C'est le CHRIST qui nous le dit en la vivant. Notre chemin vers Dieu ne peut être que le sien: Ayez en vous les sentiments qui sont dans le Christ Jésus, lui qui . . . . Nous apprenons, étonnés, que c'est par l'humilité que nous pouvons être divinisés, rendus semblables à Dieu, le vieux rêve susurré par le serpent" (translation draws on Scholl, "Christian de Chergé," 194).

52. Chergé, *Dieu pour tout jour*, 261: "Voilà pourquoi s'attacher au Christ et s'attacher à l'humilité, c'est tout UN."

53. Chergé, *Dieu pour tout jour*, 261.

for it in God. Jesus came to invite us to that unexpected course. It could even be said that he did nothing else. Everything in him is a demonstration of HUMILITY, and not of power. The proper mode of humility in Christ is OBEDIENCE."[54]

In these first talks, then, Christian builds secure foundations for a theology of humility. For Christian, as in much of the tradition behind him, humility is not simply a matter of the distance between the divine and the human. As Bernard of Clairvaux, for example, moves from "cold" to "warm" humility, Christian similarly understands humility in a fundamentally positive way. Humility is part of the life of God, the way in which God is God. Again, like the tradition behind him, he recognizes its christological basis. He also understands the irreducible, if uncomfortable, relationship between obedience and humility. Christ, obedience, and humility are integrally linked. Divine humility is expressed in the joyful obedience of the Son.

5.5 The Eschatological Horizon: Hope and Humility

When Christian went to speak at the *Journées Romaines* in September 1989, he had already over the space of six months prepared and delivered almost fifty talks to his community on the subject of humility. The fruit of this journey with the Rule of Saint Benedict is evident in his presentation to this interfaith conference, forming the foundations for his theology of dialogue. He places humility firmly in the context of eschatology, playing with a series of vivid metaphors (journey, horizon, ladder) to express his optimistic

---

54. Chergé, *Dieu pour tout jour*, 261; December 10, 1988: "Ne pouvant trouver l'humilité du côté de l'homme, nous la cherchons du côté de Dieu. Jésus est venu nous inviter à cette démarche inattendue. On pourrait même dire qu'il n'a fait que cela. Tout en lui est démonstration d'HUMILITÉ . . . et non de puissance. Le mode propre de cette humilité, dans le Christ, c'est l'OBÉISSANCE" (trans. Scholl, "Christian de Chergé," 195) (Christian's emphasis). Christian then goes on to explore the idea of modes of humility, offering a trinitarian scheme. If obedience is the mode of humility in the Son, silence is the mode of the Spirit; he draws here on RB 6, *De taciturnitate*, "On Restraint of Speech." Christian then speculates, from an Advent perspective, that perhaps waiting is the mode of the Father.

vision of human destiny. Here he articulates his theology of hope: a theme that, as theologian Christian Salenson observes, is central to his life and thought.[55]

5.5.1 "I Place Death before My Eyes"

Christian prefaces his lecture with a quotation from the beginning of Paul's second letter to the Corinthians, with Paul writing out of the experience of suffering and defeat: "We had received the sentence of death. Thus our trust could no longer be based in ourselves, but in God who raises the dead. It is He who rescued us from such a death. . . . In him we have this our hope, that he will rescue us again!" (2 Cor 1:9-10).[56]

Why did Christian choose this text? Certainly these words prophetically express the response of the monastic community of Tibhirine to the increasingly perilous situation of its last years. Here, though, he was thinking of 1975, when the Algerian authorities had given the community eight days to leave.[57] The directive was withdrawn, but that sense of having received "the sentence of death" remained. The community understood itself to be in a state of contingency. By 1989, however, five years after Christian's election as prior, the community was no longer destabilized by this permanent provisionality but secure in its vocation as a community of *priants parmi d'autre priants* (praying among others who pray).

This precariousness, and its fruitfulness, was noticed by Philippe Hémon, a monk of the Cistercian abbey of Tamié, when he first visited Tibhirine for Christophe Lebreton's ordination in 1990:

55. Christian Salenson, *Christian de Chergé: une théologie de l'espérance* (Paris: Bayard, 2009), 245–46.

56. Translating directly from the French text. Chergé, "L'échelle mystique," 1: "Nous avions reçu notre arrêt de mort. Ainsi, notre confiance ne pouvait plus se fonder sur nous-mêmes, mais sur Dieu qui ressuscitate les morts. C'est Lui qui nous a arrachés à une telle mort . . . en Lui nous avons cette espérance qui est nôtre, il nous en arrachera encore! (2 Co 1,9-10)."

57. Chergé, "L'échelle mystique," 1. The version of this lecture edited by Bruno Chenu and reprinted in *L'invincible espérance* does not include the Corinthians text.

I had scarcely arrived in that house, their house, so poor and so full of warmth at the same time, when I perceived forming within me, coming from I know not where, the profound conviction that they were the real monks of the present time. Everything in their existence was stamped with the seal of precariousness. The precariousness of their situation as foreigners several times expelled and brought back, the precariousness of the country's political and economic situation, the precariousness of their status as a religious minority. And I thought of what Jean-Baptist Metz had written once, so fittingly: religious life can never be understood apart from that precariousness which demonstrates its eschatological openness. Without that condition as its foundation it installs itself in the transitory . . . and dies as a result. What freedom I felt with those men, stripped of all, able to offer only that in themselves which made them day by day more human. Was I not told recently by a monk who had seen other communities that to his mind they were the poorest community in the Order?[58]

One is reminded here of Arnold of Bonnevaux's description of the monks of Clairvaux as "ragged men, bearing a rough cross" and of the astonishment expressed by the visiting papal party at the Cistercian way of life.[59] At Tibhirine an eschatological orientation (living with hope in the context of the "sentence of death") was not simply a theoretical possibility but was tangibly manifest in the fragility of their lives. Commenting on its fruitfulness, Salenson wonders why it is that "such precariousness is rarely considered as a form of evangelical poverty, something which offers a chance of greater gospel authenticity."[60] Precariousness is here, I suggest, closely related to humility: an awareness of one's utter dependence, as a creature of the Creator, an awareness that

58. Philippe Hémon, "An En-Visaged Good-by-E," CSQ 34, no. 2 (1999): 203–18, here 208.

59. William of Saint-Thierry, et al., *St. Bernard of Clairvaux: The Story of His Life as Recorded in the "Vita Prima Bernardi" by Certain of His Contemporaries, William of St. Thierry, Arnold of Bonnevaux, Geoffrey and Philip of Clairvaux, and Odo of Deuil*, trans. Geoffrey Webb and Adrian Walker (London: Mowbray, 1960), 79.

60. Salenson, "Monastic Life," 25.

is difficult to comprehend from a position of material (political, social, and physical) security. Precariousness, like poverty, throws one toward the mercy of God.

This "eschatological openness," which is founded on an embrace of provisionality or dependence, resonates too with the desert monastic tradition. The desert *ammas* and *abbas* lived with a similar precariousness, on the margins, in the desert. They too understood existentially their dependence on the mercy of God. Death and hope are linked. Amma Sarah comes to mind again here: "I put out my foot to ascend the ladder, and I place death before my eyes before going up it."[61] For Amma Sarah, and later for Cassian and Benedict, this "fear of God," or eschatological humility, constitutes the necessary, first step in the journey toward God.

5.5.2 Pilgrims of the Horizon

It is clear from the *Journées Romaines* lecture that Christian understands the vocation of his monastic community in an eschatological frame. Indeed, for Christian, monastic life is essentially defined by its orientation to the end, to hope, and this eschatological orientation constitutes monasticism's primary gift to the world: "If a monk thinks he has anything to say here, it's less in the role of an efficient builder of the human city (even though he might do much on this level . . .) than as a resolute adherent of a way of being in the world that is senseless apart from what we call the ultimate ends—the eschatology—of hope."[62] None of this is new, of course, but this orientation, lived out in a Muslim context, resulted in an "eschato-

61. *The Sayings of the Desert Fathers: The Alphabetical Collection*, trans. Benedicta Ward, rev. ed., CS 59 (Kalamazoo, MI: Cistercian Publications, 1984), 230 (Sarah 6).

62. Chergé, "L'échelle mystique," 3: "Et si le moine croit avoir son mot à dire ici, c'est moins comme constructeur efficace de la cité des Hommes (encore que . . .), que comme adepte résolu d'une façon d'être au monde, qui n'aurait aucun sens en dehors de ce que nous appelons les 'fins dernières' (eschatologie) de l'espérance" (trans. Salenson, "Monastic Life," 32). Desert monasticism's flight from "city to desert" resonates in Christian's choice of language here.

logical openness" that significantly pushed conservative theological boundaries—and conventional Cistercian monastic practice.

Openness means precisely that, with all the attendant risk of not knowing everything in advance. It implies an existential humility. In his lecture Christian indicates that he is fully aware of this implication but sees it quite simply as a continuation of the reforming work of Vatican II. Living "in the *house of Islam*," he says, makes one aware of both the difficulty and the urgency of its agenda. He lists the "*nouveautés* of the Gospel," the particular contributions of the Gospel, now being taken out from its "treasure house": "the practice of non-violence, the necessity of justice, religious freedom, the refusal to proselytize, the spirituality of dialogue, respect for difference, without forgetting continued solidarity with the poor."[63] All this must be implemented, he says, without expecting that "the other" will do the same. The danger he perceives, however, is that Christians will grow weary of taking the lead and call a halt. Once more he frames this Gospel-inspired agenda in eschatological terms: "Aren't we," he asks, "already indebted for the astonishing initiative taken by the One *who has loved us to the extreme [jusqu'à l'extrême]*?"[64] If Christians are to live in this Gospel way, they must escape the persistent tendency to expect something equal in return.[65] Instead, Christian urges a route that is open to the horizon: "going toward the other and going toward God, it's all one, and I cannot do without either." The same attitude of freely giving (*gratuité*) is necessary.[66] Living in this

63. Chergé, "L'échelle mystique," 7.

64. Chergé, "L'échelle mystique," 7. Christian is alluding to John 13:1 here. In *La Bible de Jérusalem* the text ends with *la fin*. It is possible that he has deliberately modified this to *l'extrême* for emphasis.

65. Chergé, "L'échelle mystique," 7: "talion du *donnant-donnant*." The phrase Christian uses here suggests the ubiquitous law of "an eye for an eye," the antithesis of the Gospel.

66. Chergé, "L'échelle mystique," 7: "Aller vers l'autre et aller vers Dieu, c'est tout un, et je ne peux m'en passer. Il y faut la même gratuité." Christian uses the same expression, "c'est tout un," in a chapter talk to describe the relationship between Christ and humility: "to attach oneself to Christ and to attach oneself to humility, is all ONE" (Chergé, *Dieu pour tout jour*, 261; trans. Scholl, "Christian de Chergé," 195).

direction, open to the horizon, he continues, reshapes the nature of mission, creating a "qualitative change in the atmosphere of life" (he quotes Jürgen Moltmann here). And here he is able to report on the experience of the Tibhirine community and its commitment to learning "to walk together" with the *house of Islam.*

On the feast of All Saints in 1980 the Alawiyines of Médéa, a group of Sufi, joined the *Ribât* for the first time. They had already come to pray with the monastic community. When they joined the *Ribât* for conversation they brought with them a verse from the Qur'an:

We will show them our Signs,
on the horizons and within themselves. (Qur'an 41:53)[67]

The metaphor of the horizon echoes Christian's own theology, confirming his embrace of eschatological openness. The Alawiyines, Christian reports, made it clear that they had no wish to engage in dogmatic discussion, where the barriers erected by humans are so great, but, they said, "We wish here to leave to God the possibility of creating between us something new. And this can only be done in prayer."[68]

It is evident here that the ground for the dialogue had shifted. No longer was it the monastic community walking toward the other; rather the monks became, with their Sufi brothers, fellow "pilgrims of the horizon." Here, paradoxically, "eschatological openness" was already fruiting: it had a (partly) realized quality. If one is open to "the horizon" it is possible that something new will be born. Such expectancy is at the heart of Christian hope.

Both Christian and the Alawiyines were clear that this new thing is most likely to emerge in prayer, "beyond the horizon of our reason where God comes to us."[69] For Christian, the "beyond"

67. Chergé, "L'échelle mystique," 7: "Nous leur montrerons bientôt nos Signes, aux horizons et en eux-mêmes . . . (Coran 41, 53)." The English here is a direct translation of Christian's French quotation of the Qur'an. I have altered "Coran" to *Qur'an.*

68. Chergé, "L'échelle mystique," 7.

69. Chergé, "L'échelle mystique," 7: "par-delà l'horizon de notre raison que Dieu nous vient."

of the horizon, with its unknowing, remains. It invokes in him a deep curiosity, but not fear: "For thirty years I have carried within myself the existence of Islam as a nagging question. I have an immense curiosity regarding the place it holds in God's mysterious design. Only death will provide me, I think, with the response I am waiting for. I am sure that I will be able to fathom it, dazzled, in the paschal light of Him who presents himself to me as the only possible Muslim [*le seul musulman possible*] because he is nothing but *yes* to the Father's will."[70]

It is worth noting three things here. First, the experience of humility is radical. Christian understands, both rationally and existentially, the limits of human capacities. In one of his chapter talks he comments on this idea in relation to the sayings of Saint Anthony. The way of the desert, Christian says, involves "the humility of the intelligence": an acceptance that not all can be known or understood. One is ultimately a mystery to oneself.[71]

Second, the horizon is oriented toward hope. Eschatological openness is met by "paschal light." Christian always understands the "ultimate ends" in terms of the Easter mystery, the death and resurrection of Jesus Christ. Finally, this hopeful horizon has the shape of humility: the obedience of the Son to the Father. Christian expresses this obedience daringly: Christ is the only Muslim.[72] Only in the Son is there perfect submission to the will of God.

---

70. Chergé, "L'échelle mystique," 6: "Depuis trente ans que je porte en moi l'existence de l'Islam comme une question lancinante, j'ai une immense curiosité pour la place qu'il tient dans le dessein mystérieux de Dieu. La mort seule, je pense, me fournira la réponse attendue. Je suis sûr de la déchiffrer, ébloui, dans la lumière pascale de Celui qui se présente à moi comme le seul *musulman* possible, parce qu'il n'est que *oui* à la volonté du Père" (trans. based on Salenson, "Monastic Life," 28).

71. Chergé, *Dieu pour tout jour*, 270; January 17, 1989: "Le chemin du desert est donc celui de l'humilité de l'intelligence: l'homme accepte de ne pas tout savoir, de ne pas tout comprendre, de rester à lui-même un mystère même lorsqu'il prête ATTENTION à ce qu'il est."

72. Chergé, "L'échelle mystique," 21. The Arabic word *islâm*, before being used to designate a faith, means "submission to God."

5.5.3 Reimagining Benedict's Ladder: The Chapter Talks

This sense of a common journey, shared by Christians and Muslims, inspires Christian to an imaginative recasting of the metaphor of the ladder, a metaphor that has been central to the development of the monastic theology of humility. The foundations of this thinking can be found in Christian's exploration of the metaphor in the context of his chapter talks, where he takes considerable time exploring its place in the Rule of Saint Benedict and in the Judeo-Christian tradition. This work underpins his reappropriation for the purposes of interfaith dialogue.

Taking his cue from Benedict (RB 7.6), Christian begins by exploring the story of Jacob's dream of angels descending and ascending a ladder that stretches from earth to heaven (Gen 28:12). He takes care to set this story and metaphor on a larger theological stage. He notes, for example, the ubiquitous presence of antonyms of height and depth (*bas-haut, abaisser-élever, en-haut, au-dessus*) in biblical, and indeed in all religious, language and its correlation with heaven and earth, the divine and the human ("the heavenly world, that of God," and "the terrestrial world where man evolves").[73] Christian understands too that, while we are physically tied to the earth, human nature is also spiritual, and that our vocation is a heavenly one.[74] It is no wonder, he says, that we have invented the ladder (or stairs, or towers) in order to escape the earth, where we are as humans inevitably stuck, and to find a way to the heavens where we ultimately belong.

Our problem is that inevitably we overstretch ourselves, displacing God, building towers of Babel (Gen 11:4-7). So what begins as a positive, indeed God-given, vocation becomes disordered by human pride. The remedy, Christian proposes, is to secure the ladder in the same way as in Jacob's dream, at *both* ends. Jacob's ladder is secure in the heavens because God holds it "higher than the starry vault." But, equally, the ladder must be secured on the earth, or otherwise it will slip. In Jacob's dream, the rock that

<hr/>

73. Chergé, *Dieu pour tout jour*, 269; January 14, 1989: "le monde dit céleste, celui de Dieu, et le monde terrestre où l'homme évolue."
74. Chergé, *Dieu pour tout jour*, 269, 273; January 14 and 30, 1989.

serves as his pillow offers this earthly anchor. This image of the rock, says Christian, is identified by a number of the church fathers as Christ.[75] There is a wonderful symmetry in this imagery: Christ is at the base and at the summit (*du côté de l'abaissement comme du côté de l'élèvement*).[76]

Elsewhere Christian equates Christ with the ladder itself. He draws attention to the echoes of Jacob's ladder in the Johannine description of the true disciple: "you will see heaven opened and the angels of God ascending and descending upon the Son of Man" (John 1:51). Christian finds it curious that Benedict has neglected this text, which makes Christ the necessary way (*le passage obligé*), the pivot on which everything rests: "The Son of Man becomes the necessary passageway between heaven and earth, the center of gravity of that circumincession of all creation, the communion between the spiritual and material worlds, symbolized by the angels ascending and descending."[77]

Christian expands this understanding of Christ as ladder in a number of directions. He understands Christ as the meeting place of the divine and the human (in the desert "he was with the wild beasts; and angels waited on him," Mark 1:13), but he also offers another, vivid image. The Son of Man, he says, plays perfectly on two keyboards—Christian alludes here to the twin keyboards or registers of an organ. The music that comes from this perfect harmony of the divine and the human is that of humility. Humility, Christian reminds us, is a divine virtue, which has allowed itself to be deciphered in terms of creation: *humus*, soil, ground.[78]

75. In fact this metaphor is used of Christ by Saint Paul, 1 Cor 10:4.

76. Chergé, *Dieu pour tout jour*, 273.

77. Chergé, *Dieu pour tout jour*, 269: "Curieusement, Benoît semble ignorer ce dernier texte qui fait du Fils de l'homme le passage obligé entre ciel et terre, le centre de gravité de cette circumincession de toute la création, les anges symbolisant cet intermédiaire d'un monde spirituel créé ayant sa subsistance propre entre le monde dit céleste, celui de Dieu, et le monde terrestre où l'homme évolue, animal et végétal tout à la fois." (trans. Scholl, "Christian de Chergé," 198).

78. Chergé, *Dieu pour tout jour*, 269–70.

The ladder thus speaks of the two natures of Christ and of the dual nature of humanity. The ladder becomes, as a whole, the ladder of humility. It is the divine music, the divine climate (*climat*).

Christian is, not surprisingly, uncomfortable with Benedict's "steps of humility," preferring Cassian's "indications."[79] He reminds his monks of the danger of tracking progress: "One day we say, *tiens*, I have gone from the second to the fourth degree; the next day we lament having fallen backwards. This comes from our annoying habit of paying more attention to where we are putting our feet than to what our eyes are looking for. Our feet are on the ladder, but Jesus said: 'You will SEE.' "[80] The orientation is always eschatological for Christian.

If the whole ladder stands for Christ and for humility, Christian is also clear that its ultimate shape is cruciform. The ladder of humility, as Benedict suggests, is the form of "this present life" (RB 7.5) and is composed of alternate abasements (*abaissements*) and elevations (*relèvements*). It is God, Christian notes, who raises us "if the heart has done its work, which is to *s'humilier*."[81] The French verb *humilier* generally means "to humiliate," and there is no separate verb *to humble* as there is in English.[82] Christian has this stronger sense in mind here. He highlights the phrase *humiliato corde* (RB 7.8) and suggests resonances with Psalm 50 [51], where the Vulgate uses *humiliatus*, meaning "crushed" (*broyé*). He has no problem understanding the wounded heart as a humiliated heart and notes that the psalmist points to God's part in the crushing. How so? Pride will inevitably lead to a hardening of the heart. The humble heart, on the other hand, will be soft: "If the heart is the natural seat of the Spirit of love, one is able to understand that it intervenes and that this fractures something in

79. Chergé, *Dieu pour tout jour*, 277; February 11, 1989.

80. Chergé, *Dieu pour tout jour*, 276; February 7, 1989: "Un jour, on dira: tiens, je suis passé du 2ᵉ au 4ᵉ degré; un autre, on se désolera d'être dégringolé, avec cette fâcheuse habitude d'être plus attentif à l'endroit où nous posons les pieds qu'à celui que nous cherchons des yeux. Les pieds se posent sur l'échelon mais Jésus a dit: Vous VERREZ" (trans. Scholl, "Christian de Chergé," 199).

81. Chergé, *Dieu pour tout jour*, 275; February 4, 1989.

82. Cf. *se rabaisser*, "to put oneself down."

us if we let the immense heart of God find a place in ours for all his own. Through this fracture the Cross enters in."[83]

Christian is pressing into the heart of the paschal mystery here, which for him is not a remote doctrine but the ground of what it means to be fully human. So this cruciform ladder continues to shape his theological anthropology: "This cross, this new ladder of Jacob is not a perch or a rope. Man is not a monkey (he does not mount to the heavens as a monkey in a tree!). He invents the stairs or the ladder, and this has two uprights."[84]

Christian perceives two related meanings in these two uprights. They are a reminder that the way of the ladder is not one way but two, up and down. Following Benedict here (RB 7.9), but aware of the dangerous dualist inheritance of Greek philosophy, Christian also notes that the two uprights represent body and soul. He points out that the two sides of the ladder are always held together in exact correspondence.[85] Again he sees this pattern in Christ and completes his chapter talk with a text from Saint Paul: "He who descended is the same one who ascended far above the heavens, so that he might fill all things" (Eph 4:10). The universe is filled, Christian says, in a way that is analogous to the indivisibility of body and soul.[86]

83. Chergé, *Dieu pour tout jour*, 275: "Si le coeur est le siège naturel de l'Esprit d'amour, on peut comprendre qu'il intervienne et que cela broie quelque chose en nous que de laisser le coeur immense de Dieu se chercher une place dans le nôtre pour tous les siens. C'est par cette fracture que la Croix pénètre."

84. Chergé, *Dieu pour tout jour*, 275: "Cette Croix, cette échelle nouvelle de Jacob n'est pas une perche, ni une corde. L'homme n'est pas un singe (il ne monte pas au ciel comme un singe à l'arbre!). Il invente l'escalier ou l'échelle, et celle-ci a deux montants."

85. The slightly obscure analogy Christian uses here is that of the two columns of mercury in a maximum-minimum thermometer. At any time of the day, the level of the mercury in the two columns corresponds exactly, but they also record the maximum and minimum temperatures reached since last being reset. It is not unreasonable to imagine there having been such a thermometer at Tibhirine.

86. Chergé, *Dieu pour tout jour*, 275: "il remplit l'univers à la façon du corps et de l'âme indissociables."

Christian returns to this idea in a later talk. The symbol of the ladder is valuable, he suggests, not so much in its vertical function, but in the way in which it emphasizes the "transverse." He concludes by placing this kenotic, humble way in the heart of the life of the Trinity:

> The rungs of a ladder are inserted into the sides, and hold them together; but it is the sides that give the direction: the rungs assure correspondence between the two sides. At each step, we can find what pertains to the body and what to the soul, made as inseparable in each effort of humility as the two natures of Christ in the kenosis of the Son. That unity is a fruit of the Spirit, who is a spark of fire, creating a circuit of love between the Father bent toward the Son and the Son turned toward the Father. The wings of the dove unite the voice which descends from the cloud and the Son who rises from the deepest waters of the earth.[87]

5.5.4 The Mystical Ladder of Dialogue: The Journées Romaines Lecture

In the *Journées Romaines* lecture, Christian makes a final, bold, though irresistible move in his use of the metaphor of the ladder. Having already identified the Alawiyines of Médéa as fellow "pilgrims of the horizon,"[88] he now begins to describe the two faiths, Islam and Christianity, as "two parallel posts" with their "point of meeting in the infinite": both are made in the earth, "fertilized by

---

87. Chergé, *Dieu pour tout jour*, 277: "Les barreaux d'une échelle s'emboutent, s'insèrent dans les deux montants qu'ils relient; ce sont les montants qui donnent la direction, les barreaux assurent la correspondance entre ces deux montants, une liaison d'unité. Nous pouvons retrouver à chaque niveau où s'arrête Benoît ce qui relève du corps et ce qui se reçoit de l'âme, rendus aussi indissociables dans chaque effort d'humilité que les deux natures du Christ dans la kénose du Fils. Cette unité est un fruit de l'Esprit, qui est étincelle de feu, créant le circuit d'amour entre le Père penché vers le Fils et le Fils tourné vers le Père. Les ailes déployées de la colombe unissent la voix qui descend des nuées et le Fils qui remonte des eaux les plus basses de la terre" (trans. Scholl, "Christian de Chergé," 199).
88. Chergé, "L'échelle mystique," 7: "pèlerins de l'horizon."

the same dung, suffering, sickness, death"; both are oriented toward the same hope, both are pointed "towards the heavens."[89] Here he evokes Jacob, who, like all human beings, has his bed on the earth and "nose in the air" and yet dreams of the ladder. This dream is common ground for all humanity. Christian's theological anthropology extends, necessarily, to his Muslim brothers. So he repeats and elaborates an image he has already used in his chapter talks: "Man is not a monkey who would be satisfied with a perch. He has been created from above: he invents the stair [*scala*] to support his climb; with two uprights, precisely, and the crossings [*passage*] from one to another [*de l'un à l'autre*], for support, at more or less regular intervals. Why not imagine climbing them in two lines, this common ladder whose uprights could be our respective faiths?"[90]

Christian's circuitous description of the rungs of the ladder— *des passages de l'un à l'autre*—is deliberate. *L'autre*, "the other," is used throughout his lecture to signify difference from oneself. Christian, schooled in continental philosophy as well as theology, is using the language popularized by the work of Emmanuel Levinas.[91] So Christian uses the phrase *les uns et les autres* to speak of Christians and Muslims. But he is always pressing toward mutuality: in his reimagining of Benedict's ladder, "the one" and "the other" (*l'un et l'autre*) are linked horizontally; neither has precedence. The related phrase *l'un l'autre* (and *les uns les autres*), meaning "one another," is one that also has strong theological resonances, particularly in the Johannine language of love, and these resonances are never very far from Christian's thinking.[92]

89. Chergé, "L'échelle mystique," 8.
90. Chergé, "L'échelle mystique," 9: "L'homme n'est pas un singe pour se suffire d'une perche. Il a été créé debout; il invente la *scala* pour l'accompagner dans ses montées; avec deux montants, précisément, et des passages de l'un à l'autre, pour prendre appui, à intervalles plus ou moins réguliers. Pourquoi ne pas imaginer de la monter sur deux files, cette échelle commune dont les montants seraient nos fois respectives?"
91. Christian refers to the death of Levinas and to his thought in a late homily (Chergé, *L'AUTRE que nous attendons*, 486).
92. John 13:34: "Je vous donne un commandement nouveau: vous aimer les uns les autres; comme je vous ai aimés, aimez-vous les uns les autres."

Christian's writing, then, contains a secure theology of hope. He shares with the monastic tradition behind him a commitment to an end that is hopeful because it is bathed in "paschal light." Indeed one could say that, for Christian, hope is bathed in humility, since the heart of the paschal mystery is to be found in the self-offering or the "kenosis of the Son." To live with eschatological openness is not only to live toward this hopeful end (*telos*) but also to live out the humble, self-giving way of Christ. For Christian, a significant consequence of living out this commitment in a Muslim environment was the loosening of certainties. The precariousness and provisionality of the community's life in Algeria challenged the monks to face and embrace their existential humility. Like Paul, they experienced a radical dependence on God. Moreover, living alongside others who prayed challenged Christian to reimagine this eschatological orientation in a larger frame. If all human beings bear the divine imprint, then his Muslim neighbors became fellow "pilgrims of the horizon." And while for Christian the *telos* was secure, he was prepared to live with a radical openness to the *narrative*, the new story that might unfold along this journey.

5.6 *L'AUTRE que nous attendons*: "The OTHER for Whom We Wait"

How then does Christian understand "the other"? What are the implications of this eschatological openness?

While Christian imagines Christianity and Islam as two poles pointed in the same direction, they are two poles: he does not conflate the two identities. His impatience with theological discourse as a means of interfaith dialogue arises from the concrete experience of living with the other. The monastic community experienced difference, often painfully, in the existential, in the daily discipline of life together. Indeed they faced the challenge of living with difference internally, within the community, as well as externally, side by side with their Muslim neighbors.

Bible quotations in French, other than those taken directly from the texts being quoted, use *La Bible de Jérusalem*.

But the continued presence of a Cistercian monastery in a Muslim country had a deeper significance, as Armand Veilleux points out. Veilleux was procurator general of the Order at the time and traveled to Algeria with the abbot general to bury the remains of the murdered monks. "Their presence in Algeria," he said, "affirmed the right to be different, in opposition to all forms of exclusion and the eradication of the Other."[93] From this perspective the monastic community itself was "the Other." Undeniably, the community of Tibhirine deeply experienced its difference from the surrounding religious culture. But as the monastic community found its vocation, found the shared ground (*priants parmi d'autre priants*), the monks became simply "others" among "others." This shift in self-understanding was important: while difference was not dissolved, the destabilizing of their identity opened the way for fruitful meeting—that is, for the possibility of something new to emerge.[94]

Christian did not fear difference—and here his biography, with his formative positive encounters with Muslims, helped him. Indeed he read difference sacramentally. As Salenson suggests, "interreligious dialogue forces one to address the fact of difference with radical seriousness."[95] The issue of difference and unity (or communion) is one that Christian considered in an article published in 1984.[96] In it he reflects on the possibility that the source of difference is in God: "What if difference takes its meaning from

93. Armand Veilleux, "The Witness of the Tibhirine Martyrs," *Spiritus* 1, no. 2 (2001): 205–16, here 206. Veilleux says that "shortly before his death [Christian] said that one of the motives for remaining where he was, as a Christian and a European, was to affirm the right of the local common people to their own differences" (214).

94. Compare Kitchen's view that Bernard of Clairvaux renders the neighbor a "second self," thereby eliminating otherness (John Kitchen, "Bernard of Clairvaux's *De Gradibus Humilitatis et Superbiae* and the Postmodern Revisioning of Moral Philosophy," in *Virtue and Ethics in the Twelfth Century*, ed. István P. Bejczy and Richard G. Newhauser [Leiden and Boston: Brill, 2005], 95–117, here 100–105).

95. Salenson, "Monastic Life," 34.

96. "Chrétiens et musulmans: nos differences ont-elles le sens d'une communion?" Reprinted in Chergé, *L'invincible espérance*, 109–66.

the revelation that God makes us of what He Himself is? Nothing then could prevent us from accepting difference in the way we accept faith, that is as a *gift* from God."[97]

Christian wants to locate diversity, otherness, firmly in God. Is this part of the trinitarian life of God? His question as to whether "God makes us of what He Himself is" (*Dieu nous fait de ce qu'Il est*) he understands as speculative, but it inspires his next thoughts. If this is so, "one would attribute a quasi-sacramental function to the differences between Christians and Muslims, regarding these as dependent on a reality that is vaster, more secret, this union for which all people carry within themselves a nostalgia."[98]

As Salenson suggests, here Christian is thinking of difference as "a sacrament of unity," which invites us to move beyond our certainties, opening out a more expansive vision of God. Such a vision is not just a matter of having different perspectives on the same reality, or simply of God always being other than our limited conceptions, though these realizations are not unrelated. Difference, for Christian, ultimately points to otherness in God: "When God expresses himself in another way, he is not expressing himself as something other, but as the Completely Other [*Tout-Autre*]: in other words, something other than all the others."[99] Christian is stretching the capacities of language here in an attempt to express the connection between difference and unity in the life of God: "to speak of God differently [*autrement*] is not to speak of another God [*un autre Dieu*]."[100] God is always, as he

97. Chergé, *L'invincible espérance*, 112: "Et si la différence prenait son sens dans la Révélation que Dieu nous fait de ce qu'Il est? Rien ne saurait empêcher alors de la recevoir comme la foi elle-même, c'est-à-dire comme un *don* de Dieu" (trans. Salenson, "Monastic Life," 34). *Gift* (*don*) is italicized in the orginal French but not in Salenson's translation.

98. Chergé, *L'invincible espérance*, 113: "On prêterait alors aux différences entre chrétiens et musulmans une fonction quasi sacramentelle les situant en dépendance d'une réalité plus vaste et plus secrète, cette union dont chacun porte en soi la nostalgie" (trans. Salenson, "Monastic Life," 35).

99. Chergé, *L'invincible espérance*, 127: "quand Dieu se dit autrement, il ne se dit pas autre, mais Tout-Autre, c'est-à-dire autrement que tous les autres" (trans. Salenson, "Monastic Life," 35).

100. Chergé, *L'invincible espérance*, 128.

says in a late Advent homily, "the OTHER for whom we wait" (*l'AUTRE que nous attendons*).[101]

Before the Completely Other, human difference is not relativized but instead sacramentalized: it is a signal of the divine, the life of God. Salenson summarizes this insight helpfully: "The mystery of divine oneness expresses itself through difference."[102] So "the other" is a gift of God. And, as Christian says in his *Journées Romaines* lecture, if we neglect this mysterious gift of the faith of "the other" we "miss contemplating the work of the Spirit and the part that we might take in it."[103]

Christian expresses this position definitively in his testament, opened on May 26, 1996, after his death (written in two stages: in Algiers, December 1, 1993, and at Tibhirine, January 1, 1994). Anticipating his death at the hand of a Muslim, Christian confidently expects that his "curiosity [about the place of Islam] will be set free":

> This is what I should be able to do, please God:
> immerse my gaze in that of the Father
> to contemplate with him His children of Islam
> just as he sees them, all shining with the glory of Christ,
> the fruit of His Passion, filled with the Gift of the Spirit
> whose secret joy will always be to establish communion
> and restore the likeness, playing with the differences.[104]

Communion, divine likeness (to the image of God), and difference are held together and, indeed, reflected in the life of God.

5.6.1 Space for "the Other"

This understanding of difference as gift and of God as the Completely Other has existential, and ethical, implications. It makes space not only for God to be God but also for "the other"

101. Chergé, *L'AUTRE que nous attendons*, 482.
102. Salenson, "Monastic Life," 35.
103. Chergé, "L'échelle mystique," 13: "Le [ce don de la foi de l'autre] négliger, c'est manquer à la contemplation du travail de l'Esprit et à la part qui nous en revient."
104. Olivera, *How Far to Follow*, 128–29.

to be other. Christian invites us to resist our impoverished versions of the community God intends for us ("our temples made with human hands"[105]): "We will always have to be entering into a vaster design that is constantly making us leap over the poor boundaries of our hasty barriers and our intransigencies, because *God really does want all human beings to be saved* [1 Tim 2:4]."[106]

In the *Journées Romaines* lecture, Christian takes up the notion of space, the "vaster design." He secures the radical otherness of God by his use of the metaphor of the "horizon," always beyond our view and grasp. Eschatological openness allows space for the new—and for "the other" to be "the other." Christian also plays with the idea of space in relation to the metaphor of the ladder, at one point imagining the angels confidently climbing up and down the ladder that is secured between the earth and the heavens. They take up this space that has been given to them. Human beings, by contrast, fumble around for the rungs of the ladder.[107]

But there is another model for us: Christ. It is, paradoxically, by relinquishing space, by radical self-offering, in fact by humility that it is possible to bridge the distance between heaven and earth, between the divine and the human. Christian again draws attention to Benedict's ladder of humility and imagines the monk standing on the lowest rung: "Isn't it there that he risks being joined by the One who has humbled himself even lower than the ladder, taking the last place that no one ever takes for himself? To unite ourselves with Him in this abasement is to be stretched to fill, with Him, the whole space of the degrees to the last step, that of the love which casts out fear."[108]

105. Chergé, *L'invincible espérance*, 147: "nos temples faits de main d'homme."

106. Chergé, *L'invincible espérance*, 147: "Nous aurons toujours à entrer dans un dessein plus vaste qui, sans cesse, fait sauter les pauvres frontières de nos exclusives rapides et de nos intransigeances; car, vraiment, 'Dieu veut que tous les hommes soient sauvés' (1 Tm 2,4)" (trans. Salenson, "Monastic Life," 35).

107. Chergé, "L'échelle mystique," 9.

108. Chergé, "L'échelle mystique," 13: "N'est pas là qu'il risque d'être rejoint par Celui qui s'est humilié lui-même jusqu'au plus bas de l'échelle, prenant cette dernière place que personne ne lui ravira jamais? S'unir à Lui

The monk simply follows Christ in bending the self in the face of the other. The goal here is at the very heart of the monastic vocation: to be able to live, to "humbly honor," what the name "monk" (from the Greek root *monos*) implies, that is, "to be one with the Unique and a beloved turned toward the One."[109] Making space for "the other" opens the way to "the Wholly Other," to love.

Preaching at the monks' memorial Mass in Algiers on June 2, 1996, Bernardo Olivera interpreted the deaths of Christian and his brother monks in precisely this way:

> The monks' testimony, like that of every believing Christian, can only be understood as a prolongation of the testimony of Christ himself. Our life following Christ should manifest with total clarity the divine liberality of the good news of the gospel which we desire to live. This good news is that a life given and offered is never lost. It is always found again in Him who is the Life. We must enter into the world of the other, whether that person be Christian or Muslim. In fact if the "other" does not exist as such, there is no space for true love. We need to be disturbed and enriched by the existence of the other. Let us remain open and sensitive to every voice that challenges us. Let us choose love, forgiveness and communion against every form of hatred, vengeance and violence. Let us believe without flinching in the deep desire for peace which resides in the depth of every human heart.[110]

This stance, of self-abasement or humility, is for Christian not simply theory but a lived practice—the ground for what he calls "existential dialogue" (*dialogue existential*).[111] "We would cease to be Christians or even men," he says, "if we were to mutilate others in their hidden dimension, for the sake of a so-called 'purely human encounter,' which refers—let us be clear about this—to

---

en cet abaissement, c'est tendre à remplir avec Lui tout l'intervalle des degrés jusqu'au dernier échelon, celui de l'amour qui bannit la crainte."

109. Chergé, "L'échelle mystique," 13: "être un avec l'Unique et bien-aimé tourné vers l'Un."

110. Olivera, *How Far to Follow*, 34–35.

111. Chergé, "L'échelle mystique," 2.

an expurgated humanity purified of any personal, and therefore unique, relation to the Wholly Other [*Tout-Autre*]. Dialogue, then means to keep our feet firmly planted on the ground (or even the manure) but our head exploring the heavens."[112]

5.7 Practicing Humility in "the School of the Other"[113]

What practices support this way of humility in the presence of the other? The themes already examined in this study are all present in the story of the Tibhirine monks: work and prayer, community, hospitality and service, commitment to the daily offices and *lectio divina*, poverty and simplicity. They are all of a piece, woven like a cloth that draws on the heritage, the lived wisdom, of Benedictine and Cistercian monasticism. The most radical difference between this heritage and Tibhirine was, however, the permeability of the monastery wall. The presence of the other was precisely a *presence*—not shut out but welcomed as a gift of God, even a revelation of God. What evolved, then, was the practical outworking of eschatological openness. The cloth did not have neatly hemmed edges; indeed it was still being woven. Certainly this openness was the basis of the distinctive *vivre ensemble*, living together, that emerged at Tibhirine. It probably also determined its end.

5.7.1 Hospitality and the Monastery Wall

Holding open a space for the other, offering "hospitality without boundaries" (*l'hospitalité sans frontières*),[114] was central to

---

112. Chergé, "L'échelle mystique," 2: "Nous cesserions d'être chrétiens et tout simplement hommes, s'il nous arrivait de mutiler l'autre dans sa dimension cachée, pour ne le rencontrer soi-disant que 'd'homme à homme', entendez dans une humilité expurgée de toute référence à Dieu, de toute relation personnelle et donc unique avec le Tout-Autre. Dialogue qui entend bien garder les pieds sur terre (et même dans le fumier), mais la tête chercheuse" (Christian Salenson, *Christian de Chergé: A Theology of Hope*, trans. Nada Conic, CS 247 [Kalamazoo, MI: Cistercian Publications, 2012], 56).

113. Chergé, "L'échelle mystique," 7: "l'école de l'autre."

114. Christian uses this phrase to describe the practice of hospitality shared by Christians and Muslims (Chergé, "L'échelle mystique," 11).

Christian's sense of vocation in Algeria. He once said to a friend, "I don't believe I have the right to live simply as a cloistered monk here."[115] To what extent did his brother monks share this view? In the decade before his election as prior in 1984, Christian had been guest master (*hôtelier*), a position that enabled him to offer hospitality to all who sought retreat or spiritual conversation, Muslims as well as Christians. But in his early years at Tibhirine, not all his fellow monks shared Christian's radical openness to Islam. Kiser suggests that Christian went "too native for the taste of many of the brothers": keeping Ramadan, taking his shoes off before entering the chapel, and proposing an alternate service with an Arabic liturgy (a suggestion that the community rejected at the time).[116] Their unanimous acceptance of his solemn profession in 1976, though, told a different story. In his petition to the community, Christian expressed his sense of vocation clearly: "to live in PRAYER in the service of the Church of Algeria, listening to the Moslem soul, God willing, unto the final gift of my death."[117] The formal visitation report to the abbot general of the Order from this time spoke of the acceptance of Christian's profession as a turning point for the community: "This vote was like a spark setting fire to the whole." The report represented Christian's calling as a providential gift to the community and noted his leadership potential, stating: "This religious . . . seems to be the most qualified at the present time to direct the future of Our Lady of Atlas."[118]

Yet by 1979, Christian was struggling with whether Tibhirine was after all the place for him to live out his very specific vocation and was actively exploring other options. He made an extended retreat to Asskrem, in the footsteps of Charles de Foucauld (1858–1916), who had lived out a similar vocation among the Tuareg in

---

115. Kiser, *Monks of Tibhirine*, 76.

116. Kiser, *Monks of Tibhirine*, 46.

117. Quoted in English translation in Olivera, "Monk, Martyr, and Mystic," 324. No source cited. Profession formulas are generally held in the archives of the monastic house where solemn profession is made or, perhaps, in the archives of the Order.

118. Quoted, in English translation, in Olivera, "Monk, Martyr, and Mystic," 325. The original source is the Visitation Report of November 2, 1976.

Algeria. Christian returned, however, with his Trappist vocation
settled.[119] His election as prior in 1984 confirmed the direction of
the whole community, but in his first term as leader some felt that
the needs of the monastic community came second to his interfaith agenda, especially as his passion and growing expertise in
interfaith matters often took him away from the monastery. (Kiser
says, "Christian was becoming the Saint Bernard of Algeria."[120])
The monastery wall, the interface between the life of the monastery and the life of the exterior world, was the central issue here.
What is the monastery for? How is monastic life differentiated
from life outside the monastic enclosure? How should it relate
to that life? As he matured, Christian grew in sensitivity to these
questions. So, for example, in 1993 as he shared with his fellow
monastic leaders the "modulations" from Cistercian practice evident in the Tibhirine community, Christian acknowledged the
tension between monastic enclosure and openness, saying that
the community was "in a perpetual search for the right balance
in our relations with our neighbors."[121]

Questions of monastic purpose and identity continued to surface, but as the community stabilized under Christian's leadership
(he was reelected prior in 1990 and 1996), the monks developed
a deepening sense of confidence in their shared vocation. In June
1991 Bernardo Olivera, then abbot general of the Order, made an
extended visit to the Tibhirine monks to learn more about the
community and to offer support to its members.[122] The question
of the continued presence of the monastery in Algeria was clearly
still a lively one that weighed heavily in his own mind. One night

119. Kiser, *Monks of Tibhirine*, 50–51.
120. Kiser, *Monks of Tibhirine*, 76.
121. Chenu, ed., *Sept vies*, 87: "D'autre part, cette particularité qui est nôtre
nous amène inévitablement à 'moduler' certaine constantes du charisme
cistercien en fonction de notre environnement: association dans le travail, et
non pas simple salariat; clôture et ouverture, en perpétuelle recherche d'un
juste équilibre dans nos relations avec le voisinage; interpellation au niveau
des expressions de la prière et de la vie foi pour rejoindre, quand faire se
peut, ce qui se pratique en fidélité musulmane."
122. Kiser, *Monks of Tibhirine*, 103.

during his stay, he dreamed that one monk was violently attacking another, shouting, "First, you are wasting your life in this Muslim world that asks nothing of you and ridicules you. There is so much to do elsewhere, so many people who wait only for your witness to enter the contemplative life and to grow your community. . . . Second, you poor fool, our Order really has no use for a foundation like yours—you're deadweight!"[123]

On waking, Olivera wrote a response to this inner critic, strongly affirming the community's own sense of vocation. Christian told the story of the dream and quoted Olivera's reply when, at Olivera's invitation, he addressed the Order's general chapter in 1993:

> You have a mission to inculturate the Cistercian charism so that the expression of this monastic commitment may be enriched by what you will have gleaned from the local culture. . . . This inculturation may provoke a reaction of fear, fear that you will lose your monastic identity. In order not to experience this fear or to liberate yourself from it, the first thing you need to do is to deepen your monastic culture.[124]

In his response, Olivera articulated the community's vocation, the embrace of the permeable monastery wall with all its inherent risk and the foundational priority in forging the way ahead, a deepening of its own monastic culture. Was there an implied criticism in Olivera's instructions? Did Olivera think that the

123. Chenu, ed., *Sept vies*, 84: "Primo, tu perds ta vie face à ce monde musulman qui ne te demande rien et se moque bien de toi, alors qu'il y a tant à faire ailleurs, tant de peuples qui n'attendent que ton témoignage pour accéder à la vie contemplative et venir grossir ta communauté. . . . Secundo, pauvre de toi, notre Ordre n'a vraiment que faire d'une fondation comme la tienne; quel poids mort!" (translation draws on Kiser, *Monks of Tibhirine*, 107).

124. Chenu, ed., *Sept vies*, 88: "Vous avez la mission d'inculturer le charisme cistercien afin que les manifestations de ce monachisme puissent s'enrichir de ce que vous aurez glané dans la culture locale. . . . Cette inculturation peut provoquer une réaction de peur, celle de perdre votre identité monastique. Pour ne pas éprouver cette peur, ou pour s'en libérer, la première chose à faire est d'approfondir votre culture monastique" (translation based on Salenson, "Monastic Life," 29).

community's monastic practice had thinned? It seems unlikely. He clearly respected Christian and this tiny monastic community, but he was deeply aware of the risks—both physical and spiritual—for the brothers themselves. He revealed a pastoral eye. But this open space, the permeable monastery wall, was not regular territory for the Cistercian Order, with its contemplative rather than apostolic charism. Nevertheless, Christian clearly took his advice to heart.

5.7.2 Monasticism and Islam

Christian shared Olivera's confidence in "monastic culture," the deep tradition of monastic practices that provide the vehicle for spiritual, indeed human, growth. This shared confidence is evident in the 1989 *Journées Romaines* lecture. If this heritage provided a well-trod route for the traditional enclosed monastic community in Europe, Christian was also confident that it offered a secure path for life in this very different cultural context. For Christian, monastic practice offered a vehicle for interreligious dialogue—it offered a way, a way *par excellence*, to live and journey together. Further, for Christian, the motivation for the deepening of monastic culture came from both his own tradition and that which now surrounded him. He found the immersion in a Muslim milieu "an undeniable stimulus" to faithfully living out his monastic profession.[125]

Christian was not alone in observing links between monasticism and Islam and their potential significance in Christian-Muslim relations. Cardinal Duval believed, "It is monasticism that is best placed to help Islam understand what the Church's deepest instinct is."[126] Kiser finds in the story of the Tibhirine monks a hopeful "common thread between Muslim and Christian worlds," providing "a window into the communal values of Islam and the importance of faith as a defining source of identity."[127] Indeed,

125. Chergé, "L'échelle mystique," 11: "un stimulant indéniable."
126. Salenson, "Monastic Life," 30.
127. John W. Kiser, "An Algerian Microcosm: Monks, Muslims, and the Zeal of Bitterness," CSQ 38, no. 3 (2003): 337–54, here 337.

Kiser suggests, from the perspective of the local population, "the monks were holy fathers who lived like good Muslims."[128]

Kiser elaborates on some visible aspects of this "affinity," which he says "was natural from the beginning":

> An Algerian in his long, hooded robe, or *abaya*, is virtually indistinguishable from a monk in his white prayer cowl. Both monk and Muslim pray communally and with formalistic regularity. Like the natives they lived with, the monks existed only as a part of an extended family; alone one is nothing. . . . The architecture of the cloister was one of interiorized space. Like the veil and the Algerian *gourbi* (mud houses common in the countryside) with its inner courtyard, monasteries present to the world a protective exterior that shelters an inner privacy. Both worlds separate women and men in places of worship and everyday life. . . . And, like the Trappists, the traditional Muslim . . . places great importance on the virtue of hospitality. Indeed it is a sacred duty.[129]

If there is a natural affinity, though, this common ground was noticed, valued, and cultivated deeply under Christian's leadership. He saw clear parallels between the pillars of Islam and monastic practices, and in his *Journées Romaines* lecture he describes them as "successive rungs" for "a common ascent." And, he discovered, "It is when you try to define these *levels* of authentic spiritual progress, that you are suddenly surprised to find yourself so near [*proches*]."[130]

Christian lists the observances or practices shared by the two traditions:

> The gift of oneself to the Absolute, regular prayer, fasting, the sharing of alms, the conversion of the heart, the ceaseless remembering of the Presence which bears a Name (*dhikr*, ejaculatory

128. Kiser, "Algerian Microcosm," 342.

129. Kiser, "Algerian Microcosm," 342–43.

130. Chergé, "L'échelle mystique," 11: "C'est quand on s'essaie à définir ces *niveaux* d'un authentique progrès spirituel qu'on s'étonne tout à coup de se trouver si proches."

prayer, the Jesus prayer), trust in Providence, the urgent need for
hospitality without limits, the call to spiritual combat, to a pilgrimage which is also interior. . . . In all this, how can one fail
to recognise the Spirit of holiness, of which it is said that one does
not know from where it comes nor where it goes (John 3:8), from
where it descends nor to where it ascends? Its role is always to
bring about birth from on high (John 3:7).[131]

The practices of the spiritual journey, then, offer a fruitful place
of dialogue with the other, between the two traditions (*l'une et
l'autre*). This was, Christian reports, precisely the experience of the
Ribât: the most productive conversations occurred when the subject was connected with the lived life of their respective faiths.[132]
These conversations were, however, for Christian really a bonus:
the real work of dialogue was to be found in the dailiness of *vivre
ensemble*, in living together. Christian calls this shared life, as we
have already noted, "existential dialogue."[133]

5.7.3 La "grisaille" du quotidian: *Ordinary Time*

At the beginning of the *Journée Romaines* lecture Christian emphasizes his conviction that the *quotidian*, the ordinary business of
daily life, is the authentic arena for interreligious dialogue. And
he immediately links the *quotidian* with humility: "Nothing can
be understood apart from a steadfast communal presence, and
the faithfulness of each to the humble reality of daily life [*l'humble*

---

131. Chergé, "L'échelle mystique," 11: "le don de soi à l'Absolu de Dieu,
la prière régulière, le jeûne, le partage de l'aumône, la conversion du coeur,
le mémorial incessant de la Présence qui port un Nom (*dhikr*, oraison jacula-
toire, prière de Jésus), la confiance en la Providence, l'urgence de l'hospitalité
sans frontières, l'appel au combat spirituel, au pèlerinage qui est aussi intérieur. . . . En tout cela, comment ne pas reconnaître l'Esprit de Sainteté,
dont nul ne sait d'où il vient ni où il va (Jn 3,8), d'où il descend ni par où il
monte. Son office est toujours de *faire naître d'en haut* (Jn 3,7)" (trans. draws
on Salenson, "Monastic Life," 29–30).

132. Chergé, "L'échelle mystique," 12.

133. Chergé, "L'échelle mystique," 2.

réalité quotidienne], from the gate to the garden, from the kitchen to the 'lectio divina.' "[134]

This is a theme to which Christian returns again and again in the lecture and had already considered in his series of chapter talks on the subject of humility. In January 1989, following the celebration of Christmas, he resumes the series with the subject of Ordinary Time. Liturgically the anticipatory feel of the Advent season and the great festivals of the Christmas season were now behind the monastic community, leaving them with humdrum ferial days, with what Christian calls the *"grisaille" du quotidian*, literally the "greyness" of the daily—what in English might be called the grind of daily routines.[135]

In this context, in the ordinary or *quotidian*, Christian wishes to place the mystery of the incarnation. It is important, he says, not to confuse the "sauce" with the "main course" (*le plat de résistance*). The main course, solid nourishment, is humility, which is seen in the life of God: "In the luminous joy of the mystery of Christmas, we have celebrated this: the humiliation of God coming to take the last place at the table of humanity."[136] The connection between ordinary daily life and humility is reinforced when Christian notes that Jesus' (paradoxical) authority is the fruit of "thirty years or more of ordinary time, absolutely ferial," marked by "littleness, modesty, abasement."[137] There is, no doubt, a pastoral element

134. Chergé, "L'échelle mystique," 2: "Rien ne saurait s'expliquer en dehors d'une présence commune constante, et de la fidélité de chacun à l'humble réalité quotidienne, de la porte au jardin, de la cuisine à la 'lectio divina.' " The version of the lecture edited by Chenu adds "et l'office des Heures," "and the office of the hours" (see Chergé, *L'invincible espérance*, 168).

135. Chergé, *Dieu pour tout jour*, 267; January 10, 1989.

136. Chergé, *Dieu pour tout jour*, 267; January 10, 1989: "Dans la joie lumineuse du mystère de Noël, nous n'avons célébré que cela: l'humiliation d'un Dieu venant prendre la dernière place à la table de l'humanité" (trans. draws on Scholl, "Christian de Chergé," 196–97). Scholl translates *l'humiliation* as "abasement." I have chosen to retain the linguistic connection to humility by using *humiliation*.

137. Chergé, *Dieu pour tout jour*, 268: "trente années et plus de temps ordinaire, absolument férial. Tout dans ce qui a précédé porte la marque de la petitesse, de la modestie, de l'abaissement."

to Christian's talk: this affirmation of the ordinary as the locus of humility (the locus of the life of God) is intended to encourage the community as it faces the *"grisaille" du quotidian*. But it is also a conviction that Christian is coming to hold and live out more deeply for himself.

When Christian returns to this same theme twelve months later, he stresses the continuity between Ordinary Time and eternity: there is no rupture. The *quotidian* has an eschatological quality: "Humility begins when I realize I have only this brief day, today, to give to him who calls me for all days [*TOUT JOUR*] but how can I tell him 'yes' for always [*TOUJOURS*] if I don't give him this little day. . . . God has a thousand years to make a day; I have but one day to make eternity—today!"[138]

This theological connection between humility and the *quotidian* both underpins Christian's understanding of and informs the practice of *vivre ensemble*, living together. The ladder (of humility, of dialogue), as Christian remarks in his *Journées Romaines* lecture, "is stowed in our common clay."[139]

5.7.4 Ora et Labora

What is the shape of this daily life together? How has the presence of "the other" informed and even remolded the practice of this community that shares a "common clay"? Christian draws on his Benedictine heritage. *Ora et labora*, prayer and work, are the *mamelles*, the udders—that is, the source of nourishment—for Benedictine monastic life. Equally, he argues, they are the key to existential dialogue in a Muslim setting. Historically, he notes, "the temptation is often to privilege one over the other, sometimes

---

138. Chergé, *Dieu pour tout jour*, 312–13: "L'humilité commence quand je sais n'avoir que ce petit jour d'aujourd'hui à donner à Celui qui m'appelle pour TOUT JOUR mais comment lui dire oui pour toujours si je ne lui donne pas ce petit jour-ci. . . . Dieu a mille ans pour faire un jour; je n'ai qu'un seul jour pour faire de l'éternel, c'est aujourd'hui!" (trans. based on Scholl, "Christian de Chergé," 213).

139. Chergé, "L'échelle mystique," 17: "Voilà notre échelle bien arrimée dans notre glaises commune."

at the expense of the second." At Tibhirine, Christian continues, the monks have been feeling their way around, aware that they will need to improvise in both directions.[140] The Benedictine tradition offers a framework; the new context requires a fleshing out and experimentation. Here, then, is the inculturation later endorsed by Olivera.

5.7.5 Work: The Monastery Garden

The monastery at Tibhirine, like all Cistercian monasteries, was an economic unit, responsible for producing sufficient income to support the monks and maintain its assets. The changing fortunes of the Cistercians in Algeria have already been traced from the halcyon days at Staouëli in the nineteenth century to their increasingly precarious presence at Tibhirine after Algerian independence in 1962. Under Christian's leadership the small community, subsisting on a remnant of its former lands, nonetheless made a decision to reshape radically its method of engaging agricultural labor.[141] Instead of hiring local workers to assist them, the monks established a cooperative model, whereby four or five locals were given access to rotating plots in exchange for a portion of the harvest. As Hémon reflected after the monks' deaths, "they had decided to be neither more nor less than their neighbors, to cultivate the earth like them—with them, even," and, he added, alluding to their costly embrace of stability, "not necessarily to escape at the first alarm."[142] Here in the garden, both literally and metaphorically, the monastic community had its feet in the clay and manure, the *humus*, of the *quotidian*.

That is not to say that this route was easy. Hémon describes both the gift and challenge of the garden, this place of humility: "That garden was a legendary place and at the same time a very real place with its tillage, its manure, the pruning of trees, the row

---

140. Chergé, "L'échelle mystique," 19.
141. As Kiser notes, a key motivation for Christian was the elimination of residual colonialism (Kiser, *Monks of Tibhirine*, 81).
142. Hémon, "En-Visaged Good-by-E," 207–8.

of hives, the harvests, and so on. It was a privileged place also for inculturation, and I assure you that it was something quite different from what is described in books, and that the good will of each person was often sorely tried by reality. That meant, very concretely, identifying oneself with the other person, with his ideas, his habits, and especially his rhythm."[143]

These were real people engaged in a real garden. Fr. Christophe, not practical by nature, was in charge of the garden enterprise: Hémon records that he expressed "sighs of impatience and even utmost despair" when "confronted with so many differences and especially with the associates' besetting sin, which often threatened the future of their patches—absenteeism." Christophe's frustration with Ali's ever-escaping cow, which would then consume the salad greens, finally caused him to get tough and impose a fine for each transgression. Later, when he was curious as to why Ali's niece always paid the fine, Christophe discovered that she was asking Fr. Amédée to provide the funds.[144] The monastic economy continued to bend toward the other.

The garden was the locale for significant meeting, between "the one and the other," *l'un et l'autre.* Among the snatches of conversation recorded in Christophe's journal are these words spoken by M., a Muslim neighbor, words that are clearly the fruit of their common agricultural enterprise: "You know, it is like the same blood flowing through us, irrigating us together."[145] And a conversation between Christophe (C.) and another neighbor (A.) speaks to the heart of this enterprise that sought to incarnate the way of humility:

> A: "In your opinion, with what does one extinguish a fire, with water or petrol?"
> C: "With water!"
> A: "Well then, you see, there is only one who does not seek to seize power, and that is he, God."[146]

143. Hémon, "En-Visaged Good-by-E," 211.
144. Hémon, "En-Visaged Good-by-E," 212.
145. Quoted in Hémon, "En-Visaged Good-by-E," 213. Hémon does not name the Muslim neighbors for security reasons.
146. Hémon, "En-Visaged Good-by-E," 213.

One could hardly imagine a better definition of humility. Here is Christian's existential dialogue in operation.

It is also worth noting the resonances with Benedict's embrace of "humble" manual work and his agenda of social reordering. RB 48.7 seems especially pertinent in this postcolonial context, where the monastery found itself in diminished circumstances: "[The brothers] must not become distressed if local conditions or their poverty should force them to do the harvesting them-selves." As Hémon observed, the monastery was materially poor. Similarly, it is possible, in Hémon's account of the community, to glimpse something of Benedict's egalitarian monastic *polis*, here extended beyond the enclosure. The monks lived in solidarity with their neighbors, living, as they did, by working the land. They lived with, not above, their neighbors. The garden was, perhaps like Benedict's kitchen, the place where mutual service was performed. Mutuality was extended beyond the monastic community as monks and their neighbors worked side by side, learning to "bear one another's weaknesses" (RB 72.5).

In desert monasticism and in the Benedictine and Cistercian traditions, humility has a material face and social resonances. Indeed, the loss of these material manifestations of humility often inspires reform. It is no coincidence, then, that Hémon's first en-counter with the community at Tibhirine led him to "the profound conviction that they were the real monks of the present time."[147]

5.7.6 Prayer: The Daily Office

It was perhaps the shared rhythm of prayer and work, *ora et labora*, that constituted the clearest point of contact between the Cistercian monastic community and their Muslim neighbors. From a Muslim perspective, the monks were, in a very real sense, nothing special. They were Christians who, unlike the Christians in the secular West, visibly lived out their faith with their days, like those of the Muslim, punctuated by prayer.

---

147. Hémon, "En-Visaged Good-by-E," 208.

In this rhythm of work and prayer, the discipline of the daily office remained central to the lives of the Tibhirine monks, and in his chapter talks, Christian makes a strong connection between the commitment to this practice and the growth of humility.

He notices that Benedict moves straight from his consideration of humility in RB 7 to a lengthy discussion of the structure and content of the offices.[148] He draws attention to the parallels between Benedict's first degree of humility (the fear of God) in RB 7 and the instructions regarding the conduct of the Divine Office in RB 19. In the first step of humility, Benedict exhorts the monk to remember that "he is always seen by God in heaven, that his actions everywhere are in God's sight . . . that our thoughts are always present to God" (RB 7.13-14). Benedict echoes and builds on this understanding in his brief instructions on the intent of psalmody in the offices: "We believe that the divine presence is everywhere. . . . But beyond the least doubt we should believe this to be especially true when we celebrate the divine office" (RB 19.1-2). If God is present, then we should be present: "the presence of God calling for one's presence to God" (the French is more elegant here: *présence de Dieu appelant la présence à Dieu*).[149]

Christian knows the struggle of keeping the spirit and voice, the heart and mind, aligned. The gift of the Office is designed to address precisely this. For Benedict, he says, the Office is "a way to practice, from the timeless precision of the psalmody, harmony between lips, life, and heart."[150] The Office both "calls for and maintains humility." In fact for Benedict, Christian says, it became "a good school of humility."[151] Humility is the "antiphon," the refrain of the Office: it sets the tone, but it is also the content. The

---

148. I have made a similar observation regarding Vigils in chap. 3, section 3.4.

149. Chergé, *Dieu pour tout jour*, 288; June 10, 1989.

150. Chergé, *Dieu pour tout jour*, 287; June 8, 1989: "une façon de pratiquer, hors du temps précis de la psalmodie, l'harmonie entre les lèvres, la vie et le cœur."

151. Chergé, *Dieu pour tout jour*, 288; June 10, 1989: "On peut en déduire que l'Office appelle et entretient l'humilité. L'OFFICE aura été une bonne école d'humilité pour Benoît."

psalms themselves are the prayers of the "humble of the earth"; their main lesson is humility.[152]

The gift of the Daily Office, then, is twofold. Its discipline assists the monk in the practice of the first step of humility: being present to the presence of God. This practice is simultaneously reinforced by the content of the offices: the psalms themselves offer a pedagogy of humility. The regular rhythm of the Office day by day, then, immerses the members of the monastic community in a *climat* (to use Christian's earlier term) of humility.

It is worth noting here the lowly shape of this enterprise at Tibhirine: a handful of monks with meager resources endeavoring to maintain a tradition of communal prayer that had developed in much larger-scale, better-resourced monasteries. Indeed, the regular visits by Philippe Hémon to Tibhirine from Tamié were intended to address this deficit.[153] Hémon was a gifted musician and liturgist who came to help the monks reshape a liturgical repertoire that had become "a strain on their throats—and their patience."[154] But while Hémon initially imagined that the revision would involve major cuts to the quantity as well as simplifying the repertoire, he found a quite different reality: "In that community liturgical prayer occupied a large place. It was perhaps, together with the work they shared with their neighbours, the only reason they had for being there and staying there, as authentic men of prayer in a land of people who pray. The repertory had to be enlarged, not reduced, lest the penury so trying in all domains of their daily life should weigh upon them in church also."[155] The first call, then, for these *priants parmi d'autre priants* was to pray authentically themselves. How did the presence of *les autre priants* shape, or reshape, the monastic community?

---

152. Chergé, *Dieu pour tout jour*, 288; June 12, 1989: "C'est aussi que l'humilité est la leçon principale des Psaumes . . . elle donne le sens de cette prière qui est bien celle des humbles de la terre."

153. Hémon's first visit to Tibhirine was for Christophe Lebreton's ordination as a priest on New Year's Day 1990. Christophe had been a brother of Tamié.

154. Hémon, "En-Visaged Good-by-E," 210.

155. Hémon, "En-Visaged Good-by-E," 210.

5.7.7 Priants parmi d'autre priants

For Christian the exploration of prayer with the other had long been a significant priority. His own experience had confirmed his belief in this possibility. In the middle of Ramadan in 1975, Christian, who was praying in the monastery chapel, was joined by a Muslim. Over the space of three hours, in what he later called "the night of fire," the two joined together in prayers of praise and thanksgiving.[156] This experience continued to motivate Christian's desire for common prayer.

In his *Journées Romaines* lecture Christian gives an account of the journey of his monastic community toward prayer with the other. For the Tibhirine monks the road to prayer with the other began with the welcome of Muslim guests in the retreat house, on the condition (common to other guests) that "they respect what they were coming to seek, an atmosphere of silence, of solitude, and of participation in work, if they desired."[157] It was this hospitality, the opened space, that inspired the Alawiyines of Médéa to seek "a meeting of prayer" with the monks.[158]

In 1988 the community took another, more daring step and offered their neighbors a large room to serve as a provisional mosque while they awaited the construction of the one planned nearby. Here the monastery wall was literally breached as they invited the neighbor to share not only the garden but also the work of prayer. As Christian describes the interaction of the twin calls to prayer, the image of the two uprights of the ladder, with Christians and Muslims climbing rung by rung, comes to mind: "Bell and muezzin correspond or succeed each other, in the interior of the same enclosure, and it is difficult not to welcome the call to prayer from wherever it comes, as a reminder of the communion

---

156. Christian's account, *Nuit de feu*, is reproduced in Chergé, *L'invincible espérance*, 33–38.

157. Chergé, "L'échelle mystique," 19: "ils respectent ce qu'ils venaient chercher, un climat de silence, de solitude, et de participation au travail s'ils le désiraient." An undated information sheet for retreat house guests is reproduced in Chenu, ed., *Sept vies*, 23–25.

158. "une rencontre de prière" (Chergé, "L'échelle mystique," 19).

which prevails in the heart of the One to whom we turn with the same abandon."[159]

The practice of the other is also a practice of humility, a turn away from the self toward the Creator. For Hémon this side-by-side call to prayer powerfully revealed the presence of God:

> About six o'clock in the morning, I opened my window, which looked out on the Tamesguida mountains. The day that was dawning was promising to be fine. After the storms of the previous day, the sky was clear, and it was somewhat fresh. Soon there would be the office of Lauds; I was preparing for it when, suddenly—and to this day, it is perhaps one of the most overwhelming emotions of my life—I heard, rising in the silence and the blue sky, the natural voice of a muezzin, a fine voice, prayerful and pacific. I thought at that moment that truly God is present when his people praise him.[160]

This sense of communion, the respectful climbing together, was, however, delicate, like a newly planted seedling. As Christian says, "A new world is in gestation."[161] As the local area came under the influence of Islamists, the atmosphere changed. The new mosque was being built directly opposite the monastery gates, and loudspeakers were directed toward the monastery, broadcasting at full volume. As Hémon remembers, during his last visit to the community during Ramadan 1996, it "literally drowned the brothers' prayers toward the end of Vespers." The monks' faces, he says, displayed "something more than consternation."[162]

For Christian, though, this side-by-side prayer was a stage along a longer journey. One thinks here of the observation in

---

159. Chergé, "L'échelle mystique," 19–20: "Cloche et muezzin se correspondent ou se succèdent, à l'intérieur du même enclos, et il est difficile de ne pas accueillir l'appel à la prière d'où qu'il vienne, comme un rappel de la communion qui prévaut au cœur de Celui vers qui nous nous tournons avec le même abandon."

160. Hémon, "En-Visaged Good-by-E," 209.

161. Chergé, "L'échelle mystique," 6: "Un nouveau monde est en gestation."

162. Hémon, "En-Visaged Good-by-E," 210.

developmental psychology that children initially engage in parallel play before eventually engaging directly with each other. When Christian speaks of prayer together, not just parallel prayer, the image he uses is one of humility: prostration. He acknowledges the difficulty of moving from being together for prayer (*ensemble pour prier*) to praying together (*prier ensemble*). He is sensitive to accusations of syncretism and acknowledges the church's caution. But he is clearly confident in the ultimate revelation of the Holy Spirit, which, he says, will accord with the Song of the Lamb ("All nations will come and worship before you," Rev 15:3-4). The Tibhirine community had substantial experience in common prayer (*une prière commune*; rather than *ensemble*, Christian uses the strong *commune*, with its connotations of unity). He lists their shared practices: making invocations and chants, listening, holding silence, and sharing in fellowship (*les partages*).[163] The foundation of this prayer together is a common understanding of their place before God, their existential humility.

Christian pictures the Tibhirine prayer together as the prayer of a single prostrate community (*une seule communauté prosternée*). He takes the image of prostration from a verse in the Qur'an:

O you who believe. Bow, prostrate yourself,
worship your Lord, do good works.
Perhaps then you will be happy. (Qur'an 22:77)[164]

Christian does not draw attention here to the ritual prostrations that are characteristic of Muslim prayer.[165] Clearly this resonance

---

163. Chergé, "L'échelle mystique," 20.

164. Chergé, "L'échelle mystique," 20: "O vous qui croyez! Inclinez-vous, prosternez-vous, adorez votre Seigneur, faites le bien. Peut-être serez-vous heureux (Coran 22, 77)" (again translating directly from Christian's text).

165. In his 1993 address to the Cistercian general chapter, Christian spoke positively about this practice: "The ritual prayer of a Moslem is short, it engages the body, turns all one's attention towards the One source of all life, is said by heart, and greatly resembles the Office of our former Lay brothers. Some of us would certainly like our Office to recover some of this stripped-down simplicity, without ever losing its character of being the prayer of the Church" (Chenu, ed., *Sept vies*, 87). Trans. Christian de Chergé, "Conference

sits behind his deliberate choice of words, but Christian's key concern is to demonstrate how humility offers the common ground for the meeting of Muslim and Christian before God. He consequently links the Qur'anic text with two gospel texts, both connected to the stance or practice of humility, and weaves the texts into a story, an example of existential dialogue.

In 1986, together with some of the community's Muslim friends, Christian had attended the World Day of Prayer called by John Paul II at Assisi. The gospel set for the day before their departure was the story of the Pharisee and the publican (Luke 18:9-14). In his homily to the monastic community, Christian remarked that the pilgrims to Assisi would need to join in the prayer of the publican: "Take pity on me, a sinner!" When they returned from the conference and assembled for a shared time of prayer, one of the Muslim friends began with the same cry—in Arabic: *Rabbî, irhamnâ.*[166]

For Christian, the question of whether this sharing in prayer was prayer together or being together for prayer had been overtaken: "We were one single community prostrate in the attitude of the publican."[167] Practice had outrun theology. The common ground here is humility, and we know that, for Christian, humility is the *climat* that speaks of divine love. There is no question in his mind regarding the divine source of this sharing in prayer; it is consistent with his own experience on "the night of fire."

Christian draws attention, briefly, to the second prostration evident in the text from the Qur'an, that of good works, again noting parallels between the Christian and Muslim revelations. He recalls the "quasi-sacramental" nature of service to one's neighbor, seen in the light of Jesus' washing of his disciples' feet. Even Judas was included, he notes. We are commanded, Christian impli', to imitate Jesus' prostration in service, even before those '¹⁰ betray us. Christian completes this section of his *Journées R* ᵘⁱⁿᵉˢ

_____   ᵎ Dialogue
Given to General Chapter of Trappist Order," *Monastic Interrel*=492.
Bulletin 55, May 1996; http://www.monasticdialog.com/aᶠerence, see
    166. Chergé, "L'échelle mystique," 20. For the pre-Asᵛ
Chergé, *L'AUTRE que nous attendons*, 205–6; October 2ᶠᵉ communauté
    167. Chergé, "L'échelle mystique," 20: "Nous étions⁄
prosternée dans l'attitude du publicain."

lecture by repeating Duval's conviction that "the Holy Spirit is in the work of all free gestures of fraternal love . . . more surely perhaps than in all prayer."[168] He does not expand this thought, but one immediately thinks of Brother Luc's dispensary and the monastery garden, as well as, ultimately, the brothers' choice to stay at Tibhirine in solidarity with their neighbors and their final prostration before the hostile other.

5.8 Martyrdom: The End of Humility?

The deaths of the seven Tibhirine monks immediately raised two critical questions. Why did they stay? Are they martyrs? The second question is of particular interest to this study, since in early Christianity humility and martyrdom are often closely linked. But the questions are related, and indeed the most helpful discussions of the question of martyrdom find their securest ground in addressing the question of the monks' continued presence in Algeria.[169] Paradoxically, as the vocation of the community became more certain, the monks' existence became more and more precarious. They were, in a very tangible way, invited to and chose to live out a narrative of humility.

5.8.1 Loving to the End

The events of late 1993 represented a watershed for the community. In October the GIA had issued an ultimatum warning foreigners to leave Algeria within a month. In November Christian refused the offer of armed assistance for the monastery but agreed to close the monastery gate at night. At the beginning of December, as the ultimatum expired, four foreign nationals were assassinated. The first half of Christian's testament was composed in the wake of these killings on December 1, while he was visiting

168. C tout geste "L'échelle mystique," 21: "l'Esprit-Saint est à l'oeuvre en prière." d'amour fraternel . . . plus sûrement peut-être qu'en toute
169. For e
Olivera, "Monk, Martyr, and Mystic."

Algiers. On December 14, twelve Catholic Croatians had their throats cut at Tamesguida, a few kilometers from the monastery. They were known to the monks, visiting at Easter and Christmas, and their deaths deeply shocked the community. On December 19, Christian was again called to the local prefecture and advised that the monks should either temporarily leave or accept armed assistance. Again Christian refused, but he accepted an improved telephone line and the need for greater vigilance.[170]

On Christmas Eve, however, the monastery was visited by a band of armed GIA militia, led by the Sayat-Attiya, who had been responsible for the slaughter of the Croatians. He demanded medical aid, supplies, and money. Christian argued with him, refusing anything beyond the usual open door of the monastery to those in medical need and reminding the visitors that the monastery was a place of peace and that indeed that evening they were preparing to celebrate the birth of the prince of peace. The group withdrew, with the promise of a return.[171]

As Olivera says: "This visit signals a before and an after in the life of Christian and his brothers."[172] In the following days the community discussed their response. At the community meeting, held on December 26, the majority of the monks voted for immediate departure, believing that there was no time now "to make provision for the future" and agreeing that cooperation with the "revolutionary movement" would not have been moral. The following day Archbishop Tessier visited the community, urging them to consider the impact of their actions on Christians in Algeria and on the neighboring area: if they were to withdraw they should carefully stage their departure. Over the next few days the monks reconsidered their position and on December 31 clarified their decisions: they would not collaborate with the rebels, three of the brothers would withdraw, but six would stay, "keeping the possibility of remaining if there is no obstacle."[173]

170. Olivera, *How Far to Follow*, 54–55, 66.
171. Olivera, *How Far to Follow*, 55–56, 64–73.
172. Olivera, "Monk, Martyr, and Mystic," 3?
173. Olivera, *How Far to Follow*, 56–57.

Why did they stay? Fr. Jean-Pierre further explained their thinking in his report to Olivera. Their vow of stability was central. If they had to flee, Jean-Pierre says, "we would reassemble somewhere else with the intention of pursuing there our common vocation together, giving priority to presence among the Muslims."[174] Similarly, their vow of stability united them with the suffering of the church of Algeria and with their Muslim Algerian neighbors. They stayed as a demonstration of love for their neighbors, one might say, in solidarity with the humiliated. Staying was, ultimately, a matter of obedience:

> Our Lord and Master, from whom we have received our mission in this place, is the one to whom our vow of obedience binds us. We weren't obliged by the orders of the GIA. So long as the neighboring people do not make us feel their desire to have us leave, we will remain with them as a covenant of love, sharing their difficult situation and trying to bear it with them. The choice to remain unarmed and unprotected by any armed security measures, or by fleeing to the town . . . was a shared decision to follow the gospel "as lambs in the midst of wolves," our only arms being fidelity in charity, and faith in the power of the Holy Spirit working in human hearts.[175]

This is obedience understood in precisely the kenotic, Christlike way that Christian had spoken of in his chapter talks. It is an imitation of the Son's joyful obedience to the Father, to the way of love. The monks' actions arose from freedom; they were, one could say, "a demonstration of humility, and not power."[176] Christian named the paschal shape of this obedience: "The enclosure in fact marks a space of welcome for [our neighbors]; it represents an open heart, wounded by the suffering of this world. For us, our stability in this place posits a resolve of crucified love in the face of our enemies."[177]

174. Olivera, *Ho[...]*
175. Olivera, *How to Follow*, 74.
176. Christian's ph[...] *Follow*, 74–75.
Dieu pour tout jour, 261)[...]d in a chapter talk and quoted above (Chergé,
177. Hémon, "En-Visag[...]
[...]-by-E," 218.

This declaration of freely offered life enabled Olivera to interpret the killing of the monks as martyrdom: "When martyrdom
is understood in the context of a spirituality of self-offering, the
death of any disciple of Christ is not related so much to the violence of the assassin, but rather to the free, conscious gift of one's
own life. So the martyr can say, in communion with Christ: *No
one takes my life from me, but I lay it down on my own* (Jn 10:18)."[178]
Olivera suggests that Christian martyrdom is both "a gift and a
vocation," not in the sense of something to be sought, but rather in
the way in which the disciple walks an interior path that enables
this free offering. It "implies increasing freedom and awareness
in relation to this divine work which is taking place from within
the depth of the person's heart."[179]

After the event, this reading of a "vocation to martyrdom"
seems unnecessary. Certainly the monks' resolve to stay was difficult and costly. Each found himself facing his own weakness
and fearfulness. The monks remained at Tibhirine for a little over
two years with "death before their eyes." As Christian wrote, a
few months before they were kidnapped, "The presence of death.
Traditionally this is a constant companion of the monk. This com-
panionship has taken on a more concrete clarity with the direct
threats we have received, the assassinations very close at hand,
and certain visits. It is present to us as a useful test of truth, even
though an inconvenient one."[180]

For Christian and for his brother monks, while the possibility
of martyrdom hung over their increasingly precarious lives, their
own self-understanding was one of continuity with and deeper
embrace of their monastic, indeed Christian, vocation. It was simply a further working out of the way of humility. In response to a
question posed in a Cistercian circular ("In the present situation,
how do we live out the charism of our order?"), the community
responded, "The violent death—of one of us or of all together—

---

178. Bernardo Olivera, "Tibhirine Today: Circular Letter to the Members
of the Order on the 10th Anniversary of the Passage of Our Brothers of Our
Lady of Atlas," *Ordo Cisterciensis S.O.* Prot. N° 01/AG/06 (May 21, 2006): 6.1.

179. Olivera, "Tibhirine Today," 6.1.

180. Olivera, *How Far to Follow*, 76–77.

would only be *the* result of our choice to live in the following of Christ."[181]

The focus of this living remained resolutely in the daily (*quotidien*). During the Easter Triduum and on the feast of Pentecost 1994, in the shadow of the Christmas visit of 1993, Christian delivered a series of homilies on martyrdom. Here he faced with his community the situation in which they found themselves: the deaths of foreigners, of fellow religious, and of Muslim neighbors, and the threats to their own lives. The reality of the paschal mystery must have sounded deeply in the community's celebrations. Christian's thinking here is careful and courageous but not dramatic or heroic. Instead he points back to the ordinary, daily challenges (the martyrdom) of monastic life. He understands Jesus' death as a "martyrdom of love." He recognizes, though, that human capacity to live out of love is severely limited and that "we cannot pretend our life to be a witness to love, a 'martyrdom' of love." The evidence of our limits is in the daily:

> We know from experience that often the small gestures of love are more difficult, especially when you have to repeat them every day. We can wash the feet of the brothers on Holy Thursday because it is soon over with, but what if we had to do it every day and to everybody? When Father Bernardo tells us that "the Order has more need of monks than of 'martyrs'," he is not speaking about this particular martyrdom of the monk through all these little things. . . . Putting on an apron, like Jesus did, can be as important and as solemn an act as giving one's own life . . . and vice versa: giving one's life can be just as simple as putting on an apron.[182]

Similarly, at the Easter Vigil Christian tells the community that they are invited to share in a "martyrdom of hope" that is "not at all glorious or breathtaking" but is grounded in the daily: "It

181. Olivera, "Tibhirine Today," 6.2.5. Olivera quotes from a community document dated November 21, 1995.

182. Chergé, *L'AUTRE que nous attendons*, 420, March 31, 1994; trans. Olivera, "Tibhirine Today," 6.2.6.

fits exactly the dimensions of our daily living [*quotidien*]. And it has always defined the monastic state of life: step by step, drop by drop, word for word, shoulder to shoulder . . . and having to begin the regular life again every morning, and every evening too: having to keep ruminating, correcting, discerning and, above all, waiting."[183]

In choosing to stay, the brothers chose each day to continue the journey they began when they became monks. They chose to walk the way of humility, orienting themselves toward the One *who has loved us to the extreme*. They knew that this way would and did reveal their weaknesses: it was humiliating. And that this daily choice opened the possibility of a violent death—of the extreme humiliation of the cross. But they were also convinced that this way of self-offering was the choice for love. As Christian wrote in a circular letter dated April 25, 1995,

> I am certain that God loves the Algerians, and that he has chosen to prove it to them by giving them our lives. So then, do we truly love them? Do we love them enough? This is a moment of truth for each one of us, and a heavy responsibility in these times when our friends feel so little loved. Slowly, each one is learning to integrate death into this gift of self and, with death, all the other conditions of this ministry of living together, which is necessary for total selflessness. On certain days, all this appears hardly reasonable: as unreasonable as becoming a monk.[184]

5.8.2 Humility and the Hostile Other

The monks' choice to remain at Tibhirine, living out their monastic vocation in solidarity with their neighbor, exposed them to the presence of the hostile other. This presence was only physically manifested again with the arrival of their kidnappers in the early hours of March 27, 1996. But living with the sentence of death

183. Chergé, *L'AUTRE que nous attendons*, 426; April 2–3, 1994; trans. Olivera, "Tibhirine Today," 2.6.2.

184. Olivera, *How Far to Follow*, 99–100.

meant that this vicious other was, in a sense, always present. This was a final breach of the monastery wall. Their decision to remain can perhaps be read as a radical act of hospitality: openness to the other even when that other is hostile. How is this possible? Christian believed that the heart of this openness is found in forgiveness. So he rehearsed the moment when he would stand before his killer and expressed the desire to forgive. In fact he had already faced such a killer on Christmas Eve in the person of Sayat-Attiya and reflected on the possibility of forgiveness.[185]

To this "other," the one who would violently take his life, Christian addressed the final lines of his testament, written on January 1, 1994, after the Christmas Eve visit of Sayat-Attiya and the community's decision to stay:

> And also you, my last-minute friend,
> who will not have known what you were doing:
> Yes, I want this THANK YOU and this "A-DIEU"
> to be for you, too,
> because in God's face I see yours.
> May we meet again as happy thieves
> in Paradise, if it please God, the Father of us both.[186]

In these lines Christian again rehearsed his intention to forgive his killer, intentionally echoing the words of Jesus from the cross: "Father, forgive them; for they do not know what they are doing" (Luke 23:34). But while the model of forgiving love is Christ, Christian identifies himself as a thief, again drawing on

---

185. Olivera, "Monk, Martyr, and Mystic," 335–36.

186. Olivera, *How Far to Follow*, 129. Edith Wyschogrod's definition of a saintly life resonates here: "A saintly life is defined as one in which compassion for the Other, irrespective of cost to the saint, is the primary trait. Such lives unfold in tension with institutional frameworks that may nevertheless later absorb them. Not only do saints contest the practices and beliefs of institutions, but in a more subtle way they contest the order of narrativity itself. Their lives exhibit two types of negation: the negation of the self and the lack of what is needful but absent in the life of the Other" (Edith Wyschogrod, *Saints and Postmodernism: Revisioning Moral Philosophy*, Religion and Postmodernism series [Chicago: University of Chicago Press, 1990], xxiii).

Luke's telling of the crucifixion. The happy thief is the one who admits his guilt ("we have been condemned justly"), begs Jesus for a place in his kingdom, and is promised a place in Paradise. Christian is aware of his own complicity with evil and his own need for forgiveness. So, earlier in the testament, he says:

> I would like, when the time comes,
> to have a moment of spiritual clarity
> which would allow me to beg forgiveness of God
> and of my fellow human beings,
> and at the same time forgive with all my heart
> the one who will strike me down.[187]

Christian made the same point when reflecting on the deaths of two religious, Sister Paul-Hélène and Brother Henri. Before the death of Jesus, he wrote, the thief witnessed to his innocence ("this man has done nothing wrong," Luke 23:41), but "faced with *that martyrdom*, the saint and the assassin are just two thieves dependent on the same forgiveness."[188] Christian viewed his killer, then, as a brother. They were fellow thieves in need of God's mercy. And they were, simultaneously, bearers of the divine likeness ("in God's face I see your face"). The enemy became a "last-minute friend."

5.9 Conclusion

This is a strong and moving narrative. In the unfolding journey of Christian de Chergé and the monks of Tibhirine, one really does sense the starkness and vulnerability that arises from the radical stripping back of all securities. This was a desert within a desert. As the monks walked toward their deaths, they had, as Christian had said in his chapter talks on humility, only "this little day" to offer to God. Humility had indeed become the *climat* in which the monks lived, precariously, day after day.

187. Olivera, *How Far to Follow*, 127.
188. Olivera, "Monk, Martyr, and Mystic," 336. Christian made this observation in the context of a homily preached on the feast of the first martyrs of Africa (Chenu, ed., *Sept vies*, 136).

But objections also clamor in the mind. What could this martyrdom of love mean in the face of 9/11 and the further rise of militant Islam? How would Christian have responded?

The monks' commitment, in the end, was quite simple: they were living out their monastic vocation, and this vocation called them to humility and love. They were endeavoring to practice *caritas*, the love of neighbor, and love required that they bend before the other. Christian's last documented chapter talk, delivered on March 16, 1996, recapitulates the fundamentals of their monastic vocation, drawing on the bookends of the Rule of Saint Benedict: the Prologue and chapter 72, the tradition that formed the brothers as individuals and as a community. They were participants in Benedict's "school for the Lord's service," which is, Christian reminds the brothers, a school of love. They were called to patience, stability, perseverance, and "participation in the sufferings of Christ," their "martyr" of love and of hope. Especially hope: Benedict envisions the community journeying together in the hope of participation in the kingdom of God.[189]

Christian closed this last talk by reading the penultimate chapter of the Rule, "The Good Zeal of Monks." A good zeal, it must be said, leads to love, not violence. The final words of Benedict's chapter speak poignantly of the path these twentieth-century monks had embraced: "Let them prefer absolutely nothing to Christ, and may he lead us all together to everlasting life" (RB 72.12).

---

189. Chergé, *Dieu pour tout jour*, 549–50; March 16, 1996.

Conclusion

Reclaiming Humility for the Twenty-First Century

I stand here today humbled.

—Barack Obama, Presidential Inauguration Speech,
    January 20, 2009

Jesus' trial, as the Gospel of John tells it, presents an encounter between human power and divine self-emptying. For his final appearance before Pilate, the embodiment of Roman power, Jesus has been dressed in a purple robe and a crown of thorns. This vesting is an act of humiliation that is played out to its end in the execution by crucifixion that follows. "Here is the man!" says Pilate in words that echo through human history. Now picture a cold winter's day in early 2009, and an African-American, standing in front of the biggest ever presidential inauguration gathering in history, and listen to the words of his first speech as the President of the United States: "My fellow citizens. I stand here today humbled . . ."

It is not entirely fair to stop the sentence there. Barack Obama, in fact, paused briefly after the word *humbled* and continued, "by the task before us." But the choice to evoke humility must have been intentional. There is a touch of the linguistic brilliance of a Bernard of Clairvaux here. One might detect a rhetorical move, a note of false humility perhaps: "I have just been elected to one of the most powerful political offices in the world, but I am still a lowly citizen."

But such a reading misses the deeper story here. Barack Obama is the first African-American to hold the office of president. A long and painful history of oppression and humiliation sits behind this moment. Video footage of the inauguration ceremony repeatedly focuses on ordinary African-Americans in the crowd. Obama's "I stand here today" is a declaration of victory over oppression. A reversal is at play here: the humiliated have been elevated. The foundational Christian story is not irrelevant: the picture of the humiliated Jesus standing before Pilate is played out again and again in the humiliating story of slavery. But there is no slave mentality here. The ground that these stories share is that of human dignity affirmed and God's solidarity with the humiliated.

While Obama evokes humility in this opening sentence he plays its resonances carefully. If the audience expects a rhetorical claim to humility he shifts ground immediately; Obama is "humbled . . . *by the task*." He makes no claim to the possession of a (problematic, ambiguous) virtue. Obama perhaps recognizes the treacherous nature of humility and its relationship to humiliation. Too many African-Americans have been "humbled," humiliated. Claiming to be "humbled . . . by the task *before us*" is, rather, to stand with the neighbor, on equal ground, oriented toward the hard road that they will travel together.

As a word, *humility* still retains its accumulated ambiguity. Perhaps in the modern world as Enzo Bianchi suggests, it is too dangerous to preach humility. Different people will hear the word differently: preaching humility will have no effect on those with blown-up egos and may damage those who already suffer from low self-esteem.[1] But, as a theology and practice, its reclamation is both possible and necessary for contemporary Christianity.

Reclaiming the Way of Humility

I began this inquiry by examining the complicated roots of the notion of humility as it emerged in the Christian tradition and

---

1. Enzo Bianchi, *Words of Spirituality: Towards a Lexicon of the Inner Life*, trans. Christine Landau (London: SPCK, 2002), 94.

its ambiguous identification as a virtue. Amid the difficulties, though, the meeting of virtue and humility is not entirely negative. Utilizing the language of virtue enabled early Christian communities to recast pagan ethics in countercultural ways. Humility, which is never a virtue in the Greco-Roman world, came in the early Christian era to signal a radically different way of conceiving the human journey and its social outworkings. Its trajectory found a place in the theology and practice of Western monastic expressions. This monastic tradition never separates humility from concrete existence, from the lived life. At its best, this monastic tradition is able to speak helpfully of a way of cultivating humility, which is, ultimately, simply a Christian way—a way of imitating the humble Christ. At its best, this tradition protects the graced nature of this quality, which can never be found by human effort but is the by-product of a life oriented toward God. Recalling the teaching of the desert *abbas*, Dorotheus of Gaza, in the sixth century, clearly understood this reality: "What is humility? . . . Humility is a great and divine work and the road to humility is labor, bodily labor, while seeking to know oneself and to put oneself below everyone else and praying to God about everything: this is the road to humility, but humility itself is something divine and incomprehensible."[2]

This interface between "the road," or way, and "the divine" appears throughout the monastic tradition. It thwarts attempts to define humility, making them feel one-dimensional. Christian de Chergé's contribution, built from the accumulated wisdom of his Cistercian inheritance, comes close to expressing the subtle yet dynamic nature of humility: humility is *un climat*, a climate, "which is not human, but upon which man is dependent if he wants to breathe freely."[3] This metaphor helpfully retains the distinction between human effort and divine grace; we choose and (painfully) learn how to breathe this new sort of air, but the

2. Dorotheus of Gaza, *Discourses and Sayings*, trans. Eric P. Wheeler, CF 33 (Kalamazoo, MI: Cistercian Publications, 1977), 101.

3. Christian de Chergé, *Dieu pour tout jour: Chapitres de Père Christian de Chergé à la communauté de Tibhirine (1985–1996)*, 2nd ed. (Montjoyer: Abbaye Notre-Dame d'Aiguebelle, 2006), 260.

atmosphere itself is pure gift. It is simply who God is. It captures too the liberative quality of this *climat*, how it frees us to be simply the beloved of God, to be truly ourselves.

Three further themes might also contribute to reclaiming humility in the twenty-first century: the foundation of an eschatological orientation, the reclamation of the material face of humility, and the need to reintegrate humility and humiliation.

Reclaiming an Eschatological Orientation

In the preface to the third edition of *After Virtue*, Alasdair MacIntyre reflects on his own intellectual journey in the twenty-seven years since its initial publication. In this time, he has returned to Catholicism and discovered and embraced Aquinas's appropriation of Aristotle. Reviewing his earlier project in the light of this new direction, he stresses the teleological nature of human existence: "My attempt to provide an account of the human good purely in social terms, in terms of practices, traditions, and the narrative unity of human lives, was bound to be inadequate until I had provided it with a metaphysical grounding. It is only because human beings have an end towards which they are directed by reason of their specific nature, that practices, traditions, and the like are able to function as they do."[4]

The monastic expressions I have examined all understand human life as oriented toward such an end (*telos*), variously expressed as the vision of God, the kingdom of heaven, eternal life, purity of heart, and love. Human life is lived not only toward this end but also in front of this end—with judgment in view. So the desire for God is met by a sense of the distance between the divine and the human, an eschatological humility. Human beings are limited, broken creatures with a divine vocation. Paradoxically, in facing and acknowledging these limits we are able to transcend them. When we ask, with Abba Anthony, what can

---

4. Alasdair MacIntyre, *After Virtue: A Study in Moral Theory*, 3rd ed. (London: Duckworth, 2007), ix.

get us through the snares of the enemy, the answer we receive is "Humility."[5]

Importantly, this eschatological orientation is different from, and richer than, a narrow belief in heavenly reward after one's physical death. It concerns an "open heaven," the way in which divine life opens to human existence, the way in which eternity is (partly) realized in the present. Athanasius's *Life of Anthony* tells this optimistic story, pitting it against the worldly vision of human flourishing found in the Greeks. Schongauer's engraving *The Temptation of Saint Anthony* depicts the monk's free, if perilous, passage toward the heavens. Benedict offers a manual for living out this orientation in the communal setting of the monastery; again, he offers an optimistic vision, oriented toward the eternal, with the expectation of the experience of "the sweetness of love" along the way. Bernard of Clairvaux dreams this vision on a larger scale, hoping for a church and a society transformed by the vision of God. In Filippino Lippi's painting, a Florentine merchant joins Bernard: with their feet planted on the earth, both are oriented toward the eternal, an orientation that relativizes human efforts. The monks of Tibhirine lived this eschatological orientation to a costly end but saw themselves as simply living out their ordinary monastic vocation.

That life is oriented toward such a *telos* is, of course, contested in the modern world, but in the absence of such an end, the Christian tradition argues, human life is untethered and meaningless. What the monastic project offers, from its very beginnings, is clarity about this end. The monk is so named because he or she has a single orientation: the monk is a *monos*. The monk dances for God only.

Reclaiming the Material Face of Humility

In its passage through Western history, particularly in its identification as a virtue, the notion of humility loses much of the

5. *The Sayings of the Desert Fathers: The Alphabetical Collection*, trans. Benedicta Ward, rev. ed., CS 59 (Kalamazoo, MI: Cistercian Publications, 1984), 2 (Anthony 7).

material resonance that was central to its understanding in the Greco-Roman world. The countercultural reading of humility that emerged in early Christianity, a reading that turned Greco-Roman scorn of humility on its head, retained this resonance. It finds continued expression in the monastic movement that first flourished in the fourth century. The way of humility has always had material and social implications.

The monastic journey begins with the renunciation of the world, including one's material possessions, social identity, family, and status. While the texts I have examined never simplistically equate humility and poverty, the monastic tradition consistently recommends a life founded on material simplicity. The principal danger of wealth lies in its potential to impart a sense of self-sufficiency; material poverty encourages dependence on God. The provisionality of the Tibhirine community vividly illustrates this understanding. But the idea of material humility as a form of solidarity with the poor (or humiliated) and of minimizing social distance also recurs throughout the tradition.

Similarly, renunciation implies the relinquishment of one's place in the social order of the world, the relinquishment of honor and status. While the need for social ordering does not disappear in the monastery, the community rethinks this ordering in the light of the gospels and the witness of the Acts of the Apostles. But such reordering is by no means an easy task. Human propensity for rivalry—competition for goods perceived as limited—often thwarts human attempts to live together differently. Monastic life is ordered in a way intended to minimize this competitive spirit, simultaneously opening out a better prospect: the unlimited love of God. The foundational model for life together is the foot-washing Christ, who chooses lowly service (*ministerium*), even sordid labor, rather than power over the other (*dominum*). Christ demonstrates that love is in fact not a scarce resource subject to competition but, rather, the product of self-offering. Humility gives birth to compassion.

In the monastic tradition too, humility is cultivated—in the sense of the ground's being softened for its growth—by quite tangible practices. Interior conversion is facilitated by commitment to practices such as exposing one's thoughts to one's *abba*, chanting the psalms, serving in the kitchen, working in a shared garden, and offering radical, and costly, hospitality. In all of these practices, the self is "given away"—to God, to the other.

Renunciation is an unfashionable idea in the modern world, but historically, the material face of humility has been periodically rediscovered through the prophetic voices of reformers and reform movements. In a world scarred by material and social inequality, its recovery may already be overdue.

Reintegrating Humility and Humiliation

In the monastic traditions I have considered, humility and humiliation are necessarily, if dangerously, related. Linguistically, discomfort with the relationship between the two has led to an English mapping of their connotations (the first positive, the second negative) as if they had no root connection. In turn, this separation of the two has sometimes resulted in an understandable reluctance to use the word *humiliation* in translating monastic texts. It is not possible, however, to appreciate fully the christological foundations of humility without reintegrating humiliation.

The monk is encouraged to face his limits, his ontological and existential humility. In fact, in our daily lives, we are continually confronted with our limitations: with the wounds we carry through our life's journey, often from childhood, with our inability to remake ourselves, with our personal and public failures, with the physical limits of our bodies, with our mortality, indeed with our inability to be God. To be human is, in one sense, to be in a state of humiliation. We are powerless to save ourselves. If we are, as Christian de Chergé reminds us, pointed toward the divine, to the heavens, we are also bound to the earth—we have clay feet— so we inevitably experience frustration and pain. Acceptance of this state of humiliation enables a paradoxical shift from what Bernard calls "cold humility" to "warm humility," a humility infused with love. The crushed heart is softened by love. This shift is made possible by God's own embrace of humiliation, in the life and death of Jesus Christ. Here ontological and existential humility meets Christ, so that we experience humility itself as divine.

Humiliations, however, often come to us by human hands, from those who exercise power over us: we are lowered by them. In this case, the experience of humiliation has the potential to damage both one's sense of self and one's relationships. The humiliated person can feel disempowered, exposed, destabilized, and isolated.

It is here that the monastic tradition inhabits dangerous territory. In entering the monastery, the monk relinquishes power to an other (the *abba* or abbot) and, in the case of cenobitic monasticism, to others (the monastic community), so that, together, they can seek God. The embrace of obedience in the monastic tradition is intended to assist the individual to relinquish self-will, or ego (so that the self is given fully to God), and to enable the monk to find in God an interior stability—a God-sufficiency, rather than self-sufficiency. This stability, in fact, offers a certain immunity from the negative consequences of humiliations. (Abba Anoub's vivid enacted parable illustrates this well: the stone statue that he alternately stones and then kneels before, begging forgiveness, is moved by neither abuse nor flattery.)

The hope is to imitate the self-giving, kenotic obedience of Christ—his joyful, free "YES to the Father,"[6] an obedience that is actually an expression of love, albeit costly love, rather than power. In the monastery, training in obedience has the same end in view. One bends before another, because Christ bends to wash our feet, bends even to death on a cross.

Still, this *is* dangerous ground. Submission remains an understandably suspect notion. As feminist critics of humility have long contended, the requirement of obedience has often left women and children the suffering victims of abusive human power. There is a significant difference between a self freely offered and a self compelled to submit to another.

When *Time* magazine chose Pope Francis as its 2013 Person of the Year, it put humility at center stage. "How do you practice humility from the most exalted throne on earth?" asked managing

---

6. Chergé, *Dieu pour tout jour,* 260.

editor Nancy Gibbs.[7] Alert to the possibility of false humility, Gibbs nonetheless listed Pope Francis's early actions as signals of a shift in the "tone and temperament" of the papacy: his decision to live in a Vatican guest house rather than the lavish papal apartments, his choice to dress more simply than his predecessors (no red shoes, the simple iron pectoral cross), his kissing a severely disfigured man, his washing a Muslim woman's feet on Maundy Thursday. In his review of the pope's first year in office, Paul Vallely counted these as "gestures of ostentatious humility." "No pope," he said, "had ever before dared to take the name of Francis."[8]

By evoking the memory of Saint Francis of Assisi, the pope is signaling a whole program of reform. In his biography of Pope Francis, Vallely quotes the twice-silenced liberation theologian Leonardo Boff: "Francis is more than a name—it's a plan. It's a plan for a poor Church, one that is close to the people, gospel-centered, loving and protective towards nature."[9] Close to the *humus*.

Vallely suggests that humility is "a mode of behavior" that Pope Francis has adopted deliberately. His discussion, however, would have been helped by the distinction, seen in the monastic traditions considered in this book, between practices that soften the ground of human hearts and the divine grace that allows humility to grow and flourish. For Pope Francis humility is simply the humble way of Jesus, a way that all Christians are called to imitate. As the monastic traditions consistently teach, Christian humility arises from the very nature of God.

The seventh-century hermit Isaac the Syrian understood this divine foundation and its implications for the human vocation: "Humility is the raiment of the Godhead. The Word who became human clothes himself in it, and he spoke to us in our body.

---

7. Nancy Gibbs, "The Choice," *Time*, December 11, 2013, http://poy.time .com/2013/12/11/pope-francis-the-choice/?iid=poy-article-featured-content -widget.

8. Paul Vallely, "Pope Francis—The First Year: Is the Rebel too Good to Be True?" *Independent*, March 8, 2014, http://www.independent.co.uk /news/world/europe/pope-francis--the-first-year-is-the-rebel-too-good-to -be-true-9172000.html.

9. Paul Vallely, *Pope Francis: Untying the Knots* (London: Bloomsbury, 2013).

Everyone who has been clothed with humility has truly been made like unto Him who came down from his own exaltedness and hid the splendour of his majesty and concealed his glory with humility, lest creation be utterly consumed by the contemplation of him."[10] Clothed with such humility, it is possible not only to stand fully human but also to stand with paradoxical confidence before God, and with compassion beside one another. Perhaps it is time to reclaim this way of humility.

10. Quoted in Hilarion Alfeyev, *The Spiritual World of Isaac the Syrian*, CS 175 (Kalamazoo, MI: Cistercian Publications, 2000), 112.

References

Primary Sources

Apophthegmata Patrum [The Greek *Alphabetical Collection*]. Edited by Jean-Baptiste Cotelier. 1647. Repr. PG 65:71–440. Paris, 1857–1866.

Aristotle. *The Ethics of Aristotle: The Nicomachean Ethics.* Translated by J. A. K. Thomson. Rev. ed. Harmondsworth, UK: Penguin, 1976.

———. *The Nicomachean Ethics.* Translated by H. Rackham. Loeb Classical Library. London: William Heinemann, 1926.

Athanasius. Contra Gentes *and* De Incarnatione. Translated by Robert W. Thomson. Oxford: Clarendon Press, 1971.

———. *The Life of Antony and the Letter to Marcellinus.* Translated by Robert C. Gregg. London: SPCK, 1980.

———. *Vita Antonii* [*Life of Antony*]. PG 26:835–976. Paris, 1857–1866.

Augustine. *The City of God.* Translated by Henry Bettenson. London: Penguin, 1984.

———. *Confessions.* Translated by R. S. Pine-Coffin. Harmondsworth, UK: Penguin, 1961.

———. *Expositions of the Psalms (1–32).* Translated by Maria Boulding. The Works of Saint Augustine: A Translation for the 21st Century, pt. 3, v. 15. Hyde Park, NY: New City Press, 2000.

———. *Sermons (341–400) on Various Subjects.* Translated by Edmund Hill. Edited by John E. Rotelle. The Works of Saint Augustine: A Translation for the 21st Century; pt. 3, v. 10. Hyde Park, NY: New City Press, 1995.

Bartelink, G. J. M., ed. *Athanase d'Alexandrie: Vie d'Antoine.* SCh 400. Paris: Éditions du Cerf, 1994.

Bernard of Clairvaux. *Bernard of Clairvaux: Selected Works.* Translated by G. R. Evans. New York: Paulist Press, 1987.

———. *Five Books on Consideration: Advice to a Pope.* Translated by John D. Anderson and Elizabeth T. Kennan. CF 37. Kalamazoo, MI: Cistercian Publications, 1976.

————. *Homilies in Praise of the Blessed Virgin Mary.* Translated by Marie-Bernard Saïd. CF 18A. Kalamazoo, MI: Cistercian Publications, 1993.

————. *In Praise of the New Knighthood: A Treatise on the Knights Templar and the Holy Places of Jerusalem.* Translated by M. Conrad Greenia. CF 19B. Kalamazoo, MI: Cistercian Publications, 2000.

————. *The Letters of St. Bernard of Clairvaux.* Translated by Bruno Scott James. Stroud, UK: Sutton Publishing, 1953. Reprint, 1998.

————. *The Life and Death of Saint Malachy the Irishman.* Translated by Robert T. Meyer. CF 10. Kalamazoo, MI: Cistercian Publications, 1978.

————. *On Baptism and the Office of Bishops.* Translated by Pauline Matarasso. CF 67. Kalamazoo, MI: Cistercian Publications, 2004.

————. *Sermons on the Song of Songs.* Translated by Kilian Walsh and Irene Edmonds. 4 vols. CF 4, 7, 31, 40. Kalamazoo, MI: Cistercian Publications, 1971–1980.

————. *The Steps of Humility.* Translated by George Bosworth Burch. Notre Dame, IN: University of Notre Dame Press, 1963.

————. *The Steps of Humility and Pride.* Translated by M. Ambrose Conway. CF 13A. 1973; Kalamazoo, MI: Cistercian Publications, 1989.

Biblia Sacra: iuxta Vulgatam versionem. Edited by Bonifatius Fisher, Robert Weber, and Roger Gryson. Stuttgart: Deutsche Bibelgesellschaft, 1994.

The Book of the Elders: Sayings of the Desert Fathers: The Systematic Collection. Translated by John Wortley. CS 240. Collegeville, MN: Cistercian Publications, 2012.

Cassian, John. *The Conferences.* Translated by Boniface Ramsey. New York: Paulist Press, 1997.

————. *The Institutes.* Translated by Boniface Ramsey. New York: Newman Press, 2000.

————. *Jean Cassien: institutions cénobitiques.* Edited by Jean-Claude Guy. SCh 109. Paris: Éditions du Cerf, 1965.

Chenu, Bruno, ed. *Sept vies pour Dieu et l'Algérie.* 2nd ed. Paris: Bayard, 1996.

Chergé, Christian de. "Conference Given to General Chapter of Trappist Order." *Monastic Interreligious Dialogue Bulletin* 55, May 1996. http://www.monasticdialog.com/a.php?id=492.

————. *Dieu pour tout jour: Chapitres de Père Christian de Chergé à la communauté de Tibhirine (1985–1996).* 2nd ed. Montjoyer: Abbaye Notre-Dame d'Aiguebelle, 2006.

————. *L'AUTRE que nous attendons: Homélies de Père Christian de Chergé (1970–1996).* Montjoyer: Abbaye Notre-Dame d'Aiguebelle, 2006.

————. "L'échelle mystique du dialogue." *Islamochristiana* 23 (1997): 1–26. Repr. and rev. by Bruno Chenu. *Lettre de Ligugé* 256 (1991–1992): 18–28.

———. *L'invincible espérance*. Edited by Bruno Chenu. Paris: Bayard, 2010.

The Desert Fathers: Sayings of the Early Christian Monks. Translated by Benedicta Ward. London: Penguin, 2003.

Dickens, Charles. *David Copperfield*. Edited by Nina Burgis. Oxford: Clarendon Press, 1981.

Dorotheus of Gaza. *Discourses and Sayings*. Translated by Eric P. Wheeler. CF 33. Kalamazoo, MI: Cistercian Publications, 1977.

Evagrius Ponticus. *The Praktikos* [;] *Chapters on Prayer*. Translated by John Eudes Bamberger. CS 4. Kalamazoo, MI: Cistercian Publications, 1981.

Flaubert, Gustave. *The Temptation of Saint Anthony*. Translated by Kitty Mrosovsky. Harmondsworth, UK: Penguin, 1983.

The Greek New Testament. Edited by Barbara Aland, et al. 4th rev. ed. Stuttgart: Deutsche Bibelgesellschaft, 1993.

Grégoire de Nazianze. *Discours 20–23*. SCh 270. Paris: Éditions du Cerf, 1980.

———. "Oration 43 or The Panegyric on S. Basil." In *Select Orations of Saint Gregory Nazianzen, Sometime Archbishop of Constantinople; S. Cyril of Jerusalem, S. Gregory Nazianzen*. Translated by Charles Gordon Brown and James Edward Swallow. Nicene and Post-Nicene Fathers, second series. Grand Rapids, MI: Eerdmans, 1955. 7:395–422.

Gregory the Great. *The Life of Saint Benedict by Gregory the Great: Translation and Commentary*. Translated by Terrence G. Kardong. Collegeville, MN: Liturgical Press, 2009.

Kardong, Terrence G. *Benedict's Rule: A Translation and Commentary*. Collegeville, MN: Liturgical Press, 1996.

La Bible de Jérusalem: la Sainte Bible traduite en français sous la direction de l'école biblique de Jérusalem. Rev. and enlarged ed. Paris: Éditions du Cerf, 1998.

Les Apophtegmes des Pères: collection systématique. Edited and translated by Jean-Claude Guy. SCh 387, 474, 498. Paris: Éditions du Cerf, 1993, 2003, 2005.

Lucian of Samosata. "The Dream or Lucian's Career." In *Lucian*. Vol. 3. Translated by A. M. Harmon. 8 vols. Loeb Classical Library. London: William Heinemann, 1921. Reprint, 1960.

Machiavelli, Niccolò. *Discourses*. Translated by Leslie J. Walker. 2 vols. London: Routledge, 1991.

Palladius. *The Lausiac History*. Translated by Robert T. Meyer. Westminster, MD: Newman Press, 1965.

The Rule of the Master (Regula Magistri). Translated by Luke Eberle. CS 6. Kalamazoo, MI: Cistercian Publications, 1977.

Rule of Saint Benedict 1980. Edited by Timothy Fry. Collegeville, MN: Liturgical Press, 1981.

Sancti Bernardi Opera. Edited by Jean Leclercq, C. H. Talbot, and Henri M. Rochais. 8 vols. Rome: Editiones Cistercienses, 1957–1977.

The Sayings of the Desert Fathers: The Alphabetical Collection. Translated by Benedicta Ward. Rev. ed. CS 59. Kalamazoo, MI: Cistercian Publications, 1984.

Silvas, Anna. *The Asketikon of St Basil the Great*. Oxford Early Christian Studies. Oxford: Oxford University Press, 2005.

Vasari, Giorgio. *The Lives of the Artists: A Selection*. Translated by George Bull. Rev. ed. Harmondsworth, UK: Penguin, 1971.

Verba Seniorum. Edited by Heribert Rosweyde, 1615. PL 73:855–1022. Paris, 1844–1864.

Vivian, Tim. "Coptic Palladiana 2: *The Life of Evagrius (Lausiac History 38)*." *Coptic Church Review* 21, no. 1 (2000): 8–23.

Vivian, Tim, and Rowan A. Greer. *Four Desert Fathers: Pambo, Evagrius, Macarius of Egypt, and Macarius of Alexandria: Coptic Texts Relating to the "Lausiac History" of Palladius*. Crestwood, NY: St. Vladimir's Seminary Press, 2004.

Vogüé, Adalbert de, ed. *Gregoire le Grand: Dialogues*. Vol. 2. SCh 260. Paris: Éditions du Cerf, 1979.

———. *La règle du Maître*. 2 vols. SCh 105, 106. Paris: Éditions du Cerf, 1964–1965.

William of Saint-Thierry, et al. *The First Life of Bernard of Clairvaux*. Translated by Hilary Costello. CF 76. Collegeville, MN: Cistercian Publications, forthcoming 2015.

———. *St. Bernard of Clairvaux: The Story of His Life as Recorded in the Vita Prima Bernardi by Certain of His Contemporaries, William of St. Thierry, Arnold of Bonnevaux, Geoffrey and Philip of Clairvaux, and Odo of Deuil*. Translated by Geoffrey Webb and Adrian Walker. London: Mowbray, 1960.

———. *Vita prima Sancti Bernardi Claraevallis Abbatis, Liber primus*. Edited by Paul Verdeyen. CCCM 89B. Turnhout: Brepols, 2011.

The Wisdom of the Desert Fathers: Apophthegmata Patrum from the Anonymous Series. Translated by Benedicta Ward. Oxford: SLG Press, 1975.

The World of the Desert Fathers: Stories and Sayings from the Anonymous Series of the Apophthegmata Patrum. Translated by Columba Stewart. Kalamazoo, MI: Cistercian Publications, 1986.

Secondary Sources

Adnès, Pierre. "Humilité." In *Dictionnaire de spiritualité*. 1969 ed.

Alfeyev, Hilarion. *The Spiritual World of Isaac the Syrian.* CS 175. Kalamazoo, MI: Cistercian Publications, 2000.

Astell, Ann W. *Eating Beauty: The Eucharist and the Spiritual Arts of the Middle Ages.* Ithaca, NY: Cornell University Press, 2006.

Auerbach, Erich. *Literary Language and Its Public in Late Latin Antiquity and the Middle Ages.* Translated by Ralph Manheim. Princeton, NJ: Princeton University Press, 1965.

Barry, Patrick. *The Benedictine Handbook.* Norwich, UK: Canterbury Press, 2003.

Barton, John. "Virtue in the Bible." *Studies in Christian Ethics* 12, no. 1 (1999): 12–22.

Bianchi, Enzo. *Words of Spirituality: Towards a Lexicon of the Inner Life.* Translated by Christine Landau. London: SPCK, 2002.

Böckmann, Aquinata. *Around the Monastic Table—RB 31–42: Growing in Mutual Service and Love.* Translated by Matilda Handl and Marianne Burkhard. Collegeville, MN: Liturgical Press, 2009.

———. *Perspectives on the Rule of St. Benedict: Expanding Our Hearts in Christ.* Translated by Matilda Handl and Marianne Burkhard. Collegeville, MN: Liturgical Press, 2005.

Bonomo, Carol. *Humble Pie: St. Benedict's Ladder of Humility.* Harrisburg, PA: Morehouse Publishing, 2003.

Brakke, David. "The Making of Monastic Demonology: Three Ascetic Teachers on Withdrawal and Resistance." *Church History* 70, no. 1 (2001): 19–48.

Bredero, Adriaan H. *Bernard of Clairvaux: Between Cult and History.* Translated by Reinder Bruinsma. Grand Rapids, MI: Eerdmans, 1996.

The British Museum, Trustees of. "Martin Schongauer, *The Temptation of St Anthony*, a copperplate engraving." British Museum. http://www.britishmuseum.org/explore/highlights/highlight_objects/pd/m/martin_schongauer,_the_temptat.aspx.

Brown, Peter. *The Body and Society: Men, Women and Sexual Renunciation in Early Christianity.* New York: Columbia University Press, 1988.

———. *The World of Late Antiquity.* London: Thames and Hudson, 1971.

Burch, George Bosworth. "Introduction: An Analysis of Bernard's Epistemology." In Bernard of Clairvaux, *The Steps of Humility.* Notre Dame, IN: University of Notre Dame Press, 1963. 1–117.

Burke, Jill. *Changing Patrons: Social Identity and the Visual Arts in Renaissance Florence.* University Park, PA: Pennsylvania State University Press, 2004.

Burton-Christie, Douglas. *The Word in the Desert: Scripture and the Quest for Holiness in Early Christian Monasticism.* New York: Oxford University Press, 1993.

Butler, Cuthbert. *Benedictine Monachism: Studies in Benedictine Life and Rule.* London: Longmans, Green, and Co., 1919.

Button, Mark. "'A Monkish Kind of Virtue?' For and Against Humility." *Political Theory* 33, no. 6 (2005): 840–68.

Bynum, Caroline Walker. *Holy Feast and Holy Fast: The Religious Significance of Food to Medieval Women.* Berkeley: University of California, 1987.

Casey, John. *Pagan Virtue: An Essay in Ethics.* Oxford: Clarendon Press, 1990.

Casey, Michael. "Bernard of Clairvaux: Forty Years of Scholarship." In *Saint Bernard of Clairvaux: The Man,* edited by John Stanley Martin. Melbourne: Dept. of Germanic Studies and Russian, University of Melbourne, 1991. 31–45.

———. "Bernard of Clairvaux: The Man behind the Image." *Pacifica* 3, no. 3 (1990): 269–87.

———. "Bernard of Clairvaux, St., 1090–1153." In *Encyclopedia of Monasticism,* edited by William M. Johnson. Chicago: Fitzroy Dearborn Publishers, 2000.

———. *Truthful Living: Saint Benedict's Teaching on Humility.* Leominster, UK: Gracewing, 2001.

Chiarini, Marco. "Giovanni di Consalvo." Grove Art Online; Oxford Art Online. http://www.oxfordartonline.com/subscriber/article/grove/art/T032524.

Chittister, Joan D. *Heart of Flesh: A Feminist Spirituality.* Grand Rapids, MI: Eerdmans, 1998.

———. *The Rule of Benedict: Insights for the Ages.* New York: Crossroad, 1992. Reprint, 1997.

———. *Twelve Steps to Inner Freedom: Humility Revisited.* Erie, PA: Benetvision, 2003.

Chitty, Derwas J. *The Desert a City: An Introduction to the Study of Egyptian and Palestinian Monasticism under the Christian Empire.* Oxford: Basil Blackwell, 1966.

Clark, David L. "Filippino Lippi's *The Virgin Inspiring St. Bernard* and Florentine Humanism." *Studies in Iconography* 7–8 (1981–1982): 175–87.

Coakley, Sarah. *Powers and Submissions: Spirituality, Philosophy and Gender.* Oxford: Blackwell, 2002.

Cordner, Christopher. "Aristotelian Virtue and Its Limitations." *Philosophy* 69, no. 269 (1994): 291–316.

Dawes, Stephen B. "Anāwa in Translation and Tradition." *Vetus Testamentum* 41, no. 1 (1991): 38–48.

———. "Humility: Whence This Strange Notion?" *Expository Times* 103, no. 3 (1991): 72–75.

Dawtry, Anne Frances. "Benedictine Order. " Grove Art Online; Oxford Art Online. http://www.oxfordartonline.com/subscriber/article/grove/art/T007854.

Delatte, Paul. *The Rule of St. Benedict: A Commentary*. Translated by Justin McCann. London: Burns, Oates, and Washbourne, 1921.

Dickson, John P., and Brian S. Rosner. "Humility as a Social Virtue in the Hebrew Bible?" *Vetus Testamentum* 54, no. 4 (2004): 459–79.

Dreyer, Elizabeth A. "Humility." In *The New Westminster Dictionary of Christian Spirituality*, edited by Philip Sheldrake. Louisville, KY: Westminster John Knox Press, 2005.

Drobner, Hubertus R. *The Fathers of the Church: A Comprehensive Introduction*. Translated by Siegfried S. Schatzmann, with bibliographies updated and expanded for the English edition by William Harmless and Hubertus R. Drobner. Peabody, MA: Hendrickson Publishers, 2007.

Dumont, Charles. *Pathway of Peace: Cistercian Wisdom according to Saint Bernard*. Translated by Elizabeth Connor. CS 187. Kalamazoo, MI: Cistercian Publications, 1999.

Dunn, Marilyn. *The Emergence of Monasticism: From the Desert Fathers to the Early Middle Ages*. Malden, MA: Blackwell Publishing, 2000.

———. "The Master and St Benedict: A Rejoinder." *English Historical Review* 107, no. 422 (1992): 104–11.

———. "Mastering Benedict: Monastic Rules and Their Authors in the Early Medieval West." *English Historical Review* 105, no. 416 (1990): 567–94.

Evans, G. R. *Bernard of Clairvaux*. New York: Oxford University Press, 2000.

Foot, Philippa. *Virtues and Vices, and Other Essays in Moral Philosophy*. Berkeley: University of California Press, 1978.

Forman, Mary. "Benedict's Use of Scripture in the Rule: Introductory Understandings." *American Benedictine Review* 52, no. 3 (2001): 324–45.

Fortin, John R. "Social Class in Saint Benedict's Monastery." CSQ 43, no. 2 (2008): 199–215.

Frame, Tom. "Humility: The Despised Virtue?" *Quadrant* 51, no. 4 (2007): 36–42.

France, James. *Medieval Images of Saint Bernard of Clairvaux*. CS 210. Kalamazoo, MI: Cistercian Publications, 2007.

Frank, Daniel H. "Humility as a Virtue: A Maimonidean Critique of Aristotle's *Ethics*." In *Moses Maimonides and His Time*, edited by Eric L. Ormsby. Washington, DC: Catholic University of America Press, 1989. 89–99.

Friedrich, Gerhard, ed. *Theological Dictionary of the New Testament*. Translated by Geoffrey W. Bromiley. Grand Rapids, MI: Eerdmans, 1972.

Gibbs, Nancy. "The Choice." *Time* December 11, 2013. http://poy
.time.com/2013/12/11/pope-francis-the-choice/?iid=poy-article
-featured-content-widget.

Gilmore, Peter. "Atlas: Reawakened Memories and Present-Day Reflections." CSQ 35, no. 2 (2000): 231–38.

Gould, Graham. "Recent Work on Monastic Origins: A Consideration of
the Questions Raised by Samuel Rubenson's *The Letters of St. Antony.*"
Studia Patristica 5 (1993): 405–16.

A Greek-English Lexicon. Compiled by Henry George Liddell and Robert
Scott. 9th ed. Oxford: Oxford University Press, 1925.

Grundmann, Walter. "Ταπεινος." In *Theological Dictionary of the New Testament*, edited by Gerhard Friedrich and translated by Geoffrey W.
Bromiley. Grand Rapids, MI: Eerdmans, 1972.

Hall, Marjorie Jean, and John N. Lupia. "Cloister." Grove Art Online;
Oxford Art Online. http://www.oxfordartonline.com/subscriber
/article/grove/art/T018230.

Harmless, William. *Desert Christians: An Introduction to the Literature of
Early Monasticism.* Oxford: Oxford University Press, 2004.

Hart, Patrick, ed. *Survival or Prophecy? The Correspondence of Jean Leclercq
and Thomas Merton.* MW 17. Collegeville, MN: Cistercian Publications, 2008.

Hémon, Philippe. "An En-Visaged Good-by-E." CSQ 34, no. 2 (1999):
203–18.

Hogan, Linda. "Virtue." In *The New Westminster Dictionary of Christian
Spirituality*, edited by Philip Sheldrake. Louisville, KY: Westminster
John Knox Press, 2005. 636–37.

Honderich, Ted, ed. *The Oxford Companion to Philosophy.* Oxford: Oxford
University Press, 1995.

Hume, David. *Enquiries Concerning Human Understanding and Concerning
the Principles of Morals.* 3rd ed. Oxford: Clarendon Press, 1975.

Jamison, Christopher. *Finding Sanctuary: Monastic Steps for Everyday Life.*
London: Weidenfeld and Nicolson, 2006.

Judge, Edwin A. "The Earliest Use of *Monachos* for 'Monk' and the Origins
of Monasticism." *Jahrbuch für Antike und Christentum* 20 (1977): 72–89.

Kardong, Terrence G. "The Achievement of André Borias, Exegete of
Benedict's Rule." ABR 44, no. 2 (1993): 179–220.

———. "Benedict's Insistence on Rank in the Monastic Community: RB
63.1-9 in Context." CSQ 42, no. 3 (2007): 243–65.

———. "Benedict's Prior: RB 65." CSQ 40, no. 2 (2005): 117–34.

———. Preface to Gregory the Great, *The Life of Saint Benedict by Gregory
the Great.* Collegeville, MN: Liturgical Press, 2009. ix–xii.

———. "Who Wrote the Dialogues of Saint Gregory? A Report on a
Controversy." CSQ 39, no. 1 (2004): 31–39.

Katos, Demetrios S. "Humility as the Harbinger of Imageless Prayer in the Lausiac History." *St Vladimir's Theological Quarterly* 51, no. 1 (2007): 107–21.

Keller, David G. R. *Oasis of Wisdom: The Worlds of the Desert Fathers and Mothers*. Collegeville, MN: Liturgical Press, 2005.

Kennan, Elizabeth T. "Introduction." In Bernard of Clairvaux, *Five Books on Consideration: Advice to a Pope*. Translated by John D. Anderson and Elizabeth T. Kennan. CF 37. Kalamazoo, MI: Cistercian Publications, 1976. 3–18.

Keys, Mary M. "Humility in the Monastic Polis: The Rule of St. Benedict." *Conference Papers—Midwestern Political Science Association* (2007): 1–42.

Kiser, John W. "An Algerian Microcosm: Monks, Muslims, and the Zeal of Bitterness." CSQ 38, no. 3 (2003): 337–54.

———. *The Monks of Tibhirine: Faith, Love, and Terror in Algeria*. New York: St. Martin's Griffin, 2002.

Kitchen, John. "Bernard of Clairvaux's *De Gradibus Humilitatis et Superbiae* and the Postmodern Revisioning of Moral Philosophy." In *Virtue and Ethics in the Twelfth Century*, edited by István P. Bejczy and Richard G. Newhauser. Brill's Studies in Intellectual History. Leiden and Boston: Brill, 2005. 95–117.

Kline, Francis. *Lovers of the Place: Monasticism Loose in the Church*. Collegeville, MN: Liturgical Press, 1997.

Larmann, Marian. "The Meaning of *omnes pariter* in RB 49.3." ABR 29, no. 2 (1978): 153–65.

A Latin Dictionary. Edited by Charleton T. Lewis and Charles Short. Oxford: Clarendon Press, 1879.

Lavere, George J. "Virtue." In *Augustine through the Ages: An Encyclopedia*, edited by Allan D. Fitzgerald. Grand Rapids, MI: Eerdmans, 1999.

Leclercq, Jean. *Bernard of Clairvaux and the Cistercian Spirit*. Translated by Claire Lavoie. CS 16. Kalamazoo, MI: Cistercian Publications, 1976.

———. "General Introduction to the Works of Saint Bernard (1)." Translated by Elias Dietz. CSQ 40, no. 1 (2005): 3–25.

———. "General Introduction to the Works of Saint Bernard (2)." Translated by Elias Dietz. CSQ 40, no. 3 (2005): 243–51.

———. "General Introduction to the Works of Saint Bernard (3)." Translated by Elias Dietz. CSQ 40, no. 4 (2005): 365–93.

———. *The Love of Learning and the Desire for God: A Study of Monastic Culture*. Translated by Catherine Misrahi. 2nd ed. New York: Fordham University Press, 1974.

———. *A Second Look at Bernard of Clairvaux*. Translated by Marie-Bernard Saïd. CS 105. Kalamazoo, MI: Cistercian Publications, 1990.

Lendon, J. E. *Empire of Honour: The Art of Government in the Roman World*. Oxford: Oxford University Press, 1995. Reprint, 2005.

Lesher, Melinda Kay. "St. Bernard of Clairvaux and the Republic of Florence in the Late Middle Ages." *Cîteaux* 35 (1984): 258–67.

Louf, André. *The Way of Humility*. Translated by Lawrence S. Cunningham. MW 11. Kalamazoo, MI: Cistercian Publications, 2007.

Louth, Andrew. "The Literature of the Monastic Movement." In *The Cambridge History of Early Christian Literature*, edited by Frances M. Young, Lewis Ayres, and Andrew Louth. Cambridge: Cambridge University Press, 2004. 373–81.

———. *The Origins of the Christian Mystical Tradition: From Plato to Denys*. Oxford: Clarendon Press, 1981.

MacIntyre, Alasdair. *After Virtue: A Study in Moral Theory*. 3rd ed. London: Duckworth, 2007.

Marr, Andrew. *Tools for Peace: The Spiritual Craft of St. Benedict and René Girard*. Lincoln, NE: iUniverse, 2007.

Martin, Luther H. "Graeco-Roman Philosophy and Religion." In *The Early Christian World*, edited by Philip F. Esler. London: Routledge, 2000. 53–79.

Martin, Ralph P. *A Hymn of Christ: Philippians 2:5-11 in Recent Interpretation and in the Setting of Early Christian Worship*. Downers Grove, IL: InterVarsity Press, 1997.

Martin, Ralph P., and Brian J. Dodd, eds. *Where Christology Began: Essays on Philippians 2*. Louisville, KY: Westminster John Knox Press, 1998.

"Martin Schongauer." Grove Art Online. Oxford University Press. http://www.oxfordartonline.com.ezproxy.csu.edu.au/subscriber/article/grove/art/T076738pg1#T076739.

McGinn, Bernard. *The Foundations of Mysticism: Origins to the Fifth Century*. New York: Crossroad Publishing, 1991.

———. *The Growth of Mysticism: Gregory the Great through the Twelfth Century*. New York: Crossroad Publishing, 1994.

McGlynn, Donald. "Atlas Martyrs." CSQ 32, no. 2 (1997): 149–94.

McGuckin, John Anthony. *The Westminister Handbook to Patristic Theology*. Louisville, KY: Westminster John Knox Press, 2004.

McGuire, Brian Patrick. "Writing about the Difficult Saint: Bernard of Clairvaux and Biography." CSQ 44, no. 4 (2009): 447–61.

Meeuws, Marie-Benoît. " 'Ora et Labora': Devise Bénédictine?" *Collectanea cisterciensia* 54 (1992–1993): 193–219.

Merton, Thomas. *The Last of the Fathers: Saint Bernard of Clairvaux and the Encyclical Letter* Doctor Mellifluus. London: Catholic Book Club, 1954.

Murphy, Nancey, Brad J. Kallenberg, and Mark Thiessen Nation, eds. *Virtues and Practices in the Christian Tradition: Christian Ethics after MacIntyre*. Harrisburg, PA: Trinity Press International, 1997.

Murray, Alexander. Review of *Bernard of Clairvaux and the Shape of Monastic Thought: Broken Dreams*, by M. B. Pranger. *Journal of Ecclesiastical History* 47, no. 1 (1996): 149–51.

Newman, Martha G. *The Boundaries of Charity: Cistercian Culture and Ecclesiastical Reform, 1098–1180*. Stanford, CA: Stanford University Press, 1996.

———. "Contemplative Virtues and the Active Life of Prelates." In Bernard of Clairvaux, *On Baptism and the Office of Bishops*. Kalamazoo, MI: Cistercian Publications, 2004. 11–36.

Nietzsche, Friedrich. "Maxims and Arrows." In *Twilight of the Idols* and *The Anti-Christ*. Harmondsworth, UK: Penguin, 1968. 23–27.

O'Daly, Gerard J. P. *Augustine's Philosophy of Mind*. Berkeley: University of California Press, 1987.

Olivera, Bernardo. *How Far to Follow: The Martyrs of Atlas*. CS 197. Kalamazoo, MI: Cistercian Publications, 1997.

———. "Monk, Martyr, and Mystic: Christian de Chergé (1937–1996)." CSQ 34, no. 3 (1999): 321–38.

———. "Tibhirine Today: Circular Letter to the Members of the Order on the 10th Anniversary of the Passage of Our Brothers of Our Lady of Atlas." *Ordo Cisterciensis S.O.* Prot. N° 01/AG/06 (May 21, 2006).

Oxford English Dictionary Online. http://www.oed.com:80/Entry/89375.

Pardue, Stephen T. *The Mind of Christ: Humility and the Intellect in Early Christian Theology*. London: Bloomsbury, 2013.

Peifer, Claude. "5. Monastic Formation and Profession." In *RB 1980: The Rule of St. Benedict*, edited by Timothy Fry. Collegeville, MN: Liturgical Press, 1981. 437–66.

———. "The Rule of St. Benedict." In *RB 1980: The Rule of St. Benedict*, edited by Timothy Fry. Collegeville, MN: Liturgical Press, 1981. 65–112.

Pennington, M. Basil. Introduction to Bernard of Clairvaux, *The Steps of Humility and Pride*, translated by M. Ambrose Conway. CF 13A. Kalamazoo, MI: Cistercian Publications, 1973. 1–24.

———. *Listen with Your Heart: Spiritual Living with the Rule of Saint Benedict*. Brewster, MA: Paraclete Press, 2007.

Porter, Jean. "Virtue." In *The Oxford Handbook of Theological Ethics*, edited by Gilbert Meilaender and William Werpehowski. Oxford: Oxford University Press, 2005. 205–19.

———. "Virtue Ethics." In *The Cambridge Companion to Christian Ethics*, edited by Robin Gill. Cambridge: Cambridge University Press, 2001. 96–111.

Pranger, M. B. *Bernard of Clairvaux and the Shape of Monastic Thought: Broken Dreams*. Leiden: E. J. Brill, 1994.

Ramsey, Boniface. "Cassian, John." In *Encyclopedia of Monasticism*, edited by William M. Johnson. Chicago: Fitzroy Dearborn Publishers, 2000.

Ray, Marie-Christine. *Christian de Chergé, prieur de Tibhirine.* 2nd ed. Paris: Bayard, 1998.

Rich, Antony D. *Discernment in the Desert Fathers: Diakrisis in the Life and Thought of Early Egyptian Monasticism.* Bletchley, Milton Keynes, UK: Paternoster, 2007.

Richards, Norvin. *Humility.* Philadelphia: Temple University Press, 1992.

————. "Is Humility a Virtue?" *American Philosophical Quarterly* 25, no. 3 (1988): 253–59.

Roberts, Robert C. *Spiritual Emotions: A Psychology of Christian Virtues.* Grand Rapids, MI: Eerdmans, 2007.

Rubenson, Samuel. "Evagrius Ponticus." In *Encyclopedia of Monasticism,* edited by William M. Johnson. Chicago: Fitzroy Dearborn Publishers, 2000.

————. *The Letters of St. Antony: Monasticism and the Making of a Saint.* Studies in Antiquity and Christianity. Minneapolis, MN: Fortress Press, 1995.

Ruddy, Deborah Wallace. "A Christological Approach to Virtue: Augustine and Humility." PhD dissertation, Boston College, 2001.

Saiving, Valerie. "The Human Situation: A Feminine View." In *Womanspirit Rising: A Feminist Reader in Religion,* edited by Carol P. Christ and Judith Plaskow. San Francisco, CA: Harper and Row, 1979. 25–42.

Salenson, Christian. *Christian de Chergé: A Theology of Hope.* Translated by Nada Conic. CS 247. Kalamazoo, MI: Cistercian Publications, 2012.

————. *Christian de Chergé: une théologie de l'espérance.* Paris: Bayard, 2009.

————. "Monastic Life, Interreligious Dialogue, and Openness to the Ultimate: A Reflection on the Tibhirine Monks' Experience." *The Way* 45, no. 3 (2006): 23–37.

Salzman, Michele R. "Pagans and Christians." In *The Oxford Book of Christian Studies,* edited by Susan Ashbrook Harvey and David G. Hunter. Oxford: Oxford University Press, 2008. 186–202.

Scarlett, Brian. "Humility: A Monkish Virtue." Preprint Series. Department of Philosophy, University of Melbourne. No. 14/94 (1994): 1–20.

Scholl, Edith. "Christian de Chergé on Humility." CSQ 41, no. 2 (2006): 193–215.

Sena, Lorenzo. "The History of the Interpretation of the Rule of Saint Benedict." ABR 56, no. 4 (2005): 394–417.

Sheldrake, Philip, ed. *The New Westminster Dictionary of Christian Spirituality.* Louisville, KY: Westminster John Knox Press, 2005.

Silvas, Anna. "Edessa to Cassino: The Passage of Basil's *Asketikon* to the West." *Vigiliae Christianae* 56, no. 3 (2002): 247–59.

Sommerfeldt, John R. *Bernard of Clairvaux on the Life of the Mind.* New York: Newman Press, 2004.

————. *Bernard of Clairvaux on the Spirituality of Relationship*. New York: Newman Press, 2004.

————. *The Spiritual Teachings of Bernard of Clairvaux: An Intellectual History of the Early Cistercian Order*. CS 125. Kalamazoo, MI: Cistercian Publications, 1991.

Špidlík, Tomáš. *The Spirituality of the Christian East: A Systematic Handbook*. Translated by Anthony P. Gythiel. CS 79. Kalamazoo, MI: Cistercian Publications, 1986.

Stewart, Columba. "Anthony of the Desert." In *The Early Christian World*, edited by Philip F. Esler. New York: Routledge, 2000. 1088–1101.

————. *Cassian the Monk*. Oxford: Oxford University Press, 1998.

————. "Desert Fathers." In *Encyclopedia of Monasticism*, edited by William M. Johnson. Chicago: Fitzroy Dearborn Publishers, 2000.

————. "In Community." In *The Benedictine Handbook*, edited by Patrick Barry, et al. Norwich, UK: Canterbury Press, 2003. 279–86.

————. *Prayer and Community: The Benedictine Tradition*. London: Darton, Longman, and Todd, 1998.

————. "Radical Honesty about the Self: The Practice of the Desert Fathers." *Sobornost* 12, no. 1 (1990): 25–39.

Stiegman, Emero. "An Analytical Commentary." In Bernard of Clairvaux, *On Loving God*. CF 13B. Kalamazoo, MI: Cistercian Publications, 1995. 45–195.

————. "Bernard of Clairvaux, William of St. Thierry, the Victorines." In *The Medieval Theologians*, edited by G. R. Evans. Oxford: Blackwell Publishing, 2001. 129–55.

Theissen, Gerd. *A Theory of Primitive Christian Religion*. Translated by John Bowden. London: SCM Press, 1999.

Vallely, Paul. "Pope Francis—the First Year: Is the Rebel too Good to be True?" *Independent*, March 8, 2014. http://www.independent.co.uk/news/world/europe/pope-francis--the-first-year-is-the-rebel-too-good-to-be-true-9172000.html.

————. *Pope Francis: Untying the Knots*. London: Bloomsbury, 2013.

Veilleux, Armand. "The Witness of the Tibhirine Martyrs." *Spiritus* 1, no. 2 (2001): 205–16.

Verbaal, Wim. "The Sermon Collection: Its Creation and Edition." In Bernard of Clairvaux, *Sermons for Advent and the Christmas Season*, edited by John Leinenweber, translated by Irene Edmonds, et al. CF 51. Kalamazoo, MI: Cistercian Publications, 2007. vii–lxiv.

Vogüé, Adalbert de. *Community and Abbot in the Rule of St. Benedict*. CS 5. Kalamazoo, MI: Cistercian Publications, 1979.

————. Introduction to *The Rule of the Master*. Translated by Luke Eberle. CS 6. Kalamazoo, MI: Cistercian Publications, 1977. 7–10.

———. *La Règle de saint Benoît.* Vols. 1, 5. SCh 181, 185. Paris: Éditions du Cerf, 1971.

———. "The Master and St. Benedict: A Reply to Marilyn Dunn." *English Historical Review* 107, no. 422 (1992): 95–103.

———. *The Rule of Saint Benedict: A Doctrinal and Spiritual Commentary.* Translated by John Baptist Hasbrouck. CS 54. Kalamazoo, MI: Cistercian Publications, 1983.

Volf, Miroslav, and Dorothy C. Bass, eds. *Practicing Theology: Beliefs and Practices in Christian Life.* Grand Rapids, MI: William B. Eerdmans, 2002.

Wengst, Klaus. *Humility: Solidarity of the Humiliated: The Transformation of an Attitude and Its Social Relevance in Graeco-Roman, Old Testament-Jewish and Early Christian Tradition.* Translated by John Bowden. London: SCM Press, 1988.

Williams, Rowan. *Silence and Honey Cakes: The Wisdom of the Desert.* Oxford: Lion Publishing, 2003.

———. *The Wound of Knowledge: Christian Spirituality from the New Testament to St. John of the Cross.* 2nd ed. Cambridge, MA: Cowley Publications, 1991.

Wilson, Jonathan R. *Living Faithfully in a Fragmented World: Lessons for the Church from MacIntyre's* After Virtue. Harrisburg, PA: Trinity Press International, 1997.

Wilson, Robert, producer. *St. Anthony.* Music by Bernice Johnson Reagon. http://www.changeperformingarts.com/Wilson/st.anthony.html.

Wink, Walter. *Engaging the Powers: Discernment and Resistance in a World of Domination.* Minneapolis, MN: Fortress Press, 1992.

Wyschogrod, Edith. *Saints and Postmodernism: Revisioning Moral Philosophy.* Religion and Postmodernism series. Chicago: University of Chicago Press, 1990.

Zelzer, Michaela. "Gregory's *Life of Benedict*: Its Historico-Literary Field." CSQ 43 (2008): 327–37.

Zizioulas, John D. *Communion and Otherness: Further Studies in Personhood and the Church.* London: T. and T. Clark, 2006.